# INGLÊS
## MINIDICIONÁRIO ESCOLAR

# INGLÊS
## MINIDICIONÁRIO ESCOLAR

PORTUGUÊS / INGLÊS • INGLÊS / PORTUGUÊS

**COPYRIGHT © 2023 – EDITORA VALE DAS LETRAS**

Todos os direitos reservados e protegidos pela lei 9.610/1998. Nenhuma parte deste livro, sem autorização prévia por escrito da editora, poderá ser reproduzida ou transmitida, sejam quais forem os meios empregados: eletrônicos, mecânicos, fotográficos, gravações ou quaisquer outros.

**Autor:** Melânia B. Klug
**Coordenação editorial:** Thaís Regina
**Revisão:** Ana Paula Aragão, Michele de Souza Lima, Sueli Brianezi Carvalho e Silvana Pierro
**Capa e projeto gráfico:** Editora Vale das Letras

```
Dados  Internacionais  de  Catalogação  na  Publicação  (CIP)
                  Angélica Ilacqua CRB-8/7057
```

```
  Inglês : minidicionário escolar : português/inglês,
inglês/português / [Melânia B. Klug ; coordenado por Thaís
Regina]. - 6. ed. - Blumenau : Vale das Letras, 2023.
   352 p. (Minidicionários Escolar)


  ISBN 978-85-7661-627-6


  1. Língua inglesa - Dicionários - Português I. Klug, Melânia B.
II. Regina, Thaís III. Série

23-2353                                            CDD 423.69
```

```
        1. Língua inglesa - Dicionários - Português
```

Rua Bahia, 5115 - Salto Weissbach - CEP: 89032-001 - Blumenau/SC
CNPJ: 05.167.347/0001-47 - SAC: +55 (47) 3340-7045
editora@valedasletras.com.br / www.valedasletras.com.br

# FALSOS COGNATOS/False Friends

Em inglês existem alguns vocábulos que têm a ortografia e a fonética similares aos vocábulos em português, mas não têm o mesmo significado. Esses vocábulos são chamados de falsos cognatos ou falsos amigos. Abaixo estão alguns deles:

- **appointment**: encontro, consulta (apontamento: note);
- **attend**: assistir a, frequentar (atender: answer);
- **cigar**: charuto (cigarro: cigarette);
- **college**: faculdade, universidade (colégio: high school);
- **comprehensive**: completo, abrangente (compreensivo: understanding);
- **estate**: bens, propriedades (estado: state);
- **eventually**: finalmente (eventualmente: casually, accidentally);
- **exit**: saída (êxito: success);
- **exquisite**: refinado, requintado (esquisito: odd, strange);
- **fabric**: tecido (fábrica: factory, plant);
- **hazard**: risco, perigo (azar: bad luck, misfortune);
- **ingenious**: criativo, engenhoso (ingênuo: naïve);
- **large**: grande (largo: wide);
- **lecture**: conferência (leitura: reading);
- **library**: biblioteca (livraria: bookstore, bookshop);
- **notice**: aviso (notícia: news);
- **novel**: romance (novela: soap-opera);
- **ore**: minério (ouro: gold);
- **parents**: pais (parentes: relatives);
- **particular**: determinado, específico (particular: private);
- **physician**: médico (físico: physicist);
- **policy**: política, prática (polícia: police);
- **prejudice**: preconceito (prejuízo: damage, loss);
- **pretend**: fingir (pretender: intend);
- **push**: empurrar (puxar: pull);
- **realize**: perceber, compreender (realizar: perform, carry out);
- **scholar**: erudito, letrado, estudioso (escolar: student, schoolboy/schoolgirl);
- **sensible**: sensato (sensível: sensitive);
- **tenant**: inquilino (tenente: lieutenant).

# NÚMEROS/Numbers

| | NUMERAIS CARDINAIS Cardinal Numbers | NUMERAIS ORDINAIS Ordinal Numbers |
|---|---|---|
| 1 | one | first |
| 2 | two | second |
| 3 | three | third |
| 4 | four | fourth |
| 5 | five | fifth |
| 6 | six | sixth |
| 7 | seven | seventh |
| 8 | eight | eighth |
| 9 | nine | ninth |
| 10 | ten | tenth |
| 11 | eleven | eleventh |
| 12 | twelve | twelfth |
| 13 | thirteen | thirteenth |
| 14 | fourteen | fourteenth |
| 15 | fifteen | fifteenth |
| 16 | sixteen | sixteenth |
| 17 | seventeen | seventeenth |
| 18 | eighteen | eighteenth |
| 19 | nineteen | nineteenth |
| 20 | twenty | twentieth |
| 30 | thirty | thirtieth |
| 40 | forty | fortieth |
| 50 | fifty | fiftieth |
| 60 | sixty | sixtieth |
| 70 | seventy | seventieth |
| 80 | eighty | eightieth |
| 90 | ninety | ninetieth |

| 100 | hundred | hundredth |
|---|---|---|
| 101 | a/one hundred and one | hundred and first |
| 200 | two hundred | two hundredth |
| 300 | three hundred | three hundredth |
| 400 | four hundred | four hundredth |
| 500 | five hundred | five hundredth |
| 600 | six hundred | six hundredth |
| 700 | seven hundred | seven hundredth |
| 800 | eight hundred | eight hundredth |
| 900 | nine hundred | nine hundredth |
| 1.000 | a/one thousand | thousandth |
| 1.001 | a/one thousand and one | thousand and first |
| 2.000 | two thousand | two thousandth |
| 10.000 | ten thousand | ten thousandth |
| 100.000 | a/one hundred thousand | hundred thousandth |
| 1.000.000 | a/one million | millionth |

# VERBOS IRREGULARES/Irregular Verbs

| PRESENT TENSE | SIMPLE PAST | PAST PARTICIPLE | TRADUÇÃO |
|---|---|---|---|
| abide | abided, abode | abided, abode | morar, habitar |
| arise | arose | arisen | elevar-se, surgir |
| awake | awoke | awoken | acordar |
| be | was/were | been | ser, estar |
| bear | bore | born, borne | suportar, aguentar |
| beat | beat | beat, beaten | bater, derrotar |
| become | became | become | tornar-se, ficar |
| begin | began | begun | começar |
| bend | bent | bent | dobrar, curvar-se |
| bet | bet, betted | bet, betted | apostar |
| bid | bade, bid | bidden, bid | fazer uma oferta, ordenar |
| bind | bound | bound | ligar, atar |
| bite | bit | bitten, bit | morder |
| bleed | bled | bled | sangrar |
| blow | blew | blown | soprar, ventar |
| break | broke | broken | quebrar, romper |
| breed | bred | bred | criar, gerar |
| bring | brought | brought | trazer |
| broadcast | broadcast | broadcast | difundir, emitir |
| build | built | built | construir |
| burn | burnt, burned | burnt, burned | queimar |
| burst | burst | burst | explodir |
| buy | bought | bought | comprar |
| cast | cast | cast | lançar, moldar |
| catch | caught | caught | pegar |
| choose | chose | chosen | escolher |
| cling | clung | clung | agarrar |
| clothe | clad, clothed | clad, clothed | vestir |

| PRESENT TENSE | SIMPLE PAST | PAST PARTICIPLE | TRADUÇÃO |
|---|---|---|---|
| come | came | come | vir, chegar |
| cost | cost | cost | custar |
| creep | crept | crept | rastejar |
| cut | cut | cut | cortar |
| deal | dealt | dealt | negociar, lidar |
| dig | dug | dug | cavar |
| do | did | done | fazer |
| draw | drew | drawn | desenhar |
| dream | dreamt, dreamed | dreamt, dreamed | sonhar |
| drink | drank | drunk , drunken | beber |
| drive | drove | driven | dirigir |
| dwell | dwelt, dwelled | dwelt, dwelled | habitar |
| eat | ate | eaten | comer |
| fall | fell | fallen | cair |
| feed | fed | fed | alimentar |
| feel | felt | felt | sentir |
| fight | fought | fought | brigar |
| find | found | found | encontrar |
| flee | fled | fled | fugir, escapar |
| fling | flung | flung | arremessar, lançar |
| fly | flew | flown | voar |
| forbid | forbade, forbad | forbidden | proibir |
| foresee | foresaw | foreseen | prever |
| foretell | foretold | foretold | predizer |
| forget | forgot | forgotten | esquecer |
| forgive | forgave | forgiven | perdoar |
| forsake | forsook | forsaken | abandonar |
| freeze | froze | frozen | congelar |
| get | got | got, gotten | obter |

| PRESENT TENSE | SIMPLE PAST | PAST PARTICIPLE | TRADUÇÃO |
|---|---|---|---|
| give | gave | given | dar |
| go | went | gone | ir |
| grind | ground | ground | moer, afiar |
| grow | grew | grown | crescer, cultivar |
| hang | hung | hung | pendurar |
| have | had | had | ter, possuir |
| hear | heard | heard | ouvir |
| hide | hid | hid, hidden | esconder |
| hit | hit | hit | bater, atingir |
| hold | held | held | segurar |
| hurt | hurt | hurt | magoar, ferir |
| keep | kept | kept | guardar |
| kneel | knelt | knelt | ajoelhar-se |
| know | knew | known | conhecer, saber |
| lay | laid | laid | deitar |
| lead | led | led | guiar, conduzir |
| lean | leant, leaned | leant, leaned | inclinar-se |
| learn | learnt, learned | learnt, learned | aprender |
| leave | left | left | sair |
| lend | lent | lent | emprestar |
| let | let | let | permitir, deixar |
| lie | lay | lain | jazer |
| lie | lied | lied | mentir |
| light | lit, lighted | lit, lighted | acender, iluminar |
| lose | lost | lost | perder |
| make | made | made | fazer, fabricar |
| mean | meant | meant | significar |
| meet | met | met | encontrar |
| mistake | mistook | mistaken | enganar-se |

| PRESENT TENSE | SIMPLE PAST | PAST PARTICIPLE | TRADUÇÃO |
|---|---|---|---|
| overcome | overcame | overcome | superar, vencer |
| pay | paid | paid | pagar |
| put | put | put | colocar, pôr |
| quit | quit, quitted | quit, quitted | abandonar |
| read | read | read | ler |
| rend | rent | rent | rasgar |
| ride | rode | ridden | cavalgar, andar de |
| ring | rang | rung | tocar, soar |
| rise | rose | risen | levantar-se, subir |
| run | ran | run | correr |
| saw | sawed | sawed, sawn | serrar |
| say | said | said | dizer |
| see | saw | seen | ver |
| seek | sought | sought | procurar |
| sell | sold | sold | vender |
| send | sent | sent | enviar |
| set | set | set | fixar, estabelecer |
| sew | sewed | sewed, sewn | costurar |
| shake | shook | shaken | agitar, sacudir |
| shed | shed | shed | derramar |
| shine | shone | shone | brilhar |
| shoot | shot | shot | atirar |
| show | showed | showed, shown | mostrar |
| shrink | shrank, shrunk | shrunk | encolher |
| shut | shut | shut | fechar |
| sing | sang | sung | cantar |
| sink | sank | sunk | afundar |
| sit | sat | sat | sentar |
| sleep | slept | slept | dormir |
| slide | slid | slid | escorregar |

| PRESENT TENSE | SIMPLE PAST | PAST PARTICIPLE | TRADUÇÃO |
|---|---|---|---|
| smell | smelt, smelled | smelt, smelled | cheirar |
| smite | smote | smitten | golpear |
| speak | spoke | spoken | falar |
| speed | sped, speeded | sped, speeded | acelerar |
| spend | spent | spent | gastar |
| spill | spilt, spilled | spilt, spilled | derramar |
| spit | spat, spit | spat, spit | cuspir |
| split | split | split | dividir-se |
| spoil | spoilt, spoiled | spoilt, spoiled | estragar, mimar |
| spread | spread | spread | espalhar, difundir |
| spring | sprang | sprung | brotar, saltar |
| stand | stood | stood | ficar em pé |
| steal | stole | stolen | roubar |
| stick | stuck | stuck | colar, afixar |
| sting | stung | stung | picar, ferroar |
| stink | stank | stunk | cheirar mal |
| strike | struck | struck | golpear, atingir |
| string | strung | strung | enfileirar |
| strive | strove | striven | lutar, esforçar-se |
| swear | swore | sworn | jurar |
| sweep | swept | swept | varrer |
| swim | swam | swum | nadar |
| swing | swung | swung | balançar |
| take | took | taken | tomar, pegar |
| teach | taught | taught | ensinar |
| tear | tore | torn | rasgar |
| tell | told | told | dizer |
| think | thought | thought | pensar |
| throw | threw | thrown | arremessar, lançar |
| thrust | thrust | thrust | empurrar, furar |

| PRESENT TENSE | SIMPLE PAST | PAST PARTICIPLE | TRADUÇÃO |
|---|---|---|---|
| tread | trod | trodden | pisar, andar |
| understand | understood | understood | compreender |
| wake | woke | woken | acordar |
| wear | wore | worn | usar, vestir |
| weep | wept | wept | chorar, prantear |
| wet | wet, wetted | wet, wetted | molhar |
| win | won | won | ganhar, vencer |
| wind | wound | wound | enrolar, dar corda |
| withdraw | withdrew | withdrawn | retirar |
| write | wrote | written | escrever |

## ALFABETO/Alphabet

A a [ei] – B b [bi] – C c [si] – D d [di] – E e [i] – F f [ef] – G g [gi]
– H h [eidi] – I i [ai] – J j [jei] – K k [kei] – L l [el] – M m [em]
– N n[en] – O o [ou] – P p [pi] – Q q [kiu] – R r [ar] – S s [es]
– T t [ti] – U u [iu] – V v [vi] – W w [dabliu] – X x [ekis] – Y y [uai]
– Z z [zi-ou-zet]

## FRUTAS/Fruits

abacaxi – pineapple
ameixa – plum
amora – blackberry
banana – banana
caju – cashew
cereja – cherry
damasco – apricot
framboesa – raspberry
goiaba – guava
laranja – orange
limão – lemon
maçã – apple
mamão – papaya
manga – mango
melancia – watermelon
melão – melon
morango – strawberry
pera – pear
tangerina – tangerine
uva – grape

## CORES/Colors

amarelo – yellow
azul – blue
branco – white
castanho, marrom – brown
cinza – grey, gray
cor-de-rosa – pink
laranja – orange
preto – black
roxo – purple
verde – green
vermelho – red

## ANIMAIS/Animals

abelha – bee
bezerro – calf
boi – ox, bull
cachorrinho – puppy
cachorro – dog
cavalinho – foal
cavalo – horse
cobra – snake
ganso – goose
gatinho – kitten
gato – cat
leão – lion
ovelha – sheep
passarinho – bird
peixe – fish
pombo – pigeon
rato – mouse
tigre – tiger
vaca – cow
veado – deer

# MESES/Months

janeiro – January
fevereiro – February
março – March
abril – April
maio – May
junho – June
julho – July
agosto – August
setembro – September
outubro – October
novembro – November
dezembro – December

# ESTAÇÕES DO ANO/Seasons

inverno – winter
outono – autumn, fall
primavera – spring
verão – summer

# DIAS DA SEMANA/Days of the Week

domingo – Sunday
segunda-feira – Monday
terça-feira – Tuesday
quarta-feira – Wednesday
quinta-feira – Thursday
sexta-feira – Friday
sábado – Saturday

# FRASES ÚTEIS/Useful Phrases

A conta, por favor – Please bring the bill
Adeus – Goodbye
Até amanhã! – See you tomorrow
Até logo! – See you later!
Bem, obrigado – I am fine, thank you.
Bem-vindo – Welcome
Boa sorte – Good luck
Boa tarde – Good afternoon
Bom apetite – Enjoy your meal
Bom dia – Good morning
Como está? – How are you?
Cuide-se – Take care!
Divirta-se – Have fun!
Felicidades – Best wishes
Feliz aniversário! – Happy birthday
Feliz Ano Novo! – Happy New Year
Feliz Natal – Merry Christmas
Oi – Hello!
Onde é…? Onde está…? – Where is…?
Onde você mora? – Where do you live?
Para onde você vai? – Where are you going?
Parabéns! – Congratulations!
Prazer em conhecê-lo – Pleased to meet you
Quanto custa? – How much does this cost?
Que é isto? – What is this?
Saudações – Greetings
Saúde (brinde) – Cheers!
Saúde (ao espirrar) – Bless you
Tchau – Bye
Tudo bem? – How is it going?

# FRAÇÕES E PORCENTAGEM
## Fractions and Percentage

100% Cem por cento – A hundred per cent
10% Dez por cento – Ten per cent
½ Metade – One half/Half
¾ Três quartos – Three quarters
3,5 Três vírgula cinco – Three point four
0,5 Zero vírgula cinco – Zero point five

## AS HORAS/The time

### Que horas são? / What time is it?

É meio dia – It's midday/Twelve o'clock
É meia-noite – It's midnight
São três horas – It's three o'clock
Uma e dez – Ten past one
Duas e meia – Half past two/Two thirty
Quinze para as três – A quarter to three/Three forty-five
São quase nove horas – It's nearly nine o'clock

### A que horas? / At what time?

À uma hora – At one
Às duas e quinze – At quarter past two
Às três e pouco – Just after three (o'clock)
Por volta das quatro e meia – At about half past four
Às cinco em ponto – At five sharp
Em dez minutos – In ten minutes
Há vinte minutos – Twenty minutes ago

# PARTES DO CORPO HUMANO
## Parts of the Human Body

Cabelo – Hair
Cabeça – Head
Sobrancelha – Eyebrown
Olho – Eye
Nariz – Nose
Boca – Mouth
Pescoço – Neck
Ombro – Shoulder
Braço – Arm
Cotovelo – Elbow
Pulso – Wrist
Mão – Hand
Dedos – Fingers
Polegar (mão) – Thumb
Barriga – Belly
Quadril – Hip
Perna – Leg
Coxa – Thigh
Joelho – Knee
Tornozelo – Ankle
Calcanhar – Kneel
Pé – Foot
Dedão – Big Toe

# PALAVRAS ÚTEIS/Useful words

aberto – open
água – water
almoço – lunch
amanhã – tomorrow
aniversário – birthday
ano – year
banco – bank
banheiro – bathroom
batata – potato
bebida – berage
bife – steak
café – coffee
café da manhã – breakfast
carne – meat (alimento)
carne de boi – beef
cartão-postal – postcard
cerveja – beer
chá – tea
chegada – arrival
colina – hill
correio – post office
curto, curta – short
despensa – larder
dia – day
direita – right
direto, reto – straight
escola – school
esquerda – left
estacionamento – parking

farmácia – drugstore
fechado – closed
fruta – fruit
garage – garage
hoje – today
hospital – hospital
hotel – hotel
igreja – church
jantar – dinner
lago – lake
loja – store, shop
longe – far
longo, longa – long
mapa – map
mês – month
metrô – subway
montanha – mountain
muito – a lot
museu – museum
oceano – ocean
ônibus – bus
ontem – yesterday
pão – bread
para baixo, abaixo – down
para cima, cima – up
partida – departure
passaporte – passport
perto – near
pimenta – pepper
piscina – swimming pool
polícia – police

ponte – bridge
pouco – little
praça – square
praia – beach
quarto – bedroom
restaurante – restaurant
rio – river
rua – street
sal – salt
sala – room
salada – salad
selo – stamp
semana – week
sobremesa – dessert
sorvete – ice-cream
suco, sumo – juice
todo, toda, tudo – all
torre – tower
trem – train
vale – valley
vegetariano – vegetarian
verdura, legume – vegetable
vinho – wine

# Aa

**A, a** *s.* the first letter of the Portuguese alphabet / *art. def.* the / *pron. pess.* her (ela), it (coisa) / *prep.* at, in, on (lugar).
**a.ba.ca.te** *s.* avocado.
**a.ba.ca.xi** *s.* pineapple.
**a.ba.de** *s.* abbot.
**a.ba.fa.do** *adj.* stuffy.
**a.ba.far** *v.* to suffocate.
**a.bai.xar** *v.* to lower (preço); to reduce (luz, som).
**a.bai.xo** *adv.* down / *prep.* below; under.
**a.ba.jur** *s.* lampshade.
**a.ba.la.do** *adj.* loose, shaky.
**a.ba.lar** *v.* to shake, to upset.
**a.ba.li.za.do** *adj.* eminent.
**a.ba.lo** *s.* shock.
**a.ba.nar** *v.* to shake.
**a.ban.do.nar** *v.* to leave; to reject.
**a.bar.car** *v.* to cover.

**a.bar.ro.ta.do** *adj.* crammed full.
**a.bar.ro.tar** *v.* to cram-full.
**a.bas.ta.do** *adj.* wealthy.
**a.bas.tan.ça** *s.* abundance.
**a.bas.tar.dar** *v.* to corrupt.
**a.bas.te.cer** *v.* to supply.
**a.bas.te.ci.men.to** *s.* supply.
**a.ba.ter** *v.* to slaughter.
**a.bau.la.do** *adj.* convex.
**a.bau.lar-se** *v.* to bulge.
**ab.di.ca.ção** *s.* abdication.
**ab.di.car** *v.* to abdicate.
**ab.dô.men** *s.* abdomen.
**a.be.ce.dá.rio** *s.* alphabet.
**a.be.lha** *s.* bee.
**a.be.lhu.do** *adj.* nosy.
**a.ben.ço.a.do** *adj.* blessed.
**a.ben.ço.ar** *v.* to bless.
**a.ber.ra.ção** *s.* aberration.
**a.ber.to** *adj.* open, exposed.

abertura     24     acabar

## A

**a.ber.tu.ra** *s.* opening.

**a.bes.ta.lha.do** *adj.* stupid.

**a.bi.lo.la.do** *adj.* crazy.

**a.bis.ma.do** *adj.* astonished.

**a.bis.mo** *adj.* abysis, chasm / *s.* abyss, chasm.

**ab.je.ção** *s.* baseness.

**ab.je.to** *adj.* abject.

**ab.ne.ga.ção** *s.* self-denial.

**ab.ne.ga.do** *adj.* self-sacrificing.

**ab.ne.gar** *v.* to renounce.

**a.bó.ba.da** *s.* vault.

**a.bo.ba.lha.do** *adj.* foolish, silly.

**a.bó.bo.ra** *s.* pumpkin.

**a.bo.bri.nha** *s.* courgette.

**a.bo.li.ção** *s.* abolition.

**a.bo.lir** *v.* to abolish.

**a.bo.mi.na.ção** *s.* abomination.

**a.bo.mi.nar** *v.* to loathe.

**a.bo.nar** *v.* to guarantee.

**a.bo.no** *s.* guarantee, bonus, surplus.

**a.bor.da.gem** *s.* approach.

**a.bor.dar** *v.* to board.

**a.bo.rí.ge.ne** *s.* aborigine.

**a.bor.re.cer** *v.* to annoy, to bore.

**a.bor.tar** *v.* to have a miscarriage (acidentalmente); to have an abortion (voluntariamente).

**a.bo.to.a.du.ra** *s.* cufflink.

**a.bo.to.ar** *v.* to button up.

**a.bra.çar** *v.* to hug, to embrace.

**a.bran.dar** *v.* to reduce.

**a.bran.ger** *v.* to cover (assunto); to reach (alcançar).

**a.bra.sar** *v.* to burn.

**a.bre.vi.ar** *v.* to abbreviate.

**a.bri.dor** *s.* opener.

**a.bri.gar** *v.* to shelter.

**a.bri.go** *s.* shelter.

**a.bril** *s.* April.

**a.brir** *v.* to open.

**a.bro.lho** *s.* thorn.

**ab.rup.to** *adj.* abrupt.

**abs.ces.so** *s.* abscess.

**ab.si.de** *s.* shrine.

**ab.so.lu.ta.men.te** *adv.* absolutely.

**ab.so.lu.to** *adj.* absolute.

**ab.sol.ver** *v.* to absolve.

**ab.sor.ção** *s.* absorption.

**ab.sor.ven.te** *adj.* absorbent, absorbing / *s.* absorvent.

**abs.ten.ção** *s.* abstention.

**abs.tra.to** *adj.* abstract.

**ab.sur.do** *adj.* absurd.

**a.bun.dân.cia** *s.* abundance.

**a.bu.sar** *v.* to abuse.

**a.bu.so** *s.* abuse.

**a.bu.tre** *s.* vulture.

**a.ca.ba.do** *adj.* finished.

**a.ca.ba.men.to** *s.* finish, finishing.

**a.ca.bar** *v.* to finish, to complete.

**acabrunhado** · 25 · **acomodar**

**a.ca.bru.nha.do** *adj.* depressed, distressed, melancholic.

**a.ca.bru.nhar** *v.* to depress, to distress.

**a.ca.de.mi.a** *s.* academy.

**a.ça.frão** *s.* saffron.

**a.ca.len.tar** *v.* to rock to sleep, to cherish.

**a.cal.mar** *v.* to calm.

**a.cam.pa.men.to** *s.* camping.

**a.ção** *s.* action.

**a.ca.ra.jé** *s.* a Bahian delicacy beans paste fried in dendê palm oil.

**a.ca.ri.ci.ar** *v.* to caress.

**a.car.re.tar** *v.* to result in.

**a.ca.so** *s.* chance luck.

**a.ca.tar** *v.* to respect.

**a.cei.tar** *v.* to accept.

**a.ce.le.ra.do** *adj.* quick.

**a.ce.le.ra.dor** *s.* accelerator.

**a.ce.le.rar** *v.* to accelerate.

**a.ce.nar** *v.* to wave.

**a.cen.de.dor** *s.* lighter.

**a.cen.der** *v.* to light.

**a.ce.no** *s.* sign.

**a.cen.to** *s.* accent.

**a.cer.ca** *prep.* about.

**a.certar** *v.* to put right.

**a.cer.vo** *s.* collection.

**a.ces.sar** *v.* to access.

**a.ces.sível** *adj.* accessible.

**a.ces.so** *s.* access.

**a.ces.só.rio** *adj.* accessory / *s.* accessory.

**a.cha.do** *s.* find, discovery.

**a.cha.que** *s.* ailment.

**a.char** *v.* to find.

**a.cha.tar** *v.* to squash.

**a.ci.den.tal** *adj.* accidental.

**a.ci.den.te** *s.* accident.

**a.ci.dez** *s.* acidity.

**á.ci.do** *adj.* acid.

**a.ci.ma** *adv.* above.

**a.cin.te** *s.* provocation.

**a.ci.o.nar** *v.* to set in motion.

**a.ci.o.nis.ta** *s.* shareholder.

**a.cir.ra.do** *adj.* tough.

**a.cir.rar** *v.* to incite.

**a.cla.ma.ção** *s.* acclamation.

**a.cla.mar** *v.* to acclaim.

**a.ço** *s.* steel.

**a.coi.tar** *v.* to shelter.

**a.çoi.tar** *v.* to whip.

**a.co.lá** *adv.* over there.

**a.col.cho.a.do** *s.* quilt.

**a.col.cho.ar** *v.* to quilt.

**a.co.lhe.dor** *adj.* welcoming, cosy.

**a.co.lher** *v.* to welcome.

**a.co.me.ter** *v.* to attack.

**a.co.mo.da.ção** *s.* accommodation.

**a.co.mo.dar** *v.* to accommodate.

**acompanhamento** 26 **adivinhar**

**a.com.pa.nha.men.to** *s.* attendance, follow-up.

**a.com.pa.nhan.te** *s.* companion.

**a.com.pa.nhar** *v.* to go with; to accompany (música).

**a.con.che.gan.te** *adj.* cosy.

**a.con.che.gar** *v.* to bring near.

**a.con.che.go** *s.* cuddle.

**a.con.di.ci.o.nar** *v.* to condition.

**a.con.se.lhar** *v.* to advise.

**a.con.te.cer** *v.* to happen.

**a.cor.dar** *v.* to wake up.

**a.cor.de** *s.* chord.

**a.cor.de.ão** *s.* accordion.

**a.cor.do** *s.* agreement.

**a.cor.ren.tar** *v.* to chain.

**a.cos.ta.men.to** *s.* hard shoulder.

**a.cos.tu.ma.do** *adj.* used, accustmed.

**a.cos.tu.mar** *v.* to accustom.

**a.co.to.ve.lar** *v.* to jostle.

**a.çou.gue** *s.* butchery, butcher shop.

**a.co.var.dar(-se)** *v.* to lose courage, to cower.

**a.cre.di.tar** *v.* to believe.

**a.cres.cen.tar** *v.* to add.

**a.cres.cer** *v.* to increase.

**a.crí.li.co** *s.* acrylic.

**a.cro.ba.ta** *s.* acrobat.

**a.çú.car** *s.* sugar.

**a.çu.de** *s.* dam.

**a.cu.dir** *v.* to help, to assist.

**a.cu.mu.lar** *v.* to accumulate.

**a.cu.sa.ção** *s.* accusation.

**a.cu.sar** *v.* to accuse.

**a.cús.ti.ca** *s.* acoustics.

**a.cús.ti.co** *adj.* acoustic / *s.* acoustics.

**a.da.ga** *s.* dagger.

**a.dap.ta.ção** *s.* adaptation.

**a.dap.tar** *v.* to adapt.

**a.de.ga** *s.* cellar.

**a.de.qua.do** *adj.* appropriate.

**a.de.quar** *v.* to adapt.

**a.de.ren.te** *adj.* adhesive.

**a.de.rir** *v.* to adhere.

**a.de.são** *s.* adhesion; entry.

**a.de.si.vo** *adj.* adhesive.

**a.des.tra.do** *adj.* skilled.

**a.des.tra.dor** *s.* trainer.

**a.des.trar** *v.* to train.

**a.deus** *s.* goodbye / *interj.* goodbye.

**a.di.a.men.to** *s.* postponement.

**a.di.an.ta.do** *adj.* advanced.

**a.di.an.ta.men.to** *s.* progress, advance.

**a.di.an.tar** *v.* to advance.

**a.di.an.te** *adv.* in front.

**a.di.ar** *v.* to postpone.

**a.di.ção** *s.* addition.

**a.di.vi.nha.ção** *s.* riddle.

**a.di.vi.nhar** *v.* to guess.

**adjetivo**     27     **afirmativo**

**ad.je.ti.vo** *s.* adjective.

**ad.jun.to** *adj.* joined / *s.* adjunct.

**ad.mi.nis.tra.ção** *s.* administration.

**ad.mi.nis.tra.dor** *s.* administrator.

**ad.mi.nis.trar** *v.* to administer.

**ad.mi.ra.ção** *s.* amazement (espanto); admiration (respeito).

**ad.mi.ra.do** *adj.* astonished.

**ad.mi.rar** *v.* to admire.

**ad.mis.são** *s.* admission.

**ad.mi.tir** *v.* to admit.

**ad.mo.es.ta.ção** *s.* admonition.

**a.do.ção** *s.* adoption.

**a.do.çar** *v.* to sweeten.

**a.do.e.cer** *v.* to fall ill, to fall sick.

**a.doi.da.do** *adj.* crazy.

**a.do.les.cen.te** *adj.* adolescent / *s.* adolescent, teenager.

**a.do.rar** *v.* to adore.

**a.dor.me.cer** *v.* to fall asleep.

**a.do.tar** *v.* to adopt.

**ad.qui.rir** *v.* to obtain.

**a.du.bar** *v.* to manure.

**a.du.lar** *v.* to flatter.

**a.dul.te.rar** *v.* to adulterate.

**a.dul.té.rio** *s.* adultery.

**a.dul.to** *adj.* adult / *s.* adult.

**ad.ven.to** *s.* advent.

**ad.vér.bio** *s.* adverb.

**ad.ver.sá.rio** *s.* adversary, opponent.

**ad.ver.tên.cia** *s.* warning.

**ad.ver.tir** *v.* to warn.

**ad.vo.ga.do** *s.* lawyer.

**ad.vo.gar** *v.* to advocate.

**a.é.reo** *adj.* air, aerial.

**a.e.ro.bar.co** *s.* hovercraft.

**a.e.ro.na.ve** *s.* aircraft.

**a.e.ro.por.to** *s.* airport.

**a.e.ros.sol** *s.* aerosol.

**a.fa.gar** *v.* to caress.

**a.fa.nar** *v.* to nick, to pinch.

**a.fas.ta.do** *adj.* remote.

**a.fas.ta.men.to** *s.* removal.

**a.fas.tar** *v.* to remove.

**a.fa.zer** *v.* to accustom.

**a.fei.ção** *s.* affection.

**a.fe.rir** *v.* to check.

**a.fe.tar** *v.* to affect.

**a.fe.to** *s.* affection.

**a.fi.a.do** *adj.* sharp.

**a.fi.ar** *v.* to sharpen.

**a.fi.lha.do(a)** *s.* godson, *fem.* goddaughter, godchild (sem distinção de sexo).

**a.fim** *adj.* similar.

**a.fi.na.do** *adj.* in tune.

**a.fi.nal** *adv.* finally.

**a.fin.co** *s.* tenacity.

**a.fi.ni.da.de** *s.* affinity.

**a.fir.ma.ção** *s.* affirmation.

**a.fir.mar** *v.* to affirm.

**a.fir.ma.ti.vo** *adj.* affirmative.

# A

**a.fi.xar** *v.* to stick.

**a.fli.ção** *s.* affliction.

**a.fli.gir** *v.* to distress.

**a.flu.ir** *v.* to flow.

**a.fo.ba.ção** *s.* fluster, panic.

**a.fo.ba.do** *adj.* flustered.

**a.fo.bar** *v.* to fluster, to hurry.

**a.fo.gar** *v.* to drown.

**a.foi.to** *adj.* bold, daring.

**a.fres.co** *s.* fresco.

**a.fun.dar** *v.* to sink.

**a.gar.rar** *v.* to seize.

**a.ga.sa.lhar** *v.* to shelter, to protect, to cover.

**a.ga.sa.lho** *s.* coat, warm clothing.

**a.gên.cia** *s.* agency, office.

**a.gen.ci.ar** *v.* to negotiate, to procure.

**a.gen.da** *s.* agenda, diary.

**a.gen.te** *s.* agent.

**á.gil** *adj.* agile.

**a.gi.o.ta** *s.* moneylender.

**a.gir** *v.* to act.

**a.gi.ta.ção** *s.* agitation.

**a.gi.ta.do** *adj.* agitated.

**a.gi.tar** *v.* to agitate.

**a.glo.me.ra.ção** *s.* gathering.

**a.glo.me.rar** *v.* to heap up.

**a.go.ni.a** *s.* agony.

**a.go.ra** *adv.* now.

**a.gos.to** *s.* August.

**a.gou.rar** *v.* to predict.

**a.gou.ro** *s.* omen.

**a.gra.dar** *v.* to please.

**a.gra.dá.vel** *adj.* pleasant.

**a.gra.de.cer** *v.* to thank.

**a.grá.rio** *adj.* agrarian.

**a.gra.van.te** *adj.* aggravating.

**a.gra.var** *v.* to aggravate.

**a.gre.dir** *v.* to attack.

**a.gres.são** *s.* attack.

**a.gres.si.vo** *adj.* aggressive.

**a.gres.te** *adj.* rural, rustic.

**a.gri.ão** *s.* watercress.

**a.grí.co.la** *adj.* agricultural.

**a.gri.cul.tor** *s.* farmer.

**a.gri.cul.tu.ra** *s.* agriculture.

**a.gro.no.mia** *s.* agronomy.

**a.gro.pe.cu.á.ria** *s.* farming.

**a.gru.par** *v.* to group.

**á.gua** *s.* water.

**a.gua.do** *adj.* watery.

**a.guar.dar** *v.* to wait for.

**a.gu.do** *adj.* sharp.

**a.guen.tar** *v.* to hold on, to put up with.

**á.guia** *s.* eagle.

**a.gu.lha** *s.* needle.

**a.in.da** *adv.* still, yet.

**ai.po** *s.* celery.

**a.jo.e.lhar** *v.* to kneel down.

**a.ju.da** *s.* help, assistance.

**a.ju.dar** *v.* to help.

# ajustar 29 alô

**a.jus.tar** *v.* to adjust.
**a.jus.te** *s.* agreement.
**a.lar.me** *s.* alarm.
**a.las.trar** *v.* to scatter.
**a.la.van.ca** *s.* lever.
**al.ber.gue** *s.* shelter, lodging house.
**ál.bum** *s.* album.
**al.ça** *s.* strap.
**al.can.çar** *v.* to reach.
**al.can.ce** *s.* reach.
**al.ca.trão** *s.* tar.
**ál.co.ol** *s.* alcohol.
**al.co.rão** *s.* Koran.
**al.co.va** *s.* bedroom, alcove.
**al.cu.nha** *s.* nickname.
**al.dei.a** *s.* village.
**a.le.crim** *s.* rosemary.
**a.le.gre** *adj.* cheerful.
**a.le.gri.a** *s.* happiness.
**a.lém** *adv.* over there.
**A.le.ma.nha** *s.* Germany.
**a.le.mão(ã)** *s.* German.
**a.ler.gi.a** *s.* allergy.
**a.ler.ta** *adj.* alert.
**al.fa.be.ti.zar** *v.* to teach to read and write.
**al.fa.be.to** *s.* alphabet.
**al.fa.ce** *s.* lettuce.
**al.fai.a.te** *s.* tailor.
**al.fân.de.ga** *s.* customs.
**al.fa.ze.ma** *s.* lavender.

**al.fi.ne.te** *s.* pin.
**al.ga.ris.mo** *s.* numeral, digit.
**al.go** *adv.* somewhat / *pron. indef.* something, anything.
**al.go.dão** *s.* cotton.
**al.guém** *pron.* someone, somebody.
**al.gum(a)** *pron.* some, any.
**a.lhei.o** *adj.* someone else's.
**a.lho** *s.* garlic.
**a.li.a.do** *adj.* allied.
**a.li.an.ça** *s.* alliance.
**a.li.ar** *v.* to ally.
**a.li.ás** *adv.* besides.
**á.li.bi** *s.* alibi.
**a.li.ca.te** *s.* pliers.
**a.li.cer.ce** *s.* foundation.
**a.li.e.na.ção** *s.* alienation.
**a.li.e.na.do** *adj.* alienated / *s.* alienate.
**a.li.e.nar** *v.* to alienate.
**a.li.men.ta.ção** *s.* food.
**a.li.men.tar** *v.* to feed.
**a.li.men.to** *s.* food.
**a.lí.vio** *s.* relief.
**al.ma** *s.* soul.
**al.mo.çar** *v.* to have lunch.
**al.mo.ço** *s.* lunch.
**al.mo.fa.da** *s.* cushion.
**al.môn.de.ga** *s.* meat ball.
**al.mo.xa.ri.fa.do** *s.* storeroom.
**a.lô** *s.* hello / *interj.* hello.

**alpinismo** / **anotação**

**al.pi.nis.mo** *s.* mountaineering.
**al.tar** *s.* altar.
**al.te.ra.ção** *s.* alteration.
**al.te.rar** *v.* to alter.
**al.ter.na.ti.va** *s.* alternative.
**al.to(a)** *adj.* high.
**al.to-fa.lan.te** *s.* loudspeaker.
**al.tu.ra** *s.* height.
**a.lu.gar** *v.* to rent.
**a.lu.no** *s.* student.
**al.vo** *s.* target.
**al.vo.ra.da** *s.* dawn.
**al.vo.re.cer** *v.* to dawn / *s.* dawn, daybreak.
**a.mal.di.ço.ar** *v.* to curse.
**a.ma.nhã** *adv.* tomorrow / *s.* tomorrow.
**a.ma.nhe.cer** *v.* to dawn / *s.* dawn.
**a.man.sar** *v.* to tame.
**a.man.te** *s.* lover.
**a.mar** *v.* to love.
**a.ma.re.lo** *adj.* yellow / *s.* yellow.
**a.mar.gar** *v.* to make bitter.
**a.mar.go** *adj.* bitter.
**am.bi.ção** *s.* ambition.
**am.bos(as)** *num.* both.
**am.bu.lân.ci.a** *s.* ambulance.
**am.bu.la.tó.ri.o** *s.* outpatient department.
**a.me.a.ça** *s.* threat.
**a.mei.xa** *s.* plum.

**a.mên.do.a** *s.* almond.
**a.men.do.im** *s.* peanut.
**A.mé.ri.ca** *s.* America.
**a.mi.go(a)** *s.* friend / *adj.* friendly.
**a.mi.za.de** *s.* friendship.
**a.mo.le.cer** *v.* to soften.
**a.mor** *s.* love.
**a.mo.ra** *s.* blackberry.
**a.mos.tra** *s.* sample.
**a.nal.gé.si.co** *s.* analgesic.
**a.na.li.sar** *v.* to analyse.
**an.dar** *v.* to walk.
**an.do.ri.nha** *s.* swallow.
**a.nel** *s.* ring.
**a.ne.xar** *v.* to annex.
**an.fí.bi.o** *adj.* amphibious / *s.* amphibian.
**an.gús.ti.a** *s.* anguish.
**a.ni.ma.ção** *s.* liveliness.
**a.ni.mal** *s.* animal.
**a.ni.mar** *v.* to liven up.
**â.ni.mo** *s.* courage.
**a.ni.ver.sá.ri.o** *s.* anniversary, birthday.
**an.jo** *s.* angel.
**a.no** *s.* year.
**a.noi.te.cer** *v.* to grow dark / *s.* nightfall.
**a.no.ma.li.a** *s.* anomaly.
**a.nô.ni.mo** *adj.* anonymous.
**a.no.ta.ção** *s.* annotation.

# anotar — aquarela

**a.no.tar** *v.* to annotate.

**ân.sia** *s.* anxiety.

**an.si.e.da.de** *s.* anxiety.

**an.si.o.so** *adj.* anxious.

**an.te.ce.den.te** *adj.* preceding / *s.* antecedent

**an.te.ce.der** *v.* to precede.

**an.te.ci.pa.ção** *s.* anticipation.

**an.te.na** *s.* antenna.

**an.te.on.tem** *adv.* the day before yesterday.

**an.te.ri.or** *adj.* previous.

**an.tes** *adv.* before.

**an.ti.go** *adj.* old.

**an.ti.gui.da.de** *s.* antiquity.

**an.ti.qua.do** *adj.* antiquated.

**a.nu.lar** *v.* to cancel.

**a.nun.ci.an.te** *s.* advertiser.

**a.nun.ci.ar** *v.* to announce.

**a.nún.cio** *s.* announcement.

**a.on.de** *adv.* where.

**a.pa.gar** *v.* to put out (fogo); to erase (com borracha); to switch off (luz).

**a.pai.xo.na.do** *adj.* passioned.

**a.pa.re.cer** *v.* to appear.

**a.pa.re.lho** *s.* apparatus.

**a.pa.rên.ci.a** *s.* appearance, aspect.

**a.pe.li.do** *s.* nickname.

**a.pe.nas** *adv.* only.

**a.per.tar** *v.* to press (botão, interruptor); to shake (mãos); to tighten (parafuso, tampa, nó).

**a.pe.sar** *prep.* in spite of, although.

**a.pe.ti.te** *s.* appetite.

**a.pli.ca.ção** *s.* application.

**a.pli.car** *v.* to apply.

**a.po.dre.cer** *v.* to rot.

**a.poi.o** *s.* support.

**a.pós** *prep.* after.

**a.po.sen.ta.do** *adj.* retired / *s.* pensioner.

**a.po.sen.tar** *v.* to retire.

**a.po.sen.to** *s.* room.

**a.pos.ta** *s.* bet.

**a.pos.tar** *v.* to bet.

**a.pren.der** *v.* to learn.

**a.pre.sen.ta.ção** *s.* presentation.

**a.pre.sen.tar** *v.* to present.

**a.pres.sa.do** *adj.* hurried.

**a.pres.sar** *v.* to hurry.

**a.pro.fun.dar** *v.* to deepen.

**a.pro.va.ção** *s.* approval.

**a.pro.var** *v.* to approve.

**a.pro.vei.tar** *v.* to take advantage.

**a.pro.xi.mar** *v.* to bring closer (coisas); to bring together (pessoas); to approach (aproximar-se).

**a.qua.re.la** *s.* watercolour.

Aquário     **32**     atrasado

**A.quá.rio** *s.* Aquarius (astrologia).

**a.quá.rio** *s.* aquarium.

**a.quá.ti.co** *adj.* aquatic.

**a.que.cer** *v.* to heat.

**a.qui** *adv.* here.

**a.qui.lo** *pron.* that.

**á.ra.be** *adj.* Arab, Arabian / *s.* Arab, Arabian.

**A.rá.bia** *s.* Arabia.

**a.ra.me** *s.* wire.

**a.ra.nha** *s.* spider.

**ar.co-í.ris** *s.* rainbow.

**ar.der** *v.* to burn.

**ar.di.do** *adj.* hot.

**a.rei.a** *s.* sand.

**a.re.na** *s.* arena.

**Ar.gé.lia** *s.* Algeria.

**Ar.gen.ti.na** *s.* Argentina.

**Á.ri.es** *s.* Aries (astrologia).

**ar.gi.la** *s.* clay.

**ar.ma.di.lha** *s.* trap, snare.

**ar.má.ri.o** *s.* wardrobe.

**ar.qui.te.to** *s.* architect.

**ar.qui.var** *v.* to file.

**ar.qui.vo** *s.* file.

**ar.re.ben.tar** *v.* to break, to burst.

**ar.re.pen.der-se** *v.* to repent, to regret.

**ar.ris.car** *v.* to risk.

**ar.ro.gân.cia** *s.* arrogance.

**ar.ro.tar** *v.* to belch, to burp.

**ar.roz** *s.* rice.

**ar.ti.go** *s.* article.

**ar.tis.ta** *s.* artist.

**ár.vo.re** *s.* tree.

**as.sar** *v.* to roast.

**as.sas.si.nar** *v.* to murder.

**as.sen.tar** *v.* to seat.

**as.sim** *adv.* like this (deste modo); so, therefore (portanto).

**as.si.nar** *v.* to sign, to subscribe.

**as.si.na.tu.ra** *s.* signature, subscription.

**as.sis.ten.te** *adj.* assistant, assisting / *s.* assistant, helper.

**as.si.stir** *v.* to attend.

**as.som.brar** *v.* to astonish.

**as.sun.to** *s.* subject.

**as.sus.ta.dor** *adj.* startling, frightening, alarming.

**as.sus.tar** *v.* to frighten.

**a.ta.car** *v.* to attack.

**a.ta.que** *s.* attack.

**a.té** *prep.* until.

**a.ten.ção** *s.* attention.

**a.ten.der** *v.* to attend.

**a.ten.ta.do** *s.* attack.

**a.ten.to** *adj.* attentive.

**a.tes.ta.do** *s.* certificate.

**a.tin.gir** *v.* to reach.

**a.tra.ção** *s.* attraction.

**a.trás** *adv.* behind.

**a.tra.sa.do** *adj.* late.

atraso · azulejo

**a.tra.so** *s.* delay.
**a.tra.vés** *adv.* across, through.
**a.tra.ves.sar** *v.* to cross.
**a.tri.bu.ir** *v.* to attribute, to assign.
**a.tri.bu.to** *s.* attribute.
**a.triz** *s.* actress.
**a.tu.al** *adj.* current.
**a.tum** *s.* tuna.
**au.di.ên.ci.a** *s.* audience.
**au.la** *s.* class, lesson.
**au.men.tar** *v.* to extend, to increase.
**au.ro.ra** *s.* dawn.
**au.sên.ci.a** *s.* absence.
**Aus.trá.lia** *s.* Australia.
**Áus.tria** *s.* Austria.
**au.tên.ti.co** *adj.* authentic.
**au.to.di.da.ta** *adj.* self-taught.
**au.to.es.co.la** *s.* driving school.
**au.to.es.tra.da** *s.* expressway.
**au.to.mó.vel** *s.* car.
**au.to.no.mi.a** *s.* autonomy.

**au.to.ri.da.de** *s.* authority.
**au.xi.li.ar** *adj.* auxiliary / *s.* assistant.
**a.va.li.a.ção** *s.* evaluation, estimation.
**a.ve** *s.* bird.
**a.ve.ni.da** *s.* avenue.
**a.ven.tu.ra** *s.* adventure.
**a.ves.truz** *s.* ostrich.
**a.vi.ão** *s.* airplane.
**a.vi.sar** *v.* to warn.
**a.vô(ó)** *s.* grandfather, *fem.* grandmother.
**a.vós** *s.* grandparents.
**a.vul.so** *adj.* separate, detached, sundry.
**a.xi.la** *s.* armpit.
**a.zar** *s.* bad luck.
**a.ze.dar** *v.* to turn sour.
**a.zei.te** *s.* olive-oil.
**a.zei.to.na** *s.* olive.
**a.zi.a** *s.* heartburn.
**a.zul** *adj.* blue / *s.* blue.
**a.zu.le.jo** *s.* glazed tile.

# Bb

**B, b** *s.* the second letter of the Portuguese alphabet.

**ba.ba.ca** *adj.* stupid / *s.* fool, stupid.

**ba.ba.do** *s.* frill.

**ba.ba.dor** *s.* bib.

**ba.bar** *v.* to dribble.

**ba.ca.lhau** *s.* cod, codfish, salt cod.

**ba.ca.na** *adj.* great, nice.

**ba.cha.rel** *s.* graduate, bachelor.

**ba.ci.a** *s.* basin.

**ba.ço** *adj.* dull / *s.* spleen.

**bac.té.ria** *s.* germ, bacterium, microbe.

**ba.da.lar** *v.* to ring.

**ba.der.na** *s.* commotion, riot.

**ba.bá** *s.* babysitter, nanny.

**ba.du.la.que** *s.* trinket.

**ba.fe.jar** *v.* to blow.

**ba.fo** *s.* breath.

**ba.ga.ço** *s.* pulp.

**ba.ga.te.la** *s.* trinket.

**ba.gu.lho** *s.* trash.

**ba.gun.ça** *s.* mess.

**ba.gun.ça.do** *adj.* messy.

**ba.gun.çar** *v.* to mess up.

**ba.í.a** *s.* bay.

**bai.la.do** *s.* dance.

**bai.lar** *v.* to dance.

**bai.le** *s.* dance, ball.

**bair.ro** *s.* neighborhood.

**bai.xa** *s.* decrease.

**bai.xar** *v.* to lower.

**bai.xo(a)** *adj.* low, short / *s.* bass (instrumento musical).

**ba.la** *s.* bullet, shot (arma); candy, sweet (doces).
**ba.la.da** *s.* ballad; party.
**ba.lai.o** *s.* straw basket.
**ba.lan.ça** *s.* scales.
**ba.lan.çar** *v.* to swing.
**ba.lan.ço** *s.* swing.
**ba.lão** *s.* balloon.
**ba.la.ús.tre** *s.* banister, baluster.
**bal.bu.ci.ar** *v.* to babble, to stammer.
**bal.búr.di.a** *s.* uproar, disorder, tumult.
**bal.cão** *s.* balcony, counter.
**bal.de** *s.* bucket.
**bal.de.a.ção** *s.* transfer.
**ba.lé** *s.* ballet.
**ba.lei.a** *s.* whale.
**ba.li.za** *s.* post, mark, landmark.
**bal.ne.á.ri.o** *s.* bathing resort.
**ba.lo.fo(a)** *adj.* plump (coloquial).
**bal.sa** *s.* raft.
**bál.sa.mo** *s.* balm.
**ba.lu.ar.te** *s.* rampart.
**bam.ba** *s.* expert.
**bam.bo** *adj.* loose.
**bam.bo.le.ar** *v.* to swing.
**bam.bu** *s.* bamboo.
**ba.nal** *adj.* banal.
**ba.na.na** *s.* banana.
**ban.car** *v.* to finance.
**ban.car.ro.ta** *s.* bankruptcy.

**ban.co** *s.* bench (assento); bank (comercial).
**ban.da** *s.* band, side, flank.
**ban.dei.ra** *s.* flag.
**ban.de.ja** *s.* tray.
**ban.di.do** *s.* bandit, gangster, outlaw.
**ban.do** *s.* band, gang.
**ban.ga.lô** *s.* bungalow.
**ba.nha** *s.* fat, lard.
**ba.nhar** *v.* to bathe, to wet.
**ba.nhei.ra** *s.* bathtub.
**ba.nhei.ro** *s.* bathroom.
**ba.nho** *s.* shower (de chuveiro), bath (de banheira).
**ba.nir** *v.* to banish.
**ban.quei.ro(a)** *s.* banker.
**ban.que.ta** *s.* stool.
**ban.que.te** *s.* banquet.
**bar** *s.* bar, pub.
**ba.ra.lho** *s.* pack of cards.
**ba.rão** *s.* baron.
**ba.ra.ta** *s.* cockroach.
**ba.ra.to(a)** *adj.* cheap.
**bar.ba** *s.* beard.
**bar.ban.te** *s.* string.
**bar.be.a.dor** *s.* shaver.
**bar.be.ar** *v.* to shave.
**bar.bei.ro** *s.* barber.
**bar.ca** *s.* barge.
**bar.co** *s.* boat.
**bar.ga.nha** *s.* bargain.

barômetro 36 Bélgica

**ba.rô.me.tro** *s.* barometer.

**bar.quei.ro** *s.* boatman.

**bar.ra** *s.* bar.

**bar.ra.ca** *s.* tent.

**bar.ra.gem** *s.* dam.

**bar.ran.co** *s.* ravine.

**bar.rar** *v.* to bar.

**bar.rei.ra** *s.* barrier.

**bar.ri.ca.da** *s.* barricade.

**bar.ri.ga** *s.* belly.

**bar.ril** *s.* barrel.

**bar.ro** *s.* clay.

**ba.ru.lhen.to** *adj.* noisy.

**ba.ru.lho** *s.* noise.

**ba.se** *s.* base.

**bá.si.co** *adj.* basic.

**bas.que.te** *s.* basketball.

**bas.tan.te** *adj.* enough.

**bas.tão** *s.* stick.

**bas.tar** *v.* to be enough.

**bas.tar.do(a)** *adj.* bastard
/ *s.* bastard, illegitimate child.

**bas.ti.dor** *s.* embroidery, frame.

**ba.ta.lha** *s.* battle.

**ba.ta.ta** *s.* potato.

**ba.te-bo.ca** *s.* row, bawling,
quarrel.

**ba.te.dei.ra** *s.* beater, mixer.

**ba.te.dor** *s.* beater.

**ba.ten.te** *s.* doorpost.

**ba.te-pa.po** *s.* chat.

**ba.ter** *v.* to beat.

**ba.te.ri.a** *s.* battery;
drums (instrumento musical).

**ba.ti.da** *s.* beat.

**ba.ti.na** *s.* cassock.

**ba.tis.mo** *s.* baptism, christening.

**ba.ti.zar** *v.* to baptize,
to christen.

**ba.tom** *s.* lipstick.

**ba.tu.ca.da** *s.* dance percussion
group.

**ba.tu.car** *v.* to drum.

**ba.tu.ta** *s.* baton, wand.

**ba.ú** *s.* trunk.

**bau.ni.lha** *s.* vanilla.

**ba.zar** *s.* bazaar.

**be.a.to(a)** *adj.* prous person,
devout.

**bê.ba.do(a)** *adj.* drunk.

**be.bê** *s.* baby.

**be.be.dou.ro** *s.* drinking
fountain.

**be.ber** *v.* to drink.

**be.co** *s.* alley.

**be.ge** *adj.* beige / *s.* beige.

**bei.ço** *s.* lip.

**bei.ja-flor** *s.* hummingbird.

**bei.jar** *v.* to kiss.

**bei.ra** *s.* edge.

**bei.rar** *v.* to be at the edge.

**be.le.za** *s.* beauty.

**bel.ga** *adj.* Belgian / *s.* Belgian.

**Bél.gi.ca** *s.* Belgium.

**be.lis.cão** *s.* pinch.

**be.lo** *adj.* beautiful; handsome.

**bem** *adv.* well, good, nice / *s.* the good, goodness.

**bem-es.tar** *s.* well-being, comfort.

**bem-vin.do** *adj.* welcome.

**bên.ção** *s.* blessing.

**ben.di.to(a)** *adj.* blessed.

**be.ne.fi.cên.cia** *s.* beneficence, charity.

**be.ne.fi.ci.ar** *v.* to benefit.

**be.ne.fí.ci.o** *s.* benefit.

**ben.ga.la** *s.* walking stick.

**be.nig.no** *adj.* benign.

**bens** *s.* goods.

**ben.to(a)** *adj.* sacred.

**ben.zer** *v.* to bless, to consecrate.

**ber.ço** *s.* cradle.

**be.rin.je.la** *s.* aubergine.

**Ber.lim** *s.* Berlin.

**ber.rar** *v.* to bellow, to cry, to shout.

**be.sou.ro** *s.* beetle.

**bes.ta** *adj.* stupid / *s.* mare, mule.

**be.ter.ra.ba** *s.* beetroot.

**be.to.nei.ra** *s.* cement mixer.

**be.tu.me** *s.* asphalt.

**be.xi.ga** *s.* bladder.

**be.zer.ro** *s.* calf.

**bí.blia** *s.* Bible.

**bi.bli.o.gra.fi.a** *s.* bibliography.

**bi.bli.o.te.ca** *s.* library.

**bi.ca** *s.* tap.

**bi.car** *v.* to peck.

**bi.cho** *s.* animal.

**bi.ci.cle.ta** *s.* bicycle.

**bi.co** *s.* beak.

**bi.dê** *s.* bidet.

**bi.fe** *s.* steak.

**bi.go.de** *s.* moustache.

**bi.gor.na** *s.* anvil.

**bi.ju.te.ri.a** *s.* costume jewellery.

**bi.lhar** *s.* billards.

**bi.lhe.te** *s.* ticket (passagem); note (recado).

**bi.lín.gue** *adj.* bilingual.

**bin.go** *s.* bingo, game of chance.

**bi.o.gra.fi.a** *s.* biography.

**bi.o.lo.gi.a** *s.* biology.

**bi.om.bo** *s.* screen.

**bi.ru.ta** *adj.* crazy, lunatic / *s.* windsock (aeronáutica).

**bi.sa.vô(ó)** *s.* great-grandfather, *fem.* great-grandmother.

**bis.ca.te** *s.* odd job.

**bis.coi.to** *s.* biscuit, cookie, cracker.

**bis.na.ga** *s.* tube.

**bis.ne.to(a)** *s.* great-grandson, *fem.* great-granddaughter.

**bis.po** *s.* bishop.

**bis.tu.ri** *s.* scalpel.

**bi.to.la** *s.* gauge.

**bi.zar.ro** *adj.* bizarre.

**blas.fe.mar** *v.* to curse.

**ble.cau.te** *s.* power cut; black-out.

**blin.da.do(a)** *adj.* armoured.

**blin.da.gem** *s.* armour, screening.

**blo.co** *s.* block.

**blo.que.ar** *v.* to blockade.

**blu.sa** *s.* blouse.

**bo.a.te** *s.* nightclub.

**bo.a.to** *s.* rumour.

**bo.ba.gem** *s.* silliness, nonsense, trash.

**bo.bi.na** *s.* reel, bobbin.

**bo.bo(a)** *adj.* silly.

**bo.ca** *s.* mouth.

**bo.ca.do** *s.* mouthful, piece, morsel.

**bo.cal** *s.* mouth, mouthpiece, nozzle.

**bo.çal** *adj.* ignorant, rude.

**bo.ce.jar** *v.* to yawn.

**bo.de** *s.* goat.

**bo.fe.ta.da** *s.* slap in the face.

**bo.fe.tão** *s.* punch, blow with the fist.

**boi** *s.* ox.

**boi.a** *s.* buoy.

**boi.a.da** *s.* herd of cattle.

**boi.ar** *v.* to float.

**boi.co.tar** *v.* to boycott.

**bo.la** *s.* ball.

**bo.la.cha** *s.* biscuit, cracker, cookies.

**bo.le.tim** *s.* report.

**bo.lha** *s.* blister, bubble.

**bo.li.che** *s.* bowling.

**Bo.lí.via** *s.* Bolivia.

**bo.lo** *s.* cake.

**bo.lor** *s.* mould.

**bol.sa** *s.* bag.

**bol.so** *s.* pocket.

**bom/boa** *adj.* good, nice.

**bom.ba** *s.* bomb.

**bom.bar.de.ar** *v.* to bomb.

**bom.be.ar** *v.* to pump.

**bom.bei.ro** *s.* fireman.

**bom.bom** *s.* chocolate.

**bon.da.de** *s.* goodness.

**bon.de** *s.* tram.

**bon.do.so(a)** *adj.* kindhearted.

**bo.né** *s.* cap.

**bo.ne.ca** *s.* doll.

**bo.ne.co** *s.* dummy, puppet.

**bo.ni.to(a)** *adj.* pretty.

**bô.nus** *s.* bonus.

**bo.qui.a.ber.to** *adj.* dumbfounded.

**bor.bo.le.ta** *s.* butterfly.

**bor.bu.lhar** *v.* to bubble.

**bor.da.do** *s.* embroidery / *adj.* embroidered.

**bor.dão** *s.* staff.

**bor.dar** *v.* to embroider.

**bor.ra.cha** *s.* rubber, eraser.

**bor.rar** *v.* to blot.

**bor.ri.far** *v.* to sprinkle.

**bos.que** *s.* forest, woods.
**bos.sa** *s.* bump, hump.
**bo.ta** *s.* boot.
**bo.tâ.ni.ca** *s.* botany.
**bo.tâ.ni.co** *s.* botanist.
**bo.tão** *s.* button.
**bo.te** *s.* boat.
**bo.te.quim** *s.* bar, tavern.
**bra.ça.da** *s.* armful.
**bra.ça.dei.ra** *s.* armband.
**bra.ce.le.te** *s.* bracelet.
**bra.ço** *s.* arm.
**bra.dar** *v.* to shout.
**bran.co(a)** *adj.* white / *s.* white.
**bran.que.ar** *v.* to whiten.
**bra.sa** *s.* hot coal.
**bra.sei.ro** *s.* brazier.
**Bra.sil** *s.* Brazil.
**bra.si.lei.ro** *adj.* Brazilian
/ *s.* Brazilian.
**bra.va.ta** *s.* bravado.
**bra.vo(a)** *adj.* angry.
**bre.car** *v.* to stop, to brake.
**bre.cha** *s.* breach, gap.
**bre.jo** *s.* marsh.
**bre.que** *s.* brake.
**bre.ve** *adj.* short.
**bri.ga** *s.* fight.
**bri.ga.da** *s.* brigade.
**bri.gar** *v.* to fight.
**bri.lhan.te** *adj.* bright
/ *s.* diamond.

**bri.lhar** *v.* to shine.
**brin.ca.dei.ra** *s.* fun.
**brin.ca.lhão(ona)** *adj.* playful
/ *s.* joker.
**brin.car** *v.* to play, to have fun.
**brin.que.do** *s.* toy.
**brio** *s.* self-respect.
**bri.sa** *s.* breeze.
**bri.tâ.ni.co** *adj.* British
/ *s.* British.
**bro.che** *s.* brooch.
**bro.chu.ra** *s.* paper-back,
brochure.
**bró.co.lis** *s.* broccoli.
**bron.ca** *s.* telling off.
**bron.co(a)** *adj.* coarse / *s.* idiot,
dunce.
**bron.qui.te** *s.* bronchitis.
**bron.ze** *s.* bronze.
**bro.tar** *v.* to produce, to sprout,
to bud.
**bro.to** *s.* youngster, bud, sprout.
**bru.tal** *adj.* brutal.
**bru.to(a)** *adj.* rude, rough,
coarse.
**bru.xa** *s.* witch.
**Bru.xe.las** *s.* Brussels.
**br.uxo** *s.* wizard.
**bu.ço** *s.* down.
**bu.dis.mo** *s.* Buddhism.
**bú.fa.lo** *s.* buffalo.
**bu.far** *v.* to puff.

**bu.fê** *s.* sideboard.
**bu.gi.gan.ga** *s.* trinket.
**bu.jão** *s.* gas cylinder.
**bul.bo** *s.* bulb.
**bu.le** *s.* teapot.
**Bul.gá.ri.a** *s.* Bulgaria.
**búl.ga.ro** *adj.* Bulgarian
/ *s.* Bulgarian.
**bun.da** *s.* backside (coloquial).
**bu.quê** *s.* bouquet, bunch.
**bu.ra.co** *s.* hole.

**bur.guês(esa)** *adj.* bourgeois
/ *s.* bourgeois.
**bur.gue.si.a** *s.* bourgeoisie.
**bu.ro.cra.cia** *s.* bureaucracy.
**bur.ro(a)** *adj.* stupid, dumb
/ *s.* donkey.
**bus.ca** *s.* search.
**bus.car** *v.* to fetch, to seek.
**bús.so.la** *s.* compass.
**bus.to** *s.* bust.
**bu.zi.na** *s.* horn.

# Cc

**C, c** *s.* the third letter of the Portuguese alphabet.

**ca.ba.na** *s.* shack, hut.

**ca.be.ça** *s.* head.

**ca.be.cei.ra** *s.* head (da mesa), headboard (da cama).

**ca.be.çu.do(a)** *adj.* bigheaded.

**ca.be.lo** *s.* hair.

**ca.ber** *v.* to fit.

**ca.bi.de** *s.* hanger.

**ca.bi.ne** *s.* cabin, cockpit.

**ca.bis.bai.xo(a)** *adj.* downcast, depressed.

**ca.bo** *s.* handle.

**ca.bra** *s.* goat.

**ca.brei.ro(a)** *adj.* suspicious.

**ca.bres.to** *s.* halter.

**ca.bri.to** *s.* young goat, kid.

**ca.ça** *s.* hunting.

**ca.ça-ní.queis** *s.* shot machine.

**ca.ção** *s.* shark.

**ca.çar** *v.* to hunt.

**ca.ca.re.jar** *v.* to cluck.

**ca.ça.ro.la** *s.* saucepan.

**ca.cau** *s.* cocoa, cacao.

**ca.ce.ta.da** *s.* blow with a club, whack.

**ca.cha.ça** *s.* white rum, sugar cane liquor.

**ca.cha.cei.ro(a)** *adj.* drunkard / *s.* drunkard.

**ca.chê** *s.* fee.

**ca.che.col** *s.* scarf.

**ca.che.pô** *s.* plant pot.

**ca.chim.bo** *s.* pipe.

**ca.cho** *s.* bunch; curl (cabelos).

**ca.cho.ei.ra** *s.* waterfall.

**ca.chor.ra** *s.* bitch, a female dog.

# cachorrinho 42 calota

**ca.chor.ri.nho(a)** *s.* puppy.
**ca.chor.ro** *s.* dog.
**ca.ci.que** *s.* chief, Indian tribal chief.
**ca.co** *s.* fragment.
**ca.ço.ar** *v.* to mock.
**ca.co.e.te** *s.* twitch.
**cac.to** *s.* cactus.
**ca.da** *adj.* each.
**ca.das.tro** *s.* register, records.
**ca.dá.ver** *s.* corpse.
**ca.dê** *adv.* where (coloquial).
**ca.de.a.do** *s.* padlock.
**ca.dei.a** *s.* chain, prison.
**ca.dei.ra** *s.* chair.
**ca.de.la** *s.* bitch.
**ca.dên.ci.a** *s.* cadence.
**ca.der.ne.ta** *s.* notebook.
**ca.der.no** *s.* notebook.
**ca.de.te** *s.* cadet.
**ca.du.car** *v.* to lapse, to expire.
**ca.fa.jes.te** *adj.* roguish
/ *s.* rogue.
**ca.fé** *s.* coffee.
**ca.fe.í.na** *s.* caffeine.
**ca.fe.tei.ra** *s.* coffee pot.
**cá.ga.do** *s.* turtle.
**ca.gar** *v.* to shit (coloquial).
**cãi.bra** *s.* cramp.
**ca.í.do(a)** *adj.* dejected, fallen.
**cai.pi.ra** *s.* peasant, yokel.
**cair** *v.* to fall.

**cais** *s.* quay.
**cai.xa** *s.* box.
**cai.xão** *s.* coffin.
**cai.xo.te** *s.* packing case.
**ca.ju** *s.* cashew nut.
**cal** *s.* lime.
**ca.la.bou.ço** *s.* dungeon.
**ca.la.do(a)** *adj.* quiet.
**ca.la.frio** *s.* shiver.
**ca.lar** *v.* to keep silent,
to get to be quiet.
**cal.ça.da** *s.* pavement, sidewalk.
**cal.ça.do** *adj.* paved
/ *s.* footwear.
**cal.ca.nhar** *s.* heel.
**cal.çar** *v.* to put on.
**cal.ças** *s.* pants.
**cal.ci.nha** *s.* panties.
**cal.cu.lar** *v.* to calculate.
**cál.cu.lo** *s.* calculation.
**cal.do** *s.* broth.
**ca.len.dá.rio** *s.* calendar.
**ca.lha** *s.* gutter.
**ca.lha.ma.ço** *s.* tome.
**cá.li.ce** *s.* wine glass.
**cal.ma** *s.* calm.
**cal.man.te** *adj.* soothing
/ *s.* tranquilizer, sedative.
**cal.mo(a)** *adj.* calm.
**ca.lor** *s.* heat, warmth.
**ca.lo.ria** *s.* calorie.
**ca.lo.ta** *s.* hubcap.

**ca.lou.ro(a)** *s.* fresher.
**ca.lú.nia** *s.* slander.
**ca.ma** *s.* bed.
**ca.ma.da** *s.* layer.
**ca.ma.ra.da** *adj.* friendly / *s.* comrade, pal, buddy.
**ca.ma.rão** *s.* shrimp.
**ca.ma.rei.ro(a)** *s.* cleaner, room servant.
**ca.ma.rim** *s.* dressing room.
**ca.ma.ro.te** *s.* cabin, box.
**cam.ba.le.ar** *v.* to stagger.
**cam.ba.lho.ta** *s.* somersault.
**ca.mi.nha.da** *s.* walk, stroll, hike.
**ca.mi.nhão** *s.* truck.
**ca.mi.nhar** *v.* to walk.
**ca.mi.nho** *s.* way.
**ca.mi.nho.nei.ro(a)** *s.* truck driver.
**ca.mi.sa** *s.* shirt.
**ca.mi.se.ta** *s.* T-shirt.
**ca.mi.si.nha** *s.* condom.
**ca.mi.so.la** *s.* night-dress.
**cam.pa.i.nha** *s.* bell.
**cam.pe.ão(ã)** *s.* champion.
**cam.pes.tre** *adj.* rural.
**cam.po** *s.* countryside; field.
**cam.po.nês(esa)** *s.* peasant.
**ca.mu.fla.gem** *s.* camouflage, disguise.
**ca.mu.flar** *v.* to camouflage, to disguise.

**ca.mun.don.go** *s.* mouse.
**ca.mur.ça** *s.* suede.
**ca.na** *s.* cane.
**Ca.na.dá** *s.* Canada.
**ca.nal** *s.* channel.
**ca.na.lha** *s.* rabble / *adj.* infamous, vile.
**ca.na.li.za.ção** *s.* plumbing.
**ca.na.li.zar** *v.* to canalize, to pipe.
**ca.na.pé** *s.* sofa.
**ca.ná.rio** *s.* canary.
**ca.na.vi.al** *s.* sugar cane plantation, reed plot.
**can.ção** *s.* song.
**can.ce.la.men.to** *s.* cancellation.
**can.ce.lar** *v.* to cross out.
**cân.cer** *s.* cancer.
**Cân.cer** *s.* Cancer (astrologia).
**can.de.la.bro** *s.* candlestick.
**can.di.da.to(a)** *s.* candidate.
**ca.ne.ca** *s.* mug.
**ca.ne.co** *s.* tankard.
**ca.ne.la** *s.* cinnamon (especiaria); shin (perna).
**ca.ne.ta** *s.* pen.
**can.gu.ru** *s.* kangaroo.
**ca.nhão** *s.* cannon.
**ca.nho.to(a)** *adj.* left-handed (pessoa).
**ca.ni.bal** *s.* canibal / *adj.* canibal.
**ca.nil** *s.* kennel.

**ca.ni.ve.te** *s.* penknife.
**can.ja** *s.* chicken broth.
**can.ji.ca** *s.* maize porridge.
**ca.no** *s.* pipe.
**ca.no.a** *s.* canoe.
**can.sa.do(a)** *adj.* tired.
**can.sar** *v.* to tire.
**can.tar** *v.* to sing.
**can.tei.ro** *s.* stone-mason
(obras); flower bed (flores).
**can.ti.ga** *s.* ballad.
**can.ti.na** *s.* canteen.
**can.to** *s.* corner; song.
**cant.or(a)** *s.* singer.
**ca.nu.di.nho** *s.* straw.
**ca.nu.do** *s.* tube.
**cão** *s.* dog.
**ca.o.lho(a)** *adj.* cross-eyed.
**caos** *s.* chaos.
**ca.pa** *s.* cape, cloak; cover.
**ca.pa.ce.te** *s.* helmet.
**ca.pa.ci.da.de** *s.* capacity.
**ca.paz** *adj.* able, capable.
**cap.ci.o.so** *adj.* tricky.
**ca.pe.la** *s.* chapel.
**ca.pim** *s.* grass.
**ca.pi.nar** *v.* to weed.
**ca.pi.tal** *adj.* capital, essential
/ *s.* capital, funds.
**ca.pi.ta.lis.mo** *s.* capitalism.
**ca.pi.tão** *s.* captain.
**ca.pí.tu.lo** *s.* chapter.

**ca.pô** *s.* bonnet.
**ca.po.ta** *s.* hood.
**ca.po.tar** *v.* to overturn.
**ca.po.te** *s.* overcoat.
**ca.pri.cho** *s.* whim.
**Ca.pri.cór.nio** *s.* Capricorn
(astrologia).
**cap.tar** *v.* to win, to pick up.
**cap.tu.ra** *s.* capture.
**ca.puz** *s.* hood.
**cá.qui** *adj.* khaki.
**ca.ra** *s.* face.
**ca.ra.col** *s.* snail (animal)
/ *adj.* curl (cabelo).
**ca.rac.te.rís.ti.co** *adj.*
characteristic.
**ca.ra de pau** *adj.* brazen.
**ca.ran.gue.jo** *s.* crab.
**ca.rá.ter** *s.* character.
**car.dá.pi.o** *s.* menu.
**car.du.me** *s.* shoal.
**ca.re.ca** *adj.* bald / *s.* baldness.
**ca.rên.cia** *s.* lack.
**ca.re.ta** *adj.* straight / *s.* grimace.
**car.ga** *s.* load.
**ca.rí.cia** *s.* caress.
**ca.ri.da.de** *s.* charity.
**cá.rie** *s.* tooth decay.
**ca.rim.bar** *v.* to stamp.
**ca.rim.bo** *s.* stamp.
**ca.ri.nho** *s.* affection.
**ca.ris.ma** *s.* charism.

# carnaval · cavaleiro

**car.na.val** *s.* carnival.

**car.ne** *s.* meat; flesh.

**car.nei.ro** *s.* sheep.

**ca.ro** *adj.* expensive.

**ca.ro.na** *s.* lift.

**car.pe.te** *s.* carpet.

**car.pin.ta.ri.a** *s.* carpentry.

**car.pin.tei.ro(a)** *s.* carpenter.

**car.ran.ca** *s.* frown.

**car.ra.pa.to** *s.* tick.

**car.ras.co** *s.* executioner.

**car.re.ga.do(a)** *adj.* loaded.

**car.re.ga.dor** *s.* porter, cartier, loader.

**car.re.ga.men.to** *s.* loading.

**car.re.gar** *v.* to load.

**car.rei.ra** *s.* career.

**car.re.ta** *s.* cart.

**car.ro** *s.* car.

**car.ro.ça** *s.* wagon, cart.

**car.ro-che.fe** *s.* main float.

**car.ro.ci.nha** *s.* tilt-car.

**car.ros.sel** *s.* merry-go-round.

**car.ru.a.gem** *s.* carriage.

**car.ta** *s.* card, playing card; letter.

**car.taz** *s.* poster.

**car.tei.ra** *s.* wallet.

**car.tei.ro** *s.* postman.

**car.tu.cho** *s.* cartridge.

**car.va.lho** *s.* oak.

**car.vão** *s.* coal.

**ca.sa** *s.* house.

**ca.sa.co** *s.* coat.

**ca.sal** *s.* couple.

**ca.sa.men.to** *s.* marriage, wedding.

**ca.sar** *v.* to marry.

**ca.sa.rão** *s.* mansion.

**cas.ca** *s.* skin.

**cas.ca.ta** *s.* waterfall.

**ca.sei.ro(a)** *adj.* homemade / *s.* housekeeper.

**ca.so** *s.* case.

**cas.pa** *s.* dandruff.

**cas.sar** *v.* to cancel.

**cas.se.te** *s.* cassette.

**cas.si.no** *s.* casino.

**cas.te.lo** *s.* castle.

**ca.tá.lo.go** *s.* catalogue.

**ca.tar** *v.* to pick up, to seek; to gather.

**ca.ta.ra.ta** *s.* waterfall.

**ca.te.dral** *s.* cathedral.

**ca.te.go.ri.a** *s.* category.

**ca.ti.var** *v.* to enslave.

**ca.ti.vo** *s.* slave.

**ca.tó.li.co** *adj.* Catholic / *s.* Catholic.

**ca.tor.ze** *num.* fourteen.

**cau.le** *s.* stalk.

**cau.sa** *s.* cause.

**cau.te.la** *s.* caution.

**ca.va.lei.ro** *adj.* horseman.

cavalheiro · 46 · chalé

**ca.va.lhei.ro** *adj.* gentleman / *s.* gentleman.
**ca.va.lo** *s.* horse.
**ca.var** *v.* to dig.
**ca.vei.ra** *s.* skull.
**ca.ver.na** *s.* cavern.
**ce.bo.la** *s.* onion.
**ce.der** *v.* to give up.
**ce.do** *adv.* early.
**ce.dro** *s.* cedar.
**cé.du.la** *s.* banknote.
**ce.gar** *v.* to blind.
**ce.go(a)** *adj.* blind.
**ce.go.nha** *s.* stork.
**cei.a** *s.* supper.
**cei.fa** *s.* harvest.
**ce.la** *s.* cell.
**ce.le.bra.ção** *s.* celebration.
**ce.le.brar** *v.* to celebrate.
**cé.le.bre** *adj.* famous.
**ce.le.bri.da.de** *s.* celebrity.
**ce.lei.ro** *s.* granary, barn.
**ce.les.te** *adj.* celestial, heavenly.
**ce.lu.lar** *adj.* cellular.
**cem** *num.* hundred.
**ce.mi.té.ri.o** *s.* cemetery.
**ce.na** *s.* scene.
**ce.nou.ra** *s.* carrot.
**cen.so** *s.* census.
**cen.su.ra** *s.* censorship.
**cen.ta.vo** *s.* cent.
**cen.tei.o** *s.* rye.

**cen.te.lha** *s.* spark.
**cen.te.na** *num.* hundred.
**cen.te.ná.ri.o** *s.* centenary.
**cen.tí.me.tro** *s.* centimetre.
**cen.tral** *adj.* central.
**cen.tro** *s.* centre, center.
**cer.car** *v.* to enclose.
**cer.co** *s.* siege.
**ce.re.al** *s.* cereal.
**cé.re.bro** *s.* brain.
**ce.re.ja** *s.* cherry.
**ce.ri.mô.ni.a** *s.* ceremony.
**cer.ne** *s.* kernel, core.
**cer.te.za** *s.* certainty.
**cer.ti.dão** *s.* certificate.
**cer.ti.fi.car** *v.* to certify.
**cer.to(a)** *adj.* certain, right.
**cer.ve.ja** *s.* beer.
**cer.vi.cal** *adj.* cervical.
**cer.vo** *s.* deer.
**ces.sa.ção** *s.* halting.
**ces.são** *s.* surrender.
**ces.sar** *v.* to cease.
**ces.ta** *s.* basket.
**ce.tro** *s.* sceptre.
**céu** *s.* sky.
**chá** *s.* tea.
**chá.ca.ra** *s.* small farm.
**cha.ci.na** *s.* slaughter.
**cha.co.ta** *s.* mockery.
**cha.fa.riz** *s.* fountain.
**cha.lé** *s.* chalet.

# chamada — ciclone

**cha.ma.da** *s.* call.

**cha.mar** *v.* to call.

**cha.ma.riz** *s.* decoy.

**chan.ce** *s.* chance.

**chan.ta.ge.ar** *v.* to blackmail.

**chan.ta.gem** *s.* blackmail.

**chão** *s.* ground.

**cha.pa** *s.* plate.

**cha.péu** *s.* hat.

**cha.ru.to** *s.* cigar.

**cha.te.ar** *v.* to bother.

**cha.ti.ce** *s.* nuisance.

**cha.to(a)** *adj.* flat (plano); boring (entediante).

**cha.ve** *s.* key.

**cha.vei.ro** *s.* keyring.

**che.car** *v.* to check.

**che.fe** *s.* chief; boss.

**che.ga.da** *s.* arrival.

**che.gar** *v.* to arrive.

**chei.o(a)** *adj.* full.

**chei.rar** *v.* to smell.

**che.que** *s.* check.

**chi.a.do** *s.* squeak.

**chi.cle.te** *s.* chewing gum.

**chi.có.ri.a** *s.* chicory.

**chi.co.te** *s.* whip.

**chi.fra.da** *s.* butt.

**chi.fre** *s.* horn.

**Chi.le** *s.* Chile.

**chim.pan.zé** *s.* chimpanzee.

**Chi.na** *s.* China.

**chi.ne.lo** *s.* slipper.

**chi.nês(esa)** *adj.* Chinese / *s.* Chinese.

**chi.que** *adj.* chic.

**chi.quei.ro** *s.* pigsty.

**cho.can.te** *adj.* shocking.

**cho.car** *v.* to hatch (ovo); to crash (colidir).

**cho.co.la.te** *s.* chocolate.

**cho.fer** *s.* driver.

**cho.pe** *s.* draught beer.

**cho.que** *s.* shock; collision.

**cho.rar** *v.* to cry, to weep.

**cho.ro** *s.* crying.

**cho.ver** *v.* to rain.

**chu.chu** *s.* chayote.

**chu.lé** *s.* foot odour (coloquial).

**chu.ma.ço** *s.* wad.

**chum.bo** *s.* lead.

**chu.par** *v.* to suck.

**chu.pe.ta** *s.* dummy.

**chur.ras.co** *s.* barbecue.

**chu.tar** *v.* to kick.

**chu.te** *s.* kick.

**chu.tei.ra** *s.* football boot.

**chu.va** *s.* rain.

**chu.vo.so** *adj.* rainy.

**ci.ca.triz** *s.* scar.

**ci.clis.mo** *s.* cycling.

**ci.clis.ta** *s.* cyclist.

**ci.clo** *s.* cycle.

**ci.clo.ne** *s.* cyclone.

# cidadania · 48 · cócoras

**ci.da.da.ni.a** *s.* citizenship.
**ci.da.dão(ã)** *s.* citizen.
**ci.da.de** *s.* town, city.
**ci.ên.cia** *v.* science.
**ci.en.te** *adj.* aware.
**ci.en.tí.fi.co** *adj.* scientific.
**ci.en.tis.ta** *s.* scientist.
**ci.ga.no(a)** *s.* gypsy.
**ci.gar.ra** *s.* cicada.
**ci.gar.ri.lha** *s.* cheroot, cigarrilo.
**ci.gar.ro** *s.* cigarette.
**ci.mei.ra** *s.* summit.
**ci.men.tar** *v.* to cement.
**ci.men.to** *s.* cement.
**cin.co** *num.* five.
**ci.ne.as.ta** *s.* film maker.
**ci.ne.ma** *s.* movies.
**cí.ni.co(a)** *adj.* cynical.
**cin.quen.ta** *num.* fifty.
**cin.to** *s.* belt.
**cin.tu.ra** *s.* waist.
**cin.za** *s.* ash / *adj.* gray.
**cin.zei.ro** *s.* ashtray.
**cir.co** *s.* circus.
**cir.cui.to** *s.* circuit.
**cir.cu.la.ção** *s.* circulation.
**cír.cu.lo** *s.* circle.
**ci.rur.gi.a** *s.* surgery.
**ci.rur.gi.ão(ã)** *s.* surgeon.
**cis.ne** *s.* swan.
**ci.tar** *v.* to quote.
**ci.ú.me** *s.* jealousy.

**ci.vil** *adj.* civil / *s.* civilian.
**ci.vi.li.za.ção** *s.* civilization.
**cla.ro** *adj.* clear; light.
**clas.se** *s.* class.
**clás.si.co(a)** *adj.* classical.
**clas.si.fi.ca.ção** *s.* classification.
**clas.si.fi.ca.do(a)** *adj.* classified, ranked.
**clas.si.fi.car** *v.* to classify.
**cláu.su.la** *s.* clause.
**cla.ví.cu.la** *s.* collar bone.
**cle.mên.cia** *s.* mercy.
**cli.en.te** *s.* customer.
**cli.ma** *s.* climate.
**clí.ni.ca** *s.* clinic.
**clu.be** *s.* club.
**co.bai.a** *s.* guinea pig.
**co.ber.ta** *s.* cover; bedspread (cama).
**co.ber.to(a)** *adj.* covered.
**co.ber.tor** *s.* blanket.
**co.ber.tu.ra** *s.* covering.
**co.bi.ça** *s.* greed.
**co.bi.çar** *v.* to covet.
**co.bra** *s.* snake.
**co.brir** *v.* to cover.
**co.ca.da** *s.* coconut sweet.
**co.çar** *v.* to scratch.
**co.cei.ra** *s.* itch.
**co.chi.char** *v.* to whisper.
**co.co** *s.* coconut.
**có.co.ras** *s.* squatting.

código 49 comportamento

**có.di.go** *s.* code.
**co.dor.na** *s.* quail.
**co.e.lho** *s.* rabbit.
**co.e.ren.te** *adj.* coherent.
**co.fre** *s.* safe.
**co.gi.tar** *v.* to contemplate.
**co.gu.me.lo** *s.* mushroom.
**co.i.bi.ção** *s.* restraint.
**coi.ce** *s.* kick.
**co.in.ci.dir** *v.* to coincide.
**coi.sa** *s.* thing.
**coi.ta.do(a)** *adj.* poor / *s.* wretch.
**co.la** *s.* glue.
**co.la.bo.ra.dor(a)** *s.* collaborator.
**co.la.bo.rar** *v.* to collaborate.
**co.lan.te** *adj.* skintight.
**co.lap.so** *s.* collapse.
**co.lar** *v.* to stick / *s.* necklace.
**col.cha** *s.* bedspread.
**col.chão** *s.* mattress.
**co.le.ção** *s.* collection.
**co.lé.gio** *s.* school.
**co.lei.ra** *s.* collar.
**co.lhei.ta** *s.* harvest.
**co.lher** *v.* to gather / *s.* spoon.
**co.li.na** *s.* hill.
**co.li.são** *s.* collision.
**col.mei.a** *s.* beehive.
**co.lo.ca.ção** *s.* act of placing, placement.
**co.lo.car** *v.* to put, to place.

**co.lô.nia** *s.* colony, community.
**co.lo.ri.do** *adj.* colourful / *s.* color, colour.
**co.lo.rir** *v.* to colour.
**co.lu.na** *s.* column.
**com** *prep.* with.
**co.man.dar** *v.* to command, to order.
**co.man.do** *s.* command, order.
**com.ba.te** *s.* combat, fight.
**com.bi.na.ção** *s.* combination.
**com.bi.nar** *v.* to combine, to match.
**com.bus.tí.vel** *s.* fuel.
**co.me.çar** *v.* to begin, to start.
**co.me.ço** *s.* beginning, start.
**co.mé.di.a** *s.* comedy.
**co.me.mo.rar** *v.* to commemorate, to celebrate.
**co.men.tar** *v.* to comment.
**co.men.tá.rio** *s.* comment, remark.
**co.mer** *v.* to eat.
**co.mer.cial** *adj.* commercial.
**co.mér.cio** *s.* commerce.
**co.mi.da** *s.* food.
**co.mi.go** *pron.* with me.
**com.pa.nhi.a** *s.* company.
**com.pe.tên.cia** *s.* competence, ability.
**com.pe.ti.ção** *s.* competition.
**com.por.ta.men.to** *s.* behaviour.

C

comprar **50** cutucar

**com.prar** *v.* to buy.
**co.mum** *adj.* common.
**co.mu.ni.ca.ção** *s.* communication.
**co.mu.ni.car** *v.* to report.
**con.cer.to** *s.* concert.
**con.de.na.ção** *s.* condemnation, conviction.
**con.di.ção** *s.* condition.
**co.ne.xão** *s.* connection.
**con.fe.rên.cia** *s.* conference, lecture.
**con.fe.rir** *v.* to check.
**con.fi.an.ça** *s.* confidence.
**con.fi.ar** *v.* to trust.
**con.fu.são** *s.* confusion, tumult, disorder.
**co.nhe.cer** *v.* to know, to meet.
**co.nos.co** *pron.* with us.
**con.quis.ta** *s.* conquest.
**cons.ci.ên.cia** *s.* conscience.
**con.se.lho** *s.* advice, opinion, council, board.
**con.se.quên.cia** *s.* consequence.
**con.ser.tar** *v.* to repair, to fix.
**con.si.de.rar** *v.* to consider.
**cons.tru.ção** *s.* building.
**con.sul.tar** *v.* to consult, to look up.
**con.ta** *s.* account, count, bill.
**con.ta.to** *s.* contact.
**con.ti.go** *pron.* with you.
**con.ti.nu.ar** *v.* to continue.
**con.trá.rio(a)** *adj.* contrary.
**con.tra.to** *s.* contract, agreement.

**con.vi.te** *s.* invitation.
**có.pia** *s.* copy.
**cor** *s.* colour, color.
**co.ra.ção** *s.* heart.
**co.ra.do** *adj.* ruddy, rosy.
**co.ra.gem** *s.* courage.
**cor.da** *s.* rope.
**cor.po** *s.* body.
**cor.rer** *v.* to run.
**cor.ri.gir** *v.* to correct.
**co.ru.ja** *s.* owl.
**cor.vo** *s.* crow, raven.
**cos.te.la** *s.* rib.
**cos.tu.me** *s.* custom, habit.
**co.xa** *s.* thigh.
**cren.ça** *s.* belief, faith.
**cres.cen.te** *adj.* growing.
**cri.an.ça** *s.* child, kid.
**cruz** *s.* cross.
**cu.e.ca** *s.* underpants.
**cui.da.do** *s.* care, precaution / *interj.* take care, look out.
**cui.dar** *v.* to take care.
**cu.jo** *pron.* whose, which.
**cu.nha.do(a)** *s.* brother-in-la.w, *fem.* sister-in-law.
**cur.rí.cu.lo** *s.* curriculum vitae, resumé.
**cur.so** *s.* course.
**cus.pe** *s.* spit.
**cus.pir** *v.* to spit.
**cus.tar** *v.* to cost.
**cu.tu.car** *v.* to prod.

# Dd

**D, d** *s.* the foutth letter of the Portuguese alphabet.

**dá.di.va** *s.* donation, gift, present.

**da.ma** *s.* lady.

**da.mas.co** *s.* apricot.

**da.na.do(a)** *adj.* damned, naughty.

**dan.ça** *s.* dance.

**dan.çar** *v.* to dance.

**da.ni.fi.car** *v.* to damage.

**da.no** *s.* damage, injury.

**da.qui** *adv.* from here.

**dar** *v.* to give.

**dar.do** *s.* dart, javelin (esporte).

**da.ta** *s.* date.

**da.ti.lo.gra.far** *v.* to type.

**de** *prep.* of; from.

**de.bai.xo** *adv.* below, under.

**de.ba.te** *s.* discussion, debate.

**de.be.lar** *v.* to subdue, to overcome.

**dé.bil** *adj.* weak.

**de.bi.tar** *v.* to debit, to bill, to charge.

**de.bo.cha.do(a)** *adj.* sardonic, mocking.

**de.bo.char** *v.* to mock.

**de.bru.çar** *v.* to bend over.

**de.bu.tar** *v.* to appear for the first time in public.

**de.bu.tan.te** *s.* debut.

**dé.ca.da** *s.* decade.

**de.ca.dên.ci.a** *s.* decadence, decline.

**de.ca.ir** *v.* to decline.

**de.ca.pi.tar** *v.* to behead.

**de.cên.cia** *s.* decency.

**de.cen.te** *adj.* decent.

**de.ce.par** *v.* to cut off.

**de.cep.ção** *s.* disappointment.

**de.ci.di.do(a)** *adj.* determined.
**de.ci.dir** *v.* to decide.
**de.ci.frar** *v.* to decipher, to decode.
**de.ci.são** *s.* decision.
**de.cla.mar** *v.* to recite, to declaim.
**de.cla.ra.ção** *s.* declaration.
**de.cla.rar** *v.* to declare.
**de.cli.nar** *v.* to decline, to reject, to refuse.
**de.cli.ve** *s.* slope, declivity.
**de.co.la.gem** *s.* take-off.
**de.co.lar** *v.* to take-off.
**de.com.por** *v.* to analyse, to decompose.
**de.com.po.si.ção** *s.* analysis, decomposition.
**de.co.ra.ção** *s.* decoration, adornment.
**de.co.rar** *v.* to decorate, to adorn; to remember, to retain.
**de.cor.rên.cia** *s.* consequence.
**de.cor.ren.te** *adj.* resulting from.
**de.cor.rer** *v.* to pass.
**de.cre.tar** *v.* to decree, to proclaim.
**de.dão** *s.* thumb (da mão), big toe (do pé).
**de.di.ca.ção** *s.* dedication.
**de.di.ca.do(a)** *adj.* dedicated.
**de.di.car** *v.* to dedicate.
**de.do** *s.* finger (da mão), toe (do pé).
**de.du.ção** *s.* deduction.

**de.du.zir** *v.* to deduct, to deduce, to reduce.
**de.fa.sa.do(a)** *adj.* out of step.
**de.fa.sa.gem** *s.* discrepancy.
**de.fei.to** *s.* defect, fault.
**de.fen.der** *v.* to defend, to protect.
**de.fen.si.va** *s.* to be on the defensive.
**de.fen.sor(a)** *s.* defender, protector.
**de.fe.sa** *s.* defence.
**de.fi.ci.en.te** *adj.* defective.
**de.fi.ni.ção** *s.* definition.
**de.fi.nir** *v.* to define.
**de.fi.ni.ti.va.men.te** *adv.* definitively.
**de.fi.ni.ti.vo(a)** *adj.* definitive.
**de.for.ma.ção** *s.* deformation.
**de.for.mar** *v.* to deform.
**de.fron.te** *adv.* opposite to, in front of.
**de.fun.to(a)** *s.* dead person / *adj.* dead, extinct.
**de.grau** *s.* step.
**de.gus.ta.ção** *s.* tasting.
**de.gus.tar** *v.* to taste.
**dei.tar** *v.* to lay down.
**dei.xar** *v.* to leave, to quit.
**de.le.ga.ção** *s.* delegation.
**de.le.ga.ci.a** *s.* police station.
**de.le.ga.do(a)** *s.* delegate, police chief.

# delegar 53 depois

**de.le.gar** *v.* to delegate.
**de.lei.tar** *v.* to delight.
**de.lei.te** *s.* delight.
**de.li.be.rar** *v.* to deliberate.
**de.li.ca.de.za** *s.* delicacy, courtesy.
**de.li.ca.do(a)** *adj.* delicate.
**de lí.cia** *s.* pleasure, delight, delicacy.
**de.li.ci.o.so(a)** *adj.* delicious.
**de.li.ne.ar** *v.* to outline.
**de.li.ran.te** *adj.* delirious, insane.
**de.li.rar** *v.* to be delirious.
**de.lí.rio** *s.* delirium, insanity.
**de.lon.ga** *s.* delay.
**de.mais** *adj.* too much
/ *adv.* besides, moreover
/ *pron.* the rest.
**de.man.da** *s.* lawsuit.
**de.mão** *s.* layer, coat.
**de.ma.si.a** *s.* excess.
**de.men.te** *adj.* insane, mad
/ *s.* lunatic.
**de.mis.são** *s.* dismissal.
**demitido(a)** *adj.* dismissed, fired.
**de.mi.tir** *v.* to dismiss.
**de.mo.cra.ci.a** *s.* democracy.
**de.mo.cra.ta** *s.* democrat.
**de.mo.li.ção** *s.* demolition.
**de.mo.lir** *v.* to demolish.
**de.mô.nio** *s.* devil, demon.
**de.mons.tra.ção** *s.* proof; demonstration.

**de.mons.trar** *v.* to demonstrate, to show, to prove.
**de.mo.rar** *v.* to delay, to detain, to retard.
**de.ne.grir** *v.* to blacken, to defame.
**de.no.mi.na.ção** *s.* denomination.
**de.no.tar** *v.* to show, to indicate.
**den.si.da.de** *s.* density.
**den.so(a)** *adj.* dense.
**den.ta.da** *s.* bite.
**den.ta.du.ra** *s.* denture, false teeth.
**den.te** *s.* tooth.
**den.tis.ta** *s.* dentist.
**den.tre** *prep.* among.
**den.tro** *adv.* in, inside.
**den.tu.ço(a)** *adj.* buck teeth.
**de.nún.ci.a** *s.* denunciation.
**de.pa.rar** *v.* to come across.
**de.par.ta.men.to** *s.* department.
**de.pen.dên.cia** *s.* dependence, dependency.
**de.pen.den.te** *s.* dependent
/ *adj.* dependent.
**de.pen.der** *v.* to depend on.
**de.pi.lar** *v.* to wax (com cera), to pluck (sobrancelhas).
**de.po.i.men.to** *s.* testimony.
**de.pois** *adv.* after, afterwards, later on, then.

**D**

**de.por** *v.* to testify.
**de.por.tar** *v.* to deport, to exile.
**de.po.si.tar** *v.* to deposit.
**de.pó.si.to** *s.* deposit.
**de.pre.ci.a.ção** *s.* depreciation.
**de.pre.ci.ar** *v.* to depreciate, to devalue.
**de.pres.sa** *adv.* fast, quickly / *interj.* hurry up.
**de.pres.são** *s.* depression.
**de.pri.men.te** *adj.* depressing.
**de.pri.mi.do(a)** *adj.* depressed.
**de.pri.mir** *v.* to depress.
**der.ra.mar** *v.* to spill.
**der.ra.par** *v.* to skid.
**der.re.ter** *v.* to melt.
**der.ro.ta** *s.* defeat.
**der.ru.bar** *v.* to knock down.
**de.sa.ba.far** *v.* to confide, to give vent to, to uncover.
**de.sa.ba.men.to** *s.* collapse.
**de.sa.bar** *v.* to collapse.
**de.sa.bri.ga.do(a)** *adj.* homeless / *s.* homeless.
**de.sa.ca.tar** *v.* to disrespect, to affront, to insult.
**de.sa.fi.ar** *v.* to challenge, to defy.
**de.sa.fi.o** *s.* challenge, defiance, competition.
**de.sa.fo.ro** *s.* insolence.
**de.sa.gra.dar** *v.* to displease.
**de.sa.gra.vo** *s.* amends, reparation, revenge, retaliation.

**de.sa.ni.mar** *v.* to dishearten, to discourage.
**de.sa.pa.re.cer** *v.* to disappear.
**de.sa.pe.go** *s.* indifference.
**de.sa.pon.tar** *v.* to disappoint.
**de.sa.pro.var** *v.* to disapprove.
**de.sar.ru.ma.do(a)** *adj.* untidy.
**de.sar.ru.mar** *v.* to mess up.
**de.sas.tra.do(a)** *adj.* clumsy.
**de.sas.tre** *s.* disaster.
**de.sa.tar** *v.* to undo, to untie.
**de.sa.ten.to** *adj.* distracted, inadvertent.
**de.sa.ti.var** *v.* to shut down.
**de.sa.tu.a.li.za.do(a)** *adj.* outdated.
**de.sa.ven.ça** *s.* quarrel.
**des.bo.ca.do(a)** *adj.* foulmouthed.
**des.bo.tar** *v.* to discolour; to fade.
**des.cal.çar** *v.* to take off.
**des.cal.ço** *adj.* barefoot.
**des.can.sar** *v.* to rest.
**des.car.ga** *s.* unloading.
**des.car.re.gar** *v.* to unload.
**des.car.tar** *v.* to discard, to get rid of.
**des.cas.car** *v.* to peel.
**des.cer** *v.* to go down, to come down, to descend.
**des.co.brir** *v.* to discover, to find, to reveal.

descolar

55

deslizar

**des.co.lar** *v.* to unglue, to unpaste.
**des.co.lo.rir** *v.* to discolour.
**des.con.fi.an.ça** *s.* suspicion.
**des.con.fi.ar** *v.* to be suspicious, to suspect.
**des.con.for.to** *s.* discomfort.
**des.con.ge.lar** *v.* to thaw, to defrost.
**des.con.tar** *v.* to deduct, to discount.
**des.con.to** *s.* discount.
**des.cren.ça** *s.* disbelief, incredulity.
**des.cren.te** *adj.* sceptical / *s.* sceptic.
**des.cre.ver** *v.* to describe.
**des.cri.ção** *s.* description.
**des.cui.dar** *v.* to neglect.
**des.cul.pa** *s.* excuse, apology.
**des.de** *prep.* from, since.
**des.dém** *s.* scorn, disdain.
**des.do.brar** *v.* to unfold.
**de.se.jar** *v.* to want, to wish.
**de.se.jo** *s.* wish, desire.
**de.sem.bar.car** *v.* to land.
**de.sem.pe.nhar** *v.* to carry out, to perform.
**de.sem.pre.ga.do(a)** *adj.* unemployed / *s.* unemployed.
**de.sem.pre.go** *s.* unemployment.
**de.sen.can.tar** *v.* to disenchant.
**de.se.nhar** *v.* to draw.

**de.se.nho** *s.* drawing.
**de.sen.vol.ver** *v.* to develop.
**de.se.qui.li.bra.do(a)** *adj.* unbalanced.
**de.se.qui.li.br ar** *v.* to throw out of balance, to unbalance.
**de.ser.tar** *v.* to desert.
**de.ses.pe.ra.do(a)** *adj.* desperate.
**de.ses.pe.rar** *v.* to despair.
**des.fal.car** *v.* to embezzle.
**des.fal.que** *s.* peculation, embezzlement.
**des.fa.vo.rá.vel** *adj.* unfavourable.
**des.fa.zer** *v.* to undo, to unmake.
**des.fi.ar** *v.* to unravel, to unknit.
**des.fi.gu.rar** *v.* to disfigure, to deform.
**des.fi.lar** *v.* to parade.
**des.for.ra** *s.* revenge, retaliation.
**des.gas.tar** *v.* to wear down.
**des.gra.ça** *s.* misfortune.
**de.sig.nar** *v.* to designate, to appoint.
**de.si.gual** *adj.* unequal.
**de.si.lu.dir** *v.* to disillusion.
**de.sin.fe.tan.te** *s.* disinfectant.
**de.sin.fe.tar** *v.* to disinfect.
**de.sis.tir** *v.* to give up, to quit.
**des.li.ga.do(a)** *adj.* off.
**des.li.gar** *v.* to disconnect.
**des.li.zar** *v.* to slide, to slip.

**deslumbrante**     **56**     **dezembro**

**des.lum.bran.te** *adj.* dazzling.

**des.lum.brar** *v.* to dazzle.

**des.mai.ar** *v.* to faint.

**des.mon.tar** *v.* to dismount, to disassemble.

**des.mo.ro.nar** *v.* to collapse.

**des.na.ta.do(a)** *adj.* skimmed.

**des.ne.ces.sá.rio** *adj.* unnecessary.

**des.nu.tri.ção** *s.* malnutrition.

**de.so.be.de.cer** *v.* to disobey.

**de.so.cu.pa.do(a)** *adj.* vacant, unoccupied.

**de.so.cu.par** *v.* to vacate.

**de.so.do.ran.te** *s.* deodorant.

**de.so.nes.to** *adj.* dishonest.

**de.sor.dem** *s.* disorder.

**de.sor.ga.ni.zar** *v.* to disorganize.

**des.pa.char** *v.* to dispatch, to send.

**des.pe.di.da** *s.* farewell.

**des.pe.dir** *v.* to dismiss.

**des.pe.jar** *v.* to pour.

**des.pen.sa** *s.* larder, store-room.

**des.per.di.çar** *v.* to waste (dinheiro); to squander.

**des.pe.sa** *s.* expense.

**des.pi.do(a)** *adj.* naked.

**des.pir** *v.* to take off, to undress.

**des.po.jar** *v.* to loot.

**des.res.pei.to** *s.* disrespect.

**des.ta.car** *v.* to point, to detach.

**des.ti.nar** *v.* to destine.

**des.ti.na.tá.ri.o(a)** *s.* addressee.

**des.ti.no** *s.* destiny.

**des.tru.i.ção** *s.* destruction.

**des.tru.ir** *v.* to destroy.

**des.vi.ar** *v.* to divert.

**des.vi.o** *s.* diversion, detour.

**de.ta.lhar** *v.* to detail, to specify.

**de.ta.lhe** *s.* detail.

**de.ter** *v.* to stop, to arrest.

**de.ter.gen.te** *s.* detergent.

**de.ter.mi.na.ção** *s.* determination.

**de.te.ti.ve** *s.* detective.

**de.to.nar** *v.* to detonate.

**de.trás** *adv.* behind.

**de.tri.men.to** *s.* detriment.

**de.tri.to** *s.* debris.

**de.tur.par** *v.* to corrupt, to distort.

**Deus** *s.* God.

**deu.sa** *s.* goddess, divinity

**de.va.gar** *adv.* slowly.

**de.va.nei.o** *s.* daydream.

**de.vas.sa** *s.* inquiry.

**de.vas.tar** *v.* to devastate.

**de.ver** *v.* to owe / *s.* duty, task.

**de.vi.do(a)** *adj.* proper / *s.* due, debt.

**de.vo.ção** *s.* devotion.

**de.vo.lu.ção** *s.* devolution.

**de.vol.ver** *v.* to give back.

**de.vo.rar** *v.* to devour.

**dez** *num.* ten.

**de.zem.bro** *s.* December.

**dezenove**     57     **discussão**

**de.ze.no.ve** *num.* nineteen.

**de.zes.seis** *num.* sixteen.

**de.zes.se.te** *num.* seventeen.

**de.zoi.to** *num.* eighteen.

**dia** *s.* day.

**di.a.be.te(s)** *s.* diabetes.

**di.a.bo** *s.* devil.

**di.a.frag.ma** *s.* diaphragm.

**di.a.go.nal** *adj.* diagonal.

**di.a.gra.ma** *s.* diagram.

**di.a.lo.gar** *v.* to talk, to dialogue.

**di.á.lo.go** *s.* dialogue.

**di.a.man.te** *s.* diamond.

**di.â.me.tro** *s.* diameter.

**di.an.te** *adv.* in front.

**di.á.ria** *s.* daily rate.

**di.á.rio** *s.* diary.

**di.ar.rei.a** *s.* diarrhoea.

**di.ca** *s.* hint, clue.

**di.ci.o.ná.rio** *s.* dictionary.

**di.dá.ti.co(a)** *adj.* didactic, educational.

**di.e.ta** *s.* diet.

**di.fa.mar** *v.* to slander.

**di.fe.ren.ça** *s.* difference.

**di.fe.ren.te** *adj.* different.

**di.fí.cil** *adj.* difficult.

**di.fi.cul.da.de** *s.* difficulty.

**di.fi.cul.tar** *v.* to make difficult.

**di.ge.rir** *v.* to digest.

**di.ges.tão** *s.* digestion.

**dig.no(a)** *adj.* worthy.

**di.lú.vi.o** *s.* flood.

**di.men.são** *s.* dimension.

**di.mi.nu.i.ção** *s.* reduction.

**di.mi.nu.ir** *v.* to reduce.

**Di.na.mar.ca** *s.* Denmark.

**D**

**di.nâ.mi.co(a)** *adj.* dynamic.

**di.na.mis.mo** *s.* dynamism.

**di.na.mi.te** *s.* dynamite.

**di.nhei.ro** *s.* money.

**di.nos.sau.ro** *s.* dinosaur.

**di.plo.ma** *s.* diploma.

**di.plo.ma.cia** *s.* diplomacy.

**di.plo.ma.ta** *s.* diplomat.

**di.re.ção** *s.* direction.

**di.rei.to(a)** *s.* right / *adj.* honest, just.

**di.re.tor(a)** *s.* director.

**di.ri.gir** *v.* to direct (filme, peça de teatro, trânsito); to drive (carro).

**dis.car** *v.* to dial.

**dis.ci.pli.na** *s.* discipline; subject (matéria).

**dis.co** *s.* disc.

**dis.cor.dar** *v.* to disagree.

**dis.cór.dia** *s.* discord.

**dis.cre.to(a)** *adj.* discreet.

**dis.cri.mi.na.ção** *s.* discrimination.

**dis.cri.mi.nar** *v.* to discriminate, to segregate.

**dis.cur.so** *s.* speech.

**dis.cus.são** *s.* discussion, debate.

**discutir** | **58** | **dragão**

**dis.cu.tir** *v.* to discuss, to argue.
**dis.far.çar** *v.* to disguise.
**dis.pen.sar** *v.* to excuse.
**dis.pli.cên.cia** *s.* negligence.
**dis.po.ní.vel** *adj.* available.
**dis.por** *v.* to arrange.
**dis.po.si.ção** *s.* arrangement.
**dis.pu.ta** *s.* dispute.
**dis.tân.ci.a** *s.* distance.
**dis.tan.te** *adj.* distant.
**dis.tin.ção** *s.* distinction.
**dis.tin.guir** *v.* to distinguish.
**dis.tor.cer** *v.* to distort.
**dis.tra.í.do(a)** *adj.* forgetful, absent-minded.
**dis.tra.ir** *v.* to distract, to amuse.
**dis.tri.bu.i.ção** *s.* distribution.
**dis.tri.bu.i.dor(a)** *s.* distributor.
**dis.tri.bu.ir** *v.* to distribute.
**di.ver.são** *s.* amusement.
**di.ver.ti.do(a)** *adj.* amusing.
**di.ver.ti.men.to** *s.* amusement.
**di.ver.tir** *v.* to amuse.
**dí.vi.da** *s.* debt.
**di.vi.dir** *v.* to divide, to share.
**di.vi.no(a)** *adj.* divine.
**di.vor.ci.ar** *v.* to divorce.
**di.vul.gar** *v.* to spread.
**di.zer** *v.* to say, to tell.
**dó** *s.* pity; do (nota musical).
**do.a.ção** *s.* donation, gift.
**do.a.dor(a)** *s.* donor.

**do.ar** *v.* to donate.
**do.brar** *v.* to double; to fold up.
**do.bro** *s.* double.
**do.ce** *adj.* sweet / *s.* sweets.
**do.cu.men.ta.ção** *s.* documentation.
**do.cu.men.to** *s.* document.
**do.çu.ra** *s.* sweetness.
**do.en.ça** *s.* illness, sickness.
**do.en.te** *adj.* sick, ill.
**do.er** *v.* to hurt, to ache.
**doi.do(a)** *adj.* mad, crazy / *s.* fool.
**do.í.do(a)** *adj.* painful.
**dois** *num.* two.
**do.lo** *s.* fraud.
**do.lo.ri.do(a)** *adj.* sore.
**dom** *s.* gift, talent.
**do.mar** *v.* to tame.
**do.més.ti.ca** *s.* maid.
**do.mes.ti.car** *v.* to domesticate.
**do.mi.cí.lio** *s.* home, residence.
**do.mi.nan.te** *adj.* dominant.
**do.mi.nar** *v.* to dominate.
**do.min.go** *s.* Sunday.
**do.no(a)** *s.* owner.
**don.ze.la** *s.* maiden.
**dor** *s.* ache, pain.
**dor.mir** *v.* to sleep.
**dou.ra.do** *adj.* golden.
**dou.tor(a)** *s.* doctor.
**do.ze** *num.* twelve.
**dra.gão** *s.* dragon.

# drama — dúzia

**dra.ma** *s.* drama.
**dri.blar** *v.* to dribble.
**drin.que** *s.* drink.
**dro.ga** *s.* drug.
**dro.ga.ri.a** *s.* drugstore.
**du.bla.gem** *s.* dubbing.
**du.blar** *v.* to dub.

**du.cha** *s.* shower.
**du.ra.ção** *s.* duration, length.
**du.ran.te** *prep.* during, while.
**du.re.za** *s.* hardness.
**dú.vi.da** *s.* doubt,
**du.zen.tos** *num.* two hundred.
**dú.zia** *s.* dozen.

**D**

# Ee

**E, e** *s.* the fifth letter of the Portuguese alphabet / *conj.* and.

**é.ba.no** *s.* ebony.

**e.bu.li.ção** *s.* ebulution.

**e.clip.se** *s.* eclipse.

**e.co.lo.gi.a** *s.* ecology.

**e.co.no.mi.a** *s.* economy.

**e.co.nô.mi.co** *adj.* economical.

**e.co.no.mis.ta** *s.* economist.

**e.co.no.mi.zar** *v.* to economize, to save.

**e.di.ção** *s.* publication, edition.

**e.di.fí.cio** *s.* building.

**e.di.tar** *v.* to publish, to edit.

**e.di.tor** *s.* publisher, editor.

**e.dre.dom** *s.* eiderdown, quilt.

**e.du.ca.ção** *s.* education.

**e.du.car** *v.* to educate, to bring up.

**e.fei.to** *s.* effect.

**e.fer.ves.cen.te** *adj.* fizzy.

**e.fe.ti.var** *v.* to carry out, to execute.

**e.fe.ti.vo** *adj.* effective.

**e.fe.tu.ar** *v.* to carry out, to accomplish.

**e.fi.caz** *adj.* efficient.

**e.fi.ci.ên.cia** *s.* efficiency.

**e.gíp.cio** *adj.* Egyptian / *s.* Egyptian.

**E.gi.to** *s.* Egypt.

**e.go.ís.mo** *s.* selfishness, egoism.

**é.gua** *s.* mare.

**ei.xo** *s.* axle.

**ela** *pron.* she.

**e.la.bo.ra.ção** *s.* working out, elaboration.

**e.la.bo.rar** *v.* to prepare, to elaborate.

**e.lás.ti.co** *adj.* elastic.

**ele** *pron.* he.

**e.le.fan.te** *s.* elephant.

elegância — 61 — empreender

**e.le.gân.ci.a** *s.* elegance.
**e.le.gan.te** *adj.* elegant.
**e.le.ger** *v.* to elect.
**e.le.gí.vel** *adj.* eligible.
**e.lei.ção** *s.* election.
**e.lei.to** *adj.* elected / *s.* elect.
**e.lei.tor** *s.* voter, elector.
**e.le.men.tar** *adj.* elementary.
**e.le.men.to** *s.* element.
**e.len.co** *s.* list, cast.
**e.le.tri.ci.da.de** *s.* electricity.
**e.le.tri.cis.ta** *s.* electrician.
**e.lé.tri.co** *adj.* electric(al)
/ *s.* electric.
**e.le.va.ção** *s.* elevation, raising.
**e.le.va.dor** *s.* elevator, lift.
**e.le.var** *v.* to lift up, to raise.
**e.li.mi.nar** *v.* to remove,
to banish.
**e.li.te** *s.* elite.
**e.lo.gi.ar** *v.* to praise.
**e.ma.gre.cer** *v.* to get thin,
to loose weight.
**e.man.ci.par** *v.* to emancipate.
**em.bai.xa.da** *s.* embassy.
**em.bai.xo** *adv.* below, under.
**em.ba.la.gem** *s.* packing up,
packaging.
**em.ba.lar** *v.* to pack (up), to rock
(criança).
**em.ba.ra.çar** *v.* to hinder,
to embarrass.

**em.bar.ca.ção** *s.* vessel, ship.
**em.bar.car** *v.* to embark, to board.
**em.bar.que** *s.* boarding.
**em.bo.ra** *conj.* though, although.
**em.bre.a.gem** *s.* clutch.
**em.bri.a.gar** *v.* to make drunk.
**em.bri.ão** *s.* embryo.
**em.bru.lhar** *v.* to wrap up,
to pack up.
**em.bru.lho** *s.* package, parcel.
**e.men.da** *s.* correction,
amendment.
**e.men.dar** *v.* to correct, to amend.
**e.mer.gên.cia** *s.* emergency.
**e.mi.gra.ção** *s.* emigration.
**e.mi.grar** *v.* to emigrate.
**e.mi.nên.cia** *s.* eminence.
**e.mis.são** *s.* emission.
**e.mi.tir** *v.* to emit, to issue.
**e.mo.ção** *s.* emotion.
**e.mo.ti.vo** *adj.* emotional,
emotive.
**em.pa.co.tar** *v.* to pack (up).
**em.pa.da** *s.* pie, patty.
**em.pa.tar** *v.* to hinder, to tie up.
**em.pe.ci.lho** *s.* obstacle.
**em.pe.nhar** *v.* to pawn.
**em.pi.lhar** *v.* to pile up.
**em.pi.nar** *v.* to raise.
**em.pol.gar** *v.* to stimulate,
to thrill.
**em.pre.en.der** *v.* to undertake.

**E**

empregado — enlatar

**em.pre.ga.do** *s.* employee / *adj.* employed.

**em.pre.ga.dor** *s.* employer.

**em.pre.gar** *v.* to employ.

**em.pre.go** *s.* job, employment.

**em.pre.sa** *s.* firm, company.

**em.pres.tar** *v.* to lend.

**em.pur.rar** *v.* to push.

**e.mu.de.cer** *v.* to silence, to still.

**en.ca.der.na.ção** *s.* binding.

**en.cai.xar** *v.* to fit in, to box.

**en.ca.lhar** *v.* to run aground.

**en.ca.mi.nhar** *v.* to direct, to conduct.

**en.ca.na.dor** *s.* plumber.

**en.can.ta.do** *adj.* delighted.

**en.can.tar** *v.* to bewitch, to charm.

**en.can.to** *s.* delight, charm.

**en.ca.par** *v.* to cover.

**en.ca.rar** *v.* to face, to stare at.

**en.chen.te** *s.* flood.

**en.cher** *v.* to fill up.

**en.co.lher** *v.* to draw up, to shrink.

**en.con.trar** *v.* to find.

**en.con.tro** *s.* meeting.

**en.co.ra.jar** *v.* to encourage.

**en.cos.tar** *v.* to lean.

**en.de.re.çar** *v.* to address.

**en.de.re.ço** *s.* address.

**en.di.rei.tar** *v.* to straighten.

**en.du.re.cer** *v.* to harden.

**e.ner.gi.a** *s.* energy.

**en.far.te** *s.* heart attack.

**ên.fa.se** *s.* emphasis.

**en.fei.tar** *v.* to decorate, to adorn.

**en.fei.ti.çar** *v.* to bewitch, to charm.

**en.fer.ma.gem** *s.* nursing.

**en.fer.mi.da.de** *s.* illness, sickness.

**en.fer.ru.jar** *v.* to rust.

**en.fiar** *v.* to put on, to thread.

**en.fim** *adv.* finally, at last.

**en.fo.que** *s.* approach, focus.

**en.for.car** *v.* to hang.

**en.fra.que.cer** *v.* to weaken.

**en.fren.tar** *v.* to face, to confront.

**en.fu.re.cer** *v.* to infuriate, to enrage.

**en.ga.jar** *v.* to engage, to take on.

**en.ga.na.do** *adj.* mistaken, wrong.

**en.ga.nar** *v.* to deceive, to cheat.

**en.ga.no** *s.* mistake, error.

**en.ge.nha.ri.a** *s.* engineering.

**en.ge.nho** *s.* inventive power; talent.

**en.go.lir** *v.* to swallow.

**en.gor.dar** *v.* to fatten.

**en.gra.ça.do** *adj.* funny.

**en.jo.a.do** *adj.* sick, bored.

**en.jo.ar** *v.* to sicken, to nauseate.

**en.jo.o** *s.* sickness, nausea.

**en.la.tar** *v.* to can, to tin.

**enlouquecer**     **63**     equipamento

**en.lou.que.cer** *v.* to drive mad, to madden.

**e.no.ja.do** *adj.* annoyed, nauseated.

**e.no.jar** *v.* to disgust, to nauseate.

**en.quan.to** *conj.* while.

**en.re.do** *s.* plot.

**en.ro.lar** *v.* to roll up.

**en.ros.car** *v.* to twist, to twine.

**en.ru.gar** *v.* to wrinkle, to crease.

**en.sai.ar** *v.* to test, to rehearse.

**en.sai.o** *s.* test, rehearsal, essay.

**en.si.na.men.to** *s.* teaching.

**en.si.nar** *v.* to teach.

**en.si.no** *s.* teaching.

**en.tão** *adv.* then.

**en.tar.de.cer** *v.* to get late / *s.* sunset.

**en.ten.der** *v.* to understand.

**en.ten.di.men.to** *s.* understanding.

**en.ter.rar** *v.* to bury.

**en.ter.ro** *s.* burial, funeral.

**en.tor.tar** *v.* to bend, to bow.

**en.tra.da** *s.* entrance, entry.

**en.trar** *v.* to go in, to enter.

**en.tre** *prep.* between.

**en.tre.ga** *s.* delivery.

**en.tre.gar** *v.* to hand over, to deliver.

**en.tre.tan.to** *conj.* however / *adv.* meantime.

**en.tre.te.ni.men.to** *s.* entertainment.

**en.tre.ter** *v.* to entertain.

**en.tre.vis.ta** *s.* interview.

**en.tu.lho** *s.* rubble, rubbish.

**en.tu.pi.do** *adj.* blocked.

**en.tu.pir** *v.* to block,

**en.tu.si.as.mar** *v.* to excite, to animate.

**en.tu.si.as.mo** *s.* enthusiasm.

**en.ve.ne.nar** *v.* to poison.

**en.ver.go.nha.do** *adj.* ashamed.

**en.ver.go.nhar** *v.* to shame.

**en.vi.ar** *v.* to send.

**en.vi.o** *s.* sending, dispatch.

**en.vol.ver** *v.* to involve, to wrap.

**en.xa.da** *s.* hoe.

**en.xa.guar** *v.* to rinse.

**en.xa.me** *s.* swarm.

**en.xa.que.ca** *s.* migraine.

**en.xer.gar** *v.* to see.

**en.xo.fre** *s.* sulphur.

**en.xo.tar** *v.* to throw out.

**en.xo.val** *s.* trousseau (de noiva), layette (de bebê).

**en.xur.ra.da** *s.* torrent.

**en.xu.to** *adj.* dry.

**e.pi.de.mi.a** *s.* epidemic.

**é.po.ca** *s.* period, time.

**e.qua.ção** *s.* equation.

**E.qua.dor** *s.* Ecuador.

**e.qua.dor** *s.* equator (linha).

**e.qui.li.brar** *v.* to balance.

**e.qui.pa.men.to** *s.* equipment.

# equipar · especial

**e.qui.par** *v.* to equip.

**e.qui.pe** *s.* team.

**e.qui.va.len.te** *adj.* equivalent.

**e.ró.ti.co** *adj.* erotic.

**er.ra.do** *adj.* wrong, mistaken.

**er.ro** *s.* mistake, error.

**er.va** *s.* herb.

**er.vi.lha** *s.* pea.

**es.ban.jar** *v.* to squander.

**es.bo.çar** *v.* to sketch, to outline.

**es.bo.fe.te.ar** *v.* to slap.

**es.ca.da** *s.* staircase, stairs.

**es.ca.la** *s.* scale.

**es.ca.lar** *v.* to climb.

**es.cân.da.lo** *s.* scandal, outrage.

**es.ca.par** *v.* to escape, to run away.

**es.cla.re.cer** *v.* to explain, to brighten.

**es.co.la** *s.* school.

**es.co.lar** *adj.* school.

**es.co.lha** *s.* choice.

**es.co.lher** *v.* to choose.

**es.col.ta** *s.* escort.

**es.con.der** *v.* to hide.

**Es.cor.pi.ão** *s.* Scorpio (astrologia).

**es.cor.pi.ão** *s.* scorpion.

**es.cor.rer** *v.* to drain.

**es.co.tei.ro** *s.* scout.

**es.co.va** *s.* brush.

**es.cra.vi.dão** *s.* slavery.

**es.cra.vo** *adj.* captive / *s.* slave.

**es.cre.ver** *v.* to write.

**es.cri.ta** *s.* writing.

**es.cri.tó.ri.o** *s.* office.

**es.cri.tu.ra** *s.* deed.

**es.cu.do** *s.* shield.

**es.cul.pir** *v.* to carve, to engrave.

**es.cu.re.cer** *v.* to darken.

**es.cu.ri.dão** *s.* darkness.

**es.cu.ro** *adj.* dark / *s.* darkness.

**es.cu.tar** *v.* to listen to.

**es.for.çar** *v.* to try hard.

**es.for.ço** *s.* effort.

**es.fre.gar** *v.* to rub, to scrub.

**es.fri.ar** *v.* to cool, chill.

**es.ga.na.do** *adj.* greedy.

**es.ga.nar** *v.* to strangle

**es.go.ta.do** *adj.* exhausted, drained.

**es.go.tar** *v.* to drain, to exhaust.

**es.go.to** *s.* drain, sewer.

**es.gri.ma** *s.* fencing.

**es.ma.gar** *v.* to crush, to squeeze.

**es.mal.te** *s.* enamel, nail polish.

**es.me.ral.da** *s.* emerald.

**es.pa.ci.al** *adj.* spatial.

**es.pa.ço** *s.* space.

**es.pa.da** *s.* sword.

**Es.pa.nha** *s.* Spain.

**es.pan.tar** *v.* to frighten.

**es.pan.to** *s.* fright.

**es.pe.ci.al** *adj.* special.

**espécie** 65 estável

**es.pé.cie** *s.* species, sort, kind.
**es.pe.lho** *s.* mirror.
**es.pe.ran.ça** *s.* hope.
**es.pe.rar** *v.* to wait for; to hope for.
**es.per.ma** *s.* sperm, semen.
**es.per.te.za** *s.* cleverness.
**es.per.to** *adj.* clever.
**es.pes.so** *adj.* thick.
**es.pe.tá.cu.lo** *s.* show.
**es.pe.to** *s.* spit.
**es.pi.ar** *v.* to spy.
**es.pi.na.fre** *s.* spinach.
**es.pi.nho** *s.* thorn.
**es.pi.o.na.gem** *s.* spying.
**es.pi.o.nar** *v.* to spy.
**es.pí.ri.to** *s.* spirit, soul.
**es.pi.ri.tu.al** *adj.* spiritual.
**es.pir.rar** *v.* to sneeze.
**es.plên.di.do** *adj.* splendid.
**es.plen.dor** *s.* splendour.
**es.pó.li.o** *s.* estate, assets.
**es.pon.ja** *s.* sponge.
**es.pon.tâ.ne.o** *adj.* spontaneous.
**es.por.te** *s.* sport.
**es.po.sa** *s.* wife.
**es.po.so** *s.* husband.
**es.pre.mer** *v.* to squeeze.
**es.pu.ma** *s.* foam, froth (de cerveja); lather (de sabão).
**es.que.cer** *v.* to forget.
**es.que.le.to** *s.* skeleton.
**es.que.ma** *s.* outline, scheme.

**es.quen.tar** *v.* to heat, to warm.
**es.quer.do** *adj.* left.
**es.qui** *s.* ski.
**es.qui.lo** *s.* squirrel.
**es.qui.na** *s.* corner.
**es.qui.si.to** *adj.* strange, weird.
**esse** *pron.* that (*pl. these*).
**es.sên.cia** *s.* essence.
**es.ta** *pron.* this (*pl. these*).
**es.ta.be.le.cer** *v.* to establish.
**es.ta.be.le.ci.men.to** *s.* establishment.
**es.ta.ção** *s.* station.
**es.ta.ci.o.na.men.to** *s.* parking, place.
**es.ta.ci.o.nar** *v.* to park.
**es.ta.da** *s.* stay.
**es.tá.di.o** *s.* stadium.
**Es.ta.do** *s.* state.
**es.ta.gi.á.rio** *s.* trainee.
**es.tá.gi.o** *s.* apprenticeship.
**es.tam.par** *v.* to print.
**es.tan.car** *v.* to stanch.
**es.tân.ci.a** *s.* ranch, farm.
**es.tan.te** *s.* bookcase.
**es.tar** *v.* to be.
**es.ta.tís.ti.ca** *s.* statistics.
**es.ta.tís.ti.co** *s.* statistician / *adj.* statistic(al).
**es.tá.tua** *s.* statue.
**es.ta.tu.ra** *s.* stature.
**es.ta.tu.to** *s.* statute.
**es.tá.vel** *adj.* stable, firm, steady.

E

**es.ten.der** *v.* to extend.

**es.ti.lo** *s.* style.

**es.ti.ma** *s.* esteem.

**es.ti.mu.lar** *v.* to stimulate.

**es.tô.ma.go** *s.* stomach.

**es.tou.ro** *s.* explosion, burst.

**es.tra.da** *s.* road, railroad, railway.

**es.tra.ga.do** *adj.* spoiled, rotten.

**es.tra.gar** *v.* to spoil, to ruin.

**es.tran.gei.ro** *adj.* foreign / *s.* foreigner.

**es.tra.nhar** *v.* to be surprised at.

**es.tra.nho** *adj.* strange / *s.* stranger.

**es.tra.té.gi.a** *s.* strategy.

**es.tre.la** *s.* star.

**es.tri.den.te** *adj.* shrill.

**es.tron.do** *s.* rumble, thundering.

**es.tru.tu.ra** *s.* structure.

**es.tu.dar** *v.* to study.

**es.tú.di.o** *s.* studio.

**es.tu.di.o.so** *adj.* studious.

**es.tu.do** *s.* study.

**es.tu.pi.dez** *s.* stupidity, foolishness.

**es.tú.pi.do** *adj.* stupid, obtuse / *s.* brute, dunce.

**es.tu.prar** *v.* to rape.

**es.tu.pro** *s.* rape.

**es.va.zi.ar** *v.* to empty.

**e.ta.pa** *s.* stage.

**e.ter.ni.da.de** *s.* eternity.

**e.ter.no** *adj.* eternal.

**é.ti.ca** *s.* ethics.

**e.ti.que.ta** *s.* etiquette, label, tag.

**eu** *pron. pess.* I.

**Eu.ro.pa** *s.* Europe.

**e.van.ge.lho** *s.* Gospel.

**e.va.po.rar** *v.* to evaporate.

**e.va.são** *s.* escape.

**e.ven.to** *s.* event.

**e.ven.tu.al** *adj.* fortuitous, occasional.

**e.vi.dên.cia** *s.* evidence.

**e.vi.tar** *v.* to avoid, to prevent.

**e.vo.lu.ção** *s.* development, evolution.

**e.vo.lu.ir** *v.* to develop, to evolve.

**e.xa.ge.rar** *v.* to exaggerate.

**e.xa.me** *s.* exam, examination.

**e.xa.mi.nar** *v.* to examine.

**e.xa.to** *adj.* right, correct, accurate, precise.

**ex.ce.ção** *s.* exception.

**ex.ce.lên.cia** *pron.* Excellence / *s.* excellence.

**ex.cên.tri.co** *adj.* eccentric.

**ex.ces.so** *s.* excess.

**ex.ci.ta.ção** *s.* excitement.

**ex.ci.ta.do** *adj.* excited.

**ex.cla.ma.ção** *s.* exclamation.

**ex.cla.mar** *v.* to exclaim.

**ex.clu.ir** *v.* to exclude.

**ex.cur.são** *s.* outing, excursion.
**e.xe.cu.tar** *v.* to execute, to perform.
**e.xe.cu.ti.vo** *s.* executive / *adj.* executive.
**e.xem.plar** *adj.* exemplary / *s.* example.
**e.xem.plo** *s.* example, model.
**e.xer.cer** *v.* to exercise.
**e.xer.cí.cio** *s.* exercise.
**e.xér.ci.to** *s.* army.
**e.xi.bir** *v.* to show.
**e.xi.gên.cia** *s.* demand.
**e.xi.gir** *v.* to demand, to urge.
**e.xis.tên.cia** *s.* existence.
**e.xis.tir** *v.* to exist.
**e.xó.ti.co** *adj.* exotic.
**ex.pan.dir** *v.* to expand.
**ex.pan.são** *s.* expansion.
**ex.pec.ta.ti.va** *s.* expectation.
**ex.pe.ri.ên.cia** *s.* experience.
**ex.pe.ri.men.tar** *v.* to taste, to try.
**ex.pli.ca.ção** *s.* explanation.
**ex.pli.car** *v.* to explain.
**ex.plo.dir** *v.* to explode, to burst.
**ex.plo.ra.ção** *s.* exploration.
**ex.por.ta.ção** *s.* export.
**ex.por.tar** *v.* to export.
**ex.pres.são** *s.* expression.
**ex.pul.sar** *v.* to expel.
**ex.te.ri.or** *adj.* outside / *s.* exterior, outside.
**ex.ter.no** *adj.* external.
**ex.tra.to** *s.* extract.
**ex.tra.va.gân.cia** *s.* extravagance.
**ex.tra.vi.ar** *v.* to mislay, to go astray.
**e.xul.tar** *v.* to rejoice.

# Ff

**F, f** *s.* the sixth letter of the Portuguese alphabet.
**fã** *s.* fan.
**fá.bri.ca** *s.* factory.
**fa.bri.ca.ção** *s.* manufacture.
**fa.bri.car** *v.* to manufacture; to make.
**fá.bu.la** *s.* fable.
**fa.bu.lo.so** *adj.* fabulous.
**fa.ca** *s.* knife.
**fa.ça.nha** *s.* exploit.
**fa.cão** *s.* carving knife.
**fac.ção** *s.* faction.
**fa.ce** *s.* face.
**fa.ce.ta** *s.* facet.
**fa.cha.da** *s.* façade, front.
**fá.cil** *adj.* easy.
**fa.ci.li.tar** *v.* to facilitate.
**fa.cul.da.de** *s.* faculty.
**fa.cul.ta.ti.vo** *adj.* optional.
**fa.da** *s.* fairy.
**fa.da.do** *adj.* predestined.
**fa.di.ga** *s.* fatigue, tiredness.
**fa.do** *s.* fate, destiny; Portuguese folk song, dance and music.
**fa.gu.lha** *s.* spark.
**fai.são** *s.* pheasant.
**fa.ís.ca** *s.* spark, flash.
**fa.is.car** *v.* to spark.
**fai.xa** *s.* belt, band, strip.
**fa.lá.cia** *s.* fallacy, fraud.
**fa.lan.te** *adj.* talkative.
**fa.lar** *v.* to speak, to talk.
**fa.la.tó.rio** *s.* talking, chit-chat.
**fal.cão** *s.* falcon, hawk.
**fa.le.cer** *v.* to die, to pass away.
**fa.lên.cia** *s.* bankruptcy.
**fa.lé.sia** *s.* sea cliff.

**fa.lha** *s.* fault, error, mistake.
**fa.lhar** *v.* to fail.
**fa.li.do(a)** *adj.* bankrupt, ruined.
**fa.lir** *v.* to fail, to go bankrupt.
**fal.sá.rlo(a)** *s.* forger.
**fal.si.da.de** *s.* falsehood.
**fal.si.fi.car** *v.* to forge.
**fal.so(a)** *adj.* false, untrue.
**fal.ta** *s.* lack; absence.
**fal.tar** *v.* to be lacking, be absent, to miss.
**fa.ma** *s.* fame.
**fa.mí.lia** *s.* family.
**fa.mi.li.ar** *adj.* family, familiar.
**fa.min.to(a)** *adj.* hungry, starving.
**fa.mo.so(a)** *adj.* famous, renowned.
**fa.ná.ti.co(a)** *adj.* fanatical / *s.* fanatic.
**fan.ta.si.a** *s.* fantasy.
**fan.ta.si.ar** *v.* to imagine.
**fan.tas.ma** *s.* ghost.
**fan.tás.ti.co(a)** *adj.* fantastic.
**fan.to.che** *s.* puppet.
**far.da** *s.* uniform.
**fa.ri.nha** *s.* flour.
**far.ma.cêu.ti.co(a)** *adj.* pharmaceutical / *s.* pharmacist.
**far.má.cia** *s.* pharmacy, drugstore.
**fa.ro** *s.* sense of smell.
**fa.rol** *s.* lighthouse.

**far.ra** *s.* binge.
**far.ra.po** *s.* rag.
**far.sa** *s.* farce.
**far.tar** *v.* to satiate.
**far.to(n)** *adj.* full.
**far.tu.ra** *s.* abundance, wealth.
**fas.ci.nan.te** *adj.* fascinating.
**fas.ci.nar** *v.* to fascinate.
**fas.cis.mo** *s.* fascismo.
**fa.se** *s.* phase, stage.
**fa.tal** *adj.* fatal.
**fa.ti.a** *s.* slice, piece.
**fa.ti.gan.te** *adj.* tiresome.
**fa.ti.gar** *v.* to tire.
**fa.to** *s.* fact.
**fa.tor** *s.* factor, agent.
**fa.tu.ra** *s.* invoice.
**fa.va** *s.* broad bean.
**fa.ve.la** *s.* slum.
**fa.vor** *s.* favour.
**fa.xi.na** *s.* brushwood.
**fa.zen.da** *s.* farm.
**fa.zer** *v.* to make, to do.
**fé** *s.* faith, creed.
**fe.bre** *s.* fever, temperature.
**fe.cha.do(a)** *adj.* shut, closed.
**fe.cha.du.ra** *s.* lock.
**fe.char** *v.* to close, to shut.
**fe.cho** *s.* fastening, zipper.
**fé.cu.la** *s.* starch, fecula.
**fe.cun.dar** *v.* to fertilize.
**fe.der** *v.* to stink.

# federação     70     fiambre

**fe.de.ra.ção** *s.* federation.
**fe.de.ral** *adj.* federal.
**fei.ção** *s.* form.
**fei.jão** *s.* bean.
**fei.o(a)** *adj.* ugly.
**fei.ra** *s.* fair.
**fei.ti.cei.ra(o)** *s.* witch.
**fei.ti.ço** *s.* charm, spell.
**fei.ti.o** *s.* shape; make, fabric.
**fei.u.ra** *s.* ugliness.
**fei.xe** *s.* bundle.
**fel** *s.* bile, gall.
**fe.li.ci.da.de** *s.* happiness.
**fe.liz** *adj.* happy.
**fel.pu.do(a)** *adj.* fuzzy, fluffy.
**fel.tro** *s.* felt.
**fê.mea** *s.* female.
**fe.mi.ni.no(a)** *adj.* feminine.
**fe.mi.nis.ta** *adj.* feminist
/ *s.* feminist.
**fen.da** *s.* slit; crack.
**fen.der** *v.* to split.
**fe.no** *s.* hay.
**fe.no.me.nal** *adj.* phenomenal.
**fe.ra** *s.* wild animal.
**fé.re.tro** *s.* coffin.
**fe.ri.a.do** *s.* holiday.
**fé.rias** *s.* holiday, vacation.
**fe.ri.da** *s.* wound.
**fe.ri.do(a)** *adj.* injured,
wounded, hurt.
**fe.ri.men.to** *s.* injury, wound.

**fe.rir** *v.* to injure, to wound.
**fer.men.tar** *v.* to ferment.
**fer.men.to** *s.* yeast.
**fe.roz** *adj.* fierce.
**fer.ra.du.ra** *s.* horseshoe.
**fer.ra.gem** *s.* hardware,
metalwork.
**fer.ra.men.ta** *s.* tool.
**fer.rei.ro** *s.* blacksmith, forger.
**fer.ro** *s.* iron.
**fer.ro.vi.a** *s.* railroad, railway.
**fer.ru.gem** *s.* rust.
**fér.til** *adj.* fertile.
**fer.ven.te** *adj.* boiling.
**fer.ver** *v.* to boil.
**fer.vi.lhar** *v.* to simmer.
**fer.vor** *s.* fervour.
**fer.vo.ro.so** *adj.* fervent.
**fes.ta** *s.* party.
**fes.te.jar** *v.* to celebrate.
**fes.tim** *s.* feast.
**fes.ti.val** *s.* festival.
**fes.ti.vi.da.de** *s.* festivity.
**fes.ti.vo(a)** *adj.* festive.
**fe.ti.che** *s.* fetish.
**fé.ti.do(a)** *adj.* stinking, rank.
**fe.to** *s.* foetus.
**fe.ve.rei.ro** *s.* February.
**fe.zes** *s.* faeces, excrements.
**fi.a.da** *s.* row, line.
**fi.a.dor(a)** *s.* backer, warrantor.
**fi.am.bre** *s.* cured cold meat.

# fiança     71     flagrar

**fi.an.ça** *s.* guarantee.

**fi.ar** *v.* to spin; to rely, to trust.

**fi.as.co** *s.* fiasco, failure.

**fi.bra** *s.* fibre.

**fi.car** *v.* to stay, to remain.

**fic.ção** *s.* fiction.

**fi.cha** *s.* ticket.

**fi.chá.rio** *s.* card index, file.

**fic.tí.cio(a)** *adj.* fictitious.

**fi.dal.go** *s.* nobleman.

**fi.de.li.da.de** *s.* fidelity, loyalty.

**fi.el** *adj.* faithful.

**fi.ga** *s.* talisman.

**fí.ga.do** *s.* liver.

**fi.go** *s.* fig.

**fi.gu.ra** *s.* figure.

**fi.gu.ran.te** *s.* extra.

**fi.gu.rar** *v.* to appear.

**fi.gu.ri.no** *s.* model.

**fi.la** *s.* row, line, queue.

**fi.la.men.to** *s.* filament.

**fi.la.te.li.a** *s.* philately.

**fi.lé** *s.* steak.

**fi.lei.ra** *s.* file, row, wing.

**fi.lho(a)** *s.* son, *fem.* daughter.

**fi.lho.te** *s.* puppy (de cachorro), cub (de leão).

**fi.li.al** *s.* branch.

**Fi.li.pi.nas** *s.* The Philippine Islands.

**fil.ma.do.ra** *s.* camcorder.

**fil.mar** *v.* to film, to shoot.

**fil.me** *s.* film.

**fi.lo.so.fi.a** *s.* philosophy.

**fil.trar** *v.* to filter.

**fil.tro** *s.* filter.

**fim** *s.* end, termination.

**fi.nal** *adj.* final / *s.* end.

**fi.nan.ças** *s.* finance.

**fin.car** *v.* to thrust in, to drive in.

**fi.ne.za** *s.* finesse.

**fin.gi.men.to** *s.* pretense, dissimulation.

**fin.gir** *v.* to pretend.

**fi.ni.to(a)** *adj.* finite / *s.* finite.

**Fin.lân.dia** *s.* Finland.

**fi.no(a)** *adj.* fine; thin, slim.

**fio** *s.* thread, twine.

**fir.ma** *s.* company.

**fir.mar** *v.* to secure, to firm.

**fir.me** *adj.* firm.

**fis.cal** *s.* custom officer, fiscal.

**fí.si.ca** *s.* physics.

**fí.si.co(a)** *adj.* physical.

**fi.sio.no.mia** *s.* expression, look.

**fi.sio.te.ra.pi.a** *s.* physiotherapy.

**fis.su.ra** *s.* crack, split.

**fi.ta** *s.* strip, band, ribbon.

**fi.tar** *v.* to stare.

**fi.ve.la** *s.* buckle.

**fi.xar** *v.* to fix.

**fi.xo(a)** *adj.* fixed, stable.

**fla.gran.te** *s.* flagrant.

**fla.grar** *v.* to catch.

**flâmula** 72 **forno**

**flâ.mu.la** *s.* pennant.
**fla.ne.la** *s.* flannel.
**flau.ta** *s.* flute.
**fle.cha** *s.* arrow.
**fle.xí.vel** *adj.* flexible.
**fli.pe.ra.ma** *s.* pinball machine.
**flo.co** *s.* flake.
**flor** *s.* flower.
**flo.res.cen.te** *adj.* flourishing.
**flo.res.cer** *v.* to flower, to bloom, to blossom.
**flo.res.ta** *s.* forest.
**flo.ri.do(a)** *adj.* flowery.
**flu.ên.cia** *s.* fluency.
**flu.i.do** *adj.* fluid / *s.* fluid, liquid.
**flu.ir** *v.* to flow.
**flu.tu.ar** *v.* to float.
**flu.vi.al** *adj.* river, fluvial.
**flu.xo** *s.* flow.
**fo.bi.a** *s.* phobia.
**fo.ca** *s.* seal.
**fo.ca.li.zar** *v.* to focus.
**fo.ci.nho** *s.* snout.
**fo.co** *s.* focus.
**fo.fo(a)** *adj.* soft, cutie (pessoa).
**fo.fo.ca** *s.* gossip.
**fo.gão** *s.* stove.
**fo.go** *s.* fire.
**fo.go.so(a)** *adj.* fiery.
**fo.gue.te** *s.* rocket.
**fol.clo.re** *s.* folklore.
**fô.le.go** *s.* breath.

**fol.ga** *s.* rest, break.
**fo.lha** *s.* leaf; page (livro), sheet (papel).
**fo.lha.gem** *s.* foliage.
**fo.li.a** *s.* revelry.
**fo.me** *s.* hunger.
**fo.ra** *adv.* out, outside.
**fo.ra.gi.do(a)** *adj.* fugitive / *s.* fugitive, outlaw.
**fo.ras.tei.ro(a)** *s.* outsider, foreigner, outlander.
**for.ca** *s.* gallows.
**for.ça** *s.* power, force, strength.
**for.çar** *v.* to force.
**for.jar** *v.* to forge.
**for.ma** *s.* form, shape, mold, cake pan.
**for.ma.ção** *s.* formation.
**for.mal** *adj.* formal.
**for.mar** *v.* to form.
**for.ma.tar** *v.* to format.
**for.mi.dá.vel** *adj.* formidable, splendid.
**for.mi.ga** *s.* ant.
**for.mo.so(a)** *adj.* beautiful, charming.
**fór.mu.la** *s.* formula.
**for.mu.lar** *v.* to formulate.
**for.mu.lá.rio** *s.* form.
**for.ne.ce.dor(a)** *s.* supplier.
**for.ne.cer** *v.* to supply, to provide.
**for.no** *s.* oven.

**for.rar** *v.* to cover.
**for.ta.le.cer** *v.* to strengthen.
**for.ta.le.za** *s.* fortress, fort.
**for.te** *adj.* strong.
**for.tui.to(a)** *adj.* accidental, casual.
**for.tu.na** *s.* fortune.
**fos.co(a)** *adj.* dull, dim, opaque.
**fós.fo.ro** *s.* match.
**fós.sil** *s.* fossil.
**fo.to** *s.* photo.
**fo.to.gra.far** *v.* to photograph.
**fo.to.gra.fia** *s.* photography.
**fo.tó.gra.fo(a)** *s.* photographer.
**foz** *s.* mouth of a river.
**fra.ção** *s.* fraction.
**fra.cas.sar** *v.* to fail.
**fra.co(a)** *adj.* weak.
**fra.ga.ta** *s.* frigate.
**frá.gil** *adj.* fragile.
**frag.men.to** *s.* fragment.
**fra.grân.cia** *s.* fragrance.
**fral.da** *s.* diaper, nappy.
**fram.bo.e.sa** *s.* raspberry.
**Fran.ça** *s.* France.
**fran.ca.men.te** *adv.* frankly.
**fran.go** *s.* chicken.
**fran.ja** *s.* fringe (enfeite), bangs (cabelo).
**fran.que.za** *s.* frankness.
**fran.qui.a** *s.* postage; franchise.
**fran.zir** *v.* to pleat.
**fra.que.za** *s.* weakness.
**fras.co** *s.* bottle, flask.
**fra.se** *s.* sentence, phrase.

**fra.tu.ra** *s.* fracture.
**frau.de** *s.* fraud.
**fre.ar** *v.* to curb, to brake.
**frei.ra** *s.* nun, sister.
**fren.te** *s.* front.
**fre.quên.cia** *s.* frequency.
**fre.quen.tar** *v.* to frequent, to attend.
**fre.quen.te** *adj.* frequent, often.
**fres.co(a)** *adj.* fresh, new.
**fres.cu.ra** *s.* freshness; fussy.
**fre.tar** *v.* to charter.
**fre.te** *s.* freight.
**fri.e.za** *s.* coldness.
**fri.gi.dei.ra** *s.* frying pan.
**frí.gi.do(a)** *adj.* frigid.
**fri.gir** *v.* to fry.
**fri.go.rí.fi.co** *s.* refrigerator.
**frio(a)** *adj.* cold / *s.* coldness.
**fri.sar** *v.* to curl, to frizzle, emphasize.
**fri.tar** *v.* to fry.
**fri.tas** *s.* chips, French fries.
**fri.to(a)** *adj.* fried.
**fro.nha** *s.* pillowcase.
**fron.te** *s.* forehead.
**fron.tei.ra** *s.* border, frontier.
**fro.ta** *s.* fleet.
**frou.xo(a)** *adj.* loose.
**frus.trar** *v.* to frustrate.
**fru.ta** *s.* fruit.
**fu.bá** *s.* corn meal.
**fu.ga** *s.* flight, escape.
**fu.gaz** *adj.* fleeting.

**fu.gir** *v.* to flee, to run away, to escape.

**fu.gi.ti.vo(a)** *adj.* fugitive / *s.* fugitive, evader.

**ful.mi.nan.te** *adj.* devastating, withering.

**fu.ma.ça** *s.* smoke.

**fu.man.te** *s.* smoker.

**fu.mar** *v.* to smoke.

**fu.mo** *s.* smoke.

**fun.ção** *s.* function.

**fun.ci.o.nar** *v.* to work, to function.

**fun.ci.o.ná.rio(a)** *s.* employee, clerk; official.

**fun.da.ção** *s.* foundation.

**fun.da.men.tal** *adj.* fundamental.

**fun.da.men.to** *s.* foundation.

**fun.dar** *v.* to found; to establish.

**fun.di.ção** *s.* fusion, melting.

**fun.dir** *v.* to fuse, to melt.

**fun.do(a)** *adj.* deep / *s.* bottom.

**fú.ne.bre** *adj.* funeral.

**fu.ne.ral** *s.* funeral.

**fu.nes.to(a)** *adj.* fatal, funest.

**fun.go** *s.* fungus.

**fu.nil** *s.* funnel.

**fu.ra.cão** *s.* hurricane.

**fu.ra.do(a)** *adj.* perforated, pierced.

**fu.rar** *v.* to bore, to perforate, to pierce, to drill.

**fur.gão** *s.* van.

**fú.ria** *s.* fury.

**fu.ro** *s.* hole.

**fur.tar** *v.* to steal.

**fu.são** *s.* fusion, merger.

**fu.sí.vel** *s.* fuse.

**fu.so** *s.* spindle, spool.

**fu.te.bol** *s.* football; soccer.

**fú.til** *adj.* futile.

**fu.ti.li.da.de** *s.* shallowness, futility.

**fu.tu.ro** *s.* future / *adj.* future.

**fu.zil** *s.* rifle, gun.

# Gg

**G, g** *s.* the seventh letter of the Portuguese alphabet.

**ga.bar** *v.* to praise / ~*se de v.* to boast.

**ga.bi.ne.te** *s.* office, cabinet.

**ga.do** *s.* livestock, cattle.

**ga.fa.nho.to** *s.* grasshopper.

**ga.fe** *s.* gaffe.

**ga.guei.ra** *s.* stutter, stammer.

**ga.gue.jar** *v.* to stutter, to stammer.

**gai.a.to(a)** *adj.* funny.

**gai.o.la** *s.* cage.

**gai.vo.ta** *s.* seagull.

**ga.jo** *s.* guy, chap.

**ga.la** *s.* gala, pomp.

**ga.lan.te** *adj.* graceful / *s.* gallant, gentleman.

**ga.lão** *s.* stripe (uniforme); gallon (medida).

**gá.la.ta** *s.* Galatian / *adj.* galatian.

**ga.lá.xia** *s.* galaxy.

**ga.le.go(a)** *s.* Galician / *adj.* Galician.

**ga.le.ra** *s.* galley.

**ga.le.ri.a** *s.* gallery.

**gal.go** *s.* greyhound.

**ga.lho** *s.* branch.

**ga.li.nha** *s.* hen, chicken.

**ga.lo** *s.* cock, rooster.

**ga.lo.cha** *s.* wellington (bota), galosh.

**ga.lo.par** *v.* to gallop.

**gal.pão** *s.* shed.

**ga.ma** *s.* scale.

**gam.bá** *s.* opossum.

**ga.na** *s.* craving, wish, hunger, hate.

# G

**ga.nân.cia** *s.* greed.

**gan.cho** *s.* hook.

**gan.gor.ra** *s.* seesaw.

**gan.gue** *s.* gang.

**ga.nha.dor(a)** *s.* winner / *adj.* winning.

**ga.nha-pão** *s.* livelihood, bread-winner.

**ga.nhar** *v.* to win; to earn.

**ga.nir** *v.* to yelp.

**gan.so(a)** *s.* gander, goose.

**ga.ra.gem** *s.* garage.

**ga.ra.nhão** *s.* stallion.

**ga.ran.ti.a** *s.* warranty, guarantee.

**ga.ran.tir** *v.* to guarantee.

**gar.bo** *s.* elegance, garb.

**gar.ça** *s.* heron.

**gar.çom** *s.* waiter.

**gar.ço.ne.te** *s.* waitress.

**gar.fo** *s.* fork.

**gar.ga.lha.da** *s.* laughter.

**gar.ga.lo** *s.* bottleneck.

**gar.gan.ta** *s.* throat.

**ga.ri** *s.* roadsweeper.

**ga.ro.a** *s.* drizzle.

**ga.ro.ta.da** *s.* the kids.

**ga.ro.to(a)** *s.* boy, *fem.* girl.

**ga.rou.pa** *s.* grouper.

**gar.ra** *s.* claw.

**gar.ra.fa** *s.* bottle.

**ga.ru.pa** *s.* hindquarters.

**gás** *s.* gas.

**ga.so.li.na** *s.* petrol, gas.

**ga.so.so(a)** *adj.* sparkling.

**gas.tar** *v.* to spend.

**gás.tri.co(a)** *adj.* gastric.

**ga.ti.lho** *s.* trigger.

**ga.to** *s.* cat.

**ga.ve.ta** *s.* drawer.

**ga.vi.ão** *s.* hawk.

**ga.ze** *s.* gauze, bandage.

**ga.ze.la** *s.* gazelle.

**ga.ze.ta** *s.* newspaper.

**ge.a.da** *s.* frost.

**ge.la.dei.ra** *s.* refrigerator, fridge.

**ge.la.do(a)** *adj.* frozen.

**ge.lar** *v.* to freeze.

**ge.la.ti.na** *s.* gelatine, jelly.

**ge.lei.a** *s.* jelly, jam.

**ge.lei.ra** *s.* glacier.

**ge.lo** *s.* ice.

**ge.ma** *s.* yolk.

**Gê.meos** *s.* Gemeni (astrologia).

**gê.meo(a)** *adj.* twin / *s.* twin.

**ge.mer** *v.* to groan, moan.

**ge.ne** *s.* gene.

**Ge.ne.bra** *s.* Geneva.

**ge.ne.ral** *s.* general.

**ge.ne.ra.li.zar** *v.* to generalize.

**gê.ne.ro** *s.* genre; type, kind.

**ge.ne.ro.si.da.de** *s.* generosity.

**ge.ne.ro.so(a)** *adj.* generous.

genética | 77 | gorila

**ge.né.ti.ca** *s.* genetics.

**gen.gi.bre** *s.* ginger.

**gen.gi.va** *s.* gum.

**ge.ni.al** *adj.* brilliant.

**gê.nio** *s.* genius.

**ge.ni.tal** *adj.* genital.

**gen.ro** *s.* son-in-law.

**gen.te** *s.* people.

**gen.til** *adj.* kind.

**geo.gra.fi.a** *s.* geography.

**ge.ra.ção** *s.* generation.

**ge.ral** *adj.* general.

**ge.râ.nio** *s.* geranium.

**ge.rar** *v.* to produce, to generate.

**ge.rên.cia** *s.* management.

**ge.ren.te** *s.* manager.

**ger.ge.lim** *s.* sesame.

**ge.ri.á.tri.co(a)** *adj.* geriatric.

**ge.rir** *v.* to manage.

**ger.me** *s.* germ.

**ges.so** *s.* plaster.

**ges.ta.ção** *s.* pregnancy.

**ges.tan.te** *s.* pregnant woman / *adj.* pregnant.

**ges.ti.cu.lar** *v.* to make gestures, to gesticulate.

**ges.to** *s.* gesture.

**gi.gan.te** *adj.* gigantic, giant / *s.* giant.

**gim** *s.* gin.

**gi.ná.sio** *s.* gymnasium.

**gi.nás.ti.ca** *s.* gymnastics.

**gi.ne.co.lo.gi.a** *s.* gynecology.

**gi.ne.co.lo.gis.ta** *s.* gynecologist.

**gi.ra.fa** *s.* giraffe.

**gi.rar** *v.* to turn.

**gi.ras.sol** *s.* sunflower.

**gi.ra.tó.rio(a)** *adj.* revolving.

**gí.ria** *s.* slang.

**giz** *s.* chalk.

**gla.ci.al** *adj.* icy.

**gla.mou.ro.so(a)** *adj.* glamorous.

**glân.du.la** *s.* gland.

**gli.ce.ri.na** *s.* glycerine.

**gli.co.se** *s.* glucose.

**glo.bal** *adj.* global.

**glo.bo** *s.* globe.

**gló.ria** *s.* glory.

**glos.sá.rio** *s.* glossary.

**goi.a.ba** *s.* guava.

**gol** *s.* goal.

**go.la** *s.* collar.

**go.le** *s.* gulp.

**go.lei.ro** *s.* goalkeeper.

**gol.fe** *s.* golf.

**gol.fi.nho** *s.* dolphin.

**gol.fo** *s.* gulf.

**gol.pe** *s.* blow.

**go.ma** *s.* gum.

**gon.go** *s.* gong.

**go.rar** *v.* to frustrate.

**gor.do(a)** *adj.* fat.

**gor.du.ra** *s.* fat; grease.

**go.ri.la** *s.* gorilla.

# gorjeta / Grécia

**gor.je.ta** *s.* tip.
**gor.ro** *s.* cap.
**gos.ma** *s.* spittle.
**gos.tar** *v.* to like.
**gos.to** *s.* taste.
**go.ta** *s.* drop.
**go.tei.ra** *s.* gutter; leak.
**go.te.jar** *v.* to drip.
**go.ver.na.dor(a)** *s.* governor.
**go.ver.na.men.tal** *adj.* government.
**go.ver.nan.ta** *s.* governess.
**go.ver.nar** *v.* to govern.
**go.ver.no** *s.* government.
**go.za.ção** *s.* mockery.
**go.za.do(a)** *adj.* funny.
**go.zar** *v.* to enjoy.
**Grã-Bre.ta.nha** *s.* Great Britain.
**gra.ça** *s.* grace.
**gra.ce.jar** *v.* to joke.
**gra.ci.o.so(a)** *adj.* charming.
**gra.da.ti.vo(a)** *adj.* gradual.
**gra.de** *s.* grating.
**gra.du.a.ção** *s.* graduation.
**gra.du.al** *adj.* gradual.
**gra.du.ar** *v.* to graduate.
**gra.fi.a** *s.* writing.
**gra.ma** *s.* gramme, gram (medida); grass (planta).
**gra.ma.do** *s.* lawn.
**gra.mar** *v.* to plant grass.
**gra.má.ti.ca** *s.* grammar.

**gra.mo.fo.ne** *s.* gramophone.
**gram.pe.a.dor** *s.* stapler.
**gram.pe.ar** *v.* to staple.
**gram.po** *s.* hairpin.
**gra.na.da** *s.* shell.
**gran.de** *adj.* big, large.
**gran.di.o.so(a)** *adj.* magnificent.
**gra.nel** *s.* in bulk.
**gra.ni.to** *s.* granite.
**gra.ni.zo** *s.* hailstone.
**gran.ja** *s.* farm, ranch.
**gra.nu.la.do(a)** *adj.* grainy.
**grâ.nu.lo** *s.* granule.
**grão** *s.* grain.
**gra.ti.dão** *s.* gratitude.
**gra.ti.fi.can.te** *adj.* rewarding.
**gra.ti.fi.car** *v.* to tip, to reward.
**grá.tis** *adj.* free.
**gra.to(a)** *adj.* grateful.
**gra.tui.to(a)** *adj.* free.
**grau** *s.* degree.
**gra.va.ção** *s.* recording.
**gra.va.dor** *s.* tape recorder.
**gra.var** *v.* to record; to engrave.
**gra.va.ta** *s.* tie.
**gra.ve** *adj.* serious.
**grá.vi.da** *adj.* pregnant.
**gra.vi.da.de** *s.* gravity.
**gra.vi.dez** *s.* pregnancy.
**gra.vu.ra** *s.* engraving.
**gra.xa** *s.* polish.
**Gré.cia** *s.* Greece.

# grelha — guloso

**gre.lha** *s.* grill.

**grê.mio** *s.* guild.

**gre.ve** *s.* strike.

**gri.far** *v.* to underline (palavras).

**gri.lo** *s.* cricket.

**gri.nal.da** *s.* garland.

**grin.go(a)** *s.* gringo.

**gri.pa.do(a)** *adj.* get a cold.

**gri.pe** *s.* flu (influenza).

**gri.sa.lho(a)** *adj.* grey.

**gri.tan.te** *adj.* glaring, gross.

**gri.tar** *v.* to shout.

**gros.sei.ro(a)** *adj.* rude.

**gros.so(a)** *adj.* thick.

**gro.tes.co(a)** *adj.* grotesque.

**gru.dar** *v.* to glue.

**gru.de** *s.* glue, paste.

**gru.den.to** *adj.* sticky.

**gru.nhi.do** *s.* grunt.

**gru.nhir** *v.* to grunt.

**gru.po** *s.* group.

**gru.ta** *s.* grotto, cave.

**guar.da** *s.* guard.

**guar.da-chu.va** *s.* umbrella.

**guar.da-ci.vil** *s.* policeman, *fem.* policewoman.

**guar.da-cos.tas** *s.* bodyguard.

**guar.da.na.po** *s.* napkin.

**guar.dar** *v.* to guard; to keep.

**guar.da-rou.pa** *s.* wardrobe.

**guar.da-sol** *s.* sunshade.

**guar.di.ão(ã)** *s.* guardian.

**guar.ni.ção** *s.* garrison (militar); garnish (culinária).

**guer.ra** *s.* war.

**guer.ri.lha** *s.* guerrilla.

**gue.to** *s.* ghetto.

**gui.a** *s.* guide, leader.

**gui.ar** *v.* to guide, to lead.

**gui.chê** *s.* ticket window.

**guin.cho** *s.* squeal (grito) / tow truck (veículo).

**guin.das.te** *s.* hoist, crane.

**gui.tar.ra** *s.* guitar.

**gu.la** *s.* gluttony, greed.

**gu.lo.di.ce** *s.* delicacy, tidbit.

**gu.lo.sei.ma** *s.* delicacy, dainties.

**gu.lo.so(a)** *adj.* greedy / *s.* glutton.

# Hh

**H, h** *s* the eighth letter of the Portuguese alphabet.

**há.bil** *adj.* skilful, clever.

**ha.bi.li.ta.ção** *s.* competence, qualification.

**ha.bi.li.ta.do(a)** *adj.* qualified.

**ha.bi.li.tar** *v.* to enable, to qualify.

**ha.bi.ta.ção** *s.* habitation, residence.

**ha.bi.tan.te** *s.* inhabitant.

**ha.bi.tar** *v.* to live.

**há.bi.to** *s.* habit, use.

**ha.bi.tu.al** *adj.* usual.

**ha.bi.tu.ar** *v.* to get used to, to familiarize.

**ha.do.que** *s.* haddock.

**há.li.to** *s.* breath.

**han.gar** *s.* hangar.

**har.mo.ni.a** *s.* harmony.

**har.mo.ni.o.so(a)** *adj.* harmonious.

**har.mo.ni.zar** *v.* to harmonize.

**har.pa** *s.* harp.

**has.te** *s.* flagpode.

**ha.va.na** *s.* light brown.

**ha.ver** *v. aux.* (*tempos compostos*) to have; there is, there are (existir).

**he.brai.co(a)** *s.* Hebrew; the Hebrew language / *adj.* Hebraic.

**he.di.on.do(a)** *adj.* hideous, dreadful.

**hé.li.ce** *s.* propeller.

**he.li.cóp.te.ro** *s.* helicopter.

**hé.lio** *s.* helium.

**he.ma.to.ma** *s.* bruise.

# hemorragia    81    honrado

**he.mor.ra.gi.a** *s.* hemorrhage.

**he.mor.roi.das** *s.* hemorrhoids.

**he.pa.ti.te** *s.* hepatitis.

**he.ran.ça** *s.* inheritance.

**her.dar** *v.* to inherit.

**her.dei.ro(a)** *s.* heir.

**he.rói** *s.* hero.

**he.ro.í.na** *s.* heroine.

**he.si.ta.ção** *s.* hesitation.

**he.si.tan.te** *adj.* hesitant.

**he.si.tar** *v.* to hesitate.

**he.te.ros.se.xu.al** *s.* heterosexual.

**hi.ber.nar** *v.* to hibernate.

**hí.bri.do(a)** *adj.* hybrid

/ *s.* hybrid.

**hi.dra.tan.te** *s.* moisturizer.

**hi.dráu.li.co(a)** *adj.* hydraulic.

**hi.dre.lé.tri.co(a)** *adj.*
hydroelectric.

**hi.dro.fo.bi.a** *s.* hidrophobia
rabies.

**hi.dro.gê.nio** *s.* hydrogen.

**hi.e.rar.qui.a** *s.* hierarchy.

**hí.fen** *s.* hyphen.

**hi.gi.e.ne** *s.* hygiene.

**hi.la.ri.an.te** *adj.* hilarious.

**hi.no** *s.* hymn; anthem.

**hi.per.mer.ca.do** *s.* hypermarket.

**hi.per.ten.são** *s.* high blood
pressure.

**hí.pi.co(a)** *adj.* riding club.

**hi.pis.mo** *s.* horseback racing.

**hip.no.tis.mo** *s.* hypnotism.

**hi.po.con.drí.a.co(a)**
*s.* hypochondriac
/ *adj.* hyponchondriac(al).

**hi.po.cri.si.a** *s.* hypocrisy.

**hi.pó.dro.mo** *s.* race-course.

**hi.po.pó.ta.mo** *s.* hippopotamus.

**hi.po.te.ca** *s.* mortgage.

**hi.pó.te.se** *s.* hypothesis.

**his.pâ.ni.co(a)** *adj.* Hispanic.

**his.te.ria** *s.* hysteria.

**his.tó.ria** *s.* history; story, tale.

**ho.je** *adv.* today.

**Ho.lan.da** *s.* Holland, Netherlands.

**ho.lo.caus.to** *s.* holocaust.

**ho.lo.fo.te** *s.* searchlight.

**ho.mem** *s.* man.

**ho.me.na.ge.ar** *v.* to pay tribute.

**ho.me.na.gem** *s.* tribute.

**ho.mi.ci.da** *adj.* homicidal
/ *s.* murderer.

**ho.mo.lo.gar** *v.* to ratify.

**ho.mos.se.xu.al** *adj.* homosexual
/ *s.* homosexual.

**Hon.du.ras** *s.* Honduras.

**ho.nes.ti.da.de** *s.* honesty.

**ho.ne.sto(a)** *adj.* honest.

**ho.no.rá.rio(a)** *adj.* honorary.

**ho.no.rá.rios** *s.* fee, pay.

**hon.ra** *s.* honour, honor.

**hon.ra.dez** *s.* honour, probity.

**hon.ra.do(a)** *adj.* honest.

**hon.rar** *v.* to honour.
**hon.ro.so(a)** *adj.* honourable.
**ho.ra** *s.* time, hour.
**ho.ri.zon.tal** *s.* horizontal / *adj.* horizontal.
**ho.ri.zon.te** *s.* horizon.
**hor.mô.nio** *s.* hormone.
**ho.rós.co.po** *s.* horoscope.
**hor.ren.do(a)** *adj.* horrendous.
**hor.ri.pi.lan.te** *adj.* horrifying.
**hor.rí.vel** *adj.* awful, horrible.
**hor.ror** *s.* horror.
**hor.ta** *s.* vegetable garden.
**hor.ta.li.ça** *s.* vegetables.
**hor.te.lã** *s.* mint.
**hor.tên.sia** *s.* hydrangea.
**hor.ti.cul.tor(a)** *s* horticultor, horticulturist.

**hor.to** *s.* plant nursery.
**hos.pe.da.gem** *s.* accomodation, lodging.
**hos.pe.dar** *v.* to put up, to lodge.
**hós.pe.de** *s.* guest.
**hos.pí.cio** *s.* madhouse, asylum.
**hos.pi.tal** *s.* hospital.
**hos.pi.ta.li.da.de** *s.* hospitality.
**hu.ma.ni.tá.rio(a)** *adj.* humane / *s.* humanitarian.
**hu.ma.no(a)** *adj.* human, humane.
**hu.mil.da.de** *s.* humility.
**hu.mil.de** *adj.* humble.
**hu.mi.lhar** *v.* humiliate.
**hu.mor** *s.* mood, humour.
**hún.ga.ro(a)** *s.* Hungarian / *adj.* hungarian.
**Hun.gri.a** *s.* Hungary.

# Ii

**I, i** *s*. the ninth letter of the Portuguese alphabet.
**i.a.te** *s*. yacht.
**i.a.tis.mo** *s*. yachting.
**i.bé.ri.co** *s*. Iberian / *adj*. iberian.
**í.co.ne** *s*. icon.
**i.da** *s*. departure.
**i.da.de** *s*. age.
**i.de.al** *s*. ideal / *adj*. ideal(istic).
**i.de.a.lis.ta** *adj*. idealist / *s*. idealist.
**i.de.a.li.zar** *v*. to idealize.
**i.dei.a** *s*. idea, thought.
**i.dem** *adj*. same.
**i.dên.ti.co** *adj*. identical.
**i.den.ti.da.de** *s*. identity.
**i.den.ti.fi.car** *v*. to identify.
**i.de.o.lo.gi.a** *s*. ideology.
**i.de.o.ló.gi.co** *adj*. ideologic(al).
**i.di.o.ma** *s*. language.

**i.di.o.ta** *adj*. idiotic(al), silly / *s*. idiot.
**i.di.o.ti.ce** *s*. stupidity.
**í.do.lo** *s*. idol.
**i.dô.neo** *adj*. competent, idoneous.
**i.do.so** *adj*. old, aged.
**i.glu** *s*. igloo.
**ig.no.rân.cia** *s*. ignorance.
**ig.no.ran.te** *adj*. ignorant.
**ig.no.rar** *v*. to ignore.
**i.gre.ja** *s*. church.
**i.gual** *s*. the same, equal / *adj*. equal.
**i.gua.lar** *v*. to equal, to level.
**i.gual.da.de** *s*. equality.
**i.gual.men.te** *adv*. equally.
**i.le.gal** *adj*. illegal.
**i.le.ga.li.da.de** *s*. illegality.
**i.lha** *s*. island.
**i.lu.são** *s*. illusion.
**i.lus.tra.ção** *s*. illustration.

**ímã** — 84 — **itinerário**

**í.mã** *s.* magnet.

**i.ma.gem** *s.* image.

**im.ba.tí.vel** *adj.* unbeatable.

**im.be.cil** *adj.* stupid, dumb / *s.* idiot, imbecile.

**i.mo.ral** *adj.* immoral.

**im.pa.ci.ên.cia** *s.* impatience.

**im.pac.to** *s.* impact.

**ím.par** *adj.* odd, uneven.

**im.pé.rio** *s.* empire.

**im.plo.rar** *v.* to beg, to implore.

**im.por** *v.* to impose.

**im.por.tân.cia** *s.* importance.

**im.pren.sa** *s.* press.

**im.pres.são** *s.* impression; print.

**im.pri.mir** *v.* to print.

**i.na.to** *adj.* innate.

**i.nau.gu.ra.ção** *s.* inauguration.

**in.ca.pa.ci.da.de** *s.* incapacity.

**in.cen.di.ar** *v.* to set fire to.

**in.cer.te.za** *s.* uncertainty, doubt.

**in.cha.do** *adj.* swollen.

**in.clu.ir** *v.* to include.

**in.co.mo.dar** *v.* to bother, to annoy.

**in.com.pe.tên.cia** *s.* incompetence.

**in.con.di.ci.o.nal** *adj.* unconditional.

**in.crí.vel** *adj.* incredible.

**in.di.ca.ção** *s.* indication.

**ín.di.ce** *s.* index.

**in.dús.tria** *s.* industry.

**i.né.di.to** *adj.* unpublished; original.

**in.fân.cia** *s.* childhood, infancy.

**in.flar** *v.* to inflate, to blow up.

**in.flu.ên.cia** *s.* influence.

**in.for.ma.ção** *s.* information.

**i.ni.mi.go(a)** *s.* enemy / *adj.* enemy.

**in.se.rir** *v.* to insert, to put in.

**ins.pe.ção** *s.* inspection.

**ins.ta.la.ção** *s.* installation.

**ins.ti.tu.i.ção** *s.* institution.

**ins.tru.men.to** *s.* instrument.

**in.te.li.gên.cia** *s.* intelligence.

**in.te.res.san.te** *adj.* interesting.

**in.te.ri.or** *adj.* inner / *s.* inland, interior.

**in.ter.nar** *v.* to intern.

**in.ter.va.lo** *s.* interval, break.

**in.ti.mi.da.de** *s.* intimacy.

**in.tri.ga** *s.* intrigue.

**in.tui.ção** *s.* intuition.

**i.nú.til** *adj.* useless / *s.* worthless person.

**in.va.dir** *v.* to invade.

**in.ve.ja** *s.* envy.

**in.ven.ção** *s.* invention.

**in.ver.no** *s.* winter.

**ir** *v.* to go.

**i.ra** *s.* anger, rage.

**ir.mã** *s.* sister.

**ir.mão** *s.* brother.

**i.ro.ni.a** *s.* irony.

**ir.ri.tar** *v.* to irritate.

**i.ti.ne.rá.rio** *s.* itinerary.

# Jj

**J, j** *s.* the tenth letter of the Portuguese alphabet.
**já** *adv.* already / *conj.* now.
**ja.ca** *s.* jack fruit.
**ja.ca.ré** *s.* alligator.
**ja.mais** *adv.* never.
**ja.nei.ro** *s.* January.
**ja.ne.la** *s.* window.
**jan.ga.da** *s.* raft, float.
**jan.tar** *s.* dinner.
**Ja.pão** *s.* Japan.
**ja.que.ta** *s.* jacket.
**jardim** *s.* garden.
**jar.dim de in.fân.cia** *s.* kindergarten.
**jar.di.na.gem** *s.* gardening.
**jar.di.nei.ro** *s.* gardener.
**jar.ro** *s.* jug.
**ja.to** *s.* jet.

**jau.la** *s.* cage.
**ja.zi.go** *s.* grave.
**jei.to** *s.* way; kind.
**ji.pe** *s.* jeep.
**jo.a.ni.nha** *s.* ladybug.
**jo.e.lho** *s.* knee.
**jo.ga.dor(a)** *s.* player.
**joi.a** *s.* jewel.
**jor.nal** *s.* newspaper.
**jor.na.lis.ta** *s.* journalist.
**jo.vem** *adj.* young / *s.* young person.
**ju.di.ar** *v.* to torment, to mistreat.
**ju.iz(íza)** *s.* judge; referee, umpire.
**ju.i.za.do** *s.* court.
**jul.ga.men.to** *s.* judgement, trial.
**ju.lho** *s.* July.
**ju.men.to** *s.* donkey.

**ju.nho** *s.* June.
**jun.ta** *s.* joint; committee.
**jun.tar** *v.* to join, connect.
**Jú.pi.ter** *s.* Jupiter.
**ju.ra** *s.* oath, vow.

**jus.ti.ça** *s.* justice.
**jus.ti.fi.car** *v.* to justify.
**jus.to** *s.* fair person / *adj.* just, right.
**ju.ven.tu.de** *s.* youth, young people.

J

# Kk

**K, k** *s.* the eleventh letter of the Portuguese alphabet.

**kai.ser** *s.* kaiser, emperor.

**ka.ra.o.ke** *s.* karaoke.

**kg** *abrev.* de kilogram.

**ki.wi** *s.* kiwi.

**Km** *abrev.* de kilometer.

# Ll

**L, l** *s.* the twelfth letter of the Portuguese alphabet.

**lá** *adv.* there, over there.

**lã** *s.* wool.

**lá.bio** *s.* lip.

**la.bo.ra.tó.rio** *s.* laboratory, lab.

**la.çar** *v.* to bind, to lace.

**la.do** *s.* side.

**la.drão(dra)** *s.* thief, robber.

**la.gar.ta** *s.* caterpillar.

**la.gar.to** *s.* lizard.

**la.gos.ta** *s.* lobster.

**lá.gri.ma** *s.* tear.

**la.ma** *s.* mud.

**lam.ber** *v.* to lick.

**la.men.tar** *v.* to lament, to regret.

**lâ.mi.na** *s.* sheet; blade.

**lâm.pa.da** *s.* lamp.

**lan.ça** *s.* spear.

**lan.ça.men.to** *s.* throwing, launching.

**lan.cha** *s.* launch, motor-boat.

**lan.che** *s.* snack.

**lan.ter.na** *s.* lantern, flashlight.

**lá.pis** *s.* pencil.

**lar** *s.* home.

**la.ran.ja** *s.* orange.

**la.tir** *v.* to bark.

**la.va.bo** *s.* washbasin.

**Le.ão** *s.* Leo (astrologia).

**leão** *s.* lion.

**le.bre** *s.* hare.

**le.gi.ão** *s.* legion.

**le.gí.vel** *adj.* legible, readable.

**le.gu.me** *s.* vegetable.

**lem.bran.ça** *s.* souvenir, gift.

**len.te** *s.* lens.

**len.to** *adj.* slow.

**le.que** *s.* fan.
**ler** *v.* to read.
**le.tra** *s.* letter.
**le.var** *v.* to take.
**le.ve** *adj.* light.
**Li.bra** *s.* Libra (astrologia).
**li.ção** *s.* lesson, homework.
**li.cen.ça** *s.* license.
**li.ga.ção** *s.* connection, relation.
**li.gar** *v.* to bind, to join, to connect.
**li.mão** *s.* lemon.
**lín.gua** *s.* tongue; language.
**lin.gua.gem** *s.* language.
**lin.gui.ça** *s.* sausage.
**li.nha** *s.* line; thread.
**li.qui.da.ção** *s.* sale; liquidation.
**li.so(a)** *adj.* smooth.
**lis.ta** *s.* list, roll.
**lis.tra** *s.* stripe.
**li.to.ral** *s.* coastline / *adj.* coastal.
**li.vra.ri.a** *s.* bookshop, bookstore.
**li.vre** *adj.* free.
**li.xo** *s.* garbage, trash.

**lo.cal** *s.* place, site / *adj.* local.
**ló.gi.co** *adj.* logical, rational.
**lo.go** *adv.* at once, soon
/ *conj.* therefore.
**lo.ja** *s.* shop, store.
**lon.ge** *adv.* far / *adj.* distant.
**lou.co(a)** *adj.* crazy, mad / *s.* mad
person.
**lou.ro(a)** *adj.* blond(e), fair.
**lou.ro** *s.* bay leaf (cozinha);
parrot (papagaio).
**lou.sa** *s.* blackboard.
**lou.var** *v.* to praise.
**lu.a** *s.* moon.
**lu.ci.dez** *s.* lucidity.
**lu.gar** *s.* place.
**lu.ne.ta** *s.* eye-glass.
**lu.ta** *s.* fight.
**lu.va** *s.* glove.
**lu.xo** *s.* luxury.
**lu.xu.o.so(a)** *adj.* luxurious.
**luz** *s.* light.

**L**

# Mm

**M, m** *s.* the thirteenth letter of the Portuguese alphabet.

**ma.çã** *s.* apple.

**ma.ca.co** *s.* monkey.

**ma.car.rão** *s.* pasta, macaroni.

**ma.cha.do** *s.* axe.

**ma.cho** *adj.* male / *s.* male.

**ma.chu.car** *v.* to crush; to smash; to wound, to hurt.

**ma.ci.o(a)** *adj.* soft, smooth, tender.

**ma.dei.ra** *s.* wood; timber.

**ma.dri.nha** *s.* godmother.

**mãe** *s.* mother.

**ma.ga.zi.ne** *s.* store; periodical.

**ma.gi.a** *s.* magic.

**ma.go** *s.* magician, wizard.

**má.goa** *s.* sorrow, grief.

**mai.o** *s.* May.

**mai.ô** *s.* swimming suit.

**mai.or** *adj.* bigger, larger.

**mais** *adj.* more, further / *adv.* more, also.

**ma.jes.ta.de** *s.* majesty.

**mal** *adv.* bad / *s.* evil, ill.

**mal.da.de** *s.* badness, wickedness.

**mal.di.ção** *s.* curse.

**ma.le.ta** *s.* suitcase.

**mal-hu.mo.ra.do(a)** *adj.* bad tempered.

**ma.lí.cia** *s.* slyness, malice.

**ma.lu.co(a)** *adj.* crazy, nutty / *s.* nut, fool.

**ma.mãe** *s.* mom, mum, mummy.

**ma.mão** *s.* papaya.

**ma.mar** *v.* to suck, take the breast.

**man.cha** *s.* stain, spot.

**man.dar** *v.* to order; to boss.

**man.dí.bu.la** *s.* jaw.

**man.di.o.ca** *s.* cassava, manioc.

# maneira — 91 — mesa

**ma.nei.ra** *s.* way, manner.
**ma.nhã** *s.* morning.
**ma.ni.fes.ta.ção** *s.* demonstration, expression.
**ma.ni.ve.la** *s.* crank, handle.
**ma.no.bra** *s.* shunting, maneuver.
**man.tei.ga** *s.* butter.
**mão** *s.* hand.
**mão de o.bra** *s.* labor, labour, workmanship.
**ma.pa** *s.* map, chart, graph.
**má.qui.na** *s.* machine.
**ma.ra.cu.já** *s.* passion fruit.
**ma.ra.to.na** *s.* marathon.
**ma.ra.vi.lha** *s.* wonder, marvel.
**mar.ca** *s.* mark; brand.
**mar.ço** *s.* March.
**mar.ga.ri.da** *s.* daisy.
**ma.ri.do** *s.* husband.
**ma.ri.nhei.ro** *s.* seaman, sailor.
**mar.rom** *adj.* brown.
**Mar.te** *s.* Mars.
**mas** *conj.* but.
**más.ca.ra** *s.* mask.
**mas.cu.li.no** *adj.* masculine.
**mas.sa.gem** *s.* massage.
**mas.ti.gar** *v.* to chew.
**ma.ta** *s.* forest, wood.
**ma.té.ria** *s.* matter, substance; subject, topic.
**ma.trí.cu.la** *s.* registration, enrollment.
**ma.tri.mô.nio** *s.* marriage, matrimony.

**má.xi.mo** *adj.* greatest / *s.* maximum.
**me.da.lha** *s.* medal.
**me.di.ci.na** *s.* medicine.
**mé.di.co(a)** *s.* doctor / *adj.* medic(al).
**me.di.da** *s.* measurement.
**me.dir** *v.* to measure.
**me.do** *s.* fear; afraid (com medo).
**mei.a** *s.* sock, stocking (de náilon).
**mei.a–noi.te** *s.* midnight.
**mei.o-di.a** *s.* midday, noon.
**mel** *s.* honey.
**me.lan.ci.a** *s.* watermelon.
**me.lão** *s.* melon.
**me.lhor** *adj.* better.
**me.lo.di.a** *s.* melody.
**mem.bro** *s.* member.
**me.mó.ria** *s.* memory.
**me.ni.no(a)** *s.* boy, *fem.* girl.
**me.nor** *adj.* smaller.
**me.nos** *adv.* less.
**men.sa.gei.ro** *s.* messenger.
**men.sa.gem** *s.* message.
**men.tir** *v.* to lie.
**mer.ca.do** *s.* market.
**Mer.cú.rio** *s.* Mercury.
**mer.cú.rio** *s.* mercury (química).
**mer.gu.lhar** *v.* to dive.
**mês** *s.* month.
**me.sa** *s.* table.

**M**

**mesmo** / **museu**

**mes.mo** *adj.* same.
**me.ta.de** *s.* half.
**me.tró.po.le** *s.* metropolis.
**meu(inha)** *pron.* my, mine.
**me.xer** *v.* to move.
**mi.cros.có.pio** *s.* microscope.
**mi.ga.lha** *s.* crumb.
**mil** *num.* thousand.
**mi.la.gre** *s.* miracle.
**mi.lha** *s.* mile.
**mi.lhão** *num.* million.
**mim** *pron. pess.* me.
**mi.ma.do(a)** *adj.* spoilt.
**mi.na** *s.* mine, quarry.
**mi.se.rá.vel** *adj.* miserable.
**mis.são** *s.* mission.
**mis.té.rio** *s.* mystery.
**mo.da** *s.* fashion.

**mo.do** *s.* way, manner.
**mo.e.da** *s.* coin.
**mon.ta.nha** *s.* mountain.
**mo.ran.go** *s.* strawberry.
**mor.rer** *v.* to die.
**mor.ta.de.la** *s.* bologna.
**mos.tar.da** *s.* mustard.
**mo.ver** *v.* to move.
**mu.dan.ça** *s.* change.
**mui.to(a)** *adj.* a lot of.
**mu.la** *s.* mule.
**mu.le.ta** *s.* crutch; support.
**mu.lher** *s.* woman.
**mul.ti.dão** *s.* crowd.
**mun.do** *s.* world.
**mu.ni.cí.pio** *s.* municipality, town.
**mu.seu** *s.* museum.

# N n

**N, n** *s.* the fourteenth letter of the Portuguese alphabet.
**na.ci.o.nal** *adj.* national.
**na.da** *pron. indef.* nothing.
**na.da.dor(a)** *s.* swimmer.
**ná.de.ga** *s.* bottock.
**na.do** *s.* swim, swimming.
**na.mo.ra.do(a)** *s.* boyfriend, *fem.* girlfriend.
**não** *adv.* no, not.
**nar.ra.ção** *s.* narration.
**nas.cer** *v.* to be born.
**na.ta.ção** *s.* swimming.
**na.tal** *adj.* native (lugar).
**Na.tal** *s.* Christmas / *adj.* Christmas.
**na.ti.vo(a)** *adj.* native / *s.* native.
**na.tu.ral** *adj.* natural.
**na.tu.re.za** *s.* nature.

**na.vi.o** *s.* ship.
**ne.bli.na** *s.* mist.
**ne.ces.sá.rio** *adj.* necessary.
**ne.gó.cio** *s.* business.
**ne.gro(a)** *adj.* black.
**nem** *conj.* neither.
**ne.nê** *s.* baby.
**neto(a)** *s.* grandson, *fem.* granddaughter.
**Ne.tu.no** *s.* Neptune.
**nin.guém** *pron. indef.* nobody.
**ni.nho** *s.* nest.
**ni.ti.dez** *s.* clearness, distinctness.
**ní.vel** *s.* level.
**no.ção** *s.* notion, idea.
**noi.va.do** *s.* engagement.
**noi.vo(a)** *s.* grom, *fem.* bride.
**no.jen.to(a)** *adj.* disgusting; filthy.

**no.me** *s.* name.
**no.ra** *s.* daughter-in-law.
**nor.ma** *s.* norm, rule; standard.
**nor.te** *adj.* northern / *s.* north, northern.
**nos** *pron. pess.* us (complemento).
**nós** *pron. pess.* we (sujeito).
**nos.so** *pron. poss.* our.
**no.ta** *s.* note, reminder.
**no.tá.vel** *adj.* remarkable.
**no.tí.cia** *s.* information; news.
**no.va.men.te** *adv.* again.

**no.ve** *num.* nine.
**no.ve.cen.tos** *num.* nine hundred.
**no.ve.la** *s.* soap-opera.
**no.vem.bro** *s.* November.
**no.ven.ta** *num.* ninety.
**no.vo(a)** *adj.* new; young.
**noz** *s.* walnut.
**nu(a)** *adj.* naked / *s.* nude.
**nu.bla.do** *adj.* cloudy.
**nun.ca** *adv.* never.
**nu.tri.ção** *s.* nutrition.
**nu.vem** *s.* cloud.

**N**

# Oo

**O, o** *s.* the fifteenth letter of the Portuguese alphabet.

**o.be.de.cer** *v.* to obey.

**ob.je.to** *s.* object.

**o.bri.ga.ção** *s.* obligation, duty.

**ob.ser.va.ção** *s.* observation.

**ob.ses.são** *s.* obsession.

**obs.tá.cu.lo** *s.* obstacle.

**o.ca.si.ão** *s.* opportunity, occasion.

**o.ce.a.no** *s.* ocean.

**o.cor.rên.cia** *s.* event, happening, incident.

**o.cu.pa.ção** *s.* occupation.

**o.di.ar** *v.* to hate.

**o.dor** *s.* smell.

**o.es.te** *s.* west.

**o.fen.der** *v.* to offend.

**o.fe.re.cer** *v.* to offer.

**o.fi.ci.al** *adj.* official / *s.* officer.

**o.fi.ci.na** *s.* workshop.

**oi.ten.ta** *num.* eighty.

**oi.to** *num.* eight.

**oi.to.cen.tos** *num.* eight hundred.

**o.lá** *interj.* hi!, hello!

**ó.leo** *s.* oil.

**o.lho** *s.* eye.

**om.bro** *s.* shoulder.

**on.ça** *s.* jaguar; ounce.

**on.da** *s.* wave.

**on.de** *adv.* where.

**ô.ni.bus** *s.* bus.

**on.tem** *adj.* yesterday.

**on.ze** *num.* eleven.

**op.ção** *s.* option, choice.

**o.por.tu.ni.da.de** *s.* opportunity.

**o.po.si.ção** *s.* opposition.

**op.tar** *v.* to choose, to decide for.

**o.ra.ção** *s.* prayer.
**or.dem** *s.* order.
**o.re.lha** *s.* ear.
**or.gâ.ni.co** *adj.* organic(al).
**or.ga.ni.za.ção** *s.* organization.
**ór.gão** *s.* organ.
**or.ques.tra** *s.* orchestra.
**or.quí.dea** *s.* orchid.
**os.so** *s.* bone.

**ó.ti.mo** *adj.* excellent.
**ou** *conj.* or, either.
**ou.sa.di.a** *s.* daring.
**ou.to.no** *s.* autumn, fall.
**ou.tro(a)** *adj.* another, other.
**ou.tu.bro** *s.* October.
**ou.vi.do** *s.* ear.
**o.ve.lha** *s.* sheep.
**o.vo** *s.* egg.

**O**

# P p

**P, p** *s.* the sixteenth letter of the Portuguese alphabet.
**pa.ci.ên.cia** *s.* patience.
**pa.co.te** *s.* packet; package.
**pac.to** *s.* pact, agreement.
**pa.da.ri.a** *s.* bakery.
**pa.drão** *s.* standard, pattern.
**pa.dri.nho** *s.* godfather; best man (de casamento).
**pa.gar** *v.* to pay.
**pá.gi.na** *s.* page.
**pai** *s.* father.
**pa.ís** *s.* country.
**pai.xão** *s.* passion.
**pa.lá.cio** *s.* palace.
**pa.la.dar** *s.* taste, palate.
**pa.la.vra** *s.* word.
**pal.co** *s.* stage.
**pa.lha** *s.* straw.
**pa.lha.ço** *s.* clown.
**pan.ca.da** *s.* blow, knock.

**pa.ne.la** *s.* pot, pan.
**pâ.ni.co** *s.* panic.
**pan.te.ra** *s.* panther.
**pão** *s.* bread.
**pa.pa.gai.o** *s.* parrot.
**pa.pai** *s.* daddy, dad.
**pa.pel** *s.* paper, role.
**par** *s.* pair, couple / *adj.* even.
**pa.ra** *prep.* for, to.
**pa.ra.béns** *s.* congratulations.
**pa.rá.gra.fo** *s.* paragraph.
**pa.rar** *v.* to stop.
**pa.re.de** *s.* wall.
**par.que** *s.* park.
**par.te** *s.* part.
**Pás.co.a** *s.* Easter.
**pas.sa.do** *s.* past / *adj.* last, past.
**pas.sa.por.te** *s.* passport.
**pas.sar** *v.* to pass.
**pas.sa.tem.po** *s.* pastime, hobby.
**pas.ta** *s.* paste; briefcase.

| | |
|---|---|
| **pa.trão** *s.* boss. | **pes.co.ço** *s.* neck. |
| **pau.sa** *s.* pause. | **pe.so** *s.* weight. |
| **paz** *s.* peace. | **pes.qui.sa** *s.* research; investigation. |
| **pé** *s.* foot. | |
| **pe.ca.do** *s.* sin. | **pês.se.go** *s.* peach. |
| **pe.da.ço** *s.* piece. | **pes.soa** *s.* person (*pl.* people). |
| **pe.di.do** *s.* order; request. | **pé.ta.la** *s.* petal. |
| **pe.dir** *v.* to ask for, to beg. | **pia** *s.* sink. |
| **pe.dra** *s.* stone. | **pi.a.da** *s.* joke. |
| **pei.xe** *s.* fish. | **pi.e.da.de** *s.* piety, mercy. |
| **Pei.xes** *s.* Pisces (astrologia). | **pí.lu.la** *s.* pill. |
| **pe.le** *s.* skin; fur. | **pi.men.ta** *s.* pepper. |
| **pe.lú.cia** *s.* plush. | **pin.cel** *s.* brush. |
| **pe.lu.do** *adj.* hairy; furry. | **pin.guim** *s.* penguin. |
| **pen.sar** *v.* to think. | **pin.tar** *v.* to paint. |
| **pen.te** *s.* comb. | **pi.or** *adj.* worse / *adv.* worse. |
| **pe.núl.ti.mo** *adj.* last but one. | **pi.ra.ta** *s.* pirate. |
| **pe.pi.no** *s.* cucumber. | **pis.ci.na** *s.* swimming pool. |
| **pe.ra** *s.* pear. | **pi.so** *s.* floor. |
| **per.dão** *s.* pardon, forgiveness; sorry. | **pla.ne.ta** *s.* planet. |
| | **plan.ta** *s.* plant. |
| **per.der** *v.* to lose. | **pla.tei.a** *s.* stalls; audience. |
| **per.do.ar** *v.* to forgive. | **po.bre** *adj.* poor. |
| **per.fil** *s.* profile. | **po.der** *s.* power / *v.* to can. |
| **per.gun.ta** *s.* question. | **po.dre** *adj.* rotten, putrid. |
| **pe.ri.go** *s.* danger. | **po.lí.cia** *s.* police. |
| **pe.ri.go.so** *adj.* dangerous. | **pol.pa** *s.* pulp. |
| **per.na** *s.* leg. | **po.lu.i.ção** *s.* pollution. |
| **per.to** *adv.* near, close / *adj.* near, close. | **pol.vo** *s.* octopus. |
| | **po.ma.da** *s.* pomade, ointment. |
| **pe.sa.de.lo** *s.* nightmare. | **pom.ba** *s.* dove, pigeon. |
| **pe.sa.do** *adj.* heavy. | **pon.te** *s.* bridge. |
| **pes.ca** *s.* fishing. | **pon.to** *s.* point, dot. |

**pôr** *v.* to put, to place.

**por.co** *s.* pig (animal) / *adj.* filthy (sujo).

**po.rém** *conj.* however.

**por.que** *conj.* because.

**por.ta** *s.* door.

**por.tan.to** *conj.* so, therefore.

**po.si.ção** *s.* position.

**po.si.ti.vo** *adj.* positive.

**pos.si.bi.li.da.de** *s.* possibility.

**po.tên.cia** *s.* power.

**pou.co** *adj.* few, not many; not much, little.

**po.vo** *s.* people.

**pra.ça** *s.* square.

**prai.a** *s.* beach.

**pra.ta** *s.* silver.

**pre.ce** *s.* prayer.

**pre.ço** *s.* price.

**pre.en.cher** *v.* to fill, to complete.

**pre.fei.to** *s.* mayor.

**pre.fe.rên.cia** *s.* preference.

**pre.gui.ça** *s.* laziness.

**pre.o.cu.pa.ção** *s.* preoccupation, worry.

**pre.pa.ra.ção** *s.* preparation.

**pre.sen.ça** *s.* presence.

**pre.si.dên.cia** *s.* presidency.

**pres.são** *s.* pressure.

**pre.sun.to** *s.* ham.

**pre.za.do(a)** *adj.* dear.

**pri.ma.ve.ra** *s.* spring.

**pri.mei.ro(a)** *adj.* first.

**pri.mi.ti.vo** *adj.* primitive.

**pri.mo(a)** *s.* cousin.

**prin.ce.sa** *s.* princess.

**prín.ci.pe** *s.* prince.

**pri.vi.lé.gi.o** *s.* privilege.

**pro.ble.ma** *s.* problem.

**pro.mes.sa** *s.* promise.ma

**pro.mo.ção** *s.* promotion.

**pro.nún.cia** *s.* pronunciation.

**pró.prio(a)** *adj.* own, proper.

**prote.í.na** *s.* protein.

**pro.va** *s.* test; proof; evidence.

**pró.xi.mo(a)** *adj.* near, next.

**pu.lô.ver** *s.* pullover.

**pul.sei.ra** *s.* bracelet.

**pul.so** *s.* wrist; pulse.

**pu.nho** *s.* fist.

**pu.re.za** *s.* purity, pureness.

**púr.pu.ra** *s.* purple.

# Qq

**Q, q** *s.* the seventeenth letter of the Portuguese alphabet.
**qua.dra** *s.* block; court.
**qua.dra.do** *adj.* square / *s.* square.
**qua.dril** *s.* hip.
**qua.dro** *s.* painting (pintura); table, schedule.
**qual** *pron.* which.
**qua.li.da.de** *s.* quality.
**qua.li.fi.ca.ção** *s.* qualification.
**qual.quer** *pron.* any.
**quan.do** *adv.* when / *conj.* when.
**qua.ren.ta** *num.* forty.
**quar.ta-fei.ra** *s.* Wednesday.
**quar.tei.rão** *s.* block.
**quar.tel** *s.* barracks, quarters.
**quar.to(a)** *s.* bedroom (de dormir) / *num.* quarter (quarta parte).
**quar.tzo** *s.* quartz.

**qua.se** *adv.* almost.
**qua.tro** *num.* four.
**qua.tro.cen.tos** *num.* four hundred.
**que** *pron.* who, that.
**que.bra-ca.be.ça** *s.* puzzle.
**que.bra.di.ço** *adj.* fragile, frail.
**que.bra-ga.lho** *s.* stopgap.
**que.bra-mar** *s.* breakwater.
**que.bra-no.zes** *s.* nutcracker.
**que.brar** *v.* to break.
**que.da** *s.* fall, drop.
**quei.jo** *s.* cheese.
**quei.ma** *s.* burning.
**quei.ma.du.ra** *s.* burn.
**quei.xa** *s.* complaint.
**quei.xo** *s.* chin, lower jaw.
**quem** *pron.* who.
**quen.te** *adj.* hot, warm.

**que.rer** *v.* to want.

**que.ri.do** *adj.* dear, darling.

**que.ro.se.ne** *s.* kerosene.

**ques.tão** *s.* question.

**ques.ti.o.nar** *v.* to question.

**qui.a.bo** *s.* okra.

**qui.e.to** *adj.* quiet, still.

**quí.mi.co(a)** *adj.* chemical / *s.* chemist.

**qui.nhen.tos** *num.* five hundred.

**quin.ta-fei.ra** *s.* Thursday.

**quin.tal** *s.* back yard, back garden.

**quin.ze** *num.* fifteen.

**quo.ta** *s.* share.

**quo.ti.di.a.no** *s.* everyday, daily.

# Rr

**R, r** *s.* the eighteenth letter of the Portuguese alphabet.

**rã** *s.* frog.

**ra.ba.ne.te** *s.* radish.

**ra.be.ca** *s.* fiddle, violin.

**ra.bi.no** *s.* rabbi.

**ra.bis.car** *v.* to scribble.

**ra.bo** *s.* tail.

**ra.bo de ca.va.lo** *s.* ponytail.

**ra.bu.do** *adj.* long-tailed, tailed; lucky.

**ra.bu.gen.to** *adj.* sullen, cross, grumpy.

**ra.ça** *s.* race (humana); breed (animal).

**ra.ção** *s.* animal food, fodder.

**ra.char** *v.* to crack, to split, to chop.

**ra.ci.o.ci.nar** *v.* to reason, to think.

**ra.ci.o.nal** *adj.* logical, reasonable.

**ra.ci.o.na.li.zar** *v.* to rationalize.

**ra.ci.o.na.men.to** *s.* rationing.

**ra.cis.mo** *s.* racism.

**racista** *adj.* racist / *s.* racist.

**ra.dar** *s.* radar.

**ra.di.a.ção** *s.* radiation.

**ra.di.a.dor** *s.* radiator.

**ra.di.a.lis.ta** *s.* broadcaster.

**rá.dio** *s.* radio (aparelho); radium (química); radius (osso).

**ra.i.nha** *s.* queen.

**rai.o** *s.* ray (de sol); spoke (de roda); lightning (relâmpago).

**rai.va** *s.* rage, fury; rabies (animal).

**ra.iz** *s.* root.

**ra.paz** *s.* boy, lad.

**ra.pi.dez** *s.* speed, quickness.

# rascunhar

**ras.cu.nhar** *v.* to sketch, to outline.
**ra.ti.fi.car** *v.* to confirm.
**ra.to** *s.* mouse.
**ra.zão** *s.* reason.
**re.a.ção** *s.* reaction.
**re.a.li.da.de** *s.* reality.
**re.a.li.za.ção** *s.* fulfilment, achievement.
**re.al.men.te** *adv.* really, indeed.
**re.bo.lar** *v.* to swing, to sway.
**re.ca.do** *s.* message.
**re.cei.o** *s.* fear, apprehension.
**re.cei.tar** *v.* to prescribe.
**re.cém** *adv.* recently.
**re.cen.te** *adj.* recent.
**re.cep.ção** *s.* reception.
**re.ci.fe** *s.* reef.
**re.ci.pi.en.te** *s.* container.
**re.co.lher** *v.* to collect.
**re.com.pen.sa** *s.* reward.
**re.con.ci.li.ar** *v.* to reconcile, to appease.
**re.co.nhe.cer** *v.* to recognize, to admit.
**re.cor.da.ção** *s.* souvenir; memory.
**re.cor.tar** *v.* to cut out.
**re.cre.a.ção** *s.* fun, recreation, amusement.
**re.cu.pe.ra.ção** *s.* recovery; retrieval.
**re.de** *s.* net; network.
**re.du.to** *s.* redoubt, stronghold.

# represa

**re.fei.ção** *s.* meal.
**re.fém** *s.* hostage.
**re.fle.xão** *s.* reflection.
**re.for.ma** *s.* reform.
**re.fres.can.te** *adj.* refreshing.
**re.fri.ge.ra.dor** *s.* refrigerator, fridge.
**re.gi.ão** *s.* region.
**ré.gua** *s.* ruler.
**re.gu.lar** *adj.* regular, constant / *v.* to control, to regulate, to rule.
**rei** *s.* king.
**rei.no** *s.* kingdom.
**re.la.ção** *s.* relationship; connection.
**re.lâm.pa.go** *s.* lightning.
**re.la.ti.vo** *adj.* relative, concerning.
**re.le.van.te** *adj.* outstanding, relevant.
**re.li.gi.ão** *s.* religion.
**re.ló.gio** *s.* clock (de parede); watch (de pulso).
**re.mar** *v.* to row.
**re.men.dar** *v.* to mend.
**re.mor.so** *s.* remorse.
**re.mo.to** *adj.* remote, distant.
**re.mo.ver** *v.* to move, to remove.
**re.pe.ti.ção** *s.* repetition.
**reple.to** *adj.* replete, filled up.
**re.po.lho** *s.* cabbage.
**re.por.ta.gem** *s.* article, newspaper report.
**re.pre.sa** *s.* dam, dike.

**R**

# réptil — ruim

**rép.til** *s.* reptile.

**re.quei.jão** *s.* cottage cheese; cream cheese.

**re.qui.si.ção** *s.* request, requisition.

**re.ser.va** *s.* reserve (natural); booking (hotel).

**re.si.dên.cia** *s.* residence, dwelling.

**re.so.lver** *v.* to resolve, solve.

**res.pei.tar** *v.* to respect.

**res.pi.ra.ção** *s.* breathing.

**res.pon.sa.bi.li.da.de** *s.* responsibility.

**res.pos.ta** *s.* answer, response.

**re.sul.ta.do** *s.* result.

**re.tor.no** *s.* return.

**reu.ni.ão** *s.* meeting.

**re.ve.la.ção** *s.* revelation.

**re.vis.ta** *s.* magazine (publicação); review (inspeção).

**re.vól.ver** *s.* gun, revolver.

**re.zar** *v.* to pray.

**ri.a.cho** *s.* stream; brook.

**ri.co(a)** *adj.* rich, wealthy.

**ri.gi.dez** *s.* rigidity, strictness.

**rim** *s.* kidney.

**ri.o** *s.* river.

**rir** *v.* to laugh.

**ro.cha** *s.* rock.

**ro.lar** *v.* to roll.

**ro.lha** *s.* cork.

**ro.mã** *s.* pomegranate.

**ro.mân.ti.co(a)** *adj.* romantic.

**ron.car** *v.* to snore.

**ro.sa** *s.* rose (flor); pink (cor).

**ros.to** *s.* face.

**ro.ta** *s.* route, direction, course.

**ró.tu.lo** *s.* tag, label.

**rou.bar** *v.* to rob; to steal.

**rou.pa** *s.* clothes.

**ro.xo** *adj.* purple, violet / *s.* purple, violet.

**ru.a** *s.* street.

**ru.í.do** *s.* noise.

**ru.im** *adj.* awful, bad.

# S s

**S, s** *s.* the nineteenth letter of the Portuguese alphabet.
**sá.ba.do** *s.* Saturday.
**sa.bão** *s.* soap.
**sa.ber** *v.* to know.
**sa.bo.ne.te** *s.* toilet soap.
**sa.bor** *s.* taste, flavour.
**sa.ca-ro.lhas** *s.* corkscrew.
**sa.co** *s.* bag, sack.
**sa.gra.do** *adj.* sacred, holy.
**sai.a** *s.* skirt.
**sa.í.da** *s.* exit, way out.
**sal** *s.* salt.
**sa.la** *s.* room; living-room.
**sa.la.da** *s.* salad.
**sal.sa** *s.* parsley.
**sal.si.cha** *s.* sausage.
**sal.va.ção** *s.* salvation.
**sal.var** *v.* to save.

**san.dá.lia** *s.* sandal.
**san.du.í.che** *s.* sandwich.
**san.gue** *s.* blood.
**san.to(a)** *s.* saint / *adj.* holy, sacred.
**sa.pa.to** *s.* shoe.
**sa.po** *s.* toad.
**sa.ram.po** *s.* measles.
**Sa.gi.tá.rio** *s.* Sagittarius (astrologia).
**sa.tis.fa.ção** *s.* satisfaction.
**Sa.tur.no** *s.* Saturn.
**sau.da.ção** *s.* greeting, salutation.
**sau.dá.vel** *adj.* healthy.
**se** *conj.* if, whether.
**se.ca.dor** *s.* drier, dryer.
**se.cre.to(a)** *adj.* secret, private.
**se.da** *s.* silk.

| | |
|---|---|
| **se.de** *s.* thirst; headquarters. | **se.te** *num.* seven. |
| **se.du.ção** *s.* seduction. | **se.te.cen.tos** *num.* seven hundred. |
| **se.gun.da-fei.ra** *s.* Monday. | **se.tem.bro** *s.* September. |
| **se.gun.do(a)** *adj.* second / *num.* second / *prep.* according to. | **se.ten.ta** *num.* seventy. |
| | **se.tor** *s.* sector; section. |
| **se.gu.ran.ça** *s.* safety; security. | **seu(ua)** *pron. adj.* his, *fem.* her. |
| **sei.o** *s.* breast. | **se.xo** *s.* sex. |
| **seis** *num.* six. | **sex.ta-fei.ra** *s.* Friday. |
| **seis.cen.tos** *num.* six hundred. | **si.gi.lo** *s.* secret. |
| **se.le.ção** *s.* selection. | **sim.pa.ti.a** *s.* affection, affinity. |
| **sel.va** *s.* forest, jungle. | **sim.ples** *adj.* simple. |
| **sel.va.gem** *adj.* wild; uncivilized. | **si.nal** *s.* sign; signal. |
| **sem** *prep.* without. | **si.no** *s.* bell. |
| **se.ma.na** *s.* week. | **sin.to.ma** *s.* symptom. |
| **se.me.lhan.ça** *s.* similarity. | **si.ri** *s.* crab. |
| **se.men.te** *s.* seed. | **sis.te.ma** *s.* system. |
| **sem.pre** *adv.* always. | **si.tu.a.ção** *s.* situation, position. |
| **se.não** *conj.* otherwise. | **só** *adj.* alone / *adv.* only, just. |
| **se.nha** *s.* password. | **so.bre** *prep.* on; about. |
| **sen.sa.ção** *s.* sensation, feeling. | **so.bre.no.me** *s.* last name, family name, surname. |
| **sen.si.bi.li.da.de** *s.* sensibility; sensitivity. | **so.bri.nho(a)** *s.* nephew, *fem.* niece. |
| **sen.tar** *v.* to seat, place. | **so.car** *v.* to hit, to punch. |
| **sen.ten.ça** *s.* sentence. | **so.ci.e.da.de** *s.* society. |
| **sen.ti.do** *adj.* grieved, touchy / *s.* sense, feeling, meaning. | **so.cor.rer** *v.* to help. |
| | **so.fá** *s.* sofa, couch. |
| **sen.tir** *v.* to feel. | **so.frer** *v.* to bear; to suffer. |
| **se.quên.cia** *s.* sequence. | **so.gro(a)** *s.* father-in-law, *fem.* mother-in-law. |
| **ser** *v.* to be / *s.* being, creature. | **sol** *s.* sun. |
| **sé.rio(a)** *adj.* serious. | **so.lu.ção** *s.* solution. |
| **ses.são** *s.* session. | **som** *s.* sound. |
| **ses.sen.ta** *num.* sixty. | **som.bra** *s.* shadow, shade. |

**so.men.te** *adv.* only.

**so.ne.ca** *s.* snooze, nap, doze.

**so.no** *s.* sleep.

**so.pa** *s.* soup.

**sor.te** *s.* luck, destiny.

**só.tão** *s.* loft, attic.

**so.zi.nho(a)** *adj.* alone.

**su.a.ve** *adj.* soft, smooth, gentle.

**subs.tân.cia** *s.* substance, matter.

**subs.ti.tu.ir** *v.* to substitute, to replace.

**su.ca.ta** *s.* scrap.

**su.í.no** *s.* swine, pig, hog / *adj.* swinish.

**su.jar** *v.* to soil.

**sul** *adj.* south / *s.* south.

**su.mir** *v.* to disappear, to vanish.

**su.or** *s.* sweat.

**su.pér.fluo** *adj.* superfluous.

**su.per.mer.ca.do** *s.* supermarket.

**su.pers.ti.ção** *s.* superstition.

**sur.do(a)** *adj.* deaf.

**sur.pre.en.den.te** *adj.* surprising, amazing, remarkable.

**sus.pei.tar** *v.* to suspect.

**sus.pen.der** *v.* to suspend, to hang.

**sus.to** *s.* fright, scare.

**S**

# Tt

**T, t** *s.* the twentieth letter of the Portuguese alphabet.
**ta.be.la** *s.* chart, list, table.
**ta.bla.do** *s.* platform, stage.
**ta.bu** *s.* taboo.
**tá.bua** *s.* board, plank.
**tal.co** *s.* talc, talcum.
**ta.len.to** *s.* talent, ability.
**tal.vez** *adv.* perhaps, maybe.
**ta.ma.nho** *s.* size / *adj.* such.
**tam.bém** *adv.* also, too, as well.
**tam.bor** *s.* drum.
**tam.pa** *s.* lid, cover(ing).
**tan.ge.ri.na** *s.* tangerine.
**tan.que** *s.* tank.
**tan.to(a)** *adj.* so much.
**tão** *adv.* so, such.
**ta.pe.te** *s.* carpet.
**ta.re.fa** *s.* job, task.
**ta.tu** *s.* armadillo.
**ta.tu.a.gem** *s.* tattoo.
**ta.xa** *s.* tax; rate.
**téc.ni.co(a)** *adj.* technical / *s.* technician.
**tei.a** *s.* web.
**tei.mar** *v.* to insist.
**te.lha** *s.* tile.
**te.ma** *s.* subject, theme, topic.
**te.mer** *v.* to fear, to dread.
**tem.pe.ra.tu.ra** *s.* temperature.
**tem.pe.ro** *s.* seasoning, condiment.
**tem.pes.ta.de** *s.* storm.
**tem.po** *s.* time; duration.
**ten.dên.cia** *s.* tendency.
**tê.nis** *s.* tennis.
**ten.ta.ção** *s.* temptation.
**ter** *v.* to have, to own.

terça-feira      **109**      trinta

**ter.ça-fei.ra** *s.* Tuesday.
**ter.cei.ro** *num.* third.
**Ter.ra** *s.* Earth.
**ter.ra** *s.* ground, land (terreno);
earth, world (mundo).
**ter.re.no** *s.* ground, land.
**ter.ri.tó.rio** *s.* territory, region.
**ter.rí.vel** *adj.* terrible, awful.
**te.sou.ra** *s.* scissors.
**tes.ta** *s.* brow, forehead.
**tes.te** *s.* test, examination, trial.
**tes.te.mu.nha** *s.* witness.
**teu(ua)** *pron. adj.* your, yours.
**tex.to** *s.* text.
**ti.ge.la** *s.* bowl.
**ti.gre** *s.* tiger.
**ti.jo.lo** *s.* brick.
**ti.mi.dez** *s.* shyness, timidity.
**tin.ta** *s.* ink; paint.
**tio(a)** *s.* uncle, *fem.* aunt.
**tí.pi.co** *adj.* typical.
**ti.ro** *s.* shot.
**to.a.lha** *s.* towel.
**to.ca-dis.cos** *s.* record-player,
CD player.
**to.da.vi.a** *conj.* yet, however.
**to.do(a)** *adj.* all / *s.* whole.
**to.le.rân.cia** *s.* tolerance.
**to.li.ce** *s.* stupidity, silliness.
**tom** *s.* tone.
**to.ma.da** *s.* socket, plug.
**to.ma.te** *s.* tomato.
**tom.bar** *v.* to fall down.
**tor.ção** *s.* twisting.

**tor.ci.da** *s.* wick.
**tor.nar** *v.* to return, to turn;
to become.
**tor.ra.da** *s.* toast.
**tor.re** *s.* tower.
**tor.to(a)** *adj.* twisted, bent.
**tor.tu.ra** *s.* torture.
**tos.se** *s.* cough.
**to.tal** *adj.* complete, full
/ *s.* total, sum.
**tou.ca** *s.* bonnet.
**Tou.ro** *s.* Taurus (astrologia).
**tou.ro** *s.* bull (animal).
**tra.çar** *v.* to draw, to delineate.
**tra.di.ção** *s.* tradition.
**tra.du.ção** *s.* translation.
**trá.fe.go** *s.* traffic.
**tra.gé.dia** *s.* tragedy.
**trans.for.ma.ção** *s.*
transformation.
**trans.mis.são** *s.* transmission.
**trans.pi.rar** *v.* to perspire, sweat.
**trans.por.tar** *v.* to transport.
**tra.tar** *v.* to treat; to deal with.
**tra.ves.sei.ro** *s.* pillow.
**tra.zer** *v.* to bring.
**trem** *s.* train.
**três** *num.* three.
**tre.vo** *s.* clover.
**tre.ze** *num.* thirteen.
**tre.zen.tos** *num.* three hundred.
**tri.go** *s.* wheat.
**trin.ta** *num.* thirty.

**T**

**tris.te** *adj.* sad, unhappy.
**tro.car** *v.* to exchange.
**tro.co** *s.* change.
**tro.féu** *s.* trophy.
**trom.ba** *s.* trunk.
**tu.ba.rão** *s.* shark.

**tu.ca.no** *s.* toucan.
**tu.do** *pron.* all, everything.
**tu.li.pa** *s.* tulip.
**tu.mul.to** *s.* tumult, disturbance.
**tú.nel** *s.* tunnel.
**tu.ris.mo** *s.* tourism.

T

# Uu

**U, u** *s.* the twenty-first letter of the Portuguese alphabet.

**úl.ce.ra** *s.* ulcer.

**ul.ti.ma.men.te** *adv.* recently, lately.

**úl.ti.mas** *s.* last moments.

**úl.ti.mo(a)** *adj.* last, preceding.

**ul.tra.je** *s.* offense, outrage.

**ul.tra.pas.sa.do** *adj.* outdated.

**ul.tra.pas.sar** *v.* to exceed.

**um(a)** *art.indef.* a / *num.* one.

**um.bi.go** *s.* navel.

**u.me.de.cer** *v.* to moisten, to humidify.

**u.mi.da.de** *s.* humidity, moisture.

**u.nâ.ni.me** *adj.* unanimous.

**u.na.ni.mi.da.de** *s.* unanimity.

**u.nha** *s.* nail.

**u.ni.ão** *s.* union, alliance.

**ú.n.ico** *s.* only.

**u.ni.da.de** *s.* unit; unity.

**u.ni.for.me** *adj.* uniform / *s.* uniform.

**u.nir** *v.* to join, to unite, to connect.

**u.ni.ver.si.da.de** *s.* university.

**u.ni.ver.si.tá.rio** *adj.* university, universitarian.

**u.ni.ver.so** *s.* universe.

**U.ra.no** *s.* Uranus.

**ur.ba.nis.mo** *s.* city planning.

**ur.ba.nis.ta** *s.* city planner / *adj.* urbanistic.

**ur.gên.cia** *s.* urgency, haste.

**u.ri.nar** *v.* to urinate.

**ur.rar** *v.* to roar.

**ur.so** *s.* bear.

**u.ru.bu** *s.* vulture.

**u.sa.do(a)** *adj.* used, usual; secondhand.
**u.si.na** *s.* plant, factory.
**u.so** *s.* use; application.

**u.su.al** *adj.* usual.
**u.su.fru.ir** *v.* to enjoy, to usufruct.
**u.va** *s.* grape.

# V v

**V, v** *s.* the twenty-second letter of the Portuguese alphabet.
**va.ca** *s.* cow (animal);
beef (carne).
**va.ci.lar** *v.* to vacillate,
to hesitate.
**va.ci.na** *s.* vaccine, inoculation.
**va.ci.nar** *v.* to vaccinate,
to inoculate with vaccine.
**va.di.ar** *v.* to idle.
**va.di.o(a)** *s.* loafer, idler.
**va.ga** *s.* vacancy.
**va.ga.bun.do(a)** *s.* roamer, idler
/ *adj.* vagabond, erratic.
**va.gão** *s.* wagon.
**va.gar** *v.* to wander, to roam.
**va.gem** *s.* green bean.
**va.gi.na** *s.* vagina.
**va.go** *adj.* empty; vague.
**vai.da.de** *s.* vanity.

**va.i.do.so** *adj.* vain.
**va.la** *s.* ditch.
**va.le** *s.* valley.
**va.le-pos.tal** *s.* money order.
**va.len.te** *adj.* brave.
**vá.li.do(a)** *adj.* valid.
**va.li.se** *s.* small suitcase, valise.
**va.lor** *s.* value.
**val.sa** *s.* waltz.
**vál.vu.la** *s.* valve.
**vam.pi.ro** *s.* vampire.
**vân.da.lo** *s.* vandal.
**van.ta.gem** *s.* advantage.
**va.por** *s.* vapour, steam.
**va.quei.ro** *s.* cowboy.
**va.ra** *s.* stick, rod.
**va.ral** *s.* clothesline.
**va.rar** *v.* to pierce, to trespass.
**va.re.jo** *s.* retail.
**va.re.ta** *s.* rod.

variedade — vulto

**va.ri.e.da.de** *s.* variety, diversity.
**va.río.la** *s.* smallpox.
**vá.rios** *adj.* several, various, many.
**var.rer** *v.* to sweep.
**va.so** *s.* vase, flowerpot.
**vas.sou.ra** *s.* brush, broom.
**va.zar** *v.* to leak.
**ve.a.do** *s.* deer (animal).
**ve.dar** *v.* to seal.
**ve.ge.ta.ção** *s.* vegetation.
**vei.a** *s.* vein.
**ve.la** *s.* candle.
**ve.la.do** *adj.* veiled.
**ve.lei.ro** *s.* sailing ship.
**ve.le.jar** *v.* to sail.
**velho** *adj.* old.
**ve.lo.ci.da.de** *s.* speed.
**ven.ce.dor** *s.* winner / *adj.* winning.
**ven.da** *s.* sale, selling.
**ven.der** *v.* to sell.
**ve.ne.no** *s.* poison.
**ven.to** *s.* wind.
**Vê.nus** *s.* Venus.
**ver** *v.* to see.
**ve.rão** *s.* summer.
**ver.bo** *s.* verb.
**ver.de** *adj.* green / *s.* green.
**ver.du.ra** *s.* greens, vegetables.
**ver.go.nha** *s.* shame.
**ver.me** *s.* worm.
**ver.me.lho** *adj.* red / *s.* red.

**ver.niz** *s.* varnish.
**ver.são** *s.* version.
**ves.ti.do** *s.* dress / *adj.* dressed.
**ves.tí.gio** *s.* sign, trace.
**ves.tir** *v.* to dress, to put on.
**vi.na.gre** *s.* vinegar.
**vin.te** *num.* twenty.
**vi.o.la.ção** *s.* violation.
**vi.o.lão** *s.* guitar.
**vi.o.lên.cia** *s.* violence.
**vir** *v.* to come.
**Vir.gem** *s.* Virgo (astrologia).
**vir.gem** *s.* virgin.
**vír.gu.la** *s.* comma.
**vi.são** *s.* vision; eyesight.
**vi.si.ta** *s.* visit.
**vi.ta.mi.na** *s.* vitamin.
**vi.tó.ria** *s.* victory, win.
**vi.va** *s.* cheer / *interj.* hooray!
**vi.ver** *v.* to live.
**vi.vo(a)** *adj.* alive; lively.
**vi.zi.nhan.ça** *s.* neighborhood.
**vo.ca.bu.lá.rio** *s.* vocabulary.
**vo.lan.te** *adj.* movable, portable / *s.* steering wheel.
**vol.ta** *s.* turn; return.
**vol.tar** *v.* to turn; to return.
**von.ta.de** *s.* will, wish.
**vo.o** *s.* flight.
**voz** *s.* voice.
**vul.cão** *s.* volcano.
**vul.to** *s.* figure; form.

# W w

**W, w** *s.* the twenty-third letter of the Portuguese alphabet.

**wal.kie-tal.kie** *s.* walkie-talkie.

**walk.man** *s.* walkman.

**w.c.** *s.* water closet.

# X x

**X, x** *s.* the twenty-fourth letter of the Portuguese alphabet.

**xa.drez** *s.* chess (jogo); chessboard (tabuleiro); *s.* check (tecido).

**xa.le** *s.* shawl.

**xam.pu** *s.* shampoo.

**xa.rá** *s.* namesake.

**xa.ro.pe** *s.* syrup.

**xe.re.ta** *adj.* nosy / *s.* gossip, disturber.

**xe.re.tar** *v.* to snoop.

**xí.ca.ra** *s.* cup.

**xin.gar** *v.* to abuse; to chide, to scold.

**xo.dó** *s.* flirtation; sweetheart.

# Yy

**Y, y** *s.* the twenty-fifth letter of the Portuguese alphabet.

**yd** *abrev.* yard (jarda).

# Z z

**Z, z** *s.* the twenty-sixth letter of the Portuguese alphabet.

**za.guei.ro** *s.* fullback.

**zan.ga.do** *adj.* angry.

**zan.gão** *s.* drone.

**zan.gar** *v.* to annoy.

**ze.ro** *num.* zero.

**zin.co** *s.* zinc.

**zí.per** *s.* zip, zipper.

**zo.ar** *v.* to buzz.

**zon.zo** *adj.* dizzy.

**zor.ra** *s.* huge mess.

# INGLÊS
## MINIDICIONÁRIO ESCOLAR

INGLÊS / PORTUGUÊS

# Aa

**A, a** *s.* primeira letra do alfabeto inglês; lá (nota musical)/*art. indef.* um(a).

**a.back** *adv.* ♦ *taken* ~ ficar surpreso, perplexo.

**a.ban.don** *v.* abandonar, desamparar.

**a.bash** *v.* embaraçar, envergonhar.

**a.bashed** *adj.* envergonhado.

**a.bate** *v.* diminuir, abater.

**ab.at.toir** *s.* matadouro.

**ab.bey** *s.* abadia, mosteiro.

**ab.bot** *s.* abade.

**ab.bre.vi.ate** *v.* abreviar; resumir.

**ab.bre.vi.a.tion** *s.* abreviação; resumo.

**ab.di.cate** *v.* abdicar, renunciar.

**ab.do.men** *s.* abdome.

**ab.duct** *v.* raptar, abduzir.

**a.bet** *v.* instigar, incitar.

**a.bey.ance** *s.* suspensão, inatividade temporária.

**a.bey.ant** *adj.* pendente, jacente.

**ab.hor** *v.* detestar, odiar.

**ab.hor.rence** *s.* aversão, repugnância.

**ab.hor.rent** *adj.* detestável, repugnante.

**a.bide** *v.* suportar; morar, residir.

**a.bil.i.ty** *s.* capacidade, habilidade, competência.

**ab.ject** *adj.* abjeto, miserável, vil, desprezível.

**a.blaze** *adj.* em chamas; inflamado.

**a.ble** *adj.* capaz, hábil, apto.

**a.bly** *adv.* habilmente.

**ab.nor.mal** *adj.* anormal; irregular.

**ab.nor.mal.i.ty** *s.* anormalidade; irregularidade.

**a.board** *adv.* a bordo.

**a.bode** *s.* domicílio; permanência, estada.

**a.bol.ish** *v.* abolir, cancelar, revogar.

**a.bom.i.na.ble** *adj.* abominável, detestável.

**a.bom.i.na.bleness** *s.* contrariedade, adversidade.

**ab.o.rig.i.ne** *s.* aborígene.

**a.bort** *v.* abortar; malograr.

**a.bound** *v.* abundar, existir em abundância.

**a.bout** *adv.* aproximadamente / *prep.* por volta de, sobre.

**a.bout-face** *s.* meia-volta (militar); reviravolta.

**a.bove** *adv.* acima / *prep.* acima de, mais de.

**ab.ra.sive** *adj.* abrasivo / *s.* abrasivo.

**a.breast** *adv.* lado a lado, estar a par de.

**a.bridge** *v.* resumir, abreviar, encurtar.

**a.broad** *adv.* estar no estrangeiro, fora do país, no exterior.

**a.brupt** *adj.* brusco.

**ab.scess** *s.* abscesso.

**ab.scond** *v.* evadir-se, fugir.

**ab.sence** *s.* ausência.

**ab.sent** *adj.* ausente.

**ab.sent-mind.ed** *adj.* distraído.

**ab.so.lute** *adj.* absoluto, inteiro, total / *s.* absoluto.

**ab.so.lute.ly** *adv.* absolutamente.

**ab.solve** *v.* absolver, isentar, perdoar.

**ab.sorb** *v.* absorver, assimilar.

**ab.sorb.ent** *adj.* absorvente.

**ab.stain** *v.* abster-se de, privar-se.

**ab.stainer** *s.* abstinente, abstêmio.

**ab.ste.mi.ous** *adj.* abstêmio.

**ab.sti.nence** *s.* abstinência.

**ab.stract** *adj.* abstrato / *s.* abstrato, resumo, sumário.

**ab.surd** *adj.* absurdo, ridículo.

**a.buse** *v.* abusar, maltratar / *s.* abuso; injúria.

**a.bu.sive** *adj.* ofensivo, insultante.

**a.bys.mal** *adj.* péssimo.

**a.byss** *s.* abismo.

**ac.a.dem.ic** *adj.* acadêmico; teórico; universitário / *s.* acadêmico.

**a.cad.e.my** *s.* academia; escola superior; conservatório.

**ac.cel.er.ate** *v.* acelerar, apressar; antecipar.

**ac.cel.er.a.tor** *s.* acelerador.

**ac.cent** *s*. acento; sotaque.

**ac.cept** *v*. aceitar; assumir.

**ac.cess** *s*. acesso / *v*. acessar, entrar.

**ac.ces.si.ble** *adj*. acessível.

**ac.ces.so.ry** *s*. acessório, suplemento / *adj*. acessório, suplementar.

**ac.ci.dent** *s*. acidente, desastre.

**ac.ci.den.tal** *adj*. acidental, inesperado.

**ac.claim** *s*. aclamação / *v*. aplaudir, aclamar.

**ac.co.lade** *s*. louvor; honra; cerimonial.

**ac.com.mo.date** *v*. alojar, acomodar.

**ac.com.mo.dat.ing** *adj*. obsequioso, complacente.

**ac.com.mo.da.tion** *s*. alojamento, acomodação.

**ac.com.pa.ny** *v*. acompanhar, escoltar.

**ac.com.plice** *s*. cúmplice.

**ac.com.plish** *v*. concluir; realizar.

**ac.com.plish.ment** *s*. realização; cumprimento.

**ac.cord** *s*. acordo / *v*. conceder; concordar.

**ac.cor.di.on** *s*. acordeão, sanfona.

**ac.cost** *v*. abordar.

**ac.count** *s*. conta / *v*. calcular, acertar contas.

**ac.count.an.cy** *s*. contabilidade.

**ac.count.ant** *s*. contador.

**ac.cred.it.ed** *adj*. autorizado, aprovado.

**ac.crue** *v*. acumular; advir, resultar.

**ac.crued in.terest** *s*. juros acumulados.

**ac.cu.mu.late** *v*. acumular.

**ac.cu.ra.cy** *s*. exatidão, precisão.

**ac.cu.rate** *adj*. correto, preciso.

**ac.cu.sa.tion** *s*. acusação; incriminação.

**ac.cuse** *v*. acusar, denunciar.

**ac.cused** *s*. acusado(a) / *adj*. acusado(a).

**ac.cus.tom** *v*. acostumar, habituar-se.

**ace** *s*. ás (carta do baralho).

**ache** *s*. dor / *v*. doer.

**a.chieve** *v*. alcançar, atingir, realizar.

**ac.id** *s*. ácido / *adj*. azedo, acre.

**ac.knowl.edge** *v*. reconhecer; admitir; confirmar o recebimento de.

**ac.me** *s*. auge, ápice.

**ac.ne** *s*. acne.

**a.corn** *s*. bolota.

**a.cous.tic** *adj*. acústico.

**a.cous.tics** *s*. acústica.

**ac.quaint** *v*. informar; familiarizar.

**ac.quaint.ance** *s.* conhecido.
**ac.qui.esce** *v.* condescender, consentir.
**ac.quire** *v.* adquirir, obter.
**ac.qui.si.tion** *s.* aquisição, obtenção.
**ac.quit** *v.* absolver, inocentar.
**ac.quit.tal** *s.* absolvição, soltura.
**a.cre** *s.* acre (medida agrária equivalente a 4.046,84 m²).
**ac.rid** *adj.* azedo.
**ac.ri.mo.ni.ous** *adj.* mordaz, cáustico, amargo.
**ac.ro.bat** *s.* acrobata.
**a.cross** *adj.* cruzado / *adv.* transversalmente / *prep.* através de.
**act** *s.* ação, ato / *v.* atuar.
**act.ing** *s.* atuação, encenação, representação / *adj.* ativo, em exercício.
**ac.tion** *s.* ação, ato.
**ac.ti.vate** *v.* acionar, ativar.
**ac.tive** *adj.* ativo, em atividade.
**ac.tive.ly** *adv.* ativamente.
**ac.tiv.ist** *s.* ativista, militante.
**ac.tiv.i.ty** *s.* atividade.
**ac.tor** *s.* ator.
**ac.tress** *s.* atriz.
**ac.tu.al** *adj.* real, verdadeiro.
**ac.tu.al.i.ty** *s.* realidade.
**ac.tu.al.ly** *adv.* na verdade, de fato, realmente.

**ac.tu.ation** *s.* acionamento; estímulo.
**a.cu.men** *s.* perspicácia.
**ad** *abrev.* de *advertisement.*
**A.D.** *abrev.* de *anno domini* (depois de Cristo)
**ad.a.mant** *adj.* inflexível, duro / *s.* pedra, magnetita.
**a.dapt** *v.* adaptar, ajustar.
**a.dapt.a.ble** *adj.* adaptável, ajustável.
**ad.ap.ta.tion** *s.* adaptação, acomodação.
**add** *v.* somar, adicionar, acrescentar.
**ad.der** *s.* víbora; máquina de somar.
**ad.dict** *s.* viciado(a).
**ad.dict.ed** *adj.* viciado(a) em; fanático(a) por.
**ad.di.tion** *s.* adição, acréscimo.
**ad.di.tive** *s.* aditivo.
**ad.dress** *s.* endereço / *v.* endereçar.
**a.dept** *adj.* hábil / *s.* perito.
**ad.e.quate** *adj.* adequado; suficiente, satisfatório.
**ad.here** *v.* aderir, grudar.
**ad.he.sive** *s.* adesivo, cola / *adj.* adesivo, aderente.
**ad.he.sive tape** *s.* fita isolante; esparadrapo.
**ad.jec.tive** *s.* adjetivo.
**ad.join** *v.* juntar, adicionar, unir.

**adjoining** / **124** / **adversity**

**ad.join.ing** *adj.* adjacente, contíguo.

**ad.journ** *v.* suspender; adiar; transferir.

**ad.just** *v.* ajustar, adaptar, arrumar.

**ad.judge** *v.* julgar; condenar.

**ad.just.ment** *s.* ajuste, regulagem.

**ad-lib** *v.* improvisar.

**ad.meas.ure** *v.* repartir, partilhar.

**ad.min.is.ter** *v.* administrar, ministrar, dirigir.

**ad.min.is.tra.tion** *s.* administração, direção.

**ad.mi.ra.ble** *adj.* admirável.

**ad.mi.ral** *s.* almirante.

**ad.mire** *v.* admirar, apreciar.

**ad.mis.sion** *s.* entrada; ingresso; confissão.

**ad.mit** *v.* admitir, deixar entrar.

**ad.mit.tance** *s.* admissão, aceitação.

**ad nau.se.am** *adv.* sem parar.

**a.do** *s.* pressa; alvoroço.

**a.do.be** *s.* barro seco; tijolo cru.

**ad.o.les.cence** *s.* adolescência, juventude.

**ad.o.les.cent** *s.* adolescente / *adj.* adolescente, juvenil.

**a.dopt** *v.* adotar, admitir.

**a.dop.tion** *s.* adoção.

**a.dop.tive** *adj.* adotivo(a).

**a.dor.a.ble** *adj.* adorável, admirável.

**a.dore** *v.* adorar.

**a.dorn** *v.* adornar, ornar.

**a.dorn.ment** *s.* adorno, enfeite.

**a.drift** *adv.* à deriva / *adj.* desgovernado(a).

**a.droit** *adj.* hábil, ágil.

**a.droit.ness** *s.* habilidade, destreza; talento.

**a.dult** *s.* adulto(a) / *adj.* adulto(a).

**a.dul.ter.er** *s.* adúltero.

**a.dul.ter.ess** *s.* mulher infiel, adúltera.

**a.dul.ter.ous** *adj.* adúltero(a).

**a.dul.ter.y** *s.* adultério.

**ad.vance** *s.* avanço / *adj.* antecipado / *v.* adiantar, avançar.

**ad.vanced** *adj.* avançado, adiantado, desenvolvido.

**ad.van.tage** *s.* vantagem, supremacia / *v.* aproveitar-se, favorecer.

**ad.van.ta.geous** *adj.* vantajoso, proveitoso.

**ad.van.ta.geous.ness** *s.* vantagem.

**ad.vent** *s.* advento, chegada.

**ad.ven.ture** *s.* aventura, façanha / *v.* aventurar-se.

**ad.ven.tur.er** *s.* aventureiro.

**ad.ver.si.ty** *s.* adversidade, dificuldade.

**advert** 125 **again**

**ad.vert** *s.* anúncio (coloquial) / *v.* advertir; chamar a atenção.

**ad.vert.ence** *s.* advertência.

**ad.ver.tise** *v.* anunciar, publicar; fazer propaganda.

**ad.ver.tise.ment** *s.* anúncio, propaganda.

**ad.ver.tis.ing** *s.* publicidade, propaganda, anúncio.

**ad.vice** *s.* conselho, aviso, parecer.

**ad.vise** *v.* aconselhar, recomendar.

**ad.vis.a.ble** *adj.* aconselhável, recomendável; oportuno.

**ad.vo.cate** *v.* advogar / *s.* advogado(a).

**Ae.ge.an** *adj.* egeu.

**aer.i.al** *s.* antena / *adj.* aéreo.

**aer.o.bics** *s.* ginástica, aeróbica.

**aer.o.plane** *s.* aeroplano, avião.

**aer.o.sol** *s.* aerossol.

**aes.thet.ic** *adj.* estético.

**a.far** *adv.* de longe; a distância.

**af.fa.ble** *adj.* afável, cortês, amável.

**af.fa.ble.ness** *s.* amabilidade, afabilidade.

**af.fair** *s.* assunto; negócio; romance.

**af.fect** *v.* afetar; comover.

**af.fect.ed** *adj.* afetado(a).

**af.fec.tion** *s.* afeto, afeição, simpatia.

**af.fec.tive** *adj.* afetivo(a).

**af.fil.i.ate** *v.* afiliar, incorporar.

**af.fin.i.ty** *s.* afinidade.

**af.fix** *v.* afixar, colar, juntar / *s.* afixo, anexo.

**af.flict** *v.* afligir.

**af.flu.ence** *s.* afluência, abundância, riqueza.

**af.flu.ent** *adj.* abundante / *s.* afluente.

**af.ford** *v.* poder gastar, ter dinheiro suficiente.

**af.ford.able** *adj.* disponível.

**af.for.est** *v.* reflorestar.

**af.for.est.ation** *s.* reflorestamento.

**af.fray** *v.* assustar / *s.* desordem.

**af.front** *s.* afronta, ofensa / *v.* insultar, ofender.

**a.field** *adv.* muito longe, afastado.

**a.float** *adj.* flutuante; inundado.

**a.foot** *adj.* andando / *adv.* a pé.

**a.fraid** *adj.* ♦ *to be* ~ assustado(a), amedrontado(a).

**a.fresh** *adv.* de novo, mais uma vez.

**Af.ri.can** *adj.* africano(a) / *s.* africano(a).

**af.ter** *adv.* depois, após / *prep.* atrás de, depois / *adj.* posterior.

**af.ter all** *adv.* apesar de tudo, afinal.

**af.ter.math** *s.* consequências.

**af.ter.noon** *s.* tarde / *adj.* à tarde.

**a.gain** *adv.* de novo, outra vez, novamente.

**against**      **126**      **airtight**

**A**   **a.gainst** *prep.* contra, contrário.
**a.gape** *adj.* boquiaberto.
**a.gaze** *adv.* contemplativamente.
**age** *s.* idade, época.
**aged** *adj.* idoso(a), velho(a).
**a.gen.cy** *s.* agência.
**a.gen.da** *s.* ordem do dia, pauta; agenda.
**a.gent** *s.* agente.
**ag.gra.vate** *v.* agravar, piorar; irritar, provocar.
**ag.gre.gate** *s.* agregado / *v.* agregar, unir.
**ag.gress** *v.* agredir, atacar.
**ag.gres.sive** *adj.* agressivo; enérgico, ativo.
**ag.grieved** *adj.* aflito; magoado.
**a.ghast** *adj.* horrorizado; espantado.
**a.gil.i.ty** *s.* agilidade.
**ag.ing** *s.* envelhecimento.
**ag.i.tate** *v.* agitar.
**a.go** *adv.* atrás, há tempo / *adj.* passado.
**a.gog** *adj.* ávido, entusiasmado, impaciente / *adv.* impacientemente.
**ag.o.ni.zing** *adj.* angustiante, agonizante.
**ag.o.ny** *s.* agonia, aflição.
**a.gree** *v.* concordar, combinar.
**a.gree.ment** *s.* acordo, contrato, consentimento.

**ag.ri.cul.tur.al** *adj.* agrícola, agrário.
**ag.ri.cul.ture** *s.* agricultura.
**a.ground** *adv.* de modo encalhado / *adj.* encalhado(a).
**a.head** *adv.* adiante, à frente.
**aid** *s.* ajuda / *v.* ajudar, auxiliar.
**aide** *s.* ajudante.
**aid.less** *adj.* sem ajuda.
**AIDS** *abrev.* de *Acquired Immune Deficiency Syndrome* (Síndrome de Imunodeficiência Adquirida).
**ail.ing** *adj.* enfermo, doente.
**ail.ment** *s.* indisposição, doença.
**aim** *v.* apontar, visar / *s.* pontaria, alvo, objetivo.
**ain't** contração de *am not, are not, is not, have not, has not* (coloquial).
**air** *s.* ar, atmosfera / *v.* arejar, ventilar.
**air-bomb** *s.* bomba aérea.
**air-brick** *s.* tijolo furado.
**air.craft** *s.* aeronave.
**air.ing** *s.* ventilação.
**air-jacket** *s.* colete salva-vidas.
**air.line** *s.* linha aérea.
**air.mail** *s.* correio aéreo.
**air.man** *s.* piloto, aviador.
**air.plane** *s.* avião, aeroplano.
**air.port** *s.* aeroporto.
**air.tight** *adj.* hermético.

**air.y** *adj.* arejado, vaporoso.

**aisle** *s.* nave de igreja; corredor, passagem.

**a.jar** *adj.* entreaberto.

**a.kin** *adj.* consanguíneo.

**alac.rity** *s.* vivacidade.

**a.larm** *s.* alarme / *v.* alarmar.

**a.larm-clock** *s.* despertador.

**alarm.ing** *adj.* alarmante.

**alas** *interj.* ai de mim!

**al.be.it** *conj.* embora, apesar de.

**al.bum** *s.* álbum.

**al.co.hol** *s.* álcool.

**al.co.hol.ic** *s.* alcoólatra / *adj.* alcoólico.

**ale** *s.* cerveja inglesa (coloquial).

**a.lert** *adj.* atento(a), alerta / *v.* alertar.

**al.ge.bra** *s.* álgebra.

**Al.ge.ri.a** *s.* Argélia.

**a.li.as** *s.* alcunha, pseudônimo / *adv.* aliás.

**al.i.bi** *s.* álibi; desculpa.

**a.li.en** *s.* estrangeiro(a); alienígena / *adj.* estranho(a).

**al.ien.ate** *v.* alienar.

**a.light** *adj.* aceso, ardente / *v.* desmontar, descer / *adv.* em chamas.

**a.lign** *v.* alinhar, enfileirar.

**a.like** *adj.* semelhante / *adv.* igualmente.

**al.i.mo.ny** *s.* pensão alimentícia; manutenção.

**a.live** *adj.* vivo(a), animado(a).

**all** *adj.* todo(s), toda(s); inteiro / *s.* totalidade, tudo.

**al.lay** *v.* acalmar.

**all clear** *s.* sinal de tudo limpo (coloquial).

**al.lege** *v.* alegar.

**al.lege.dly** *adv.* segundo dizem, supostamente.

**al.le.giance** *s.* lealdade, submissão.

**al.le.giant** *adj.* fiel, obediente.

**al.ler.gic** *adj.* alérgico(a).

**al.ler.gy** *s.* alergia.

**al.le.vi.ate** *v.* aliviar.

**al.ley** *s.* viela, ruela.

**al.li.ance** *s.* aliança.

**all in** *adj.* tudo incluído.

**all night** *adj.* toda a noite.

**al.lo.cate** *v.* alocar, partilhar, repartir.

**al.lot** *v.* distribuir proporcionalmente; outorgar, conceder.

**al.lot.ment** *s.* partilha, lote, cota.

**all-out** *adj.* total / *adv.* todo o possível.

**al.low** *v.* permitir, autorizar.

**al.low.ance** *s.* pensão, mesada, ajuda de custo.

**al.loy** *s.* liga, fusão.

**alude** — **ambassadress**

**al.lude** *v.* aludir, insinuar.

**al.lur.ing** *adj.* tentador(a), atraente.

**al.ly** *s.* aliado(a) / *v.* aliar-se.

**al.migh.ty** *adj.* onipotente, todo-poderoso.

**Al.migh.ty God** *s.* Deus Todo-Poderoso.

**al.mond** *s.* amêndoa.

**al.most** *adv.* quase, perto de.

**alms** *s.* esmola, dádiva.

**a.loft** *adv.* em cima, no alto.

**a.lone** *adj.* sozinho(a) / *adv.* somente, apenas.

**a.long** *prep.* ao longo de, por / *adv.* junto a.

**a.loof** *adj.* afastado(a), reservado(a), indiferente / *adv.* a distância, de longe.

**a.loud** *adv.* em voz alta.

**al.pha.bet** *s.* alfabeto, abecedário.

**Alps** *s.* Alpes.

**al.read.y** *adv.* já.

**Al.sa.tian** *s.* alsaciano / *adj.* alsaciano.

**Al.sa.tian dog** *s.* cão pastor.

**al.so** *adv.* também, além disso.

**al.tar** *s.* altar, mesa de sacrifício.

**al.ter** *adv.* alterar, modificar.

**al.ter.a.ble** *adj.* alterável, modificável.

**al.ter.nant** *adj.* alternante.

**al.ter.nate** *adj.* alternado(a) / *v.* alternar, revezar.

**al.ter.na.tive** *s.* alternativa, opção / *adj.* alternativo(a).

**al.ter.na.tor** *s.* alternador, gerador.

**al.though** *conj.* embora, apesar de, contudo.

**al.ti.tude** *s.* altitude.

**al.to.geth.er** *adv.* o todo, no total, inteiramente.

**a.lu.mi.num** *s.* alumínio.

**al.ways** *adv.* sempre, continuamente.

**am** *v.* *1ª* pess. sing. pres. do *v.* to be.

**a.m.** *abrev.* de *ante meridiem*.

**a.mass** *v.* acumular, amontoar.

**a.mass.able** *adj.* acumulável, amontoável.

**am.a.teur** *adj.* amador(a) / *s.* amador(a).

**a.maze** *v.* pasmar, maravilhar / *s.* assombro, estupefação.

**a.maze.ment** *s.* espanto, perplexidade.

**a.maz.ing** *adj.* surpreendente, espantoso; fantástico.

**Amazon** *s.* Amazonas.

**am.bas.sa.dor** *s.* embaixador; emissário.

**am.bas.sa.dress** *s.* embaixatriz, embaixadora.

amber      **129**      analysis

**am.ber** *s.* âmbar / *adj.* ambárico, ambarino.

**am.bi.gu.ity** *s.* ambiguidade.

**am.big.u.ous** *adj.* ambíguo, vago, incerto.

**am.bi.tion** *s.* ambição, aspiração.

**am.bi.tious** *adj.* ambicioso(a).

**am.bu.lance** *s.* ambulância.

**am.bush** *s.* emboscada, tocaia / *v.* emboscar.

**am.bush.ment** *s.* cilada.

**a.men** *s.* amém / *interj.* amém!

**a.me.na.ble** *adj.* receptivo(a), afável; responsável.

**a.mend** *v.* emendar; aperfeiçoar.

**a.mend.ment** *s.* correção; melhoramento; emenda.

**a.mends** *s.* reparação, indenização.

**a.men.i.ties** *s.* comodidades.

**a.men.i.ty** *s.* afabilidade, cortesia, gentileza.

**a.merce** *v.* multar, punir.

**A.mer.i.can** *s.* americano(a) / *adj.* americano(a).

**am.i.ca.ble** *adj.* amigável, afável.

**a.mid** *prep.* no meio de, entre.

**amiss** *adj.* defeituoso, errado / *adv.* defeituosamente.

**am.i.ty** *s.* amizade.

**am.mo.nia** *s.* amoníaco; amônia.

**am.mu.ni.tion** *s.* munição.

**a.mong** *prep.* entre vários, no meio de.

**am.o.rist** *adj.* namorador, galanteador.

**am.o.rous** *adj.* amoroso(a).

**am.ort** *adj.* desfalecido, sem vida.

**a.mount** *s.* soma, quantidade, quantia / *v.* equivaler, corresponder.

**am.pere** *s.* ampère (unidade de medida da corrente elétrica).

**am.ple** *adj.* amplo, suficiente, vasto.

**am.ple.ness** *s.* amplitude.

**am.pli.fi.er** *s.* amplificador.

**am.pli.fy** *v.* ampliar, aumentar.

**a.muck, a.mok** *adj.* cheio de fúria / *adv.* furiosamente.

**a.muse** *v.* divertir, distrair.

**a.muse.d** *adj.* divertido, entretido.

**a.muse.ment** *s.* divertimento, passatempo.

**a.mus.ing** *adj.* divertido, que causa divertimento.

**an** *art. indef.* um(a).

**an.a.log(ue)** *adj.* analógico / *s.* análogo, semelhante.

**a.nal.o.gous** *adj.* análogo, semelhante.

**a.na.lyse(-lyze)** *v.* analisar.

**a.nal.y.sis** *s.* análise.

**analyst** | 130 | **announcer**

**an.a.lyst** *s.* analista; psicanalista.

**an.ar.chist** *s.* anarquista.

**an.ar.chy** *s.* anarquia.

**a.nath.e.ma** *s.* horror; excomunhão; condenação.

**a.nat.o.my** *s.* anatomia.

**an.ces.tor** *s.* antepassado.

**an.ces.try** *s.* descendência, linhagem.

**an.chor** *s.* âncora / *v.* ancorar.

**an.chor.age** *s.* ancoradouro.

**an.cho.vy** *s.* anchova.

**an.cient** *s.* antigo, ancião / *adj.* antigo, velho, remoto.

**an.cient.ry** *s.* antiguidade.

**an.cil.lar.y** *adj.* auxiliar, assistente, subordinado.

**and** *conj.* e.

**An.des** *s.* Andes.

**An.dean** *adj.* andino.

**a.ne.mic** *adj.* anêmico, fraco.

**an.es.thet.ic** *s.* anestésico.

**an.es.the.tist** *s.* anestesista.

**a.new** *adv.* de novo; de uma forma diferente.

**an.gel** *s.* anjo.

**an.gel.face** *s.* anjo, cara de anjo. (coloquial).

**an.ger** *s.* raiva, fúria / *v.* zangar- -se, irritar-se.

**an.gina** *s.* angina.

**an.gle** *s.* ângulo; anzol.

**An.gles** *s.* anglos (tribo germânica).

**An.gli.can** *s.* anglicano(a) / *adj.* anglicano(a).

**an.gling** *s.* pesca à vara.

**An.glo-** *s.* anglo-, elemento de composição que denota inglês ou Inglaterra.

**An.gola** *s.* Angola.

**an.gri.ly** *adv.* com raiva, furiosamente.

**an.gry** *adj.* zangado(a), furioso(a), irado(a), raivoso(a).

**an.guish** *s.* sofrimento, angústia, agonia.

**an.i.mal** *s.* animal / *adj.* animal.

**an.i.mate** *v.* avivar; animar / *adj.* animado(a), vivo(a).

**an.ise** *s.* anis, erva-doce.

**an.iseed** *s.* semente de erva-doce.

**an.kle, an.cle** *s.* tornozelo.

**an.nex** *s.* anexo / *v.* anexar.

**an.nex.a.ble** *s.* anexável.

**an.ni.hi.late** *v.* aniquilar, exterminar.

**an.ni.ver.sa.ry** *s.* aniversário, festa de aniversário.

**an.nounce** *v.* anunciar, declarar.

**an.nounce.ment** *s.* aviso, comunicado, publicação.

**an.nounc.er** *s.* locutor(a); anunciante.

**annoy** 131 **anybody**

**an.noy** *v.* aborrecer, irritar.

**an.noy.ance** *s.* aborrecimento, amolação.

**an.noy.ing** *adj.* irritante, aborrecido(a), chato(a).

**an.nu.al** *adj.* anual / *s.* anual, anuário.

**an.nu.i.ty** *s.* anuidade.

**an.nul** *v.* anular; exterminar.

**a.non.y.mous** *adj.* anônimo(a), desconhecido(a).

**an.oth.er** *pron.* outro, um outro / *adj.* outro(a), um(a) outro(a).

**an.swer** *v.* responder / *s.* resposta.

**an.swer.a.ble** *adj.* responsável; respondível.

**an.swer.a.ble.ness** *s.* responsabilidade.

**ant** *s.* formiga; *abrev.* de *antiquary.*

**an.tag.o.nism** *s.* antagonismo.

**an.tag.o.nize** *v.* antagonizar, contrariar.

**Ant.arc.tic** *s.* região antártica / *adj.* antártico.

**an.te.na.tal** *s.* pré-natal / *adj.* pré-natal.

**an.te me.rid.i.e.m** *adv.* antes do meio dia.

**an.te.nupcial** *adj.* antenupcial.

**an.them** *s.* hino.

**an.thol.o.gy** *s.* antologia.

**an.ti.bi.ot.ic** *s.* antibiótico / *adj.* antibiótico.

**an.ti.bod.y** *s.* anticorpo.

**an.tic.i.pate** *v.* prever; antecipar.

**an.tic.i.pa.tion** *s.* expectativa; antecipação.

**an.ti.clock.wise** *adv.* sentido anti-horário.

**an.ti.freeze** *s.* anticongelante / *adj.* anticongelante.

**an.ti.quar.y** *s.* antiquário.

**an.ti.quat.ed** *adj.* antiquado, fora de moda.

**an.tique** *s.* antiguidade, objeto antigo.

**an.tique.ness** *s.* antiguidade.

**an.tiq.ui.ty** *s.* antiguidade.

**an.ti-Sem.i.tism** *s.* antissemitismo.

**an.ti.sep.tic** *s.* antisséptico / *adj.* antisséptico.

**an.ti.so.cial** *adj.* antissocial.

**an.tler** *s.* chifre; armação.

**an.vil** *s.* bigorna.

**anx.i.e.ty** *s.* ansiedade, ânsia, inquietação.

**anx.ious** *adj.* preocupado(a), inquieto(a).

**an.y** *pron.* qualquer um(a), algum(a) / *adj.* qualquer, quaisquer.

**an.y.bod.y** *pron.* ninguém; alguém.

**anyhow**      **132**      **appliance**

**A**

**an.y.how** *adv.* de qualquer modo.

**an.y.one** *pron.* ninguém; alguém.

**an.y.thing** *pron.* alguma coisa; qualquer coisa.

**an.y.way** *adv.* de qualquer modo.

**an.y.where** *adv.* onde quer que seja, em qualquer lugar.

**a.part** *adv.* à parte, a distância, além de.

**a.part.heid** *s.* separação.

**a.part.ment** *s.* apartamento.

**ap.a.thet.ic** *adj.* apático(a), indiferente.

**ap.a.thy** *s.* apatia, indiferença.

**ape** *s.* macaco / *v.* imitar.

**a.pe.ri.tif** *s.* aperitivo.

**ap.er.ture** *s.* abertura, orifício.

**a.pex** *s.* ápice, cume.

**a.pian** *adj.* de ou relativo a abelhas.

**a.pi.ar.y** *s.* colmeia, apiário.

**a.piece** *adv.* cada um; por cabeça; por peça.

**a.plomb** *s.* serenidade, calma; desenvoltura.

**a.pol.o.get.ic** *adj.* cheio de desculpas, apologético.

**a.pol.o.gize** *v.* pedir desculpas, desculpar-se.

**a.pol.o.gy** *s.* desculpa; defesa.

**a.pos.tle** *s.* apóstolo.

**a.pos.tro.phe** *s.* apóstrofe.

**ap.pall** *v.* horrorizar, intimidar, amedrontar.

**ap.pall.ing** *adj.* terrível, horrível, apavorante.

**ap.pa.ra.tus** *s.* aparelho, utensílio.

**ap.par.el** *s.* vestuário, traje / *v.* vestir, trajar.

**ap.par.ent** *adj.* aparente; evidente, claro.

**ap.pa.ri.tion** *s.* fantasma, espectro; aparição.

**ap.peal** *s.* apelação; simpatia; atração / *v.* apelar.

**ap.pear** *v.* aparecer, surgir.

**ap.pear.ance** *s.* aparência.

**ap.pease** *v.* apaziguar; satisfazer.

**ap.pel.lant** *adj.* apelante, suplicante / *s.* apelante, recorrente.

**ap.pen.di.ci.tis** *s.* apendicite.

**ap.pen.dix** *s.* apêndice; peça acessória de um órgão.

**ap.pe.tite** *s.* apetite.

**ap.pe.tiz.er** *s.* aperitivo, tiragosto.

**ap.pe.tiz.ing** *adj.* apetitoso(a).

**ap.plaud** *v.* aplaudir, aclamar.

**ap.plause** *s.* aplauso, aclamação.

**ap.ple** *s.* maçã.

**ap.ple pie** *s.* torta de maçã.

**ap.pli.ance** *s.* aplicação, utilização.

**ap.pli.cant** *s.* candidato(a), pretendente.

**ap.pli.ca.tion** *s.* aplicação.

**ap.plied** *adj.* aplicado, empregado, usado.

**ap.plier** *s.* aplicador.

**ap.ply** *v.* aplicar, usar, empregar.

**ap.point** *v.* nomear, designar, apontar.

**ap.point.ed** *adj.* marcado; designado, nomeado, apontado.

**ap.point.er** *s.* nomeador.

**ap.point.ment** *s.* encontro marcado; compromisso; nomeação.

**ap.por.ta.tion** *s.* dividir em partes iguais, repartir.

**ap.po.site** *adj.* adequado, apropriado.

**ap.prais.al** *s.* avaliação, cálculo.

**ap.praise** *v.* avaliar, estimar.

**ap.pre.ci.ate** *v.* apreciar, estimar, prezar.

**ap.pre.ci.a.tion** *s.* avaliação, estimativa.

**ap.pre.cia.tive** *adj.* apreciativo, compreensivo.

**ap.pre.hend** *v.* prender, deter; sentir apreensão, recear.

**ap.pre.hen.sion** *s.* apreensão, preocupação.

**ap.pre.hen.sive** *adj.* apreensivo(a), preocupado(a), receoso(a).

**ap.pren.tice** *s.* aprendiz, praticante.

**ap.pren.tice.ship** *s.* aprendizado, aprendizagem.

**ap.proach** *s.* aproximação / *v.* aproximar-se.

**ap.proach.a.ble** *adj.* acessível.

**ap.proach.a.ble.ness** *s.* acessibilidade, facilidade.

**ap.pro.pri.ate** *v.* apropriar-se, apoderar-se / *adj.* apropriado, adequado.

**ap.prov.al** *s.* aprovação, consentimento.

**ap.prove** *v.* autorizar, aprovar, apoiar.

**ap.prox.i.mate** *adj.* aproximado, quase correto / *v.* aproximar(-se).

**ap.prox.i.mate.ly** *adv.* aproximadamente.

**ap.prox.i.ma.tion** *s.* aproximação.

**ap.ri.cot** *s.* damasco.

**A.pril** *s.* abril.

**A.pril Fool's Day** *s.* dia dos bobos, 1º de abril.

**a.pron** *s.* avental.

**apt** *adj.* adequado(a); apto(a), competente.

**ap.ti.tude** *s.* aptidão, talento, habilidade.

**a.qual.ung** *s.* aparelho para respiração debaixo d'água.

**aquarium** 134 **armhole**

**a.quar.i.um** *s.* aquário.

**A.quar.i.us** *s.* Aquário (zodíaco).

**Ar.ab** *adj.* árabe / *s.* árabe.

**A.ra.bi.an** *s.* árabe. / *adj.* árabe.

**Ar.a.bic** *adj.* arábico, árabe.

**ar.a.ble** *s.* terra arável / *adj.* arável, cultivável.

**ar.bi.ter** *s.* árbitro, juiz.

**ar.bi.trar.y** *adj.* arbitrário.

**ar.bi.tra.tion** *s.* arbitragem.

**ar.bor** *s.* árvore.

**ar.bor.eal** *s.* arbóreo.

**arc** *s.* arco.

**ar.chae.ol.o.gist** *s.* arqueólogo(a).

**ar.chae.ol.o.gy** *s.* arqueologia.

**ar.ch** *s.* arco (arquitetura) / *v.* curvar.

**ar.cha.ic** *adj.* arcaico, antigo.

**arch.bish.op** *s.* arcebispo.

**arch.en.e.my** *s.* arqui-inimigo(a).

**ar.che.ol.o.gy** *s.* arqueologia.

**arch.er.y** *s.* tiro de arco; a arte de manobrar arco e flecha.

**ar.chi.tect** *s.* arquiteto(a).

**ar.chi.tec.tural** *adj.* arquitetônico, arquitetural.

**ar.chi.tec.ture** *s.* arquitetura.

**ar.chive** *s.* arquivo.

**Arc.tic Ocean, the** *s.* Oceano Ártico

**ar.dent** *adj.* ardente.

**are** *v.* 2ª *pess. sing., 1ª, 2ª* e 3ª *pess. pl. pres.* do *v. to be* / *s.* are (medida de superfície correspondente a 100 m²).

**ar.e.a** *s.* área, zona, região.

**ar.e.na.ceous** *adj.* arenoso.

**aren't** contração de *are not.*

**Ar.gen.tina** *s.* Argentina.

**ar.gil** *s.* argila, barro.

**ar.gue** *v.* discutir, argumentar, debater.

**ar.gu.ment** *s.* briga, discussão, debate.

**ar.gu.ment.ative** *adj.* argumentativo, lógico; inclinado a discussões.

**ar.id** *adj.* árido, seco.

**a.rid.i.ty** *s.* aridez, seca.

**Ar.ies** *s.* Áries (zodíaco).

**a.right** *adv.* corretamente, certamente.

**a.rise** *v.* aparecer.

**ar.is.toc.rat** *s.* aristocrata, nobre.

**a.rith.me.tic** *s.* aritmética.

**ark** *s.* arca, barco grande.

**arm** *s.* braço; arma.

**ar.ma.ment** *s.* armamento, equipamento bélico.

**arm.chair** *s.* poltrona, cadeira de braços.

**armed** *adj.* armado, munido de armas.

**arm.less** *s.* sem braço; sem armas.

**arm.hole** *s.* axila.

armor **135** aside

**A**

**ar.mor** *s.* armadura.

**ar.mored** *adj.* blindado.

**arm.pit** *s.* axila.

**arm.rest** *s.* braço de poltrona.

**ar.my** *s.* exército.

**a.ro.ma** *s.* aroma, fragrância.

**a.round** *adv.* em volta, cerca de / *prep.* em redor de, em torno de.

**a.rouse** *v.* despertar; provocar; estimular.

**ar.range** *v.* organizar, arrumar.

**ar.range.ment** *s.* acordo; disposição; combinação; arranjo.

**ar.rears** *s.* atrasos; dívidas atrasadas.

**ar.rest** *v.* prender, deter, aprisionar / *s.* apreensão, detenção, prisão.

**ar.ri.val** *s.* chegada.

**ar.rive** *v.* chegar.

**ar.ro.gant** *adj.* arrogante.

**ar.row** *s.* flecha, seta.

**ar.son** *s.* incêndio culposo.

**ar.son.ist** *s.* incendiário.

**art** *s.* arte.

**ar.te.fact** *s.* artefato.

**ar.ter.y** *s.* artéria.

**art.ful** *adj.* ardiloso; esperto.

**art gal.le.ry** *s.* museu; galeria de arte.

**ar.thri.tis** *s.* artrite.

**ar.ti.choke** *s.* alcachofra.

**ar.ti.cle** *s.* artigo.

**ar.tic.u.late** *v.* articular, expressar / *adj.* articulado, bem escrito.

**ar.ti.fi.cial** *adj.* artificial.

**ar.till.ler.y** *s.* artilharia.

**ar.ti.san** *s.* artesão(ã).

**ar.tist** *s.* artista.

**art.less** *adj.* natural; simples; sem arte.

**art school** *s.* escola de artes.

**as** *prep.* como, na qualidade de / *adv.* tão, tanto quanto.

**as.cend** *v.* subir; ascender.

**as.cen.dan.cy** *s.* predomínio; domínio; ascendência.

**as.cent** *s.* subida, ascensão.

**as.cer.tain** *v.* averiguar, verificar, apurar.

**as.cribe** *v.* atribuir algo a, designar.

**ash** *s.* cinza.

**a.shamed** *adj.* envergonhado(a).

**ash.en** *adj.* cinzento.

**a.shore** *adv.* em terra firme.

**ash.tray** *s.* cinzeiro.

**Ash Wednes.day** *s.* Quarta-feira de Cinzas.

**A.sia** *s.* Ásia.

**A.sian** *adj.* asiático(a) / *s.* asiático(a).

**a.side** *adv.* de lado, ao lado; longe, a distância.

**ask** *v.* perguntar; convidar; pedir.

**a.skance** *adv.* de soslaio, desconfiadamente.

**a.skew** *adj.* torto, retorcido.

**a.sleep** *adj.* adormecido; dormente.

**as.par.a.gus** *s.* aspargo.

**as.pect** *s.* aspecto, aparência.

**as.pect.able** *adj.* visível.

**as.per.i.ty** *adj.* aspereza, rudeza.

**as.per.sion** *s.* calúnia, difamação; borrifo, respingo.

**as.phyx.iation** *s.* asfixia, sufocamento.

**as.pi.ra.tor** *s.* aspirador.

**aspire** *v.* aspirar, ansiar, almejar.

**as.pi.rin** *s.* aspirina.

**ass** *s.* jumento, asno; imbecil (coloquial).

**as.sail.ant** *s.* assaltante / *adj.* assaltante.

**as.sas.sin** *s.* assassino.

**as.sas.si.nate** *v.* assassinar.

**as.sas.si.na.tion** *s.* assassinato.

**as.sault** *v.* assaltar, atacar / *s.* assalto, ataque.

**as.sem.ble** *v.* reunir, ajuntar, agregar; montar, armar.

**as.sem.bly** *s.* reunião, assembleia, junta.

**as.sent** *s.* aprovação, consentimento / *v.* consentir, aprovar.

**as.sert** *v.* afirmar, declarar.

**as.ser.tion** *s.* afirmação, declaração.

**as.sess** *v.* avaliar, calcular, estimar.

**as.sess.ment** *s.* avaliação; taxação.

**as.set** *s.* vantagem, trunfo.

**as.sets** *s.* espólio.

**as.sign** *v.* designar, apontar.

**as.sign.ment** *s.* tarefa; designação.

**as.sist** *v.* ajudar, auxiliar, assistir.

**as.sis.tance** *s.* ajuda, auxílio, assistência.

**as.sis.tant** *s.* assistente, auxiliar.

**as.so.ci.ate** *v.* associar / *s.* associado(a).

**as.sort** *v.* agrupar, classificar.

**as.sort.ed** *adj.* sortido, variado, classificado.

**as.sort.ment** *s.* variedade, sortimento.

**as.sume** *v.* supor, presumir; assumir.

**as.sump.tion** *s.* suposição, hipótese.

**as.sur.ance** *s.* garantia; confiança.

**as.sure** *v.* garantir, afirmar.

**as.sured** *adj.* garantido, segurado.

**asth.ma** *s.* asma.

**as.ton.ish** *v.* espantar, surpreender, pasmar.

**as.ton.ish.ment** *s.* assombro, grande surpresa, pasmo.

**as.tound** *v.* pasmar, surpreender.

**a.stray** *adj.* desviado, perdido.

**a.stride** *adj.* montado a cavalo, escarranchado / *adv.* escarranchadamente.

**as.trol.o.gy** *s.* astrologia.

**as.tro.naut** *s.* astronauta.

**as.tron.o.my** *s.* astronomia.

**as.tute** *adj.* astuto, ardiloso.

**a.sy.lum** *s.* manicômio.

**at** *prep.* em, a.

**ate** *v. pret.* do *v. to eat.*

**a.the.ist** *s.* ateísta, ateu, *fem.* ateia.

**Ath.ens** *s.* Atenas.

**ath.lete** *s.* atleta.

**ath.let.ics** *s.* atletismo.

**At.lan.tic Ocean, the** *s.* Oceano Atlântico.

**at.las** *s.* atlas.

**at.mos.phere** *s.* atmosfera.

**at.om** *s.* átomo.

**at.om.izer** *s.* pulverizador.

**a.tone** *v.* reparar; harmonizar.

**a.tro.cious** *adj.* atroz, cruel.

**at.tach** *v.* prender, fixar; anexar.

**at.ta.ché** *s.* adido, diplomata.

**at.tach.ment** *s.* acessório; anexo; ação de fixar.

**at.tack** *v.* atacar, agredir / *s.* ataque, acesso súbito; agressão.

**at.tain** *v.* alcançar, chegar a, atingir.

**at.tain.able** *adj.* atingível, alcançável.

**at.tempt** *s.* tentativa, intento / *v.* tentar.

**at.tend** *v.* cursar; assistir; prestar atenção.

**at.ten.dance** *s.* frequência; atenção.

**at.ten.dant** *s.* encarregado(a), atendente.

**at.ten.tion** *s.* atenção, cuidado.

**at.ten.tive** *adj.* atento(a), atencioso(a), cuidadoso(a).

**at.tic** *s.* sótão.

**at.ti.tude** *s.* atitude, postura.

**at.tor.ney** *s.* procurador, representante, advogado.

**at.tract** *v.* atrair; puxar para si.

**at.trac.tive** *adj.* atraente, atrativo.

**at.trib.ute** *v.* atribuir algo a / *s.* atributo, qualidade.

**at.tri.tion** *s.* atrito, fricção.

**au.ber.gine** *s.* berinjela.

**au.burn** *adj.* castanho avermelhado.

**auc.tion** *v.* leiloar / *s.* leilão.

**auc.tion.eer** *s.* leiloeiro(a).

**au.di.ble** *adj.* audível.

**au.di.ence** *s.* público, audiência.

**au.di.o.vis.u.al** *adj.* audiovisual.

**au.dit** *v.* fazer auditoria, examinar / *s.* auditoria, exame.

**au.di.tion** *s.* audição.
**au.di.tor** *s.* auditor(a).
**aug.ment** *v.* aumentar, acrescentar / *s.* aumento, acréscimo.
**au.gur** *v.* augurar, prognosticar / *s.* profeta, adivinho.
**Au.gust** *s.* agosto.
**au.gust.ness** *s.* majestade; dignidade.
**aunt** *s.* tia.
**au.ra** *s.* aura, essência.
**aus.pi.cious** *adj.* favorável, auspicioso.
**aus.ter.i.ty** *s.* severidade, austeridade.
**Aus.tra.li.a** *s.* Austrália.
**Aus.tra.li.an** *adj.* australiano(a) / *s.* australiano(a).
**Aus.tri.a** *s.* Áustria.
**Aus.tri.an** *adj.* austríaco(a).
**au.then.tic** *adj.* autêntico, genuíno.
**au.thor** *s.* autor(a).
**au.thor.i.tar.i.an** *adj.* autoritário(a) / *s.* autoritário(a).
**au.thor.i.ta.tive** *adj.* autorizado.
**au.thor.i.ty** *s.* autoridade.
**au.thor.ize** *v.* autorizar, permitir.
**au.to** *s.* automóvel.
**au.to.bi.og.ra.phy** *s.* autobiografia.

**au.to.graph** *s.* autógrafo / *v.* autografar.
**au.to.mat.ic** *adj.* automático.
**au.tom.a.ton** *s.* autômato; robô.
**au.to.mo.bile** *s.* automóvel.
**au.ton.o.my** *s.* autonomia.
**au.tumn** *s.* outono.
**aux.il.ia.ry** *adj.* auxiliar, ajudante.
**a.vail** *v.* aproveitar / *s.* proveito, lucro.
**a.vail.a.ble** *adj.* disponível, acessível.
**av.a.lanche** *s.* avalanche.
**a.vant-garde** *s.* vanguarda / *adj.* de vanguarda.
**Ave.** *abrev.* de *avenue*.
**a.venge** *v.* vingar(-se).
**a.venge.ment** *s.* vingança, desforra.
**a.veng.er** *s.* vingador.
**av.e.nue** *s.* avenida.
**av.er.age** *s.* média, proporção.
**a.vert** *v.* prevenir, evitar, desviar.
**a.vi.a.ry** *s.* viveiro de aves, aviário.
**av.id** *adj.* ávido(a), ansioso(a).
**a.vid.i.ty** *s.* avidez, cobiça.
**av.o.ca.do** *s.* abacate.
**a.void** *v.* evitar; escapar, fugir.
**a.vow** *v.* declarar francamente, confessar.

**a.vun.cu.lar** *adj.* avuncular, relativo ou semelhante a tio ou tios.

**a.wait** *v.* esperar, aguardar.

**a.wake** *v.* despertar / *adj.* acordado(a).

**a.wak.en** *v.* despertar, acordar.

**a.ward** *v.* conceder, premiar / *s.* prêmio, recompensa.

**a.ware** *adj.* informado(a), ciente; atento(a).

**a.ware.ness** *s.* consciência, conhecimento.

**a.wash** *adj.* inundado; levado pelas ondas ou pela maré.

**a.way** *adv.* fora, à distância / *adj.* ausente, distante.

**awe** *s.* terror, grande medo.

**awe.some** *adj.* imponente, temeroso.

**aw.ful** *adj.* terrível, horrível.

**a.while** *adv.* por algum tempo, pouco tempo.

**awk.ward** *adj.* desajeitado(a), inábil, embaraçoso.

**awk.ward.ness** *s.* inabilidade, inaptidão, embaraço.

**awn.ing** *s.* toldo, tenda.

**a.woke** *v. pret.* do *v. to awake.*

**a.wry** *adv.* de esguelha / *adj.* torto, oblíquo.

**axe** *s.* machado / *v.* reduzir, cortar.

**ax.le** *s.* eixo de rodas.

**ay** *adv.* sim (coloquial) / *interj.* ah! oh! ai!

**aye** *adv.* sempre, indefinidamente.

# Bb

**B, b** *s.* segunda letra do alfabeto inglês; si (nota musical).

**bab.ble** *v.* balbuciar / *s.* conversa tola, murmúrio.

**ba.by** *s.* bebê, nenê.

**ba.by.hood** *s.* infância.

**ba.by.ish** *adj.* infantil, pueril.

**ba.by.sit** *v.* pajear, cuidar de uma criança.

**ba.by-sit.ter** *s.* babá.

**bach.e.lor** *s.* bacharel; solteiro.

**bach.e.lor.hood** *s.* bacharelado; celibato.

**back** *s.* costas, dorso, parte traseira / *v.* recuar, voltar atrás.

**back.bite** *s.* calúnia / *v.* caluniar.

**back.bone** *s.* coluna vertebral; firmeza.

**back.ground** *s.* fundo; conhecimento; formação, origem.

**back.pack** *s.* mochila.

**back yard** *s.* quintal.

**ba.con** *s.* toucinho defumado.

**bad** *adj.* mau, má, ruim.

**bade** *v. pret.* do *v. to bid.*

**badge** *s.* crachá, distintivo, emblema.

**bad.ly** *adv.* mal, não bem.

**bad.ness** *s.* maldade, ruindade.

**bad-tem.pered** *adj.* mal--humorado(a), de mau humor.

**baf.fle** *v.* desconcertar, confundir / *s.* confusão.

**bag** *s.* mala; bolsa; sacola.

**bag.gage** *s.* bagagem.

**bag.man** *s.* caixeiro-viajante.

**bail** *s.* fiança / *v.* libertar sob fiança, fiançar.

**bail.er** *s.* balde.

**bait** *s.* isca / *v.* iscar; apoquentar.

**bake** *v.* assar.

**bak.er** *s.* padeiro.

**bak.er.y** *s.* padaria.

**baking** *s.* fornada / *adj.* escaldante, quente.

**bak.ing-pow.der** *s.* fermento em pó.

**bal.ance** *s.* balança; balanço; equilíbrio / *v.* equilibrar.

**bal.co.ny** *s.* varanda; balcão.

**bald** *adj.* careca, calvo.

**bale** *s.* fardo, desgraça / *v.* enfardar.

**bale.ful** *adj.* maligno, fatal.

**ball** *s.* bola; novelo; baile.

**bal.last** *s.* lastro / *v.* lastrar, colocar lastro.

**ball bear.ing** *s.* rolimã.

**bal.le.ri.na** *s.* bailarina.

**bal.let** *s.* balé.

**bal.loon** *s.* balão.

**bal.lot** *s.* votação.

**bal.lot-box** *s.* urna eleitoral.

**bal.lot pa.per** *s.* cédula eleitoral.

**ball.point pen** *s.* caneta esferográfica.

**ball.room** *s.* salão de baile.

**balm** *s.* bálsamo.

**ban** *v.* proibir, interditar / *s.* proibição.

**ba.nan.a** *s.* banana.

**band** *s.* banda; bando; faixa, fita; orquestra.

**ban.dage** *v.* enfaixar / *s.* atadura, bandagem.

**band-aid** *s.* curativo.

**band.wa.gon** *s.* carro para propaganda política; ficar na moda (coloquial).

**bang** *v.* bater / *s.* explosão, estrondo, pancada.

**ban.gle** *s.* bracelete, pulseira.

**bangs** *s.* franja (de cabelo).

**ban.ish** *v.* banir, expulsar.

**ban.is.ter** *s.* corrimão; balaústre.

**bank** *s.* banco; margem de rio / *v.* manter em banco, depositar.

**bank.ing** *s.* transações bancárias.

**bank.rupt** *adj.* falido, quebrado.

**bank.rupt.cy** *s.* falência.

**bank state.ment** *s.* extrato bancário.

**ban.ner** *s.* faixa, estandarte.

**banns** *s.* proclama de casamento.

**bap.tism** *s.* batismo.

**bap.tize** *v.* batizar.

**bar** *s.* bar; barra; vara / *v.* barrar; obstruir.

**bar.bar.ic** *adj.* bárbaro, selvagem.

**bar.be.cue** *s.* churrasco, churrasqueira.

**barbed wire** *s.* arame farpado.

**bar.ber** *s.* barbeiro, cabeleireiro de homens.

**bar.ber.shop** *s.* barbearia.

**bar code** *s.* código de barras.

**bare** *adj.* despido, nu / *v.* descobrir; expor; despir.

**bare.bone** *s.* esqueleto.

**bare.faced** *adj.* descarado(a); sem máscara.

**bare.foot.ed** *adj.* descalço.

**bare.head.ed** *s.* sem chapéu.

**bare.ness** *s.* nudez; pobreza.

**bar.gain** *v.* barganhar, pechinchar / *s.* barganha, pechincha.

**barge** *s.* barcaça / *v.* transportar em batelão.

**barge.pole** *s.* varejão.

**bark** *s.* latido; casca de árvore; embarcação, navio / *v.* latir, ladrar.

**bark-bared** *s.* descascado.

**bar.ley** *s.* cevada (grão e planta).

**barm** *s.* levedo de cerveja.

**bar.maid** *s.* garçonete.

**bar.man** *s.* garçom.

**barn** *s.* celeiro.

**ba.rom.e.ter** *s.* barômetro.

**bar.on** *s.* barão; magnata.

**bar.on.age** *s.* nobreza.

**bar.on.ess** *s.* baronesa.

**bar.rack** *s.* barraca, barracão.

**bar.racks** *s.* quartel; caserna.

**bar.rage** *s.* barragem.

**bar.rel** *s.* barril, tonel; cano de arma.

**bar.ren** *adj.* árido, estéril, improdutivo.

**bar.ri.cade** *s.* barricada / *v.* bloquear com uma barricada.

**bar.ri.er** *s.* barreira, obstáculo.

**bar.ring** *prep.* exceto, salvo.

**bar.rister** *s.* advogado(a).

**bar.row** *s.* carrinho de mão, padiola.

**bar.tend.er** *s.* garçom (de bar).

**bar.ter** *v.* trocar, permutar / *s.* comércio de troca.

**base** *v.* basear-se / *s.* base.

**base.ball** *s.* beisebol.

**base.born** *s.* nascido pobre.

**base.ment** *s.* porão.

**bash** *v.* socar, esmurrar, sussurar.

**bash.ful** *adj.* envergonhado, acanhado.

**ba.sic** *adj.* básico; mínimo.

**ba.sic.ally** *adv.* basicamente.

**ba.sics** *s.* essencial, elementos fundamentais.

**bas.il** *s.* manjericão.

**ba.sin** *s.* bacia; pia de banheiro.

**ba.sis** *s.* base.

**bask** *v.* tomar sol, aquecer-se ao sol.

**basket** 143 **beardless**

**bas.ket** *s.* cesto, cesta.
**bas.ket.ball** *s.* basquetebol.
**bass** *s.* som ou tom baixo, grave / *adj.* grave.
**bas.si.net** *s.* berço de vime.
**bas.soon** *s.* fagote.
**bas.tard** *s.* bastardo(a), filho(a) ilegítimo(a) / *adj.* bastardo(a), ilegítimo(a).
**bat** *s.* morcego; bastão / *v.* pestanejar, piscar o olho.erior
**batch** *s.* monte, lote; fornada.
**bat.ed** *adj.* contido(a), diminuído, reduzido.
**bath** *s.* banho, ato de tomar banho / *v.* banhar, lavar.
**bathe** *v.* tomar banho de mar / *s.* banho de mar.
**bath.er** *s.* banhista.
**bath.ing** *s.* banho / *adj.* de banho, relativo a banho.
**bath.robe** *s.* roupão de banho.
**bath.room** *s.* banheiro.
**baths** *s.* banhos públicos.
**bat.on** *s.* cassetete; batuta (música); bastão (esporte).
**bat.ter** *s.* massa de farinha com ovos; batedor (esporte) / *v.* bater, quebrar.
**bat.tered** *adj.* amassado, quebrado, danificado.
**bat.ter.y** *s.* pilha, bateria.

**bat.tle** *s.* batalha, combate, luta / *v.* lutar, brigar, combater.
**bat.tle.field** *s.* campo de batalha.
**bat.tle.ship** *s.* navio de guerra.
**bawd.y** *adj.* indecente, imoral.
**bawl** *v.* gritar, berrar / *s.* grito, berro.
**bay** *s.* baía, enseada; latido grave / *v.* ladrar; amarrar a caça.
**bay.leaf** *s.* louro, loureiro.
**bay win.dow** *s.* janela com sacada.
**ba.zaar** *s.* bazar.
**B.C.** *abrev.* de *before Christ* (antes de Cristo).
**be** *v.* ser, estar.
**beach** *s.* praia / *v.* encalhar.
**bea.con** *s.* farol, sinalizador, baliza.
**bead** *s.* gota; conta de rosário.
**beak** *s.* bico.
**bea.ker** *s.* copo com bico; proveta.
**beam** *s.* viga, suporte; raio, feixe de luz / *v.* sorrir.
**bean** *s.* feijão; grão; fava.
**bean.sprout** *s.* broto de feijão.
**bear** *s.* urso / *v.* suportar.
**bear.a.ble** *adj.* suportável, tolerável.
**beard** *s.* barba.
**beard.ed** *adj.* barbado, barbudo.
**beard.less** *adj.* sem barba, imberbe.

**B**

**bear.er** *s.* portador(a), carregador(a), titular.

**bear.ing** *s.* comportamento, postura; posição, rumo.

**beast** *s.* animal, besta, fera.

**beast.ly** *adj.* horrível, bestial, brutal.

**beat** *v.* bater em, tocar / *s.* batida, pancada, golpe; ritmo, compasso.

**beat.ing** *s.* surra, derrota; açoitamento.

**beat it** *interj.* pinica! fora!

**beau.ti.ful** *adj.* belo, bonito, lindo.

**beau.ti.ful.ness** *s.* beleza, formosura.

**beau.ti.ful.ly** *adv.* admiravelmente, belamente.

**beau.ty** *s.* beleza, encanto.

**beauty par.lor** *s.* salão de beleza.

**bea.ver** *s.* castor.

**be.came** *v. pret.* do *v. to become.*

**be.cause** *conj.* porque, pela razão de.

**be.cause of** *prep.* pelo motivo de, por.

**beck** *s.* sinal, aceno com a cabeça ou com as mãos / *v.* acenar, fazer sinal.

**beck.on** *v.* acenar / *s.* gesto, aceno.

**be.come** *v.* tornar-se, transformar-se em.

**be.com.ing** *adj.* elegante, vistoso.

**bed** *s.* cama.

**bed.clothes** *s.* roupa de cama.

**bed.ding** *s.* roupa de cama.

**bed.gown** *s.* camisola.

**bed.lam** *s.* confusão, tumulto.

**be.drag.gled** *adj.* molhado, ensopado; sujo.

**bed.rid.den** *adj.* acamado.

**bed.room** *s.* quarto de dormir.

**bed.side lamp** *s.* lâmpada de cabeceira.

**bed.spread** *s.* colcha.

**bed-table** *s.* mesa de cabeceira, criado-mudo.

**bed.time** *s.* hora de ir para cama.

**bee** *s.* abelha.

**beech** *s.* faia.

**beef** *s.* carne de vaca ou de boi.

**beef.burger** *s.* hambúrguer.

**beef.eat.er** *s.* guarda da torre de Londres.

**beef.steak** *s.* bife de carne bovina.

**bee.hive** *s.* colmeia.

**bee.keeper** *s.* apicultor.

**bee.line** *s.* caminho mais curto, linha reta.

**been** *v. pp.* do *v. to be.*

**beer** *s.* cerveja.

**beet** *s.* beterraba.

# beetle · 145 · below

**bee.tle** s. besouro.

**be.fore** prep. antes, antes de; diante de, na frente de.

**be.fore.hand** adv. anteriormente, antecipadamente.

**be.fore.time** adv. antigamente, anteriormente.

**beg** v. mendigar; implorar, suplicar; pedir.

**beg.gar** s. mendigo(a).

**beg.gar.y** s. pobreza, miséria, penúria.

**be.gin** v. começar, iniciar.

**be.gin.ner** s. principiante, iniciante.

**be.gin.ning** s. início, começo.

**be.gun** v. pp. do v. to begin.

**be.half** s. lado, interesse, favor
♦ in ~ of em nome de, a favor de.

**be.have** v. comportar-se, conduzir-se.

**be.hav.ior** s. comportamento, ação, conduta.

**be.head** v. decapitar, degolar.

**be.head.ing** s. decapitação.

**be.held** v. pp. do v. to behold.

**be.hind** prep. atrás de
/ adv. atrás, detrás.

**be.hold** v. contemplar, observar, notar, ver.

**beige** adj. bege / s. bege.

**Bei.jing** s. Pequim.

**be.ing** s. ser, existência.

**be.jewel** v. adornar com joias.

**be.lat.ed** adj. atrasado.

**belch** v. arrotar; vomitar / s. arroto.

**bel.fry** s. campanário, torre dos sinos.

**Bel.gian** s. belga / adj. belga.

**Bel.gium** s. Bélgica.

**be.lie** v. desmentir; dar ideia falsa de; caluniar.

**be.lief** s. opinião; crença, fé.

**be.lieve** v. acreditar, crer, confiar.

**be.liev.er** s. crente.

**be.lit.tle** v. depreciar.

**bell** s. sino, sineta; campainha.

**bell.bird** s. araponga.

**bell.boy** s. mensageiro de hotel.

**bel.lied** adj. barrigudo.

**bel.lig.er.ent** adj. agressivo, hostil / s. beligerante.

**bel.low** v. mugir, berrar / s. berro, urro, grito.

**bel.lows** s. fole.

**bel.ly** s. barriga, ventre.

**bel.ly.ache** s. dor de barriga, cólica.

**be.long** v. pertencer.

**be.long.ings** s. pertences.

**be.lov.ed** s. amado, querido
/ adj. querido.

**be.low** prep. abaixo, sob
/ adv. embaixo.

belt — beware

**belt** *s.* cinto / *v.* surrar.

**belt.way** *s.* via circular.

**be.mused** *adj.* preocupado, perturbado, confuso.

**bench** *s.* banco (assento); bancada.

**bend** *v.* dobrar.

**be.neath** *prep.* abaixo de, debaixo de, inferior a / *adv.* debaixo.

**ben.e.fac.tor** *s.* benfeitor.

**ben.e.fac.tress** *s.* benfeitora.

**ben.e.fi.cial** *adj.* benéfico(a), proveitoso(a).

**ben.e.fit** *s.* benefício, auxílio / *v.* beneficiar.

**be.nev.o.lent** *adj.* benévolo(a), bondoso(a).

**be.nign** *adj.* benigno(a), bondoso(a), gentil.

**bent** *s.* inclinação / *adj.* inclinado / *v. pp.* do *v. to bend*.

**be.quest** *s.* legado.

**be.reave** *v.* privar de; roubar.

**be.reaved** *adj.* de luto.

**be.ret** *s.* boina.

**Berlin** *s.* Berlim.

**berm** *s.* acostamento; margem de um canal.

**ber.ry** *s.* baga, fruto; semente ou grão.

**ber.serk** *adj.* frenético, furioso / *s.* guerreiro nórdico.

**berth** *v.* atracar, ancorar / *s.* beliche (navio); cabine (trem); ancoradouro.

**be.screen** *v.* cobrir, ocultar, esconder algo.

**be.seech** *v.* implorar, suplicar.

**be.set** *v.* atacar, assaltar.

**be.side** *prep.* junto de, ao lado de.

**be.sides** *prep.* além de; exceto / *adv.* além disso.

**be.siege** *v.* sitiar; assediar.

**be.sought** *v. pp.* do *v. to beseech*.

**best** *adj.* (*superl.* de *good*) melhor / *s.* ♦ *the* ~ o melhor, o máximo.

**best man** *s.* padrinho de casamento.

**be.stow** *v.* outorgar, entregar.

**bet** *v.* apostar / *s.* aposta.

**be.think** *v.* refletir, considerar.

**be.tray** *v.* trair.

**be.tray.al** *s.* traição.

**be.tray.er** *s.* traidor.

**bet.ter** *adj.* (*compar.* de *good*) melhor / *v.* melhorar.

**bet.ter.ment** *s.* benfeitoria, melhoria.

**bet.ting** *s.* aposta.

**bet.ting shop** *s.* casa de apostas.

**be.tween** *prep.* entre / *adv.* no meio dc dois.

**bev.er.age** *s.* bebida.

**be.ware** *v.* ter cuidado.

# bewilder       147       bird-cage

**be.wil.der** *v.* desnortear, confundir totalmente.

**be.wil.dered** *adj.* atordoado, confuso.

**be.witch** *v.* encantar, enfeitiçar

**be.witch.ing** *adj.* encantador(a), sedutor.

**be.witch.ment** *s.* feitiço, encantamento.

**be.wray** *v.* trair; revelar.

**be.yond** *prep.* além de / *adv.* além.

**be.yond.nature** *s.* sobrenatural.

**bib** *s.* babador.

**Bi.ble** *s.* Bíblia.

**bick.er** *v.* brigar, disputar / *s.* briga, contenda.

**bi.cy.cle** *s.* bicicleta.

**bi.cy.clist** *s.* ciclista.

**bid** *s.* lance; oferta; proposta / *v.* oferecer; propor.

**bid.der** *s.* licitante, quem oferece mais, lançador.

**bid.ding** *s.* licitação; comando; ordem.

**bide** *v.* viver, residir; aguardar.

**bi.fo.cals** *s.* óculos bifocais.

**big** *adj.* grande; volumoso(a).

**big.a.mist** *s.* bígamo.

**big dipper** *s.* montanha-russa.

**big-heart.ed** *adj.* generoso(a), bondoso(a).

**big.ot** *s.* fanático(a).

**big.ot.ed** *adj.* intolerante, fanático.

**big toe** *s.* dedão do pé.

**big top** *s.* tenda de circo.

**bike** *s.* bicicleta.

**bi.ki.ni** *s.* biquíni.

**bi.lin.gual** *adj.* bilíngue.

**bile** *s.* bílis; fel.

**bill** *s.* conta, fatura; bico de aves.

**bill.board** *s.* quadro ou moldura para cartazes.

**bil.let** *s.* alojamento, aquartelamento; boleto.

**bil.liards** *s.* bilhar / *adj.* de bilhar.

**bil.lion** *s.* bilhão.

**bin** *s.* caixa, lata, receptáculo ♦ *dust~* lata ou cesto de lixo.

**bind** *v.* amarrar, ligar, atar / *s.* faixa, cinta, atadura.

**bind.er** *s.* amarrador; fichário; encadernador; fita, tira.

**bind.ing** *s.* ligação; amarração / *adj.* que liga, que amarra.

**binge** *s.* bebedeira; farra.

**bin.go** *s.* bingo.

**bin.oc.u.lars** *s.* binóculos.

**bi.o.chem.is.try** *s.* bioquímica.

**bi.og.ra.phy** *s.* biografia.

**bi.ol.o.gy** *s.* biologia.

**birch** *s.* bétula.

**bird** *s.* pássaro, ave.

**bird-cage** *s.* gaiola.

**biro** *s.* caneta esferográfica.
**birth** *s.* nascimento; parto.
**birth.day** *s.* aniversário.
**birth.place** *s.* local do nascimento.
**birth.rate** *s.* taxa de natalidade.
**bis.cuit** *s.* biscoito, bolacha.
**bi.sect** *v.* dividir ao meio.
**bish.op** *s.* bispo.
**bit** *s.* pedaço / *v. pret.* do *v. to bite.*
**bitch** *s.* cadela; vagabunda (coloquial).
**bite** *s.* mordida; picada / *v.* morder.
**bite.r** *s.* mordedor.
**bit.ter** *adj.* amargo.
**bit.ter.ness** *s.* rancor, mágoa, amargura.
**blab** *v.* tagarelar, falar muito / *s.* tagarelice, tagarela.
**blab.ber** *s.* tagarela.
**black** *adj.* preto, negro / *s.* preto, negro.
**black.ber.ry** *s.* amora silvestre.
**black.board** *s.* quadro-negro, lousa.
**black.en** *v.* denegrir, difamar; pretejar.
**black.mail** *s.* chantagem, extorsão / *v.* chantagear, extorquir.
**black.ness** *s.* negridão, negrura.

**black-out** *s.* apagamento, escurecimento.
**black pepper** *s.* pimenta-do-reino.
**black sheep** *s.* ovelha negra.
**blad.der** *s.* bexiga.
**blade** *s.* lâmina.
**blame** *s.* culpa / *v.* culpar.
**blame.less** *adj.* inocente, sem culpa.
**bland** *adj.* brando, suave; insosso.
**blank** *s.* espaço vazio, espaço em branco / *adj.* em branco, sem nada escrito.
**blank check** *s.* cheque em branco.
**blank.ness** *s.* brancura, claridade.
**blan.ket** *s.* cobertor, manta de lã / *v.* cobrir por completo.
**blast** *s.* rajada de vento; estrondo, explosão / *interj.* droga!
**bla.tant** *adj.* descarado, barulhento, ruidoso.
**blaze** *s.* fogo; labareda; chama / *v.* arder; resplandecer.
**blaz.er** *s.* casaco esportivo, jaqueta.
**bleach** *s.* água sanitária / *v.* branquear, alvejar.
**bleach.ed** *adj.* oxigenado.
**bleach.ers** *s.* arquibancada descoberta.
**bleak** *adj.* sombrio, desolado, deserto.

**bled** *v. pret.* do *v. to bleed.*

**bleed** *v.* sangrar.

**bleed.ing** *s.* hemorragia / *adj.* que está sangrando.

**blem.ish** *s.* mancha; marca; defeito / *v.* manchar, sujar, desfigurar.

**blend** *s.* mistura / *v.* misturar.

**bless** *v.* abençoar; benzer; glorificar.

**bless.ed** *adj.* sagrado, santificado, abençoado.

**bless.ing** *s.* bênção, graça divina.

**blew** *v. pret.* do *v. to blow.*

**blight** *v.* fazer secar (planta), arruinar / *s.* ferrugem; inseto ou pulgão.

**bli.mey** *interj.* caramba! nossa!

**blind** *adj.* cego / *v.* cegar, encobrir / *s.* cortina, persiana; cego.

**blind.ed** *adj.* cego.

**blind.ness** *s.* cegueira; ignorância.

**blink** *v.* piscar / *s.* piscadela.

**bliss** *s.* felicidade, alegria, êxtase.

**blis.ter** *s.* bolha; vesícula.

**blithe.ly** *adv.* contentemente, alegremente.

**blitz** *s.* bombardeio; guerra relâmpago; ataque repentino.

**bliz.zard** *s.* nevasca; temporal com neve e frio.

**bloat.ed** *adj.* inchado.

**blob** *s.* gota, bolha.

**bloc** *s.* coligação política ou partidária.

**block** *s.* bloco; quadra, quarteirão / *v.* obstruir, bloquear.

**block.ade** *s.* bloqueio.

**block.age** *s.* obstrução; bloqueio; impedimento.

**block.buster** *s.* livro ou filme que é sucesso de vendas.

**block.head** *s.* cabeça-dura.

**block let.ter** *s.* letra de forma.

**bloke** *s.* cara, sujeito.

**blond** *adj.* louro(a) / *s.* claro, louro.

**blood** *s.* sangue.

**blood.bank** *s.* banco de sangue.

**blood.thirst.y** *s.* sanguinário, cruel.

**blood re.la.tive** *s.* parente consanguíneo.

**blood.shed** *s.* matança, carnificina.

**blood.y** *adj.* sangrento / *v.* sangrar, fazer sangrar.

**bloom** *s.* flor / *v.* florescer.

**bloom.ing** *adj.* florido; viçoso, exuberante.

**blos.som** *s.* florescência / *v.* florescer, florir.

**blot** *s.* borrão de tinta, mancha / *v.* borrar, rasurar.

**blotchy** / **bona fide**

**blotch.y** *adj.* manchado.
**blot.ting pa.per** *s.* mata-borrão.
**blouse** *s.* blusa.
**blow** *v.* soprar / *s.* golpe; soco; florescência.
**blow.ing** *s.* sopro, assopro.
**blow-up** *s.* explosão.
**blue** *adj.* azul; deprimido, triste (coloquial) / *s.* azul.
**bluff** *v.* blefar, enganar / *s.* blefe; logro.
**blun.der** *s.* gafe, asneira / *v.* cometer uma gafe, errar.
**blunt** *adj.* cego, sem corte (faca); obtuso.
**blur** *s.* borrão; nódoa; falta de clareza / *v.* embaçar.
**blurb** *s.* sinopse; resumo; sumário.
**blurt out** *v.* falar sem pensar.
**blush** *v.* corar / *s.* rubor.
**blus.ter.ing** *adj.* fanfarrão; fanfarrona; estrondoso.
**boar** *s.* javali; porco não castrado.
**board** *s.* quadro de avisos; tábua; prancha.
**boast** *v.* gabar-se / *s.* ostentação.
**boat** *s.* bote, barco.
**boat.er** *s.* chapéu duro de palha; barqueiro.
**boat.ing-trip** *s.* viagem de barco.
**bobby** *s* policial, tira (coloquial).
**bob.sleigh** *s.* trenó duplo / *v.* andar de trenó.

**bod.i.ly** *adj.* corporal / *adv.* à força.
**bod.y** *s.* corpo; cadáver.
**bod.y.build.ing** *s.* musculação.
**bod.y.guard** *s.* guarda-costas.
**bod.y.work** *s.* lataria, carroceria de automóvel.
**bog** *s.* pântano, brejo / *v.* atolar.
**bo.gus** *adj.* falso, adulterado / *s.* falsificação, adulteração.
**boil** *v.* ferver / *s.* ebulição, fervura; furúnculo, tumor.
**boi.ler** *s.* caldeira para aquecer líquido.
**boi.ler suit** *s.* macacão.
**bois.ter.ous** *adj.* tumultuoso, impetuoso; violento, rude.
**bold** *adj.* corajoso, valente; atrevido; nítido, claro; negrito (tipografia).
**Bo.liv.i.a** *s.* Bolívia.
**bol.lard** *s.* poste de amarração de navio.
**bolt** *s.* trinco; pino; parafuso; ferrolho.
**bomb** *s.* bomba / *v.* bombardear.
**bomb.er** *s.* avião de bombardeio; a pessoa que coloca bombas.
**bomb.shell** *s.* bomba, granada explosiva.
**bo.na fi.de** *adj.* genuíno, legítimo / *adv.* de boa fé.

**bond** *s.* compromisso; vínculo; bônus; título / *v.* unir, ligar.

**bond.age** *s.* escravidão, servidão.

**bone** *s.* osso; chifre; espinha de peixe / *v.* desossar.

**bone-i.dle** *adj.* extremamente preguiçoso.

**bon.fire** *s.* fogueira.

**bon.net** *s.* capô; touca usada por mulheres.

**bo.nus** *s.* bônus, bonificação; bênção.

**bon.y** *adj.* ossudo.

**boo** *v.* vaiar / *s.* vaia / *interj.* u!

**boo.by-trap** *s.* armadilha para pregar uma peça em alguém.

**book** *s.* livro / *v.* reservar, registrar.

**book.case** *s.* estante para livros.

**book.ing of.fice** *s.* bilheteria.

**book.keep.er** *s.* guarda-livros.

**book.keep.ing** *s.* contabilidade.

**book.let** *s.* folheto, livreto, apostila.

**book.mak.er** *s.* agenciador de apostas.

**book.man** *s.* livreiro; estudioso.

**book.mark** *s.* marcador de páginas.

**book re.view** *s.* crítica literária.

**book.sell.er** *s.* livreiro, vendedor de livros.

**book.shelf** *s.* prateleira para livros.

**book.stall** *s.* banca para venda de livros.

**book.store** *s.* livraria.

**book.worm** *s.* traça que destrói livros.

**boom** *s.* barulho; estrondo / *v.* retumbar.

**boon** *s.* benefício; bênção.

**boost** *s.* estímulo, aumento, impulso / *v.* estimular, impulsionar, aumentar.

**boost.er** *s.* propugnador; dínamo.

**boot** *v.* carregar (coloquial) / *s.* bota; porta-malas de carro; vantagem.

**boot.black** *s.* engraxate.

**booth** *s.* barraca, tenda; cabine.

**boot.less** *adj.* descalço; inútil.

**boot.mak.er** *s.* sapateiro.

**boo.ty** *s.* saque; pilhagem.

**booze** *s.* bebida alcoólica (coloquial); bebedeira.

**bor.der** *s.* margem, borda; fronteira, limite / *v.* limitar-se com.

**bor.der.line** *adj.* fronteiriço; limítrofe / *s.* linha divisória.

**bore** *v.* entediar; perfurar (buraco) / *s.* chato; buraco.

**bored** *adj.* entediado, chateado.

**bore.dom** *s.* tédio, enfado, aborrecimento.

**bore.some** *adj.* cansativo, enfadonho.

**bor.ing** *adj.* chato(a), enfadonho(a) / *s.* perfuração, furagem, sondagem.

**born** *v.* ♦ *to be* ~ nascer; *pp.* do *v. to bear* / *adj.* nascido.

**borne** *v. pp.* do *v. to bear.*

**bo.rough** *s.* município; vila com plenos direitos políticos.

**bor.row** *v.* pedir algo emprestado / *s.* empréstimo.

**Bos.ni.a and Her.ze.go.vi.na** *s.* Bósnia-Herzegóvina.

**bos.om** *s.* peito.

**bos.om friend** *s.* amigo íntimo.

**boss** *s.* chefe, patrão / *v.* mandar, dirigir, controlar.

**boss.y** *adj.* mandão(ona), dominante.

**bos.un** *s.* contramestre de barco ou navio.

**bot.a.ny** *s.* botânica.

**botch** *v.* estropiar, estragar / *s.* remendo mal feito.

**both** *adj.* ambos(as) / *pron.* ambos(as) / *conj.* não só, tanto que.

**both.er** *v.* atrapalhar, incomodar; preocupar / *s.* preocupação; incômodo.

**both.er.some** *adj.* aborrecido, amolante.

**bot.tle** *s.* garrafa / *v.* engarrafar.

**bot.tle.neck** *s.* gargalo de garrafa; passagem estreita.

**bot.tle nose** *s.* nariz vermelho.

**bot.tle o.pen.er** *s.* abridor de garrafas.

**bot.tom** *s.* fundo; parte mais baixa.

**bot.tom.less** *adj.* ilimitado; sem fundo.

**bough** *s.* ramo; galho de árvore.

**bought** *v. pret.* e *pp.* do *v. to buy.*

**boul.der** *s.* pedra grande, rocha.

**bounce** *v.* saltar, quicar; ser devolvido / *s.* salto, pulo.

**bound** *s.* pulo / *v.* pular; *pret.* e *pp.* do *v. to bind* / *adj.* com destino a.

**bound.a.ry** *s.* fronteira, limite.

**bound.less** *adj.* ilimitado, sem limites, infinito.

**bou.quet** *s.* ramalhete, buquê; aroma de vinho, fragrância.

**bour.geois** *adj.* burguês, da classe média / *s.* pessoa da classe média, burguês.

**bout** *s.* ataque, combate.

**bow** *s.* arco para atirar flechas; reverência / *v.* fazer reverência, curvar-se.

**bow.el** *s.* intestino.

**bow.er** *s.* caramanchão.

**bowl** *s.* tigela, bacia; boliche / *v.* arremessar a bola.

**bow.leg.ged** *adj.* de pernas tortas.
**bowl.er** *s.* lançador da bola no críquete.
**bowl.ing** *s.* jogo de boliche; críquete.
**bowl.ing-green** *s.* gramado para jogo de críquete.
**bowls** *s.* jogo de bolas, partida de boliche.
**bow-tie** *s.* gravata borboleta.
**box** *s.* caixa; tabefe; bofetada / *v.* encaixotar; boxear.
**box.er** *s.* pugilista, boxeador; boxer (raça de cachorro).
**box.ing** *s.* pugilismo, boxe.
**boy** *s.* menino, moço, rapaz.
**boy.cott** *s.* boicote / *v.* boicotar.
**boy.friend** *s.* namorado, amigo.
**boy.ish** *adj.* jovial, pueril, infantil.
**bra** *s.* sutiã.
**brace** *s.* aparelho odontológico; braçadeira / *v.* suportar, apoiar; fixar.
**brace.let** *s.* pulseira, bracelete.
**brac.ing** *adj.* tonificante, fortificante / *s.* amarração, suporte, esteio.
**brack.en** *s.* samambaia.
**brack.et** *s.* suporte; parêntese.
**brag** *v.* gabar-se.
**braid** *s.* trança de cabelo; cadarço / *v.* trançar, entrelaçar.

**brain** *s.* cérebro, miolo; inteligência.
**brain.child** *s.* ideia, obra.
**brain-fag** *s.* cansaço cerebral.
**brain.less** *s.* sem cérebro, desmiolado.
**brain.wash.ing** *s.* lavagem cerebral.
**brain.wave** *s.* inspiração, ideia brilhante.
**brain.y** *adj. coloq.* inteligente, esperto.
**braise** *v.* refogar, guisar.
**brake** *v.* frear, brecar / *s.* freio, breque; matagal.
**braky** *adj.* cheio de mato.
**bram.ble** *s.* amoreira preta.
**bran** *s.* farelo.
**branch** *s.* galho; ramo de árvore; filial.
**branch-bank** *s.* filial de banco.
**brand** *s.* marca de fábrica, marca registrada / *v.* marcar (gado).
**bran.dish** *v.* brandir / *s.* brandimento.
**brand-new** *adj.* novo em folha.
**bran.dy** *s.* conhaque.
**brash** *adj.* frágil, quebradiço; grosseiro, impetuoso / *s.* indisposição, mal-estar.
**brass** *s.* latão, metal.
**brass.ard** *s.* distintivo, emblema.

**brass.band** *s.* orquestra de instrumentos de metal.

**brat** *s.* pirralho, fedelho.

**bra.va.do** *s.* bravata, desafio.

**brave** *adj.* valente, corajoso / *s.* bravo (pessoa valente) / *v.* desafiar.

**brav.er.y** *s.* coragem, bravura.

**braw** *adj.* fino, bonito, elegante.

**brawn.y** *adj.* musculoso, vigoroso.

**bray** *v.* zurrar / *s.* zurro, ornejo.

**braze** *v.* revestir ou decorar com metal.

**bra.zen** *adj.* descarado, atrevido; de latão / *v.* tornar atrevido.

**bra.zi.er** *s.* caldeireiro; braseiro.

**Bra.zil** *s.* Brasil.

**Bra.sil.i.a** *s.* Brasília.

**Bra.zil.i.an** *adj.* brasileiro(a).

**Bra.zil nut** *s.* castanha-do-pará.

**breach** *s.* brecha, abertura; ruptura, quebra, violação.

**bread** *s.* pão.

**bread bin** *s.* caixa de pão.

**bread.crumb** *s.* migalha de pão.

**breadth** *s.* largura, amplitude.

**bread.win.ner** *s.* arrimo de família, ganha-pão.

**break** *s.* quebra; brecha; fenda; interrupção, intervalo / *v.* quebrar, fraturar.

**break.down** *s.* avaria; colapso, crise (de nervos); análise.

**break.fast** *s.* café da manhã.

**break.ing** *s.* fratura; ruptura; bancarrota.

**break.through** *s.* avanço; ruptura das linhas inimigas.

**break-up** *s.* decaída, colapso; separação; fim; dissolução.

**break.water** *s.* quebra-mar.

**breast** *s.* peito.

**breast-feed** *v.* amamentar.

**breath** *s.* fôlego; hálito; respiração.

**breathe** *v.* respirar, inspirar, inalar.

**breath.ing** *s.* respiração; aspiração.

**breath.less** *adj.* sem fôlego, ofegante; esbaforido.

**breath.tak.ing** *adj.* emocionante; excitante; extraordinário.

**bred** *v. pret. e pp.* do *v. to breed.*

**breed** *v.* criar (gado); reproduzir-se / *s.* raça (animal), casta, criação.

**breed.ing** *s.* procriação, geração, parição.

**breeze** *s.* brisa, vento leve; pó de cinza.

**breez.y** *adj.* vivaz, alegre; com brisa.

**brew** *s.* bebida fervida ou fermentada / *v.* fazer cerveja, fazer bebida para fervura.

**brew.age** *s.* ato de fazer cerveja.

**brew.er** *s.* cervejeiro.

brewery     **155**     brochure

**brew.er.y** *s.* cervejaria.

**brew.ing** *s.* preparação; fábrica de bebida fermentada.

**bribe** *s.* suborno / *v.* subornar.

**bribe.less** *adj.* insubornável.

**brick** *s.* tijolo; bloco para construção.

**brick.built** *s.* construído de tijolos.

**brick.en** *s.* feito de tijolo.

**brick.lay.er** *s.* pedreiro.

**brick.wall** *s.* muro de tijolos.

**bri.dal** *adj.* nupcial, de noiva / *s.* casamento.

**bride** *s.* noiva.

**bride.groom** *s.* noivo.

**brides.maid** *s.* dama de honra.

**bridge** *s.* ponte.

**bri.dle** *s.* freio (de cavalo), rédea / *v.* colocar rédea ou freio.

**brief** *adj.* breve, curto / *s.* sumário, síntese / *v.* instruir, fazer resumo.

**brief.case** *s.* pasta executiva.

**brief.ing** *s.* instruções resumidas.

**brief.ly** *adv.* rapidamente, resumidamente, brevemente.

**briefs** *s.* cueca ou calcinha.

**bright** *adj.* claro; brilhante; inteligente.

**bright.en** *v.* iluminar; clarear ♦ *~up* animar-se.

**bright.ness** *s.* brilho, luminosidade; inteligência.

**bril.liance** *s.* brilho, luminosidade, claridade.

**bril.liant** *adj.* brilhante, luminoso; genial / *s.* diamante; brilho, resplendor.

**brim** *s.* borda, aba.

**brim.less** *s.* sem borda, sem aba.

**brine** *s.* salmoura / *v.* salgar.

**bring** *v.* trazer.

**brink** *s.* beira de precipício.

**brisk** *adj.* vigoroso, enérgico; ativo / *v.* estimular, animar.

**bris.tle** *s.* cerda / *v.* eriçar, arrepiar.

**Brit.ain** *s.* Grã-Bretanha.

**Brit.ish** *adj.* britânico / *s.* britânico.

**Bri.ton** *adj.* britânico nasce ou habita a Grã-Bretanha; bretão.

**brit.tle** *adj.* frágil, quebradiço, inseguro.

**broach** *v.* abordar um assunto; perfurar, espetar / *s.* furador, alargador, espeto.

**broad** *adj.* amplo, vasto; largo.

**broad.cast** *v.* transmitir, difundir / *s.* transmissão.

**broad.brim** *s.* chapéu de aba larga.

**broc.co.li** *s.* brócolis.

**bro.chure** *s.* folheto, panfleto; brochura.

**broil** *v.* grelhar.

**broke** *v. pret.* do *v. to break* / *adj.* sem dinheiro, quebrado.

**bro.ken** *v. pp.* do *v. to break* / *adj.* quebrado; partido.

**bro.ken down** *adj.* desmoronado, decaído; deprimido.

**broker** *s.* corretor(a), agente, intermediário(a).

**brol.ly** *s.* guarda-chuva.

**bron.chi.tis** *s.* bronquite.

**bronze** *s.* bronze / *v.* bronzear-se.

**brooch** *s.* broche.

**brood** *s.* ninhada, filhotes; prole numerosa / *v.* chocar.

**brook** *s.* riacho, córrego / *v.* tolerar, sofrer, aguentar.

**broom** *s.* vassoura / *v.* varrer.

**broom.stick** *s.* cabo da vassoura.

**broth** *s.* caldo, sopa.

**broth.el** *s.* bordel, prostíbulo.

**broth.er** *s.* irmão; confrade; irmandade.

**broth.er-in-law** *s.* cunhado.

**brought** *v. pret.* e *pp.* do *v. to bring.*

**brow** *s.* fronte, testa; sobrancelha.

**brown** *adj.* castanho, marrom / *s.* castanho, marrom.

**brown.ie** *s.* bolo de chocolate com amêndoas; bandeirante (menina).

**brown pa.per** *s.* papel pardo, papel de embrulho.

**brown su.gar** *s.* açúcar mascavo.

**browse** *v.* pastar (gado) / folhear, ler algumas páginas de livro / *s.* brotos tenros.

**bruise** *s.* hematoma, contusão, pisadura / *v.* contundir, machucar.

**bru.nette** *adj.* morena, de cabelo escuro / *s.* mulher de cabelo escuro.

**brunch** *s.* refeição que se toma ao acordar tarde, misto de café da manhã e almoço (*breakfast + lunch*).

**brunt** *s.* ímpeto; força.

**brush** *s.* escova, escovão; pincel, broxa / *v.* escovar; varrer.

**brush.wood** *s.* lenha; mato; gravetos.

**brusque** *adj.* ríspido, brusco, rude.

**Brus.sels** *s.* Bruxelas.

**Brus.sels sprouts** *s.* couve-de--bruxelas.

**bru.tal** *adj.* brutal, cruel.

**brute** *s.* bruto; besta; animal irracional / *adj.* bruto, animalesco.

**brut.ish.ness** *s.* brutalidade.

**bub.ble** *s.* bolha, borbulha / *v.* borbulhar.

**bub.ble bath** *s.* banho de espuma.

**bub.ble gum** *s.* chiclete, goma de mascar.

buck | **157** | bully

**buck** *s.* corça macho (animal); pulo; pinote; dólar (coloquial) / *v.* lutar contra, resistir.

**buck.et** *s.* balde, tina / *v.* baldear.

**buck.le** *s.* fivela; curva, dobra / *v.* afivelar; dobrar, curvar.

**bud** *s.* broto; botão de flor; origem / *v.* brotar, florescer.

**Bud.dhis.m** *s.* budismo.

**bud.ding** *adj.* em ascensão, nascente, que está emergindo.

**bud.dy** *s. coloq.* companheiro, amigo; camarada.

**budge** *v.* mover-se, mexer-se, sair do lugar.

**budg.et** *s.* orçamento; receita; verba / *v.* orçar, planejar gastos.

**buff** *adj.* da cor do couro / *s.* couro de búfalo / *v.* polir com couro.

**buf.fa.lo** *s.* búfalo; bisão.

**buff.er** *s.* para-choque; memória intermediária (informática).

**buf.fet** *s.* restaurante com bufê; lanchonete; bofetada / *v.* esbofetear.

**bug** *s.* inseto; bicho; erro, defeito, falha (informática); grampo, escuta.

**bug.gy** *s.* carrinho de bebê.

**bu.gle** *s.* corneta, clarim / *v.* tocar corneta ou clarim.

**build** *v.* construir, edificar / *s.* estatura, constituição física.

**build.ing** *s.* edifício, construção, estrutura.

**built** *v. pret.* e *pp.* do *v. to build.*

**bulb** *s.* bulbo; lâmpada elétrica.

**Bul.ga.ri.a** *s.* Bulgária.

**bulge** *s.* bojo; protuberância / *v.* inchar; bojar.

**bulk** *s.* volume; tamanho
♦ ~ *buying* compra no atacado.

**bulk.y** *adj.* volumoso; grande.

**bull** *s.* touro.

**bull-calf** *s.* bezerro macho.

**bull.dog** *s.* buldogue.

**bull.doz.er** *s.* escavadora para terraplenagem; pessoa ou arma que intimida.

**bul.let** *s.* bala de revólver, projétil.

**bul.le.tin** *s.* comunicado, boletim, publicação regular.

**bul.let-proof** *adj.* à prova de bala.

**bull.fight** *s.* tourada.

**bul.lion** *s.* ouro ou prata em barras ou lingotes.

**bul.lock** *s.* boi, bovino.

**bull.ring** *s.* praça de touros, arena.

**bull's eye** *s.* no alvo, na mosca; tiro certeiro.

**bul.ly** *s.* valentão; carne salgada (de boi) / *v.* amedrontar, provocar, intimidar.

**bum** *s.* bumbum, bunda (coloquial) / *v.* soar forte; zunir / *adj.* ordinário.

**bump** *s.* batida, baque, sacudida / *v.* bater contra.

**bump.er** *s.* para-choque / *adj.* abundante.

**bump.er car** *s.* carro de trombada (parque de diversões).

**bump.tious** *adj.* presunçoso, arrogante, convencido.

**bump.y** *adj.* acidentado, desigual; esburacado.

**bun** *s.* pão doce; coque de cabelo, birote.

**bunch** *s.* grupo; cacho de fruta; ramalhete / *v.* agrupar-se.

**bun.dle** *s.* embrulho, trouxa, maço / *v.* embrulhar, empacotar.

**bun.ga.low** *s.* chalé, bangalô.

**bun.gle** *v.* estragar; fracassar, fazer malfeito.

**bun.ion** *s.* joanete.

**bunk** *s.* beliche; bobagem, besteira (coloquial).

**bun.ker** *s.* abrigo subterrâneo, casamata.

**bun.ny** *s.* coelhinho (expressão infantil).

**buoy** *s.* boia.

**buoy.ant** *adj.* flutuante.

**bur.den** *s.* carga, peso, encargo / *v.* sobrecarregar.

**bu.reau** *s. (pl. bureaux)* escritório, repartição pública, agência; escrivaninha; cômoda.

**bu.reauc.ra.cy** *s.* burocracia.

**bur.glar** *s.* assaltante, arrombador.

**bur.gla.ry** *s.* roubo de uma casa, arrombamento.

**bur.i.al** *s.* enterro, sepultamento.

**bur.ly** *adj.* robusto, corpulento.

**Bur.ma** *s.* Birmânia.

**burn** *v.* queimar; acender; incinerar / *s.* queimadura; queimada.

**burn.er** *s.* bico de gás, maçarico, queimador.

**burn.ing** *adj.* ardente / *s.* combustão, incêndio, queimadura.

**bur.row** *s.* toca / *v.* cavar, fazer uma toca.

**bur.sar.y** *s.* bolsa de estudos; tesouraria.

**burst** *v.* arrebentar, estourar, explodir / *s.* rajada; estouro, rompimento.

**burst up** *s.* colapso.

**bur.y** *v.* enterrar, sepultar.

**bus** *s.* ônibus.

**bush** *s.* arbusto; mato, moita.

**bush.y** *adj.* espesso, cerrado, frondoso.

**bus.i.ly** *adv.* atarefadamente.

**business** | **159** | **byword**

**busi.ness** *s.* negócio; trabalho; assunto, negócio.

**busk** *s.* barbatana / *v.* pôr isca em anzol; vestir-se.

**busk.er** *s.* artista de rua.

**bus stop** *s.* ponto de ônibus.

**bust** *s.* busto, peito (escultura) / *adj.* quebrado / *v.* estourar; quebrar.

**bust.er** *s.* bebedeira; vento intenso.

**bus.tle** *s.* animação, alvoroço / *v.* apressar-se, alvoroçar-se.

**bust.ling** *adj.* movimentado.

**bus.y** *adj.* ocupado(a), atarefado, movimentado / *v.* ocupar-se com algo.

**bus.y.bod.y** *adj.* intrometido(a).

**but** *conj.* mas, porém / *adv.* apenas.

**butch.er** *s.* açougueiro; carniceiro / *v.* chacinar; abater e carnear (animal).

**butch.er.y** *s.* matadouro; carnificina.

**but.ler** *s.* mordomo.

**butt** *s.* tonel, barrica; culatra; alvo; bunda (coloquial); toco de cigarro.

**but.ter** *s.* manteiga / *v.* untar; *coloq.* bajular.

**but.ter.cup** *s.* botão-de-ouro (botânica).

**but.ter.fly** *s.* borboleta.

**but.ter.ine** *s.* margarina.

**but.tock** *s.* nádega, traseiro.

**but.ton** *s.* botao; dístlco, broche / *v.* abotoar.

**bux.om** *adj.* rechonchudo; de seios grandes; curvilíneo.

**buy** *v.* comprar / *s.* compra, aquisição.

**buy.er** *s.* comprador(a).

**buzz** *s.* zumbido, zunido; cochicho, rumor / *v.* zumbir; cochichar.

**buzz.er** *s.* cigarra, campainha elétrica.

**buzz.word** *s.* modismo.

**by** *prep.* por; de; com; via; perto de, ao lado de; pelo, pela.

**bye** *interj.* até logo, tchau!

**by-e.lec.tion** *s.* eleição suplementar.

**by.gone** *adj.* passado, antigo.

**by.pass** *s.* desvio, passagem secundária / *v.* contornar; evitar.

**by-product** *s.* derivado.

**by.stand.er** *s.* espectador.

**byte** *s. byte* (unidade necessária para o armazenamento de um caractere em informática).

**by.word** *s.* provérvio; máxima.

# Cc

**C, c** *s.* terceira letra do alfabeto inglês; dó (nota musical); representa o número 100 em algarismos romanos.

**cab** *s.* táxi; cabine (de caminhão, de trem).

**cab.a.ret** *s.* cabaré.

**cab.bage** *s.* repolho, couve.

**cab.in** *s.* cabana; camarote (náutica); cabine (aeronáutica).

**cab.i.net** *s.* gabinete; escritório.

**ca.ble** *s.* cabo; amarra.

**cache** *s.* esconderijo (de alimentos) / *v.* esconder, ocultar.

**cack.le** *v.* gargalhar; cacarejar; tagarelar / *s.* cacarejo; gargalhada; tagarelice.

**cac.tus** *s.* cacto.

**cad.dy** *s.* carregador de tacos; caixa, lata ou cofre.

**ca.det** *s.* cadete; caçula; irmão mais novo.

**ca.fe** *s.* café, restaurante.

**caf.e.te.ri.a** *s.* lanchonete, bandejão, cantina.

**cage** *s.* gaiola, jaula / *v.* engaiolar, enjaular.

**ca.goule** *s.* casaco de náilon.

**Cai.ro** *s.* Cairo.

**ca.jole** *v.* lisonjear, adular, bajular.

**cake** *s.* bolo; torta.

**ca.lam.i.ty** *s.* calamidade, catástrofe; desgraça.

**cal.cu.late** *v.* calcular, fazer cálculos, avaliar.

**cal.cu.la.tion** *s.* cálculo, avaliação, cômputo.

**cal.cu.la.tor** *s.* calculadora.

**cal.en.dar** *s.* calendário.

**calf** 161 canister

**calf** *s.* vitela; bezerro; cria, filhote; barriga da perna, panturrilha.

**cal.i.ber, cal.i.bre** *s.* calibre.

**call** *v.* chamar, gritar, telefonar, visitar / *s.* grito, chamada, visita, telefonema.

**call.box** *s.* cabine telefônica.

**call.er** *s.* visitante; pessoa que chama ao telefone.

**call.ing** *s.* vocação, tendência; chamada.

**call.ing card** *s.* cartão de visita.

**cal.lous** *adj.* cruel, insensível; calejado; endurecido.

**cal.lous.ness** *s.* calosidade; desumanidade, insensibilidade.

**calm** *s.* calma, tranquilidade / *adj.* calmo(a) / *v.* acalmar.

**calm.ness** *s.* calmaria, tranquilidade, sossego.

**cal.o.rie** *s.* caloria.

**cal.o.rif.ic** *adj.* calorífico.

**Cam.bo.di.a** *s.* Camboja.

**cam.corder** *s.* filmadora.

**came** *v. pret.* do *v. to come.*

**cam.el** *s.* camelo.

**cam.el.opard** *s.* girafa.

**cam.e.ra** *s.* máquina fotográfica.

**cam.e.ra.man** *s.* cinegrafista.

**cam.ou.flage** *s.* camuflagem / *v.* camuflar.

**camp** *s.* campo; acampamento / *v.* acampar.

**cam.paign** *s.* campanha / *v.* fazer campanha.

**camp.er** *s.* indivíduo acampado.

**cam.phor** *s.* cânfora.

**camp.ing** *s.* acampamento.

**camp.site** *s.* área de acampamento.

**camp.us** *s.* cidade universitária.

**can** *v. modal* poder, ser capaz de; enlatar / *s.* lata.

**Can.a.da** *s.* Canadá.

**Ca.na.di.an** *adj.* canadense / *s.* canadense.

**ca.nar.y** *s.* canário.

**can.cel** *v.* cancelar, invalidar / *s.* cancelamento, revogação.

**can.cel.la.tion** *s.* cancelamento, anulação, supressão.

**Can.cer** *s.* Câncer (astrologia).

**can.cer** *s.* câncer, cancro.

**can.did** *adj.* franco(a), sincero(a), ingênuo(a).

**can.di.da.cy** *s.* candidatura.

**can.di.date** *s.* candidato(a).

**can.dle** *s.* vela.

**can.dle.light** *s.* luz de vela.

**can.dle.stick** *s.* castiçal.

**can.dor** *s.* fraqueza, sinceridade.

**can.dy** *s.* doce, bala confeitada, bombom.

**can.dy floss** *s.* algodão-doce.

**cane** *s.* cana; bengala, vara; bambu ♦ *sugar* ~ cana-de-açúcar.

**can.is.ter** *s.* lata; estopim.

**can.na.bis** s. maconha.

**canned** adj. enlatado.

**canned-goods** s. pl. conservas.

**can.non** s. canhão.

**can.ny** adj. astuto(a), engenhoso(a), sagaz.

**ca.noe** s. canoa, piroga / v. navegar em canoa, remar em canoa.

**ca.noe.ist** s. canoeiro, remador de canoa.

**can o.pen.er** s. abridor de latas.

**can't** v. contração de can not.

**can.teen** s. cantina; cantil.

**can.vas** s. lona; tenda; barraca; quadro ou pintura a óleo.

**can.vass** v. sondar; fazer campanha / s. exame minucioso.

**can.yon** s. desfiladeiro.

**cap** s. gorro, boné, quepe; tampa / v. tampar; completar.

**ca.pa.bil.i.ty** s. capacidade; competência.

**ca.pa.ble** adj. capaz; competente; apto.

**ca.pac.i.ty** s. capacidade, aptidão.

**cape** s. capa; cabo, promontório.

**ca.per** s. alcaparra; salto, cambalhota / v. saltar.

**cap.i.tal** s. capital; letra maiúscula; patrimônio, ganhos.

**cap.i.tal letter** s. letra maiúscula, capitular.

**cap.i.tal.is.m** s. capitalismo.

**cap.i.tal.ist** s. capitalista / adj. capitalista.

**cap.i.tal.ize** v. capitalizar; escrever com letra maiúscula.

**Cap.ri.corn** s. Capricórnio (astrologia).

**cap.size** v. virar de cabeça para baixo, emborcar, capotar.

**cap.sule** s. cápsula.

**cap.tain** s. capitão / v. capitanear, chefiar, comandar.

**cap.tion** s. legenda (cinema, tv); cabeçalho, título; captura, prisão.

**cap.tious** adj. capcioso, ardiloso.

**cap.ti.vate** v. cativar, atrair.

**cap.tive** s. cativo(a), prisioneiro(a) / adj. cativo(a), preso(a).

**cap.tiv.i.ty** s. cativeiro.

**cap.tor** s. captor, capturador, apreensor.

**cap.ture** v. prender, capturar / s. captura, aprisionamento.

**car** s. carro, automóvel.

**ca.rafe** s. garrafa de mesa.

**car.a.mel** s. caramelo.

**car.at** s. quilate.

**car.a.van** s. trailer (veículo); caravana; cáfila.

**car.bo.hy.drate** s. carboidrato.

**car.bon** s. carbono.

**car.bu.ret.tor** s. carburador.

**car.case** s. carcaça; esqueleto (animal).

**card** *s.* cartão; carta de baralho; ficha.

**card.board** *s.* papelão; cartolina.

**car.di.ac** *adj.* cardíaco.

**car.di.gan** *s.* casaco de lã, cardigã.

**car.di.nal** *adj.* cardeal; cardinal / *s.* cardeal.

**card in.dex** *s.* fichário.

**care** *s.* cuidado, cautela, precaução / *v.* importar-se com; cuidar de.

**ca.reer** *s.* carreira, profissão / *v.* correr a toda velocidade.

**care.free** *adj.* despreocupado(a), alegre, feliz.

**care.ful** *adj.* cuidadoso(a), atento(a), meticuloso(a).

**care.ful.ly** *adv.* cuidadosamente.

**care.less** *adj.* descuidado(a), negligente, desleixado(a).

**care.less.ness** *s.* descuido, negligência, desatenção.

**ca.ress** *v.* acariciar / *s.* carícia.

**care.tak.er** *s.* zelador(a), vigia, porteiro(a).

**care.worn** *adj.* aflito(a), ansioso(a), preocupado(a).

**car.go** *s. (pl. cargoes)* carga, carregamento, frete.

**car hire** *s.* aluguel de carros.

**Car.ib.b.ean** *s.* Caribe; caraíba / *adj.* caribenho(a), caraíba.

**car.ing** *adj.* humanitário(a), afetuoso(a).

**car.nage** *s.* carnificina, massacre; amontoado de cadáveres.

**car.na.tion** *s.* cravo / *adj.* vermelho, encarnado.

**car.ni.val** *s.* carnaval; folia.

**carp** *s.* carpa.

**car park** *s.* estacionamento.

**car.pen.ter** *s.* carpinteiro.

**car.pen.try** *s.* carpintaria.

**car.pet** *s.* tapete, carpete / *v.* atapetar.

**car.pet sweep.er** *s.* limpador de tapetes.

**car phone** *s.* telefone de carro.

**car.riage** *s.* carruagem; vagão ferroviário.

**car.ri.er** *s.* firma transportadora; portador; companhia aérea.

**car.ri.er bag** *s.* sacola.

**car.rot** *s.* cenoura.

**car.ry** *v.* levar, carregar, transportar; trazer consigo.

**cart** *s.* carroça; carrinho de mão / *v.* transportar em carroça.

**cart.er** *s.* carreteiro, carroceiro.

**cart.on** *s.* caixa de papelão.

**car.toon** *s.* desenho animado; história em quadrinhos; caricatura.

**car.tridge** *s.* cartucho; rolo de filme.

**carve** *v.* esculpir, entalhar.

carving     164     cater

**carv.ing** *s.* entalhe; escultura.
**carv.ing knife** *s.* faca de trinchar.
**cas.cade** *s.* cascata, cachoeira.
**case** *s.* caso; paciente, doente; causa judicial; estojo, caixa.
**cash** *s.* dinheiro (em espécie); pagamento à vista / *v.* descontar.
**cash card** *s.* cartão de banco.
**cash dis.pens.er** *s.* caixa eletrônico.
**ca.shew** *s.* castanha de caju; cajueiro.
**cash.ier** *s.* caixa, encarregado do caixa.
**cash reg.is.ter** *s.* caixa registradora.
**cas.ing** *s.* invólucro, embalagem; cobertura; caixa.
**ca.si.no** *s.* cassino.
**cask** *s.* barril, tonel.
**cas.ket** *s.* cofrezinho; porta-joias; caixinha.
**cas.se.role** *s.* caçarola.
**cas.sette** *s.* fita cassete.
**cas.sette play.er** *s.* toca-fitas.
**cas.sette re.cor.der** *s.* gravador.
**cast** *v.* lançar, atirar / *s.* lance; elenco (teatro); molde.
**cast.a.way** *s.* náufrago(a); pária / *adj.* rejeitado(a), inútil; náufrago(a).
**cast.er sug.ar** *s.* açúcar branco refinado.

**cast.ing vote** *s.* voto decisivo.
**cast iron** *s.* ferro fundido.
**cas.tle** *s.* castelo, fortaleza; torre.
**cas.tor** *s.* castor.
**cas.tor oil** *s.* óleo de rícino ou de mamona.
**cas.u.al** *adj.* informal, esportivo / *s.* trabalhador sem vínculo empregatício.
**cas.u.al.ly** *adv.* casualmente, eventualmente.
**cas.u.al.ty** *s.* vítima; acidente, desastre, infortúnio.
**cat** *s.* gato(a).
**cat.a.logue** *s.* catálogo / *v.* catalogar, classificar.
**cat.a.lyst** *s.* catalisador.
**cat.a.pult** *s.* atiradeira; catapulta; estilingue.
**cat.a.ract** *s.* catarata, cachoeira.
**ca.tarrh** *s.* catarro.
**ca.tas.tro.phe** *s.* catástrofe.
**catch** *v.* pegar, apanhar, prender; surpreender / *s.* captura, presa.
**catch.ing** *adj.* contagioso, infeccioso.
**catch.y** *adj.* que pega fácil; atrativo.
**cat.e.go.ry** *s.* categoria, classe, série, grupo.
**ca.ter** *v.* abastecer, fornecer, suprir.

**caterer** 165 **centigrade**

**ca.ter.er** *s.* aprovisionador, fornecedor de mantimentos.
**ca.ter.ing** *s.* abastecimento.
**cat.er.pil** *s.* lagarta; esteira (de trator, tanque).
**ca.the.dral** *s.* catedral.
**Cath.o.lic** *adj.* católico, que pertence à religião católica / *s.* católico(a).
**cat.tle** *s.* gado; rebanho.
**cat.tle breed.ing** *s.* pecuária.
**cat.ty** *adj.* malévolo, maldoso; felino.
**cau.cus** *s.* comitê eleitoral, convenção de um partido político.
**caught** *v. pret.* e *pp.* do *v. to catch.*
**cau.li.flow.er** *s.* couve-flor.
**cause** *s.* causa, razão, origem / *v.* causar, originar.
**cau.tion** *s.* cautela; aviso / *v.* avisar, acautelar, advertir.
**cav.al.ry** *s.* cavalaria.
**cave** *s.* caverna, gruta, toca / *v.* ♦ ~ *in* desabar; ceder.
**cave.man** *s.* homem das cavernas, troglodita.
**cav.ern** *s.* caverna, gruta.
**cav.i.ty** *s.* cavidade; cárie.
**cd** *abrev.* de *compact disc.*
**cease** *v.* cessar, terminar, parar.
**cease-fire** *s.* cessar-fogo.

**cease.less** *adj.* incessante, contínuo.
**ce.dar** *s.* cedro.
**cede** *v.* ceder.
**ceil.ing** *s.* teto, forro.
**cel.e.brate** *v.* celebrar, festejar.
**cel.e.brat.ed** *adj.* célebre, famoso.
**cel.e.bra.tion** *s.* celebração, comemoração.
**cel.e.ry** *s.* aipo.
**cel.i.bacy** *s.* celibato.
**cell** *s.* cela; célula; pilha.
**cel.lar** *s.* adega, celeiro, porão.
**cel.lo** *s.* violoncelo.
**cell.phone** *s.* telefone celular.
**Celt** *s.* celta / *adj.* celta.
**ce.ment** *s.* cimento, argamassa / *v.* cimentar, consolidar.
**ce.ment mix.er** *s.* betoneira.
**cem.e.ter.y** *s.* cemitério.
**cen.sor** *v.* censurar / *s.* censor.
**cen.sor.ship** *s.* censura.
**cen.sure** *v.* criticar, repreender, censurar / *s.* crítica, repreensão, reprimenda.
**cen.sus** *s.* censo, recenseamento.
**cent** *s.* cêntimo, centavo.
**cen.te.na.ry** *s.* centenário.
**cen.ter, cen.tre** *s.* centro, meio, núcleo / *v.* centrar, concentrar-se.
**cen.ti.grade** *adj.* centígrado.

**cen.ti.me.ter** *s.* centímetro.

**cen.ti.pede** *s.* centopeia.

**cen.tral** *adj.* central, principal.

**cen.tral heat.ing** *s.* aquecimento central.

**cen.tu.ry** *s.* século.

**ce.ram.ic** *adj.* cerâmico, relativo a cerâmica.

**cer.e.mo.ny** *s.* cerimônia, solenidade.

**cer.tain** *adj.* seguro, certo, claro, evidente; determinado, algum.

**cer.tain.ly** *adv.* certamente, com certeza.

**cer.tain.ty** *s.* certeza, segurança, convicção.

**cer.tif.i.cate** *s.* certidão, certificado, atestado, diploma.

**cer.ti.fied mail** *s.* correio registrado.

**cer.ti.fy** *v.* certificar, atestar.

**cer.vi.cal** *adj.* cervical.

**cer.vix** *s.* cerviz, nuca, cachaço.

**cess.pit** *s.* fossa séptica.

**cess.pool** *s.* fossa, poço negro.

**chafe** *v.* roçar, atritar, friccionar / *s.* arranhão, esfoladura.

**cha.grin** *s.* desgosto, pesar, humilhação / *v.* afligir, vexar.

**chain** *s.* corrente, cordilheira, cadeia / *v.* acorrentar.

**chains** *s.* algema.

**chain store** *s.* sucursal, filial.

**chair** *s.* cadeira ♦ *the* ~ a presidência.

**chair.man** *s.* presidente de uma organização.

**chal.ice** *s.* cálice, taça.

**chalk** *s.* giz, greda.

**chal.lenge** *s.* desafio, provocação / *v.* desafiar, provocar.

**chal.leng.ing** *adj.* desafiante, desafiador, estimulante.

**cham.ber** *s.* câmara, gabinete; compartimento.

**cham.ois** *s.* camurça.

**cham.pagne** *s.* champanhe.

**cham.pi.on** *s.* campeão, vencedor.

**cham.pi.on.ship** *s.* campeonato.

**chance** *s.* oportunidade, possibilidade / *v.* arriscar a sorte.

**chan.cel.lor** *s.* chanceler.

**chan.de.lier** *s.* lustre.

**change** *v.* mudar, trocar / *s.* troca, mudança, substituição; troco (dinheiro).

**change.a.ble** *adj.* instável, mutável, inconstante.

**change.o.ver** *s.* comutação.

**chang.ing** *adj.* variável / *s.* troca, mudança; baldeação.

**chan.nel** *s.* canal / *v.* canalizar.

**chant** *s.* canto, canção / *v.* cantar, entoar.

chaos         **167**         check book

**cha.os** *s.* caos; confusão.

**chap** *s.* sujeito, cara, homem; rachadura, fenda / *v.* fender-se, rachar-se.

**chap.el** *s.* capela.

**chap.lain** *s.* capelão.

**chap.ped** *adj.* rachado.

**chap.ter** *s.* capítulo.

**char** *v.* tostar, queimar / *s.* carvão mineral.

**char.ac.ter** *s.* caráter, personalidade; reputação; personagem.

**char.ac.ter.is.tic** *adj.* característico / *s.* traço, característica.

**char.coal** *s.* carvão vegetal.

**charge** *s.* encargo; carga; acusação / *v.* carregar (bateria); acusar; cobrar.

**charge ac.count** *s.* conta corrente.

**charge.less** *adj.* de graça, sem despesa.

**charge card** *s.* cartão de crédito.

**char.i.ta.ble** *adj.* caridoso(a), bondoso(a), generoso(a).

**char.i.ty** *s.* caridade.

**char.la.dy** *s.* diarista.

**charm** *s.* charme, encanto / *v.* encantar, enfeitiçar.

**charm.ful** *adj.* encantador.

**charm.ing** *adj.* encantador(a), gracioso(a).

**chart** *s.* mapa, gráfico / *v.* traçar, mapear.

**chart.er** *s.* alvará, licença; fretamento / *v.* fretar.

**chase** *v.* perseguir, caçar / *s.* perseguição, caçada, animal caçado.

**chas.m** *s.* abismo, brecha, fenda na terra.

**chas.sis** *s.* chassi.

**chas.ti.ty** *s.* castidade; modéstia.

**chat** *v.* conversar, tagarelar, bater papo / *s.* conversa, bate-papo.

**chat show** *s.* programa de entrevistas.

**chat.ter** *s.* tagarelice, conversa fiada / *v.* tagarelar.

**chat.ty** *adj.* conversador, falador.

**chauf.feur** *s.* chofer, motorista.

**chau.vin.ist** *s.* chauvinista.

**cheap** *adj.* barato, econômico, de preço baixo; de má qualidade.

**cheap.ly** *adv.* por preço baixo.

**cheat** *v.* trapacear, enganar; colar (na prova) / *s.* trapaça; impostor, trapaceiro.

**check, cheque** *v.* verificar, conferir / *s.* inspeção, verificação; cheque.

**check.ing ac.count** *s.* conta corrente.

**check book** *s.* talão de cheques.

**cheek** *s.* bochecha; descaramento.
**cheek.y** *adj.* insolente, atrevido.
**cheep** *v.* piar / *s.* pio de passarinhos.
**cheer** *v.* aplaudir, alegrar-se / *interj.* saúde! / *s.* alegria, ânimo.
**cheer.ful** *adj.* alegre, agradável, animado.
**cheer.ful.ness** *s.* alegria, satisfação, contentamento.
**cheer.less** *adj.* triste, desanimado, melancólico.
**cheese** *s.* queijo.
**chee.tah** *s.* chita.
**chef** *s.* cozinheiro-chefe.
**chem.i.cal** *adj.* químico / *s.* produto químico.
**chem.ist** *s.* químico(a); farmacêutico(a).
**chem.is.try** *s.* química.
**chequ.ered** *adj.* acidentado.
**cher.ish** *v.* tratar com carinho, estimar.
**cher.ry** *s.* cereja.
**chess** *s.* xadrez.
**chest** *s.* peito, tórax; arca; baú.
**chest of drawers** *s.* cômoda.
**chest.nut** *s.* castanha; castanheira (árvore, madeira).
**chew** *v.* mastigar; remoer, ruminar.
**chewing gum** *s.* goma de mascar, chiclete.

**chic** *adj.* elegante, chique.
**chick** *s.* pinto, passarinho; criança; moça.
**chick.en** *s.* galinha, frango.
**chick.en.heart.ed** *adj.* medroso, covarde.
**chick.en.pox** *s.* catapora, varicela.
**chide** *v.* ralhar / *s.* repreensão.
**chief** *s.* chefe / *adj.* principal, superior.
**chief ex.ec.u.tive** *s.* diretor geral.
**chief.ly** *adv.* principalmente, sobretudo.
**chif.fon** *s.* fita.
**chil.blain** *s.* frieira.
**child** *s.* *(pl. children)* criança; filho(a).
**child.birth** *s.* parto.
**child.hood** *s.* infância, meninice.
**child.ish** *adj.* infantil, pueril; ingênuo(a), imaturo(a).
**child.like** *adj.* pueril, infantil, inocente.
**Chil.e** *s.* Chile.
**chill** *s.* friagem, frio; resfriado / *v.* congelar, esfriar, refrigerar.
**chill.i, chili** *s.* pimentão picante; pimenta malagueta.
**chill.y** *adj.* frio.
**chime** *s.* carrilhão / *v.* soar, bater (sinos).
**chim.ney** *s.* chaminé.

**chim.pan.zee** s. chimpanzé.

**chin** s. queixo.

**chi.na** s. louça, porcelana.

**China** s. China.

**Chi.nese** s. chinês(esa) / adj. chinês(esa).

**chink** s. fresta, abertura.

**chip** s. lasca, fragmento, pedaço.

**chips** s. batatas fritas.

**chi.rop.o.dist** s. pedicuro.

**chirp** v. piar, gorjear / s. gorjeio, cricri (grilo).

**chis.el** s. formão, cinzel / v. cinzelar, talhar.

**chit** s. talão, bilhete; penhor.

**chit.chat** s. conversa fiada, mexerico.

**chi.val.ry** s. cavalheirismo, bravura; cavalaria.

**chive** s. cebolinha, cebolinha verde.

**chlo.rine** s. cloro.

**chock-a-block** adj. abarrotado, repleto.

**choco.late** s. chocolate, bombom.

**choice** s. escolha, seleção / adj. de qualidade, seleto.

**choir** s. coro.

**choke** v. engasgar; estrangular, asfixiar / s. sufocação, asfixia, estrangulação.

**chol.er.a** s. cólera.

**cho.les.ter.ol** s. colesterol.

**choose** v. escolher, preferir.

**choos.y** adj. exigente, difícil de contentar.

**chop** v. picar; cortar / s. golpe; mudança.

**chop.per** s. helicóptero; cutelo, machadinha.

**chop.py** adj. agitado.

**chop.sticks** s. hashi, pauzinhos para comer.

**cho.ral** adj. coral / s. coral.

**chord** s. acorde.

**chore** s. tarefa do cotidiano.

**cho.re.og.ra.pher** s. coreógrafo(a).

**chor.tle** v. casquinar, rir / s. riso, casquinada.

**cho.rus** s. coro; estribilho, refrão.

**chose** v. pret. do v. to choose.

**Christ** s. Cristo, Jesus Cristo.

**chris.ten** v. batizar; dar nome.

**chris.ten.dom** s. cristandade.

**chris.ten.ing** s. batismo.

**Chris.tian** adj. cristão(ã) / s. cristão(ã).

**Chris.ti.an.i.ty** s. cristianismo, cristandade.

**Chris.tian name** s. nome de batismo, prenome.

# Christmas · 170 · citizen

**Christ.mas** s. Natal / adj. de Natal, natalino.

**Christ.mas Eve** s. véspera de Natal.

**Christ.mas tree** s. árvore de Natal.

**chrome** s. cromo / v. cromar.

**chron.ic** adj. crônico.

**chron.i.cle** s. crônica / v. registrar.

**chub.by** adj. gorducho, bochechudo.

**chuck** v. jogar, atirar, arremessar.

**chuck.le** s. riso contido / v. rir consigo mesmo.

**chum** s. camarada, amigo íntimo.

**chunk** s. pedaço, naco.

**church** s. igreja.

**church.go.er** s. devoto, igrejeiro, carola.

**churl** s. camponês; pessoa rude ou grosseira; avarento, sovina.

**churl.ish** adj. rude, grosseiro; avarento, sovina.

**churn** s. batedeira / v. agitar, bater violentamente.

**chute** s. rampa, ladeira íngreme; tobogã (em piscina); calha.

**chut.ney** s. molho picante.

**CIA** abrev. de Central Intelligence Agency (Agência Central de Inteligência).

**ci.der** s. sidra.

**ci.gar** s. charuto.

**cig.a.rette** s. cigarro.

**cin.der** s. cinza ♦ ~s carvão em brasa; hulha betuminosa.

**Cin.de.rel.la** s. Cinderela.

**cine-camera** s. câmera cinematográfica.

**cine-film** s. filme cinematográfico.

**cin.e.ma** s. cinema; filme.

**cin.na.mon** s. canela; casca de caneleira.

**ci.pher** s. cifra; criptograma / v. calcular; cifrar.

**cir.cle** s. círculo / v. rodear.

**cir.cuit** s. circuito; volta.

**cir.cu.lar** adj. circular, redondo / s. circular.

**cir.cu.late** v. circular.

**cir.cu.la.tion** s. circulação; tiragem (jornal), distribuição.

**cir.cum.cise** v. circuncidar.

**cir.cum.flex** s. circunflexo.

**cir.cum.spect** adj. prudente, circunspeto(a), cauteloso(a).

**cir.cum.stance** s. circunstância, condição ♦ ~s situação econômica.

**cir.cum.vent** v. burlar, lograr.

**cir.cus** s. circo.

**cis.tern** s. caixa d'água, cisterna.

**cite** v. citar, mencionar, referir-se.

**cit.i.zen** s. cidadão, civil.

**cit.i.zen.ship** *s.* cidadania.

**cit.rus fruit** *s.* fruta cítrica.

**cit.y** *s.* cidade.

**civic** *adj.* cívico; municipal.

**civ.il** *adj.* civil; gentil, cortês.

**civ.i.lized** *adj.* civilizado, educado, culto.

**civil law** *s.* direito civil.

**civil war** *s.* guerra civil.

**claim** *v.* exigir, alegar, afirmar / *s.* reclamação, reivindicação; afirmação.

**claim.ant** *s.* requerente, pretendente.

**clair.voy.ant** *s.* clarividente, vidente / *adj.* vidente, clarividente.

**clam** *s.* molusco, marisco.

**clam.ber** *v.* escalar (com dificuldade) / *s.* escalada, subida.

**clam.my** *adj.* úmido, pegajoso.

**clam.or** *v.* clamar, protestar / *s.* clamor, rebuliço.

**clamp** *v.* grampear, segurar, apertar / *s.* grampo, fixador.

**clan** *s.* clã.

**clang** *v.* retinir, soar, ressoar / *s.* tinido.

**clap** *v.* aplaudir / *s.* palmada; aplauso.

**clap hands** *v.* bater palmas.

**clapp.ing** *s.* aplausos.

**clar.i.fy** *v.* esclarecer, clarificar.

**clar.i.net** *s.* clarinete.

**clar.i.ty** *s.* clareza, lucidez.

**clash** *s.* estrondo; confronto / *v.* confrontar; enfrentar.

**clasp** *s.* gancho; fecho; abraço / *v.* afivelar, apertar, abraçar.

**class** *v.* classificar / *s.* classe, categoria; aula / *adj.* de classe.

**clas.sic** *s.* clássico / *adj.* clássico.

**class.i.fied** *adj.* secreto, confidencial.

**class.mate** *s.* colega de classe.

**class.room** *s.* sala de aula.

**clat.ter** *s.* ruído, tropel, algazarra.

**clause** *s.* cláusula.

**claw** *s.* pata; garra / *v.* arranhar.

**clay** *s.* argila, barro.

**clean** *v.* limpar / *adj.* limpo, honesto.

**clean.er** *s.* faxineiro(a).

**clean.ing** *s.* limpeza.

**clean.ness** *s.* limpeza; asseio.

**cleanse** *v.* purificar, limpar.

**cleans.er** *s.* creme de limpeza; removedor.

**clean-shav.en** *adj.* sem barba, de barba feita.

**clean-up** *s.* limpeza total.

**clear** *adj.* claro / *v.* clarear; remover, retirar.

**clear.ance** *s.* remoção; desobstrução.

# clearing — cloister

**clear.ing** *s.* clareira; roça; ajuste, acerto.

**clear.ly** *adv.* claramente.

**cleave** *v.* rachar-se, fender-se.

**cleav.er** *s.* cutelo de açougueiro.

**clef** *s.* clave.

**cleft** *s.* fissura, racha, fenda / *adj.* rachado, fendido.

**clench** *v.* agarrar, prender, cerrar / *s.* aperto.

**cler.gy** *s.* clero.

**cler.gy.man** *s.* pastor, padre, ministro da igreja, clérigo.

**cler.i.cal** *adj.* clerical, eclesiástico; de escritório / *s.* clérigo, padre.

**clerk** *s.* balconista; escrevente; auxiliar de escritório; funcionário.

**clev.er** *adj.* inteligente, esperto(a), engenhoso(a).

**clev.er.ness** *s.* inteligência; habilidade.

**clew** *s.* indício; vestígio.

**click** *v.* estalar, tinir; clicar / *s.* estalido, clique.

**cli.ent** *s.* cliente, freguês.

**cliff** *s.* penhasco, precipício.

**cli.mate** *s.* clima; condições metereológicas; atmosfera.

**cli.max** *s.* clímax.

**climb** *v.* subir, escalar, trepar / *s.* subida, escalada.

**climb.er** *s.* alpinista.

**climb.ing** *s.* alpinismo, escalamento; ascensão.

**clinch** *v.* rebitar, segurar; fechar acordo; ganhar / *s.* rebitamento; agarramento.

**cling** *v.* agarrar-se, grudar-se.

**clin.ic** *s.* clínica.

**clin.i.cal** *adj.* clínico.

**clink** *v.* tinir, tilintar / *s.* tinido, som de vidro.

**clip** *s.* tosquia, corte; clipe, grampo / *v.* tosquiar, cortar; grampear, apertar.

**clip.ping** *s.* recorte de jornal; tosquia.

**clique** *s.* panelinha, roda, grupo de pessoas.

**cloak** *s.* manto, capote; disfarce, pretexto / *v.* encobrir, mascarar.

**cloak.room** *s.* vestiário, chapelaria (teatro, restaurante).

**clock** *s.* relógio (de parede ou de mesa), medidor, taxímetro / *v.* cronometrar.

**clock.wise** *adv.* em sentido horário / *adj.* em sentido horário.

**clod** *s.* torrão de terra.

**clog** *s.* tamanco; obstáculo, obstrução / *v.* obstruir, entupir.

**clois.ter** *s.* claustro; convento, mosteiro, retiro.

**close** *adj.* próximo, íntimo / *v.* fechar; terminar.

**close-by** *adj.* perto, vizinho, adjacente.

**close.ly** *adv.* intimamente.

**clos.et** *s.* armário, quartinho, cubículo.

**close-up** *s.* primeiro plano, fotografia tirada de perto, vista (de perto).

**clo.sure** *s.* fechamento, fim, encerramento.

**clot** *s.* coágulo; imbecil (coloquial) / *v.* coagular.

**cloth** *s.* tecido, pano.

**clothe** *v.* vestir-se, pôr roupa.

**clothes** *s. pl.* roupa, traje, vestuário.

**cloth.ing** *s.* roupa, vestuário.

**cloud** *s.* nuvem.

**cloud.less** *adj.* claro, sem nuvens.

**cloud.y** *adj.* nublado.

**clout** *v.* esbofetear, dar um cascudo em / *s.* cascudo.

**clove** *s.* cravo-da-índia, ♦ *~of garlic* dente de alho.

**clo.ver** *s.* trevo, trifólio.

**clown** *s.* palhaço / *v.* fazer palhaçadas.

**cloy** *v.* fartar, saciar, saturar.

**cloy.ing** *adj.* enjoativo.

**club** *s.* clube; porrete, cacete / *v.* golpear.

**cluck** *v.* cacarejar / *s.* cacarejo.

**clue** *s.* pista, indício.

**clump** *s.* moita; torrão, pedaço.

**clum.sy** *adj.* desajeitado.

**clung** *v. pret. e pp.* do *v. to cling.*

**clus.ter** *v.* agrupar-se, apinhar-se / *s.* grupo; cacho; enxame.

**clutch** *s.* embreagem; ninhada; aperto; agarração / *v.* apertar; chocar.

**clut.ter** *v.* entulhar / *s.* desordem, bagunça.

**cm** *abrev.* de *centimeter.*

**c/o** *abrev.* de *care of* (aos cuidados de).

**coach** *s.* treinador; carruagem; ônibus / *v.* treinar, ensinar.

**coal** *s.* carvão; hulha.

**co.a.li.tion** *s.* coligação, união, coalizão.

**coal mine** *s.* mina de carvão.

**coarse** *adj.* grosseiro(a), grosso(a), vulgar; piada obscena.

**coarse.ness** *s.* aspereza, grosseria, rudeza.

**coast** *s.* costa, praia, beira-mar; litoral.

**coast.al** *adj.* costeiro, litorâneo.

**coast guard** *s.* guarda costeira.

**coast.line** *s.* litoral, contorno.

**coat** *s.* casaco; plumagem / *v.* cobrir, revestir.

**cob.ble** *s.* remendo (de sapatos); pedra de calçamento / *v.* remendar.

**cob.bler** *s.* sapateiro.

**cob.web** *s.* teia de aranha.

**co.caine** *s.* cocaína.

**cock** *s.* galo, frango; ave macho.

**cock.ney** *s.* habitante dos bairros pobres de Londres; dialeto.

**cock.pit** *s.* compartimento do piloto.

**cock.roach** *s.* barata.

**cock-sure** *adj.* absolutamente certo, convencido (coloquial).

**cock.tail** *s.* coquetel.

**cock.y** *adj.* convencido, arrogante.

**co.coa** *s.* cacau; chocolate (bebida).

**co.co.nut** *s.* coco.

**co.coon** *s.* casulo.

**cod** *s.* bacalhau.

**code** *s.* código.

**co.er.cion** *s.* coerção, repressão.

**cof.fee** *s.* café (bebida).

**coffee break** *s.* pausa para café.

**cof.fer** *s.* arca; cofre.

**cof.fin** *s.* caixão, ataúde.

**cog** *s.* dente de engrenagem.

**co.gent** *adj.* convincente, forçoso.

**co.her.ent** *adj.* coerente.

**coil** *s.* bobina, espiral, rolo; DIU (anticoncepcional) / *v.* enrolar, bobinar.

**coin** *s.* moeda.

**coin.age** *s.* sistema monetário; cunhagem.

**co.in.cide** *v.* coincidir; acontecer ao mesmo tempo.

**co.in.ci.dence** *s.* coincidência.

**coke** *s.* cocaína (coloquial); Coca-Cola; coque.

**col.an.der** *s.* coador, escorredor de macarrão.

**cold** *s.* frio; resfriado / *adj.* frio; gélido; insensível.

**cold-blood.ed** *adj.* cruel, de sangue-frio.

**cold.ly** *adv.* friamente.

**cole.slaw** *s.* salada de repolho.

**col.lapse** *s.* colapso, desabamento / *v.* desabar, ruir.

**col.laps.i.ble** *adj.* dobrável, desmontável, articulado.

**col.lar** *s.* gola; colarinho.

**col.lar.bone** *s.* clavícula.

**col.lat.e.ral** *s.* parente colateral; garantia / *adj.* paralelo, colateral.

**col.league** *s.* colega.

**col.lect** *v.* coletar, reunir, juntar; cobrar.

**col.lec.tion** *s.* coleção; arrecadação.

**college** 175 **commercial**

**col.lege** *s.* faculdade, centro de ensino superior.

**col.lide** *v.* colidir.

**col.li.sion** *s.* colisão.

**Co.lom.bi.a** *s.* Colômbia.

**co.lon** *s.* cólon, dois pontos.

**colo.nel** *s.* coronel.

**col.o.nize** *v.* colonizar.

**col.o.ny** *s.* colônia, povoação.

**col.or** *s.* cor / *v.* colorir, pintar.

**col.or-blind** *s.* daltônico.

**col.or.ful** *adj.* colorido.

**col.or.ing** *s.* coloração; corante; tez.

**colt** *s.* potro.

**col.umn** *s.* coluna.

**col.um.nist** *s.* colunista.

**coma** *s.* coma.

**comb** *s.* pente; crista (de ave, de onda); favo (de mel) / *v.* pentear.

**com.bat** *v.* combater / *s.* combate.

**com.bi.na.tion** *s.* combinação; associação.

**com.bine** *v.* combinar; unir-se, associar-se.

**come** *v.* vir; chegar; aproximar-se.

**come.back** *s.* volta, retorno / *v.* voltar, retornar.

**co.me.di.an** *s.* humorista, comediante.

**com.e.dy** *s.* comédia.

**com.fort** *s.* bem-estar, conforto / *v.* consolar.

**com.fort.a.ble** *adj.* confortável, cômodo.

**com.fort.a.bly** *adv.* confortavelmente.

**com.ic** *s.* cômico, comediante; revista em quadrinhos, gibi.

**comic strip** *s.* história em quadrinhos.

**com.ing** *s.* chegada, vinda.

**com.ma** *s.* vírgula.

**com.mand** *s.* ordem, comando / *v.* mandar, dirigir, comandar.

**com.mand.er** *s.* comandante, chefe.

**com.mand.ment** *s.* mandamento, preceito.

**com.mem.o.rate** *v.* comemorar, celebrar.

**com.mence** *v.* iniciar, começar.

**com.mend** *v.* elogiar, recomendar.

**com.men.su.rate** *adj.* compatível; proporcional; igual.

**com.ment** *s.* comentário, observação / *v.* comentar.

**com.men.tar.y** *s.* comentário, explicação.

**com.men.ta.tor** *s.* comentarista.

**com.merce** *s.* comércio.

**com.merc.ial** *s.* anúncio / *adj.* comercial; mercantil.

**com.mis.sion** *s.* comissão, encargo / *v.* encomendar; encarregar.

**com.mis.sion.er** *s.* comissário(a).

**com.mit** *v.* cometer; confinar, encerrar; comprometer-se.

**com.mit.ment** *s.* compromisso; promessa.

**com.mit.tee** *s.* comitê.

**com.mod.i.ty** *s.* mercadoria; artigo de utilidade.

**com.mon** *adj.* comum, popular, usual.

**com.mon.ly** *adv.* geralmente.

**common sense** *s.* bom senso; juízo.

**com.mo.tion** *s.* tumulto, distúrbio; agitação.

**com.mu.nal** *adj.* comum.

**com.mu.ni.cate** *v.* comunicar-se.

**com.mu.ni.ca.tion** *s.* comunicação.

**com.mun.i.on** *s.* comunhão, participação.

**com.mu.ni.qué** *s.* comunicado oficial.

**com.mun.ism** *s.* comunismo.

**com.mun.ist** *adj.* comunista / *s.* comunista.

**com.mu.ni.ty** *s.* comunidade.

**com.mute** *v.* viajar diariamente para o trabalho; comutar, trocar.

**com.pact** *adj.* compacto / *s.* caixa de pó de arroz / *v.* comprimir.

**com.pact disc** *s.* disco compacto.

**com.pan.ion** *s.* companheiro(a).

**com.pan.ion.ship** *s.* companheirismo, camaradagem.

**com.pa.ny** *s.* companhia.

**com.par.a.tive** *adj.* comparativo; relativo.

**com.par.a.tively** *adv.* relativamente, comparativamente.

**com.pare** *v.* comparar.

**com.par.i.son** *s.* comparação.

**com.part.ment** *s.* compartimento.

**com.pass** *s.* bússola.

**com.pass.es** *s.* compasso.

**compass card** *s.* rosa dos ventos.

**com.pas.sion** *s.* compaixão, piedade.

**com.pat.i.bil.i.ty** *s.* compatibilidade.

**com.pat.i.ble** *adj.* compatível, conciliável.

**com.pel** *v.* obrigar, compelir, forçar.

**com.pel.ling** *adj.* convincente; persuasivo; irresistível.

**com.pen.sate** *v.* indenizar, compensar.

**com.pen.sa.tion** *s.* indenização.

**com.pete** *v.* competir.

**com.pe.tent** *adj.* competente, capacitado.

**com.pe.ti.tion** *s.* competição, disputa.

**com.pet.i.tive** *adj.* competitivo.

**com.pet.i.tor** *s.* competidor(a).

**com.pla.cen.cy** *s.* complacência satisfação consigo próprio.

**com.plain** *v.* queixar-se; reclamar.

**com.plai.sant** *adj.* complacente, afável, cortês.

**com.plaint** *s.* queixa, denúncia, reclamação; enfermidade.

**com.ple.ment** *v.* complementar / *s.* complemento.

**com.ple.men.ta.ry** *adj.* complementar.

**com.plete** *adj.* completo, terminado / *v.* completar, terminar, concluir.

**com.plete.ly** *adv.* completamente, inteiramente, totalmente.

**com.plete.ness** *s.* perfeição; inteireza, integralidade.

**com.ple.tion** *s.* conclusão; acabamento.

**com.plex** *s.* complexo / *adj.* complexo, complicado.

**com.plex.ion** *s.* tez, cútis; caráter, natureza.

**com.pli.ance** *s.* submissão; condescendência; conformidade.

**com.pli.cate** *v.* complicar.

**com.pli.cat.ed** *adj.* complicado, complexo.

**com.pli.ca.tion** *s.* complicação.

**com.pli.ment** *s.* elogio ♦ ~s cumprimentos / *v.* elogiar; cumprimentar.

**com.pli.men.ta.ry** *adj.* lisonjeiro; grátis.

**complot** *s.* conspiração, trama.

**com.ply** *v.* cumprir; estar de acordo com; condescender.

**com.po.nent** *s.* peça; componente / *adj.* componente.

**com.pose** *v.* compor.

**com.posed** *adj.* sereno, calmo, tranquilo.

**com.pos.er** *s.* compositor(a).

**com.po.si.tion** *s.* composição; redação.

**com.post** *s.* compostagem, adubo.

**com.po.sure** *s.* serenidade, compostura, calma.

**com.pound** *adj.* composto / *s.* composto, combinação / *v.* misturar, compor.

**com.pre.hend** *v.* compreender, entender.

**com.pre.hen.sive** *adj.* abrangente, completo; compreensivo.

**com.press** *s.* compressa / *v.* comprimir, reduzir.

**com.pro.mise** *v.* comprometer, chegar a um acordo / *s.* acordo.

**compulsion** · 178 · **conduce**

**com.pul.sion** *s.* compulsão.

**com.pul.sive** *adj.* compulsivo; inveterado (jogador).

**com.pul.so.ry** *adj.* obrigatório, compulsório.

**com.put.er** *s.* computador.

**com.put.er.ize** *v.* informatizar.

**com.put.ing** *s.* computação, informática.

**com.rade** *s.* camarada, companheiro(a).

**com.rade.ship** *s.* camaradagem.

**con.ceal** *v.* omitir; esconder, ocultar.

**con.cede** *v.* reconhecer, admitir, ceder.

**con.ceit** *s.* presunção, vaidade.

**con.ceit.ed** *adj.* vaidoso, convencido.

**con.ceive** *v.* conceber.

**con.cen.trate** *v.* concentrar / *s.* concentrado.

**con.cen.tra.tion** *s.* concentração.

**con.cept** *s.* conceito.

**con.cep.tion** *s.* concepção.

**con.cern** *s.* interesse; preocupação / *v.* dizer respeito a, interessar.

**con.cern.ing** *prep.* a respeito de, acerca de, relativo a.

**con.cert** *s.* concerto.

**con.cert.ed** *adj.* conjunto, coordenado, de comum acordo.

**con.cer.ti.na** *s.* sanfona, harmônica.

**con.ces.sion** *s.* concessão.

**con.cise** *adj.* conciso, breve, resumido.

**con.clude** *v.* concluir; deduzir, inferir.

**con.clu.sive** *adj.* conclusivo, decisivo.

**con.cord** *s.* acordo; concórdia.

**con.course** *s.* saguão.

**con.crete** *s.* concreto / *adj.* concreto.

**con.cur** *v.* concordar; coincidir.

**con.demn** *v.* condenar.

**con.den.sa.tion** *s.* condensação.

**con.dense** *v.* condensar; resumir.

**con.di.ment** *s.* condimento, tempero.

**con.di.tion** *s.* condição / *v.* condicionar.

**con.di.tion.er** *s.* condicionador; amaciante (de roupas).

**con.do.lences** *s.* pêsames, condolências.

**con.dom** *s.* camisinha, preservativo.

**con.do.min.i.um** *s.* condomínio.

**con.done** *v.* perdoar, desculpar; tolerar.

**con.duce** *v.* conduzir, levar, tender.

**con.duct** *v.* conduzir, dirigir, administrar / *s.* conduta, procedimento.

**cone** *s.* cone; casquinha (sorvete); pinha.

**con.fec.tion er** *s.* confeiteiro.

**con.fer** *v.* conferir, outorgar, deliberar.

**con.fer.ence** *s.* congresso, conferência.

**con.fess** *v.* confessar.

**con.fes.sion** *s.* confissão.

**con.fes.sor** *s.* confessor.

**con.fet.ti** *s.* confete.

**con.fide** *v.* confiar.

**con.fi.dence** *s.* confiança.

**con.fi.dent** *adj.* confiante, certo, seguro.

**con.fi.den.tial** *adj.* confidencial, secreto.

**con.fine** *v.* confinar, limitar.

**con.fines** *s.* confins.

**con.fine.ment** *s.* prisão, confinamento.

**con.firm** *v.* confirmar; aprovar.

**con.fir.ma.tion** *s.* confirmação.

**con.fis.cate** *v.* confiscar / *adj.* confiscado.

**con.flict** *v.* divergir, discordar / *s.* conflito.

**con.flict.ing** *adj.* divergente, conflitante, contraditório.

**con.form** *v.* conformar-se, adaptar-se.

**con.found** *v.* confundir, desconcertar.

**con.front** *v.* enfrentar, confrontar.

**con.fron.ta.tion** *s.* confronto, acareação.

**con.fuse** *v.* confundir, desorientar.

**con.fused** *adj.* confuso, desorientado.

**con.fu.sion** *s.* confusão, desordem, balbúrdia.

**con.geal** *v.* congelar-se.

**con.ge.ni.al** *adj.* simpático; agradável; apropriado.

**con.ges.tion** *s.* congestão, congestionamento.

**con.grat.u.la.te** *v.* parabenizar.

**con.grat.u.la.tion** *s.* felicitação ♦ ~*s* parabéns.

**con.gre.gate** *v.* reunir-se.

**con.gre.ga.tion** *s.* congregação.

**con.gress** *s.* congresso.

**con.gress.man** *s.* deputado; congressista.

**con.ju.gate** *v.* conjugar; unir, ligar.

**con.jure** *v.* fazer truques; invocar; evocar; conjurar, adjurar.

**con.jur.er** *s.* mágico; conjurador.

**conk out** *v.* pifar, falhar (coloquial).

**con.man** *s.* vigarista.

**con.nect** *v.* conectar, unir, associar.
**con.nec.tion** *s.* conexão, ligação, relação.
**con.quer** *v.* conquistar, vencer.
**con.quer.or** *s.* conquistador, vencedor.
**con.quest** *s.* conquista.
**con.science** *s.* consciência.
**con.scious** *adj.* consciente, cônscio, ciente.
**con.script** *s.* recruta / *adj.* conscrito, recrutado, alistado.
**con.scrip.tion** *s.* serviço militar obrigatório.
**con.sent** *s.* consentimento / *v.* consentir.
**con.se.quence** *s.* consequência.
**con.se.quent.ly** *adv.* consequentemente.
**con.ser.va.tion** *s.* conservação.
**con.serv.a.tive** *adj.* conservador / *s.* conservador.
**con.ser.va.to.ry** *s.* conservatório (música); estufa.
**con.serve** *s.* conserva / *v.* preservar, conservar.
**con.sid.er** *v.* considerar, refletir.
**con.sid.er.a.ble** *adj.* considerável.
**con.sid.er.ate** *adj.* atencioso.
**con.sid.er.a.tion** *s.* consideração; respeito, estima.

**con.sign.ment** *s.* consignação; remessa.
**con.sist** *v.* consistir.
**con.sis.ten.cy** *s.* consistência.
**con.sis.tent** *adj.* estável, consistente, coerente.
**con.so.la.tion** *s.* conforto, consolo, consolação.
**con.sole** *s.* consolo / *v.* confortar, consolar.
**con.so.nant** *s.* consoante / *adj.* consoante, harmonioso.
**con.sort** *s.* cônjuge, consorte.
**con.sor.tium** *s.* consórcio.
**con.spir.a.cy** *s.* conspiração, trama.
**con.sta.ble** *s.* policial; condestável.
**con.stant** *adj.* constante.
**con.sti.pat.ed** *adj.* com prisão de ventre.
**con.sti.pa.tion** *s.* prisão de ventre.
**con.sti.tu.en.cy** *s.* distrito eleitoral.
**con.sti.tu.ent** *s.* eleitor(a), constituinte.
**con.sti.tute** *v.* constituir.
**con.sti.tu.tion** *s.* constituição.
**con.strain** *v.* constranger, obrigar, compelir.
**con.straint** *s.* coação; restrição; confinamento.
**con.struct** *v.* construir.

**con.struc.tion** *s.* construção.
**con.strue** *v.* interpretar; explicar.
**con.sul** *s.* cônsul.
**con.sult** *v.* consultar; prestar consultoria.
**con.sul.tant** *s.* consultor.
**con.sume** *v.* consumir.
**con.sum.er** *s.* consumidor(a).
**con.sum.er goods** *s.* bens de consumo.
**con.sump.tion** *s.* consumação.
**con.tact** *s.* contato / *v.* contatar, comunicar.
**contact lens** *s.* lente de contato.
**con.ta.gious** *adj.* contagioso.
**con.tain** *v.* conter.
**con.tain.er** *s.* recipiente, contêiner.
**con.tam.i.nate** *v.* contaminar.
**con.tem.plate** *v.* contemplar.
**con.tem.po.rar.y** *adj.* contemporâneo / *s.* contemporâneo.
**con.tempt** *s.* desprezo, desdém.
**con.tempt.i.ble** *adj.* desprezível.
**con.tent** *v.* contentar / *s.* contentamento ♦ ~*s* conteúdo.
**con.tent.ed** *adj.* contente.
**con.tent.ment** *s.* contentamento, satisfação.
**con.test** *s.* concurso, competição / *v.* disputar.
**con.tes.tant** *s.* adversário(a); concorrente.

**con.text** *s.* contexto.
**con.ti.nent** *s.* continente.
**con.ti.nen.tal** *adj.* continental.
**con.tin.gen.cy** *s.* contingência, eventualidade.
**con.tin.gent** *s.* contingente (de soldados).
**con.tin.u.al** *adj.* contínuo.
**con.tin.u.al.ly** *adv.* continuamente.
**con.tin.u.a.tion** *s.* prolongamento, continuação.
**con.tin.ue** *v.* continuar, prosseguir.
**con.tin.u.ous** *adj.* contínuo.
**con.tin.u.ous forms** *s.* formulários contínuos.
**con.tort** *v.* contorcer.
**con.tour** *s.* contorno; curva de nível.
**con.tra.band** *s.* contrabando.
**con.tract** *v.* contrair; contratar / *s.* contrato.
**con.trac.tion** *s.* contração.
**con.trac.tor** *s.* contratante, empreiteiro.
**con.tra.dict** *v.* contradizer, contestar.
**con.trap.tion** *s.* geringonça, engenhoca (coloquial).
**con.trar.y** *s.* contrário, oposto / *adj.* teimoso; desfavorável, adverso.

**contrast** 182 coordinate

**con.trast** s. contraste
/ v. contrastar; comparar.
**con.tra.vene** v. infringir,
transgredir, violar.
**con.trib.ute** v. contribuir.
**con.tri.bu.tion** s. contribuição;
donativo; taxa, tributo.
**con.trib.u.tor** s. contribuinte;
colaborador.
**con.trol** s. controle / v. controlar.
**con.trol.ler** s. controlador, fiscal,
inspetor.
**con.trol room** s. sala de controle.
**con.trol tower** s. torre de controle.
**con.tro.ver.sial** adj. polêmico,
controverso.
**con.tro.ver.sy** s. controvérsia.
**con.va.lesce** v. convalescer.
**con.vene** v. convocar; reunir-se.
**con.ve.ni.ence** s. utilidade;
conveniência; comodidade.
**con.ve.ni.ent** adj. conveniente,
apropriado; prático.
**con.vent** s. convento.
**con.ven.tion** s. convenção.
**con.ver.sa.tion** s. conversação,
conversa.
**con.verse** v. conversar
/ adj. contrário, oposto.
**con.verse.ly** adv. inversamente.
**con.ver.sion** s. conversão, troca.
**con.vert** v. converter
/ s. convertido(a).

**con.vert.i.ble** s. conversível
(carro) / adj. conversível.
**con.vey** v. transportar;
comunicar, expressar; enviar.
**con.vict** v. condenar
/ s. presidiário(a), condenado.
**con.vic.tion** s. convicção;
condenação.
**con.vince** v. convencer.
**con.vinc.ing** adj. convincente.
**con.voy** s. escolta, proteção
/ v. escoltar, comboiar.
**coo** v. arrulhar; namorar
/ s. arrulho.
**cook** v. cozinhar
/ s. cozinheiro(a).
**cook.book** s. livro de receitas
culinárias.
**cook.er** s. fogão.
**cook.e.ry** s. culinária.
**cook.ing** s. cozinha; arte
culinária / adj. de cozinha.
**cool** adj. fresco; frio; legal
(coloquial) / v. resfriar.
**cool.ness** s. frigidez, frieza.
**coop** s. gaiola; viveiro
/ v. prender, confinar, cercar.
**co.op.e.rate** v. cooperar, colaborar.
**co.op.e.ra.tive** s. cooperativa
/ adj. cooperativo(a).
**co.or.di.nate** v. coordenar
/ s. coordenadas.

**co-ownership**     183     **corruption**

**co-own.er.ship** *s.* condomínio, copropriedade.

**cop** *s.* tira, policial (coloquial).

**cop.per** *s.* cobre; tira, policial (coloquial).

**cop.u.late** *v.* ter relações sexuais, copular.

**cop.y** *v.* copiar / *s.* cópia, reprodução / *v.* copiar, reproduzir.

**cop.y.right** *s.* direitos autorais / *adj.* protegido por direitos autorais.

**cor.al** *s.* coral / *adj.* coral, coralino.

**cord** *s.* corda, cordão; fio.

**cor.di.al** *adj.* cordial / *s.* cordial.

**cor.dial.i.ty** *s.* cordialidade.

**cor.don** *s.* cordão de isolamento.

**cor.du.roy** *s.* veludo cotelê.

**core** *s.* caroço de frutas; centro, núcleo; essência.

**co.ri.an.der** *s.* coentro.

**cork** *s.* cortiça, rolha de cortiça / *adj.* de cortiça.

**cork.screw** *s.* saca-rolhas.

**corn** *s.* milho.

**corn bread** *s.* broa de fubá.

**corned beef** *s.* carne enlatada.

**cor.ner** *s.* esquina; canto; ângulo; escanteio (futebol).

**cor.net** *s.* cornetim.

**corn.field** *s.* trigal; milharal.

**corn.flakes** *s.* flocos de milho.

**corn.flour** *s.* amido de milho, maisena.

**corn.y** *adj.* granuloso, em grão.

**cor.o.na.ry** *s.* coronária / *adj.* coronário, coronal.

**cor.o.na.tion** *s.* coroação.

**cor.o.net** *s.* pequena coroa, diadema.

**cor.po.ral** *adj.* corporal / *s.* cabo (militar).

**cor.po.rate** *adj.* corporativo, coletivo.

**cor.po.ra.tion** *s.* corporação.

**corps** *s.* corpo (militar, do exército); corporação.

**corpse** *s.* cadáver, defunto.

**cor.ral** *s.* curral.

**cor.rect** *v.* corrigir; repreender / *adj.* correto, certo.

**cor.rect.ness** *s.* precisão; correção.

**cor.re.spond** *v.* corresponder.

**cor.re.spon.dence** *s.* correspondência.

**cor.re.spon.dent** *s.* correspondente.

**cor.ri.dor** *s.* corredor, passagem.

**cor.rode** *v.* corroer.

**cor.ro.sion** *s.* corrosão.

**cor.rupt** *adj.* corrupto, desonesto / *v.* corromper.

**cor.rupt.ion** *s.* corrupção.

**cor.sage** *s.* corpinho; corpete.

**cor.set** *s.* espartilho, cinta feminina.

**Cor.si.ca** *s.* Córsega.

**cos.met.ic** *s.* cosmético / *adj.* artificial; cosmético.

**cos.mos** *s.* cosmo, universo.

**cos.set** *v.* paparicar, mimar.

**cost** *v.* custar / *s.* preço, valor, custo.

**co-star** *s.* coadjuvante.

**Cos.ta Ri.ca** *s.* Costa Rica.

**cost-ef.fec.tive** *adj.* rentável.

**cost.ly** *adj.* caro.

**cost of liv.ing** *s.* custo de vida.

**cos.tume** *s.* traje, roupa nacional ou regional; fantasia.

**cos.tume-jew.elle.ry** *s.* bijuteria.

**co.sy** *adj.* aconchegante, confortável.

**cot** *s.* berço; cama estreita; choupana.

**cot.tage** *s.* casa de campo ou de verão; chalé, cabana.

**cot.tage cheese** *s.* requeijão.

**cot.ton** *s.* algodão / *adj.* de algodão.

**cot.ton-cand.y** *s.* algodão-doce.

**cot.ton wool** *s.* algodão bruto ou em rama.

**couch** *s.* sofá.

**cou.chette** *s.* leito.

**cou.gar** *s.* puma (animal).

**cough** *s.* tosse, tossidela / *v.* tossir.

**cough drop** *s.* pastilha para tosse.

**could** *v. pret.* do *v. to can.*

**coun.cil** *s.* conselho, assembleia.

**coun.cil.or** *s.* conselheiro; vereador.

**coun.cil estate** *s.* conjunto habitacional.

**coun.sel** *s.* conselho / *v.* aconselhar, recomendar.

**count** *v.* contar / *s.* conta, soma; conde.

**coun.te.nance** *v.* tolerar, aprovar / *s.* apoio, auxílio.

**coun.ter** *s.* balcão; contador; oposto, contrário / *v.* contrariar / *adj.* oposto.

**coun.ter.act** *v.* neutralizar, agir contra.

**coun.ter.bal.ance** *s.* contrapeso / *v.* contrabalançar.

**coun.ter.feit** *v.* falsificar / *s.* falsificação; imitação / *adj.* falsificado.

**coun.ter.foil** *s.* canhoto do talão.

**coun.ter.mand** *v.* revogar / *s.* revogação.

**coun.ter.part** *s.* equivalente, contraparte, duplicata.

**coun.ter.sign** *v.* autenticar, rubricar.

**count.less** *adj*. inumerável, incontável.

**coun.try** *s*. país; pátria; campo, interior; zona, região.

**country house** *s*. casa de campo.

**coun.try.man** *s*. camponês; compatriota, patrício.

**coun.try.side** *s*. campo, zona rural, interior.

**coun.ty** *s*. condado, município, comarca.

**coup** *s*. golpe de estado.

**cou.ple** *s*. par, casal, dupla.

**coup.ling** *s*. ligação, junção.

**cou.pon** *s*. cupom, bilhete, talão.

**cour.age** *s*. coragem, bravura.

**cou.ri.er** *s*. correio; mensageiro; guia.

**course** *s*. curso; rumo; direção; prato (comida).

**court** *s*. corte (de justiça, real); quadra para jogos / *v*. cortejar.

**cour.te.ous** *adj*. cortês, amável.

**cour.te.san** *s*. cortesã, meretriz.

**cour.te.sy** *s*. cortesia, favor.

**court-house** *s*. palácio de justiça.

**court-mar.tial** *s*. corte marcial; conselho de guerra.

**court.room** *s*. sala de tribunal.

**cous.in** *s*. primo(a).

**cove** *s*. enseada.

**cov.e.nant** *s*. compromisso; convenção; pacto.

**cov.er** *s*. cobertura; capa / *v*. cobrir, tampar.

**cov.er.age** *s*. cobertura.

**cov.er.ing** *s*. camada, revestimento, cobertura.

**cov.er.let** *s*. coberta, colcha.

**cov.ert** *adj*. velado, secreto, encoberto / *s*. abrigo.

**cov.et** *v*. cobiçar; desejar.

**cow** *s*. vaca / *v*. intimidar; amedrontar.

**cow.ard** *s*. covarde / *adj*. covarde, medroso.

**cow.ard.ice** *s*. covardia.

**cow.ard.ly** *adj*. covarde / *adv*. covardemente.

**cow.boy** *s*. vaqueiro, boiadeiro; trambiqueiro, picareta.

**cow.pox** *s*. vacina; varíola bovina.

**crab** *s*. caranguejo, siri.

**crack** *s*. rachadura; estalo; droga; craque (esportista) / *v*. quebrar; estalar.

**crack.brained** *adj*. louco, doido.

**crack.er** *s*. biscoito de água e sal; bombinha de São João.

**cra.dle** *s*. berço; terra natal / *v*. embalar.

**craft** *s*. nave; artesanato; ofício, profissão; técnica / *v*. elaborar.

**craftsman** 186 **cress**

**crafts.man** *s.* artesão.

**craft.y** *adj.* astuto, ladino.

**crag** *s.* penhasco, rochedo.

**cramp** *s.* grampo; cãibra, cólica.

**cramped** *adj.* apertado, espremido; espasmódico.

**crane** *s.* guindaste, grua.

**crank** *s.* manivela; pessoa excêntrica (coloquial).

**crash** *s.* batida; estampido; desastre; quebra / *v.* bater; quebrar.

**crash course** *s.* curso intensivo.

**crash he.lmet** *s.* capacete de proteção.

**crash landing** *s.* aterrissagem forçada.

**crate** *s.* caixote; engradado / *v.* encaixotar, engradar.

**cra.vat** *s.* gravata larga.

**crawl** *v.* engatinhar, arrastar-se / *s.* rastejo; estilo de natação.

**cray.fish** *s.* lagostim.

**cray.on** *s.* giz de cera, creiom.

**craze** *s.* moda, febre, interesse passageiro.

**cra.zy** *adj.* louco, maluco, doido.

**creak** *s.* rangido / *v.* ranger, estalar.

**cream** *s.* creme; nata / *adj.* de creme.

**cream cheese** *s.* queijo cremoso.

**cream.e.ry** *s.* estabelecimento para laticínios.

**cream.y** *adj.* cremoso.

**crease** *v.* amassar; vincar; enrugar / *s.* vinco, prega, dobra; ruga.

**cre.a.tor** *s.* criador, autor.

**crea.ture** *s.* criatura, ser humano; animal.

**cre.dence** *s.* crédito, crença.

**cred.i.ble** *adj.* acreditável, crível.

**cred.i.bil.i.ty** *s.* credibilidade.

**cred.it** *v.* creditar / *s.* crédito, empréstimo.

**credit card** *s.* cartão de crédito.

**cred.i.tor** *s.* credor.

**creed** *s.* credo, crença; doutrina.

**creek** *s.* riacho, córrego.

**creep** *v.* rastejar; engatinhar / *s.* ♦ ~s arrepio, calafrio.

**creep.er** *s.* trepadeira; rastreador; rastejador.

**creep.y** *adj.* horripilante, arrepiador.

**cre.mate** *v.* cremar.

**cre.ma.tion** *s.* cremação.

**crem.a.to.ri.um** *s.* crematório.

**crepe** *s.* crepe, panqueca.

**crept** *v. pret.* e *pp.* do *v. to creep.*

**cres.cent** *s.* meia-lua, crescente; quarto crescente.

**cress** *s.* agrião.

**crest** *s.* crista; topo.

**Crete** *s.* Creta.

**crev.ice** *s.* fenda, fissura.

**crew** *s.* tripulação.

**crib** *s.* berço com grades altas; manjedoura.

**crick** *s.* cãibra.

**crick.et** *s.* grilo; críquete (esporte).

**crime** *s.* crime, delito.

**crim.i.nal** *s.* criminoso / *adj.* criminoso, criminal.

**cringe** *v.* encolher-se de medo.

**crin.kle** *s.* ruga; dobra; amassadura de papel.

**crip.ple** *v.* aleijar; mutilar / *s.* aleijado(a).

**cri.sis** *s. (pl. crises)* crise.

**crisp** *adj.* torrado, crocante / *v.* encrespar; torrar.

**criss.cross** *adj.* cruzado, riscado com linhas cruzadas / *v.* riscar, marcar.

**cri.te.ri.on** *s. (pl. criteria)* critério.

**crit.ic** *s.* crítico; detrator / *adj.* crítico.

**crit.i.cal** *adj.* grave; decisivo, crucial.

**crit.i.cism** *s.* crítica; censura; desaprovação.

**crit.i.cize** *v.* criticar, censurar.

**croak** *v.* coaxar / *s.* coaxo.

**Cro.a.tia** *s.* Croácia.

**cro.chet** *s.* crochê / *v.* fazer crochê.

**crock.er.y** *s.* louça de barro.

**croc.o.dile** *s.* crocodilo.

**cro.cus** *s.* açafrão.

**croft** *s.* pequena chácara, sítio.

**cro.ny** *s.* comparsa; amigo íntimo.

**crook** *s.* vigarista, trapaceiro; curva, dobra / *adj.* torto, tortuoso; desonesto.

**croon.er** *s.* cantor de rádio.

**crop** *s.* colheita, safra / *v.* cortar, tosar.

**cross** *s.* cruz; cruzamento / *v.* cruzar.

**cross.ing** *s.* travessia; cruzamento; faixa para pedestres.

**cross.word** *s.* palavras cruzadas.

**cross.eyed** *s.* vesgo; estrábico.

**crotch** *s.* virilha.

**crouch** *s.* agachamento / *v.* agachar-se, curvar-se.

**crow** *s.* corvo, gralha; grito de alegria; canto de galo / *v.* cantar (galo).

**crow.bar** *s.* pé de cabra, alavanca.

**crowd** *s.* multidão, grupo / *v.* reunir-se, aglomerar-se.

**crowd.ed** *adj.* lotado, abarrotado, cheio.

**crown** *s.* coroa (de rei, de dente); copa de árvore / *v.* coroar.

**cru.cial** *adj.* decisivo, crucial.

**cru.ci.fix** *s.* crucifixo.

**cru.ci.fix.ion** *s.* crucificação.

**crude** *adj.* bruto, cru; rude, grosseiro.

**crude.ness** *s.* crueza, rudeza.

**cru.el** *adj.* cruel.

**cru.el.ty** *s.* crueldade.

**cruise** *s.* cruzeiro (marítimo), viagem / *v.* viajar, percorrer os mares.

**crumb** *s.* migalha; miolo do pão.

**crum.ble** *v.* esfarelar, desfazer-se, quebrar, desmoronar.

**crum.bly** *adj.* farelento, que se desfaz.

**crum.ple** *v.* amarrotar, amassar, enrugar.

**crunch** *s.* mastigação ruidosa / *v.* mastigar, morder algo (ruidosamente).

**crunch.y** *adj.* crocante.

**cru.sade** *s.* cruzada.

**crush** *v.* esmagar, espremer / *s.* aglomeração; paixão intensa e passageira.

**crust** *s.* crosta de pão, casca; borra (de vinho).

**crutch** *s.* muleta.

**crux** *s.* ponto crucial.

**cry** *v.* chorar, gritar, exclamar / *s.* grito, choro.

**cry.ing** *s.* choro, pranto, gritaria.

**cryp.tic** *adj.* enigmático; escondido, oculto.

**cry.stal** *s.* cristal.

**cub** *s.* filhote de urso ou raposa; lobinho (escoteiro).

**Cu.ba** *s.* Cuba.

**cub.by.hole** *s.* cubículo; lugar pequeno e fechado.

**cube** *s.* cubo; terceira potência / *v.* elevar ao cubo.

**cube root** *s.* raiz cúbica.

**cu.bic** *adj.* cúbico.

**cu.bi.cle** *s.* cubículo; pequeno compartimento.

**cu.cum.ber** *s.* pepino.

**cud.dle** *s.* abraço / *v.* abraçar, afagar.

**cue** *s.* taco de bilhar; sugestão, dica / *v.* dar sugestão, dica.

**cuff** *s.* bainha de calça; punho de manga; tapa, soco; algema / *v.* esbofetear.

**cui.sine** *s.* cozinha.

**cull** *v.* selecionar; abater animais.

**cul.mi.na.tion** *s.* auge, clímax.

**cu.lottes** *s.* saia-calça.

**cul.prit** *s.* culpado(a), acusado(a).

**cult** *s.* culto, veneração; moda.
**cul.ti.vate** *v.* cultivar.
**cul.ti.va.tion** *s.* cultivo.
**cul.ture** *s.* cultura.
**cul.tured** *adj.* culto; refinado.
**cum.ber.some** *adj.* desajeitado; embaraçoso.
**cun.ning** *s.* astúcia / *adj.* engenhoso, astuto.
**cup** *s.* xícara.
**cup.board** *s.* armário, guarda-louça.
**cup.ped** *s.* em forma de xícara.
**cup tie** *s.* jogo eliminatório.
**cu.ra.tor** *s.* curador(a).
**curb** *v.* refrear, restringir / *s.* freio; restrição; meio-fio.
**curd** *s.* coalho, coágulo / *v.* coagular, coalhar.
**cur.dle** *v.* coalhar; engrossar; solidificar.
**cure** *s.* cura; remédio / *v.* curar, tratar; defumar.
**cure.less** *adj.* sem cura, incurável.
**cur.few** *s.* toque de recolher.
**cu.ri.ous** *adj.* curioso.
**curl** *s.* cacho; espiral / *v.* cachear, enrolar.
**curl.er** *s.* bobe de cabelos.
**curl.y** *adj.* cacheado, enrolado, ondulado.
**cur.rant** *s.* groselha; uva-passa.

**cur.ren.cy** *s.* moeda.
**cur.rent** *s.* corrente / *adj.* atual.
**cur.rent ac.count** *s.* conta corrente.
**cur.rent.ly** *adv.* atualmente.
**cur.ric.u.lum** *s.* programa de estudos; currículo.
**cur.ric.u.lum vi.tae** *s.* currículo, histórico profissional.
**curse** *s.* maldição, praga / *v.* xingar; amaldiçoar, rogar praga.
**curs.ed** *adj.* maldito, amaldiçoado.
**cur.sor** cursor (informática).
**cur.so.ry** *adj.* superficial, apressado.
**curt** *adj.* curto, áspero; breve.
**cur.tail** *v.* restringir; reduzir.
**cur.tain** *s.* cortina.
**curve** *s.* curva / *v.* fazer a curva.
**cush.ion** *v.* amortecer / *s.* almofada; amortecedor.
**cus.tard** *s.* creme (baunilha); manjar ou pudim.
**cus.to.di.an** *s.* guardião; depositário (museu, etc.).
**cus.to.dy** *s.* custódia, tutela.
**cus.tom** *s.* costume, hábito; clientela.
**cus.tom.a.ry** *adj.* costumeiro, habitual.
**cus.tom.er** *s.* cliente.

**customs** 190 **Czech**

**cus.toms** *s.* alfândega.

**cus.toms duty** *s.* imposto alfandegário.

**cut** *v.* cortar, reduzir. / *s.* corte, redução

**cute** *adj.* gracinha, atraente.

**cu.ti.cle** *s.* cutícula.

**cut.ler.y** *s.* talheres.

**cut.ter** *s.* cortador.

**cut.ting** *adj.* cortante, afiado; mordaz / *s.* recorte de jornal.

**cy.a.nide** *s.* cianeto, cianureto.

**cy.cle** *s.* ciclo; bicicleta / *v.* andar de bicicleta.

**cy.cling** *s.* ciclismo.

**cy.clist** *s.* ciclista.

**cyl.in.der** *s.* cilindro, tambor (gás).

**cyn.ic** *s.* cínico(a), cético.

**cyn.i.cal** *adj.* cínico, cético.

**cyn.i.cism** *s.* cinismo, ceticismo.

**cy.press** *s.* cipreste.

**Cy.prus** *s.* Chipre.

**cyst** *s.* cisto, quisto.

**cyst.i.tis** *s.* cistite.

**czar** *s.* czar.

**Czech** *adj.* checo / *s.* checo, idioma checo.

# Dd

**D, d** *s.* quarta letra do alfabeto inglês; ré (nota musical); representa o número 500 em algarismos romanos.

**dab** *v.* tocar de leve / *s.* toque; perito(a), experto(a).

**dab.ble** *v.* interessar-se em (coloquial); salpicar, borrifar.

**dad, dad.dy** *s.* papai.

**daft** *adj.* tolo, ridículo.

**dag.ger** *s.* punhal, adaga.

**dai.ly** *s.* jornal diário / *adj.* diário / *adv.* diariamente.

**dain.ty** *adj.* delicado, delicioso / *s.* gulodice.

**dair.y** *s.* leiteria; estabelecimento de laticínios.

**dai.ry prod.ucts** *s.* laticínios.

**da.is** *s.* estrado, plataforma.

**dai.sy** *s.* margarida.

**dale** *s.* vale.

**dam** *s.* represa, dique / *v.* represar.

**dam.age** *v.* danificar / *s.* prejuízo; dano.

**dame** *s.* dama, mulher.

**damn** *s.* maldição / *v.* condenar, amaldiçoar.

**damn.ing** *adj.* prejudicial, condenatório.

**damp** *s.* umidade / *adj.* úmido / *v.* umedecer.

**damp.en** *v.* umedecer.

**damp.ness** *s.* umidade.

**dam.sel** *s.* rapariga; donzela.

**dam.son** *s.* ameixa pequena e roxa.

**dance** *s.* dança / *v.* dançar; bailar.

**dan.cer** *s.* dançarino(a).

**danc.ing** *s.* dança / *adj.* dançante.

**dan.de.li.on** *s.* dente-de-leão (botânica).

**dan.druff** *s.* caspa.

**Dane** *s.* dinamarquês(esa).

**dan.ger** *s.* perigo, risco.

**dan.ger.ous** *adj.* perigoso, arriscado.

**dan.gle** *v.* balançar.

**Dan.ish** *adj.* dinamarquês(esa) / *s.* dinamarquês(esa).

**dap.per** *adj.* garboso; esperto.

**dare** *v.* atrever-se, ousar / *s.* desafio, ousadia.

**dare.dev.il** *s.* atrevido; valente / *adj.* valentão, atrevido.

**dar.ing** *s.* ousadia, audácia / *adj.* ousado, atrevido.

**dark** *adj.* escuro.

**dark.en** *v.* escurecer.

**dark.ness** *s.* escuridão; trevas.

**dark.room** *s.* câmara escura.

**dar.ling** *adj.* querido(a) / *s.* querido(a).

**darn** *v.* cerzir, remendar / *s.* remendo, cerzidura.

**dart** *s.* dardo / *v.* precipitar-se, jogar dardos.

**dart.board** *s.* jogo de dardos.

**dash** *s.* hífen; colisão; movimento rápido / *v.* arremessar, colidir.

**dash.board** *s.* painel de instrumentos.

**dash.ing** *adj.* arrojado, enérgico, vivo; elegante.

**da.ta** *s.* dados, informações, detalhes.

**da.ta.base** *s.* banco de dados.

**data pro.cess.ing** *s.* processamento de dados.

**date** *s.* data; encontro; tâmara / *v.* namorar.

**dat.ed** *adj.* antiquado, fora de moda; datado.

**daub** *s.* argamassa, barro / *v.* borrar; sujar.

**daugh.ter** *s.* filha.

**daugh.ter-in-law** *s.* nora.

**daunt** *v.* amedrontar, intimidar.

**daunt.ing** *adj.* desanimador(a).

**daunt.less** *adj.* destemido(a), corajoso(a).

**dawn** *v.* amanhecer / *s.* alvorada, amanhecer, madrugada.

**day** *s.* dia.

**day.break** *s.* romper do dia, aurora, alvorada.

**day-dream** *s.* devaneio.

**day.light** *s.* luz do dia.

**day.light-sav.ing time** *s.* horário de verão.

**daze** *s.* ofuscação / *v.* aturdir, ofuscar / *adj.* aturdido, confuso.

**daz.zle** *s.* deslumbramento, fascinação / *v.* deslumbrar, encantar.

dazzling 193 decode

**daz.zling** *s.* deslumbrante, fascinante, ofuscante.

**dead** *s.* defunto / *adj.* morto.

**dead.en** *v.* amortecer, abafar (som), aliviar (dor).

**dead end** *s.* beco sem saída.

**dead.line** *s.* prazo final; data limite.

**dead.ly** *adj.* fatal, mortal.

**deaf** *s.* surdo.

**deaf.en** *v.* ensurdecer.

**deaf.ness** *s.* surdez.

**deal** *s.* negócio; acordo, trato; quantidade / *v.* negociar; tratar; lidar.

**deal.er** *s.* negociante; vendedor; traficante (drogas, armas); carteador (cartas).

**dean** *s.* reitor(a); decano, deão.

**dear.ly** *adv.* ternamente; muito.

**death** *s.* morte.

**death-bed** *s.* leito de morte.

**death pen.al.ty** *s.* pena de morte.

**de.ba.cle** *s.* fracasso, derrota.

**de.base** *v.* degradar, humilhar.

**de.bauch** *s.* deboche; bacanal, devassidão.

**de.bauch.er.y** *s.* decadência, devassidão.

**deb.it** *s.* débito; dívida / *v.* debitar.

**de.bris** *s.* escombros.

**debt** *s.* dívida.

**de.bunk** *v.* desmascarar, desiludir.

**dé.but, de.but** *s.* estreia, debute; primeira tentativa.

**dec.ade** *s.* década.

**de.cant** *v.* decantar.

**de.cay** *s.* ruína; decadência; cárie / *v.* enfraquecer; decair; cariar.

**de.cease** *s.* morte, óbito.

**de.ceive** *v.* enganar, iludir.

**De.cem.ber** *s.* dezembro.

**de.cent** *adj.* decente, honesto, apropriado.

**de.cep.tion** *s.* engano, fraude, trapaça.

**de.cep.tive** *adj.* enganoso, ilusório.

**de.cide** *v.* decidir, resolver; julgar.

**de.cid.ed** *adj.* decidido, resolvido.

**de.cid.ed.ly** *adv.* decididamente, resolutamente.

**dec.i.mal** *s.* decimal / *adj.* decimal.

**de.ci.sion** *s.* decisão, resolução.

**de.ci.sive** *adj.* decisivo.

**deck** *s.* convés, deque.

**deck.chair** *s.* espreguiçadeira.

**dec.la.ra.tion** *s.* declaração; depoimento.

**de.clare** *v.* declarar.

**de.cline** *s.* declínio, decadência / *v.* recusar, declinar.

**de.code** *v.* decifrar.

D

**de.com.pose** *v.* decompor(-se); apodrecer.

**de.cor** *s.* decoração, cenário.

**dec.o.rate** *v.* decorar.

**dec.o.ra.tion** *s.* decoração.

**dec.o.ra.tive** *adj.* decorativo.

**dec.o.ra.tor** *s.* decorador(a).

**de.co.rum** *s.* decoro, decência.

**de.coy** *s.* chamariz, isca, engodo.

**de.crease** *s.* decréscimo; diminuição, redução / *v.* diminuir, reduzir.

**de.cree** *s.* decreto / *v.* decretar.

**ded.i.cate** *v.* dedicar, consagrar.

**ded.i.ca.tion** *s.* dedicação, dedicatória.

**de.duce** *v.* deduzir, inferir.

**de.duc.tion** *s.* dedução.

**deed** *s.* escritura; ação, obra.

**deem** *v.* estimar; considerar; julgar; crer.

**deep** *adj.* profundo, fundo / *s.* profundidade.

**deep.en** *v.* aprofundar.

**deep.ly** *adv.* profundamente.

**deer** *s.* veado, cervo.

**deer-skin** *s.* camurça.

**de.face** *v.* desfigurar, deformar.

**de.fault** *s.* falta; revelia; descumprimento / *v.* faltar a alguma obrigação.

**de.feat** *s.* derrota, frustração / *v.* derrotar, frustrar.

**de.fect** *s.* defeito / *v.* desertar.

**de.fec.tive** *adj.* defeituoso.

**de.fend** *v.* defender, proteger.

**de.fend.er** *s.* defensor(a); advogado de defesa.

**de.fense** *s.* defesa, proteção.

**de.fense.less** *adj.* indefeso, desprotegido.

**de.fen.sive** *adj.* defensivo / *s.* defensiva.

**de.fer** *v.* adiar, protelar; submeter-se, condescender.

**de.fi.ance** *s.* desafio, rebeldia.

**de.fi.ant** *adj.* desafiador(a).

**de.fi.cien.cy** *s.* deficiência.

**def.i.cit** *s.* déficit.

**de.file** *s.* desfiladeiro, passagem estreita / *v.* profanar; desonrar; corromper.

**de.fine** *v.* definir, explicar.

**def.i.nite** *adj.* definitivo.

**def.i.nite.ly** *adv.* sem dúvida, definitivamente.

**de.fin.i.tive** *adj.* conclusivo; definido.

**de.flate** *v.* esvaziar, desinflar; deflacionar.

**de.fla.tion** *s.* esvaziamento; deflação.

**de.flect** *v.* desviar.

**de.for.est** *v.* desflorestar, desmatar.

**deform** v. deformar, desfigurar.
**de.for.mi.ty** s. deformidade, deformação.
**de.fraud** v. trapacear, defraudar.
**de.fray** v. custear.
**de.frost** v. descongelar, degelar.
**deft** adj. destro; esperto, hábil.
**de.funct** adj. extinto, morto.
**de.fuse** v. neutralizar; desarmar, dasativar.
**de.fy** v. desafiar, provocar.
**de.gen.er.ate** v. degenerar / adj. degenerado(a), corrompido(a).
**de.gree** s. grau; estágio, classe; diploma.
**de.hy.dra.ted** adj. desidratado.
**de.ice** v. descongelar, remover o gelo.
**de.i.ty** s. divindade, deidade.
**de.ject** v. abater, desanimar.
**de.ject.ed** adj. deprimido, desanimado.
**de.lay** s. demora, atraso / v. atrasar, demorar, retardar.
**de.lec.ta.ble** adj. gostoso, deleitável.
**del.e.gate** s. delegado(a), representante / v. delegar, encarregar.
**del.e.ga.tion** s. delegação.
**de.lete** v. eliminar; deletar (informática); apagar, excluir.

**de.lib.er.ate** v. deliberar / adj. deliberado, intencional.
**de.lib.er.ate.ly** adv. propositalmente.
**del.i.ca.cy** s. delicadeza, iguaria.
**del.i.cate** adj. delicado(a); frágil; diplomático.
**del.i.ca.tes.sen** s. guloseimas; casa de mercearias finas.
**de.li.cious** adj. delicioso, gostoso.
**de.light** s. prazer, deleite, encanto / v. encantar, deleitar.
**de.light.ed** adj. encantado(a).
**de.light.ful** adj. encantador(a).
**de.lin.quent** s. delinquente / adj. delinquente.
**de.lir.i.ous** adj. delirante.
**de.liv.er** v. entregar.
**de.liv.er.ance** s. libertação, livramento.
**de.liv.er.y** s. entrega; parto.
**de.lude** v. iludir.
**del.uge** s. dilúvio / v. inundar.
**de.lu.sion** s. ilusão, desilusão.
**de.mand** s. demanda / v. demandar, perguntar; exigir.
**de.mand.ing** adj. exigente.
**de.mean** v. rebaixar, humilhar.
**de.mean.or** s. conduta, comportamento.
**de.men.ted** adj. demente, louco.
**de.mise** s. falecimento, morte.

# demister · 196 · depressing

**de.mister** *s.* desembaçador de para-brisa.

**demo** *s.* manifestação, passeata, demonstração (coloquial).

**de.moc.ra.cy** *s.* democracia.

**dem.o.crat** *s.* democrata.

**dem.o.crat.ic** *adj.* democrático(a).

**de.mol.ish** *v.* demolir.

**dem.on.strate** *v.* demonstrar.

**dem.on.stra.tion** *s.* demonstração, manifestação.

**dem.on.stra.tor** *s.* manifestante, demonstrador(a).

**de.mor.al.** *v.* desmoralizar.

**de.mote** *v.* degradar, rebaixar de graus.

**de.mure** *adj.* recatado; acanhado.

**den** *s.* covil; espelunca.

**de.ni.al** *s.* negação, recusa.

**den.im** *s.* brim.

**Den.mark** *s.* Dinamarca.

**de.nom.i.na.tion** *s.* denominação.

**de.nounce** *v.* denunciar, delatar.

**dense** *adj.* denso; estúpido (coloquial).

**dense.ly** *adv.* densamente.

**den.si.ty** *s.* densidade.

**dent** *s.* entalhe; dente (de engrenagem, roda, pente) / *v.* dentear.

**den.tal** *adj.* dentário, dental.

**den.tist** *s.* dentista.

**den.tis.try** *s.* odontologia.

**den.tures** *s.* dentadura.

**de.ny** *v.* recusar, negar.

**de.o.dor.ant** *s.* desodorante.

**de.part** *v.* partir, sair.

**de.part.ment** *s.* departamento, seção.

**de.part.ment store** *s.* magazine, loja de departamentos.

**de.par.ture** *s.* partida, saída.

**de.pend** *v.* depender.

**de.pend on** *v.* depender de.

**de.pend.a.ble** *adj.* confiável.

**de.pend.ant** *s.* dependente.

**de.pict** *v.* retratar; pintar.

**de.plet.ed** *adj.* reduzido(a).

**de.ploy** *v.* dispor; desenrolar-se, estender-se.

**de.pop.u.lation** *s.* despovoamento.

**de.port** *v.* deportar, exilar.

**de.port.ment** *s.* comportamento, conduta.

**de.pose** *v.* depor, destituir.

**de.pos.it** *v.* depositar / *s.* depósito, fiança.

**de.pot** *s.* estação, terminal; armazém, depósito.

**de.prave** *v.* depravar, perverter.

**de.pre.ci.ate** *v.* depreciar-se.

**de.press** *v.* deprimir; humilhar.

**de.pressed** *adj.* deprimido(a).

**de.press.ing** *adj.* deprimente, depressivo(a).

depression 197 detached

**de.pres.sion** *s.* depressão.
**dep.ri.va.tion** *s.* privação; pobreza.
**de.prive** *v.* privar; destituir.
**de.prived** *adj.* carente, necessitado(a).
**depth** *s.* profundidade, profundeza; fundo.
**dep.u.ta.tion** *s.* delegação.
**dep.u.ty** *s.* deputado(a), representante.
**de.rail** *v.* descarrilar.
**de.rail.ment** *s.* descarrilamento.
**de.ranged** *adj.* transtornado(a), desordenado(a), louco(a).
**der.e.lict** *adj.* abandonado(a).
**de.rive** *v.* derivar, originar.
**der.rick** *s.* guindaste.
**de.scend.ant** *s.* descendente.
**de.scribe** *v.* descrever.
**de.scrip.tion** *s.* descrição.
**de.scrip.tive** *adj.* descritivo(a).
**des.e.crate** *v.* profanar, violar.
**de.sert** *v.* desertar / *s.* deserto.
**de.sert.er** *s.* desertor.
**de.serve** *v.* merecer.
**de.serv.ing** *adj.* digno(a).
**de.sign** *v.* projetar; desenhar / *s.* desenho; projeto; esboço.
**des.ig.nate** *v.* nomear, designar / *adj.* designado(a), nomeado(a).
**de.sign.er** *s.* artista gráfico; estilista; projetista.

**de.sire** *s.* desejo / *v.* desejar, cobiçar.
**desk** *s.* mesa, escrivaninha, carteira escolar; balcão.
**des.o.late** *adj.* deserto(a); desolado(a), triste / *v.* desolar.
**de.spair** *s.* desesperança; desespero / *v.* desesperar-se.
**des.per.ate** *adj.* desesperado, desesperador; sem esperança.
**des.per.ate.ly** *adv.* desesperadamente.
**des.per.a.tion** *s.* desespero.
**des.pi.ca.ble** *adj.* vil, desprezível.
**de.spise** *v.* desprezar.
**de.spite** *prep.* apesar de.
**de.spond** *v.* desesperar, desanimar.
**de.spon.dent** *adj.* desanimado(a), desesperado(a).
**des.sert** *s.* sobremesa.
**des.ti.na.tion** *s.* destino, destinação.
**des.tined** *adj.* destinado.
**des.ti.ny** *s.* destino; sorte.
**des.ti.tu.te** *adj.* necessitado(a); destituído(a); indigente.
**de.stroy** *v.* destruir.
**de.struc.tion** *s.* destruição.
**de.tach** *v.* separar.
**de.tach.ed** *adj.* imparcial; isolado, separado.

**D**

**detachment** | **198** | **diameter**

**de.tach.ment** *s.* distanciamento, afastamento; imparcialidade.

**de.tail** *s.* detalhe / *v.* detalhar.

**de.tain** *v.* deter.

**de.tect** *v.* perceber, detectar.

**de.tec.tion** *s.* descoberta, detecção.

**de.tec.tive** *s.* detetive, investigador.

**de.ten.tion** *s.* prisão, detenção, retenção.

**de.ter** *v.* dissuadir; intimidar.

**de.ter.gent** *s.* detergente.

**de.te.ri.o.rate** *v.* deteriorar-se, estragar.

**de.ter.mine** *v.* demarcar; determinar; decidir.

**de.ter.mined** *adj.* resoluto(a), determinado(a).

**de.test** *v.* detestar, abominar.

**det.o.nate** *v.* detonar, explodir.

**det.o.na.tor** *s.* detonador.

**de.tour** *s.* desvio.

**det.ri.men.tal** *adj.* prejudicial, danoso(a).

**de.val.ue** *v.* desvalorizar.

**dev.as.tate** *v.* devastar, arruinar.

**de.vel.op** *v.* desenvolver, progredir; elaborar; revelar.

**de.vel.op.ment** *s.* desenvolvimento, evolução; revelação.

**de.vice** *s.* aparelho, dispositivo, mecanismo.

**dev.il** *s.* diabo, demônio.

**dev.il.ish** *adj.* diabólico(a), maligno(a).

**de.vi.ous** *adj.* malandro(a), desonesto(a); tortuoso(a).

**de.vise** *v.* inventar; imaginar.

**de.vo.lu.tion** *s.* devolução, restituição.

**de.vote** *v.* devotar-se, dedicar.

**dev.o.tee** *s.* adepto(a); devoto(a); fã.

**de.vo.tion** *s.* devoção.

**de.vour** *v.* devorar.

**de.vout** *adj.* devoto; sincero, dedicado.

**dew** *s.* orvalho; sereno.

**dew.drop** *s.* gota de orvalho.

**dex.ter.i.ty** *s.* destreza, aptidão, habilidade.

**di.a.be.tes** *s.* diabetes, diabete.

**di.a.bol.i.cal** *adj.* horrível, diabólico(a).

**di.ag.no.sis** *s.* diagnóstico.

**di.ag.o.nal** *s.* diagonal / *adj.* diagonal.

**di.a.gram** *s.* diagrama.

**di.al** *s.* mostrador, indicador; disco / *v.* discar.

**di.a.lect** *s.* dialeto.

**di.al.ling code** *s.* código de área.

**di.a.logue** *s.* diálogo / *v.* dialogar.

**di.am.e.ter** *s.* diâmetro.

**di.a.mond** *s.* diamante; brilhante; losango.

**di.a.phragm** *s.* diafragma.

**di.ar.rhea** *s.* diarreia.

**di.a.ry** *s.* diário; agenda.

**dice** *s.* jogo de dados; dado / *v.* cortar em cubos.

**dic.tate** *v.* ditar; dar ordens.

**dic.ta.tion** *s.* ditado; ordem.

**dic.ta.tor** *s.* ditador(a).

**dic.ta.tor.ship** *s.* ditadura.

**did** *v. pret.* do *v. to do*.

**didn't** contração de *did not*.

**die** *v.* morrer; dado.

**die.sel** *s.* diesel.

**di.et** *s.* regime; dieta.

**dif.fer** *v.* discordar, divergir.

**dif.fer.ence** *s.* diferença.

**dif.fer.ent** *adj.* diferente, distinto.

**dif.fer.en.tly** *adv.* diferentemente, diversamente.

**dif.fi.cult** *adj.* difícil.

**dif.fi.cul.ty** *s.* dificuldade.

**dif.fuse** *v.* difundir.

**dif.fusion** *s.* difusão, propagação; dispersão.

**dig** *v.* cavar / *s.* escavação.

**di.gest** *s.* digesto; resumo / *v.* digerir.

**di.gest.i.ble** *adj.* digestível.

**di.ges.tion** *s.* digestão.

**di.ges.tive** *adj.* digestivo.

**dig.it** *s.* dígito.

**dig.i.tal** *adj.* digital.

**dig.ni.fied** *adj.* digno, honrado, nobre.

**dig.ni.fy** *v.* dignificar.

**dig.ni.ty** *s.* dignidade; decência.

**digs** *s.* pensão, alojamento, aposento.

**di.gress** *v.* divagar.

**dike** *s.* dique, barragem.

**di.lap.i.dat.ed** *adj.* arruinado.

**di.late** *v.* dilatar(-se).

**di.lem.ma** *s.* dilema.

**dil.i.gent** *adj.* diligente.

**di.lute** *v.* diluir.

**dim** *v.* ofuscar / *adj.* escuro; ofuscado(a).

**dime** *s.* moeda de dez centavos.

**di.men.sion** *s.* dimensão; tamanho; medida.

**di.min.ish** *v.* diminuir.

**di.min.u.tive** *s.* diminutivo / *adj.* diminutivo, diminuto.

**dim.mer** *s.* regulador para iluminação.

**dim.ness** *s.* obscuridade.

**dim.ple** *s.* covinha no rosto.

**din** *s.* alarido (de gente); barulhada (de máquinas).

**di.ne** *v.* jantar.

**din.er** *s.* aquele que janta; vagão restaurante.

**dinette** *s.* pequena sala de jantar.
**ding.y** *adj.* sujo(a); desbotado(a).
**dining room** *s.* sala de jantar.
**dinner** *s.* jantar; ceia.
**dip** *s.* mergulho / *v.* mergulhar; molhar.
**diph.tong** *s.* ditongo.
**di.plo.ma** *s.* diploma.
**dip.lo.mat** *s.* diplomata.
**dip.switch** *s.* interruptor.
**dire** *adj.* terrível, fatal.
**di.rect** *adj.* direto; franco / *v.* dirigir; conduzir.
**di.rec.tion** *s.* direção, sentido ♦ ~s instruções.
**di.rect.ly** *adv.* diretamente.
**di.rec.tor** *s.* diretor(a).
**dir.i.gi.ble** *s.* dirigível / *adj.* dirigível.
**dirt** *s.* sujeira.
**dirti.ness** *s.* porcaria; sujidade.
**dirt.y** *adj.* sujo / *v.* sujar.
**dis.a.bil.i.ty** *s.* incapacidade; deficiência.
**dis.a.bled** *adj.* inválido, incapacitado.
**dis.ad.van.tage** *s.* desvantagem.
**dis.af.fec.tion** *s.* desafeição, desamor, inimizade.
**dis.a.gree** *v.* discordar.
**dis.a.gree.a.ble** *adj.* desagradável.
**dis.a.gree.ment** *s.* desacordo, discordância, divergência.

**dis.ap.pear** *v.* desaparecer.
**dis.ap.pear.ance** *s.* desaparecimento.
**dis.ap.point** *v.* decepcionar, desapontar.
**dis.ap.point.ment** *s.* desapontamento, decepção.
**dis.ap.prov.al** *s.* desaprovação.
**dis.ap.prove** *v.* desaprovar, reprovar.
**dis.arm** *v.* desarmar(-se).
**dis.ar.ma.ment** *s.* desarmamento.
**dis.ar.ray** *s.* desordem; confusão.
**dis.as.ter** *s.* desastre, calamidade.
**dis.band** *v.* dispersar.
**dis.be.lief** *s.* descrença.
**disc, disk** *s.* disco.
**dis.card** *v.* descartar.
**dis.cern** *v.* identificar; discernir.
**dis.cern.ing** *adj.* perspicaz, discernente.
**dis.charge** *v.* dispensar, descarregar / *s.* descarga; dispensa.
**dis.ci.ple** *s.* discípulo(a).
**dis.ci.pline** *s.* disciplina / *v.* disciplinar.
**disc jockey** *s.* radialista; disc-jóquei.
**dis.claim** *v.* negar.
**dis.close** *v.* revelar; descobrir.
**dis.clo.sure** *s.* revelação.
**disco** *s.* discoteca.

discolored 201 disjointed

**dis.col.or.ed** *adj.* descolorado, desbotado.

**dis.com.fort** *s.* desconforto, incômodo.

**dis.con.cert** *v.* desconcertar.

**dis.con.nect** *v.* desligar, desconectar.

**dis.con.tent** *s.* descontentamento.

**dis.con.tent.ed** *adj.* descontente.

**dis.con.tin.ue** *v.* interromper.

**dis.cord** *s.* discórdia, desarmonia / *v.* discordar.

**dis.count** *s.* desconto / *v.* descontar.

**dis.cour.age** *v.* desanimar, desencorajar.

**dis.cov.er** *v.* descobrir.

**dis.cov.er.y** *s.* descoberta, descobrimento.

**dis.cred.it** *v.* desacreditar; desabonar / *s.* descrédito.

**dis.creet** *adj.* discreto.

**dis.crep.an.cy** *s.* discrepância.

**dis.cre.tion** *s.* discrição.

**dis.crim.i.nate** *v.* discriminar.

**dis.crim.i.nat.ing** *adj.* criterioso(a); perspicaz; discriminador(a).

**dis.crim.i.na.tion** *s.* discriminação.

**dis.cuss** *v.* discutir, tratar de um assunto.

**dis.cus.sion** *s.* discussão, debate.

**dis.dain** *s.* desdém / *v.* desdenhar.

**dis.ease** *s.* doença, enfermidade.

**dis.em.bark** *v.* desembarcar.

**dis.fig.ure** *v.* desfigurar.

**dis.grace** *s.* desgraça, vergonha, desonra / *v.* desonrar, desgraçar.

**dis.grace.ful** *adj.* vergonhoso(a), infame.

**dis.grun.tled** *adj.* descontente, desapontado(a).

**dis.guise** *s.* disfarce; máscara / *v.* disfarçar, mascarar.

**dis.gust** *s.* repugnância / *v.* repugnar.

**dis.gust.ing** *adj.* repugnante; desgostoso(a).

**dish** *s.* prato, travessa; iguaria.

**di.shev.eled** *adj.* despenteado(a); desalinhado(a).

**dis.hon.est** *adj.* desonesto(a).

**dis.hon.or** *s.* desonra / *v.* desonrar.

**dis.hon.or.a.ble** *adj.* desonroso.

**dish.tow.el** *s.* pano de prato.

**dish.wash.er** *s.* máquina de lavar louças.

**dis.il.lu.sion** *v.* desiludir / *s.* desilusão.

**dis.in.fec.tant** *s.* desinfetante.

**dis.in.te.grate** *v.* desintegrar.

**dis.joint.ed** *adj.* desconexo(a), deslocado(a).

D

**disk** *s.* disco; disquete (coloquial).

**disk drive** *s.* unidade de disco (informática).

**dis.kette** *s.* disquete (informática).

**dis.like** *s.* aversão, antipatia; desagrado / *v.* antipatizar.

**dis.lo.cate** *v.* deslocar.

**dis.lodge** *v.* desalojar.

**dis.loy.al** *adj.* desleal, infiel.

**dis.mal** *adj.* deprimente, triste, sombrio.

**dis.man.tle** *v.* desmontar.

**dis.may** *s.* desânimo / *v.* consternar.

**dis.miss** *v.* demitir; despedir.

**dis.miss.al** *s.* demissão.

**dis.mount** *v.* desmontar.

**dis.o.be.di.ent** *adj.* desobediente.

**dis.o.bey** *v.* desobedecer.

**dis.or.der** *s.* desordem.

**dis.or.der.ly** *adj.* desordenado, confuso / *adv.* desordenadamente.

**dis.own** *v.* repudiar; desconhecer; negar.

**dis.par.ag.ing** *adj.* depreciativo.

**dis.pa.rate** *adj.* desigual, diferente / *s.* disparate.

**dis.par.i.ty** *s.* desigualdade, disparidade.

**dis.pas.sion.ate** *adj.* imparcial, impassível, controlado.

**dis.patch** *s.* despacho; remessa / *v.* enviar.

**dis.pel** *v.* dissipar; dispersar.

**dis.pense** *v.* dispensar, atribuir, conceder.

**dis.pens.er** *s.* distribuidor automático, dispensador.

**dis.perse** *v.* dispersar, disseminar.

**dis.pir.it.ed** *adj.* desanimado, deprimido.

**dis.place** *v.* deslocar, substituir.

**dis.play** *s.* exibição / *v.* mostrar; exibir.

**dis.please** *v.* ofender; desagradar.

**dis.pleas.ure** *s.* desgosto, desprazer; aborrecimento.

**dis.pos.a.ble** *adj.* descartável, disponível.

**dis.pos.al** *s.* venda, uso; disposição, disponibilidade.

**dis.pose** *v.* dispor, arranjar, ordenar.

**dis.posed** *adj.* disposto; preparado.

**dis.po.si.tion** *s.* disposição; temperamento.

**dis.prove** *v.* refutar; contestar.

**dis.pute** *v.* questionar / *s.* disputa.

**dis.qual.i.fy** *v.* desqualificar.

**dis.re.gard** *v.* ignorar, desconsidcrar / *s.* desconsideração, indiferença.

**dis.re.spect** *s.* desrespeito, desconsideração / *v.* desrespeitar.

**dis.rupt** *v.* perturbar, interromper.

**dis.rupt.ion** *s.* interrupção, rompimento.

**dis.sat.is.fac.tion** *s.* descontentamento.

**dis.sat.is.fy** *v.* descontentar.

**dis.sect** *v.* dissecar.

**dis.sem.ble** *v.* dissimular.

**dis.ser.ta.tion** *s.* dissertação.

**dis.sim.i.lar** *adj.* diferente.

**dis.sim.u.late** *v.* dissimular, fingir.

**dis.si.pate** *v.* dissipar.

**dis.solve** *v.* dissolver.

**dis.suade** *v.* dissuadir.

**dis.taff** *s.* fuso para fiar.

**dis.tance** *s.* distância.

**dis.tant** *adj.* distante.

**dis.taste** *s.* desagrado; aversão.

**dis.taste.ful** *adj.* repugnante, desagradável.

**dis.tend** *v.* estender-se, expandir, alargar.

**dis.tend.ed** *adj.* inchado, distendido.

**dis.til** *v.* destilar.

**dis.til.le.ry** *s.* destilaria.

**dis.tinct** *adj.* distinto.

**dis.tinc.tion** *s.* distinção.

**dis.tin.guish** *v.* distinguir.

**dis.tin.guished** *adj.* distinto(a); famoso(a).

**dis.tort** *v.* distorcer; torcer; corromper.

**dis.tract** *v.* distrair.

**dis.tract.ed** *adj.* distraído.

**dis.trac.tion** *s.* distração.

**dis.tress** *s.* aflição; angustia / *v.* afligir.

**dis.tress.ing** *adj.* angustiante, penoso.

**dis.trib.ute** *v.* distribuir.

**dis.tri.bu.tion** *s.* distribuição.

**dis.trict** *s.* distrito, bairro.

**dis.trust** *s.* desconfiança / *v.* desconfiar.

**dis.turb** *v.* perturbar, incomodar.

**dis.turb.ance** *s.* distúrbio, perturbação.

**dis.turbed** *adj.* perturbado.

**dis.turb.ing** *adj.* perturbador, inquietante.

**dis.used** *adj.* abandonado(a), fora de uso.

**ditch** *v.* abandonar, livrar-se de / *s.* fosso, vala.

**dith.er** *v.* vacilar (coloquial).

**dit.to** *s.* idem, o mesmo.

**di.van** *s.* divã.

**dive** *s.* mergulho / *v.* mergulhar.

**div.er** *s.* mergulhador.

**di.vers** *adj.* diversos, vários.

**di.verse** *adj.* diverso(a), diversificado(a).

# diversify — 204 — donut

**di.ver.si.fy** *v.* diversificar.

**di.ver.sion** *s.* diversão, distração; desvio.

**di.ver.si.ty** *s.* diversidade.

**di.vert** *v.* desviar; distrair.

**di.vide** *v.* dividir, repartir.

**di.vine** *adj.* divino(a).

**div.ing** *s.* salto ornamental, mergulho.

**div.ing board** *s.* trampolim.

**di.vin.i.ty** *s.* divindade.

**di.vi.sion** *s.* divisão; seção, departamento.

**di.vor.cée** *s.* divorciada.

**di.vorce** *s.* divórcio / *v.* divorciar-se de.

**divorcé** *s.* divorciado.

**di.vorced** *adj.* divorciado.

**DIY** *abrev.* de *do-it-yourself*.

**diz.zy** *adj.* tonto(a), atordoado(a) / *v.* causar desmaios; atordoar.

**dj** *abrev.* de *disc jockey*.

**do** *v.* fazer, executar.

**do.cile** *adj.* dócil.

**dock** *s.* doca, embarcadouro / *v.* atracar (navios).

**dock.er** *s.* estivador.

**dock.yard** *s.* estaleiro.

**doc.tor** *s.* doutor(a), médico(a).

**doc.trine** *s.* doutrina.

**doc.u.ment** *s.* documento / *v.* documentar.

**doc.u.men.ta.ry** *adj.* documentário / *s.* documentário (filme).

**doe** *s.* coelha; corça.

**dog** *s.* cachorro, cão / *v.* perseguir.

**doings** *s.* atividades; ações.

**do-it-your.self** *s.* faça você mesmo.

**dole.ful** *adj.* triste; doloroso.

**doll** *s.* boneca / *adj.* mulher bonita, mas pouco inteligente.

**dol.lar** *s.* dólar.

**doll up** *v.* embonecar-se (coloquial).

**dol.phin** *s.* golfinho.

**do.main** *s.* domínio, propriedade.

**dome** *s.* cúpula, abóbada.

**do.mes.tic** *adj.* doméstico, caseiro; nacional, interno.

**do.mes.ti.cated** *adj.* domesticado(a).

**dom.i.nate** *v.* dominar.

**dom.i.neer.ing** *adj.* mandão(ona), dominador(a).

**do.min.ion** *s.* domínio, poder absoluto.

**dom.i.noes** *s.* jogo de dominó.

**do.nate** *v.* doar, contribuir.

**done** *v. pp.* do *v. to do* / *adj.* completo, pronto.

**don.key** *s.* burro, asno.

**do.nor** *s.* doador(a).

**donut** *s.* sonho (doce).

**don't** contração de *do not*.

**doom** *s.* julgamento; sentença; perdição / *v.* condenar.

**dooms.day** *s.* dia do julgamento final.

**door** *s.* porta; acesso.

**door.bell** *s.* campainha de porta.

**door-handle** *s.* maçaneta de porta.

**door-mat** *s.* capacho.

**dope** *s.* narcótico, droga / *v.* dopar, drogar.

**dop-fiend** *s.* viciado em narcóticos.

**dor.mant** *adj.* inativo, latente.

**dor.mi.to.ry** *s.* dormitório; alojamento estudantil.

**dos.age** *s.* dosagem, dose.

**dose** *s.* dose / *v.* dosar.

**dot** *s.* ponto / *v.* pontilhar.

**dote** *v.* adorar.

**dotted line** *s.* linha pontilhada.

**dou.ble** *adj.* duplo; dobro / *v.* dobrar / *s.* duplo, dobro; cópia; dublê.

**doubly** *adv.* duplamente.

**doubt** *s.* dúvida / *v.* duvidar, hesitar.

**doubt.ful** *adj.* duvidoso, incerto.

**doubt.less** *adv.* sem dúvida.

**douse** *v.* encharcar, ensopar.

**dove** *s.* pomba.

**dow.dy** *adj.* deselegante, desleixado.

**down** *s.* penugem, penas; buço / *adv.* para baixo.

**down.stairs** *adv.* embaixo, para baixo / *s.* andar térreo / *adj.* de baixo.

**down.stream** *adj.* rio abaixo.

**down.town** *s.* centro da cidade.

**dow.ry** *s.* dote.

**doze** *s.* soneca / *v.* cochilar.

**doz.en** *s.* dúzia.

**drab** *adj.* monótono, sem graça.

**draft** *s.* rascunho, esboço; saque; corrente de ar / *v.* rascunhar, esboçar.

**drag** *s.* peso, chato (coloquial) / *v.* arrastar-se.

**drag.on** *s.* dragão.

**drag.on.fly** *s.* libélula.

**drain** *s.* dreno; bueiro / *v.* drenar; escoar; enfraquecer, esvair.

**drain.age** *s.* drenagem.

**drain.pipe** *s.* cano de esgoto.

**drake** *s.* pato; marreco.

**dra.ma** *s.* drama; peça de teatro.

**drank** *v. pret.* do *v. to drink*.

**drape** *s.* cortina; cortinado / *v.* ornar; cobrir.

**dras.tic** *adj.* drástico; grave.

**draw** *v.* desenhar, traçar; empatar / *s.* empate.

**draw.er** *s.* gaveta.

**draw.ing** *s.* desenho; sorteio; saque.

**dread** *s.* terror / *v.* temer.
**dread.ful** *adj.* terrível, horrível.
**dream** *s.* sonho / *v.* sonhar.
**dream.y** *adj.* sonhador(a).
**drear.y** *adj.* monótono(a); lúgubre.
**dredge** *v.* dragar / *s.* draga.
**dregs** *s.* escória, resíduos; ralé.
**drench** *s.* remédio líquido / *v.* encharcar.
**dress** *v.* vestir; temperar / *s.* vestido.
**dress.ing** *s.* ação de vestir-se; tempero, condimento.
**dress.ing-down** *s.* surra; correção.
**dress.ing gown** *s.* roupão.
**dress.mak.er** *s.* costureira.
**dress.y** *adj.* chique.
**drew** *v. pret.* do *v.* to draw.
**drib.ble** *v.* driblar; babar / *s.* baba, saliva; drible (futebol).
**dried** *adj.* seco / *v. pret.* e *pp.* do *v.* to dry.
**drift** *v.* derivar, ir à deriva / *s.* vento; correnteza.
**drill** *v.* furar / *s.* furadeira; broca.
**drink** *s.* bebida / *v.* beber.
**drink.ing wa.ter** *s.* água potável.
**drip** *s.* gota, gotejamento / *v.* pingar, gotejar.
**drip.ping** *s.* gordura, banha; gotejamento / *adj.* gorduroso, encharcado.

**drive** *s.* passeio de carro / *v.* dirigir.
**driv.el** *s.* bobagem, disparate; baba; saliva.
**driv.en** *v. pp.* do *v.* to drive.
**driv.er** *s.* motorista.
**driv.ing** *s.* direção.
**driv.ing li.cence** *s.* carteira de motorista.
**driv.ing mirror** *s.* retrovisor.
**driv.ing school** *s.* autoescola.
**driz.zle** *s.* chuvisco, garoa / *v.* garoar.
**drone** *s.* zangão; zumbido / *v.* zunir, zumbir.
**droop** *s.* inclinação, abatimento / *v.* inclinar-se, pender; desanimar.
**droop.ing** *s.* tristeza; gotejamento / *adj.* gotejante.
**drop** *s.* gota, pingo / *v.* cair.
**drop-off** *s.* decadência.
**drop.per** *s.* conta-gotas.
**drought** *s.* seca.
**drove** *v. pret.* do *v.* to drive.
**drown** *v.* afogar-se.
**drowse** *s.* sonolência, soneca / *v.* cochilar, dormitar.
**drow.sy** *adj.* sonolento(a).
**drug** *s.* remédio; droga / *v.* drogar; ingerir drogas.
**drug-ad.dict** *s.* viciado(a) em drogas.

**drug.gist** *s.* farmacêutico(a).

**drug.store** *s.* drogaria; farmácia.

**drum** *s.* tambor, bateria; tímpano / *v.* rufar, tocar tambor.

**drum.mer** *s.* baterista.

**drunk** *adj.* bêbado(a) / *v. pp.* do *v. to drink*.

**drunk.ard** *s.* bêbado(a), ébrio.

**drunk.en** *adj.* bêbado(a), embriagado(a).

**drunk.en.ness** *s.* bebedeira; embriaguez.

**dry** *v.* secar / *adj.* seco; árido.

**dry clean.ing** *s.* lavagem a seco.

**dry.er** *s.* secador.

**dry.ness** *s.* secura, aridez; ironia.

**dry-nurse** *s.* ama-seca, aia.

**du.al** *adj.* duplo.

**dubbed** *adj.* dublado.

**du.bi.ous** *adj.* duvidoso, incerto.

**duch.ess** *s.* duquesa.

**duck** *s.* pato(a).

**duck.ling** *s.* filhote de pato.

**duct** *s.* ducto, canal, tubo.

**due** *s.* dívida / *adj.* devido.

**du.el** *s.* duelo.

**du.et** *s.* dueto, duo.

**duf.fel bag** *s.* mochila, saco de pano grosso.

**dug** *v. pret.* e *pp.* do *v. to dig*.

**duke** *s.* duque.

**dull** *adj.* enfadonho, monótono; nublado (tempo).

**dul.ly** *adv.* desanimadamente.

**du.ly** *adv.* devidamente; no tempo devido.

**dum.my** *s.* manequim; imbecil (coloquial); testa de ferro.

**dump** *s.* espelunca; depósito de lixo / *v.* esvaziar, despejar.

**dump.y** *adj.* gorducho(a), rechonchudo(a).

**dunce** *s.* estúpido, bronco.

**dune** *s.* duna.

**dung** *s.* estrume, esterco.

**dun.ga.rees** *s.* macacão, jardineira.

**dupe** *s.* incauto, ingênuo / *v.* enganar.

**du.plex** *s.* casa geminada / *adj.* duplex, duplo.

**du.pli.cate** *s.* duplicata, réplica / *v.* duplicar, copiar / *adj.* duplicado.

**du.plic.i.ty** *s.* duplicidade; fingimento, fraude.

**du.ra.ble** *adj.* durável, duradouro.

**dur.ing** *prep.* durante.

**dust** *s.* poeira, pó / *v.* tirar o pó.

**dust.y** *adj.* empoeirado.

**Dutch** *adj.* holandês(esa) / *s.* língua holandesa ♦ *the* ~ o povo holandês.

**du.ti.ful** *adj.* respeitoso, obediente.

**du.ty** *s.* dever, obrigação; taxa, imposto; tarefa, função.

**dwarf** *s.* anão(ã).

**dwell** *v.* morar, habitar, residir.

**dwell.er** *s.* morador, habitante.

**dye** *s.* tintura / *v.* tingir.

**dyer** *s.* tintureiro.

**dy.ing** *adj.* moribundo, agonizante; último.

**dyke** *s.* dique; represa.

**dy.nam.ic** *adj.* dinâmico.

**dy.nam.ics** *s.* dinâmica.

**dy.na.mite** *s.* dinamite / *v.* dinamitar

# Ee

**E, e** *s.* quinta letra do alfabeto inglês; mi (nota musical).

**each** *adj.* cada / *pron.* cada qual / *adv.* para cada um, cada um.

**ea.ger** *adj.* ávido / *v.* ansiar por algo.

**ea.ger.ness** *s.* ânsia; avidez; entusiasmo.

**ea.gle** *s.* águia.

**ear** *s.* orelha; ouvido; espiga.

**ear.ache** *s.* dor de ouvido.

**ear.deaf.en.ing** *adj.* ensurdecedor.

**ear.drum** *s.* tímpano.

**earl** *s.* conde.

**ear.li.er** *adj.* mais adiantado / *adv.* mais cedo.

**ear.ly** *adv.* cedo / *adj.* prematuro.

**earn** *v.* ganhar; render.

**ear.nest** *adj.* intenso; sério.

**earn.ings** *s.* salário, ordenado; ganhos.

**ear.phone** *s.* fone de ouvido.

**ear.ring** *s.* brinco.

**Earth** *s.* Terra, globo terrestre.

**earth.quake** *s.* terremoto.

**earth.worm** *s.* minhoca.

**ease** *s.* facilidade, conforto, alívio / *v.* facilitar, aliviar.

**ea.sel** *s.* cavalete (de pintor).

**eas.i.ly** *adv.* facilmente.

**eas.i.ness** *s.* facilidade, tranquilidade.

**east** *s.* leste, este, oriente.

**Eas.ter** *s.* Páscoa.

**eas.ter.ly** *adv.* oriundo do ou em direção leste.

**east.ern** *adj.* oriental.

**east.ward** *adv.* ao leste.

**easy** — 210 — **effuse**

**easy** *adj.* fácil; tranquilo.

**easy chair** *s.* poltrona; espreguiçadeira.

**eat** *v.* comer.

**eat.a.ble** *s.* comestíveis, víveres / *adj.* comível, próprio para comer.

**eaves** *s.* beiral do telhado.

**ebb** *s.* vazante; maré-baixa / *v.* baixar, diminuir.

**eb.on.y** *s.* ébano.

**ec.cen.tric** *adj.* excêntrico(a), extravagante.

**ech.o** *s.* eco, ressonância / *v.* ecoar.

**e.clair** *s.* bomba (doce), ecler.

**e.clipse** *s.* eclipse, escurecimento / *v.* ofuscar, eclipsar.

**e.col.o.gy** *s.* ecologia.

**ec.o.nom.ic** *adj.* econômico.

**ec.o.nom.i.cal** *adj.* rentável.

**ec.o.nom.ics** *s.* economia (ciência).

**e.con.o.mize** *v.* economizar.

**e.con.om.y** *s.* economia.

**e.con.o.my class** *s.* classe econômica; classe turística.

**ec.sta.sy** *s.* êxtase.

**Ec.ua.dor** *s.* Equador.

**edge** *s.* fio; borda, beira.

**edg.y** *adj.* inquieto(a), impaciente.

**ed.i.ble** *adj.* comestível.

**Ed.in.burgh** *s.* Edimburgo.

**ed.it** *v.* editar, revisar.

**e.di.tion** *s.* edição, revisão, publicação.

**ed.i.tor** *s.* editor(a).

**ed.i.to.ri.al** *adj.* editorial / *s.* editorial.

**ed.u.cate** *v.* educar, ensinar.

**ed.u.ca.tion** *s.* educação, ensino, estudo.

**ed.u.ca.tion.al** *adj.* educativo, educacional.

**eel** *s.* enguia.

**ee.rie** *adj.* estranho, assustador.

**ef.fect** *s.* efeito, resultado / *v.* efetuar, executar.

**ef.fec.tive** *adj.* eficaz.

**ef.fec.tive.ness** *s.* eficácia, eficiência.

**ef.fects** *s.* bens móveis.

**ef.fem.i.nate** *adj.* afeminado; delicado.

**ef.fi.ca.cy** *s.* eficácia.

**ef.fi.cien.cy** *s.* eficiência.

**ef.fi.cient** *adj.* eficiente, competente.

**ef.fort** *s.* esforço; empenho; conquista.

**ef.fort.less** *adj.* fácil, sem esforço.

**ef.fron.te.ry** *s.* descaramento, insolência.

**ef.fuse** *v.* efundir, derramar; espalhar.

effusive 211 elevator

**ef.fu.sive** *adj*. caloroso, efusivo; expansivo.

**egg** *s*. ovo.

**egg.plant** *s*. berinjela.

**egg.shell** *s*. casca de ovo / *adj*. fino.

**e.go** *s*. ego, eu.

**e.go.tism** *s*. egoísmo, egotismo, vaidade.

**E.gypt** *s*. Egito.

**E.gyp.tian** *adj*. egípcio / *s*. egípcio.

**eight** *num*. oito.

**eigh.teen** *num*. dezoito.

**eigh.teenth** *num*. décimo oitavo.

**eighth** *num*. oitavo.

**eight.i.eth** *num*. octogésimo.

**eight.y** *num*. oitenta.

**Ei.re** *s*. Irlanda.

**ei.ther** *pron*. um ou outro; cada / *adj*. qualquer (de duas alternativas), ambos.

**e.ject** *v*. expulsar; lançar; expelir.

**eke** *v*. economizar; prolongar.

**e.lab.o.rate** *v*. aperfeiçoar; elaborar; detalhar / *adj*. complicado; elaborado.

**e.lapse** *v*. transcorrer.

**e.las.tic** *s*. elástico / *adj*. flexível, elástico.

**elas.ti.city** *s*. elasticidade.

**e.lat.ed** *adj*. em júbilo, alegre / *v*. elevar, exaltar.

**e.la.tion** *s*. exaltação; elevação.

**el.bow** *s*. cotovelo.

**eld.er** *adj*. mais velho; primogênito.

**eld.er.ly** *adj*. idoso(a) / *s*. idosos.

**eld.est** *adj*. mais velho(a).

**e.lect** *s*. predestinado / *adj*. eleito, escolhido / *v*. eleger, escolher.

**e.lec.tion** *s*. eleição, votação.

**e.lec.tion.eer.ing** *s*. campanha eleitoral, propaganda eleitoral.

**e.lec.tor** *s*. eleitor(a).

**e.lec.to.rate** *s*. eleitorado.

**e.lec.tric** *adj*. elétrico; vibrante.

**e.lec.tri.cal** *adj*. elétrico.

**e.lec.tri.cian** *s*. eletricista.

**e.lec.tri.ci.ty** *s*. eletricidade.

**e.lec.tri.fy** *v*. eletrificar.

**e.lec.tro.cute** *v*. eletrocutar.

**e.lec.tron.ic** *adj*. eletrônico.

**electronic mail** *s*. correio eletrônico.

**e.lec.tron.ics** *s*. eletrônica (ciência).

**el.e.gant** *adj*. elegante, gracioso.

**el.e.ment** *s*. elemento.

**el.e.men.ta.ry** *adj*. elementar; rudimentar.

**el.e.phant** *s*. elefante.

**el.e.va.tion** *s*. elevação, altura.

**el.e.va.tor** *s*. elevador.

eleven | 212 | emigrant

**e.lev.en** *num.* onze.

**e.lev.enth** *num.* décimo primeiro; undécimo.

**elf** *s. (pl. elves)* duente; gnomo.

**e.lide** *v.* eliminar.

**el.i.gi.ble** *adj.* elegível, qualificado.

**elm** *s.* olmo.

**e.lon.gated** *adj.* alongado, comprido.

**e.lope** *v.* fugir com o namorado; escapar, evadir-se.

**e.lope.ment** *s.* fuga, evasão.

**el.o.quent** *adj.* eloquente.

**El Sal.va.dor** *s.* El Salvador.

**else** *adv.* mais; em vez de / *conj.* ou, senão / *adj.* outro, diverso.

**else.where** *adv.* em outro lugar.

**e.lude** *v.* esquivar; iludir; enganar.

**e.lu.sive** *adj.* ardiloso; evasivo(a), esquivo(a).

**e.ma.ci.a.ted** *adj.* definhado(a), emagrecido(a).

**em.a.nate** *v.* emanar, exalar.

**e.man.ci.pate** *v.* emancipar.

**e.man.ci.pa.tion** *s.* emancipação, libertação.

**em.bank.ment** *s.* aterro.

**em.bar.go** *s.* proibição, interdição.

**em.bark** *v.* embarcar.

**em.bark.ation** *s.* embarque.

**em.bar.rass** *v.* constranger; embaraçar.

**em.bar.rass.ed** *adj.* desconfortável, constrangido.

**em.bar.rass.ing** *adj.* embaraçoso, desagradável.

**em.bar.rass.ment** *s.* constrangimento; embaraço.

**em.bas.sy** *s.* embaixada.

**em.bel.lish** *v.* embelezar, enfeitar.

**em.bel.lish.er** *s.* decorador, embelezador.

**em.ber** *s.* brasa, tição.

**em.bit.ter** *v.* amargar, angustiar.

**em.bod.i.ment** *s.* incorporação; encarnação.

**em.bod.y** *v.* incorporar; personificar; encarnar.

**em.bosom** *v.* abraçar.

**em.boss** *v.* realçar, ornar com relevos.

**em.bossed** *adj.* realçado, ornado.

**em.brace** *v.* abraçar, envolver / *s.* abraço.

**em.broi.der** *v.* bordar; ornar.

**em.broi.der.y** *s.* bordado.

**em.bry.o** *s.* embrião; feto.

**em.e.rald** *s.* esmeralda.

**e.merge** *v.* emergir, aparecer.

**e.mer.gen.cy** *s.* emergência.

**e.mer.gent** *adj.* emergente.

**em.i.grant** *s.* imigrante.

**emigrate** | 213 | **encroach**

**em.i.grate** *v.* emigrar.
**em.i.nent** *adj.* eminente; notável, famoso.
**e.mis.sion** *s.* emissão.
**e.mit** *v.* emitir, liberar.
**e.mitter** *s.* emissor.
**e.mo.tion** *s.* emoção.
**e.mo.tion.al** *adj.* emocional.
**em.per.or** *s.* imperador.
**em.pha.sis** *s.* ênfase.
**em.pha.size** *v.* enfatizar.
**em.phat.ic** *adj.* enfático, categórico.
**em.phat.i.cally** *adv.* enfaticamente.
**em.pire** *s.* império.
**em.place.ment** *s.* posição; situação.
**em.ploy** *v.* empregar; usar, aplicar.
**em.ploy.ee** *s.* empregado(a), funcionário(a).
**em.ploy.er** *s.* empregador(a), patrão(oa).
**em.ploy.ment** *s.* emprego, trabalho.
**em.poison** *v.* envenenar.
**em.poison.ment** *s.* envenenamento.
**em.pow.er** *v.* autorizar; capacitar; habilitar.
**em.press** *s.* imperatriz.
**emp.ti.ness** *s.* vácuo, vazio.

**emp.ty** *adj.* vazio; inútil / *v.* esvaziar; desocupar.
**e.mul.sion** *s.* emulsão.
**en.a.ble** *v.* tornar possível; habilitar.
**en.act** *v.* representar; decretar, legalizar.
**e.nam.el** *s.* esmalte / *v.* esmaltar.
**en.am.or** *v.* enamorar.
**en.am.ored** *adj.* enamorado(a).
**en.cage** *v.* engaiolar, enjaular.
**en.case** *v.* encaixotar, encaixar.
**en.chain** *v.* acorrentar.
**en.chant** *v.* encantar, maravilhar.
**en.chant.ed** *adj.* encantado(a).
**en.chant.er** *s.* feiticeiro; mágico.
**en.chant.ing** *adj.* encantador(a).
**en.cir.cle** *v.* circundar; cercar, envolver.
**en.clasp** *v.* abraçar, cingir.
**en.clave** *s.* enclave.
**en.close** *v.* cercar; anexar.
**en.closed** *adj.* incluso, anexo; fechado.
**en.com.pass** *v.* abranger, abarcar.
**en.core** *s.* bis / *v.* pedir bis.
**en.coun.ter** *s.* encontro; conflito / *v.* encontrar, deparar.
**en.cour.age** *v.* encorajar, apoiar.
**en.cour.age.ment** *s.* encorajamento, estímulo.
**en.croach** *v.* invadir, usurpar.

**encumber**     **214**     **enough**

**en.cum.ber** *v.* embaraçar, dificultar.

**end** *s.* fim / *v.* terminar.

**en.dan.ger** *v.* arriscar; pôr em risco.

**en.dear.ing** *adj.* simpático, terno, afetuoso.

**en.deav.our** *s.* tentativa; empenho / *v.* esforçar-se.

**end.ing** *s.* conclusão, fim, término.

**en.dive** *s.* chicória.

**end.less** *adj.* infinito; infindável.

**en.dorse** *v.* endossar, aprovar.

**en.dorse.ment** *s.* aval, endosso, aprovação.

**en.dow** *v.* dotar, doar.

**en.dow.ment** *s.* doação.

**en.dur.able** *adj.* sofrível, suportável, tolerável.

**en.dur.ance** *s.* tolerância, duração, resistência.

**en.dure** *v.* aturar, suportar, resistir.

**en.dur.ing** *adj.* duradouro.

**en.e.my** *adj.* inimigo(a) / *s.* inimigo(a).

**en.fee.ble** *v.* enfraquecer, debilitar.

**en.force** *v.* fazer cumprir, obrigar, impor.

**en.force.able** *adj.* obrigatório, executável.

**en.frame** *v.* emoldurar, enquadrar.

**en.gage** *v.* comprometer-se, noivar; empenhar.

**en.gaged** *adj.* ocupado; noivo.

**en.gage.ment** *s.* noivado; compromisso.

**en.gag.ing** *adj.* atraente, sedutor(a).

**en.gine** *s.* motor; máquina.

**en.gine driv.er** *s.* maquinista.

**en.gi.neer** *s.* engenheiro(a).

**en.gi.neer.ing** *s.* engenharia.

**Eng.land** *s.* Inglaterra.

**Eng.lish** *adj.* inglês(esa) / *s.* inglês(esa).

**en.grave** *v.* gravar, estampar.

**en.grav.ing** *s.* gravura, estampa.

**en.gulf** *v.* tragar, engolfar; subjugar.

**en.hance** *v.* ressaltar; aumentar.

**en.joy** *v.* desfrutar; divertir-se; deleitar-se.

**en.joy.a.ble** *adj.* agradável, divertido.

**en.joy.ment** *s.* prazer, satisfação, divertimento.

**en.lace** *v.* envolver, enlaçar.

**en.large** *v.* ampliar, alargar.

**en.list** *v.* alistar(-se), recrutar.

**en.liv.en** *v.* avivar, animar.

**en.mi.ty** *s.* inimizade.

**e.nor.mous** *adj.* enorme.

**e.nough** *adj.* suficiente, bastante.

**enrage** 215 **equal**

**en.rage** *v.* enfurecer.
**en.rich** *v.* enriquecer.
**en.roll** *v.* matricular, inscrever.
**en.roll.ment** *s.* matrícula, inscrição.
**en.slave** *v.* escravizar.
**en.slav.er** *s.* escravocrata.
**en.sure** *v.* assegurar, segurar, garantir.
**en.ter** *v.* entrar, passar para dentro.
**en.ter.prise** *s.* empresa; empreendimento.
**en.ter.pris.ing** *adj.* empreendedor(a).
**en.ter.tain** *v.* entreter, divertir.
**en.ter.tain.ing** *adj.* divertido, interessante.
**en.ter.tain.ment** *s.* diversão, entretenimento.
**en.thu.si.asm** *s.* entusiasmo.
**en.thu.si.ast** *s.* entusiasta, apaixonado.
**en.thu.si.as.tic** *adj.* entusiástico, muito interessado.
**en.tice** *v.* atrair; incitar.
**en.tire** *adj.* inteiro, todo, completo.
**en.tire.ly** *adv.* inteiramente, totalmente.
**en.ti.tle** *v.* intitular; autorizar.
**en.ti.ty** *s.* entidade, ente.
**en.tomb** *v.* enterrar, sepultar.

**en.trails** *s. pl.* estranhas; vísceras.
**en.trance** *s.* entrada.
**en.trap** *v.* apanhar com laço; armar cilada.
**en.tre.pre.neur** *s.* empresário(a).
**en.trust** *v.* confiar algo a alguém, incumbir, encarregar.
**en.try** *s.* entrada, ingresso; apontamento; verbete (dicionário).
**en.try form** *s.* ficha de registro.
**en.ve.lope** *s.* envelope.
**en.vi.ous** *adj.* invejoso(a).
**en.vi.ron.ment** *s.* meio ambiente.
**en.vi.ron.men.tal** *adj.* ambiental.
**en.vi.rons** *s. pl.* arredores, imediações.
**en.vis.age** *v.* prever, imaginar.
**en.voy** *s.* enviado(a).
**en.vy** *s.* inveja, cobiça, ciúme / *v.* invejar, cobiçar.
**en.wrap** *v.* envolver, embrulhar.
**ep.ic** *adj.* épico, heroico / *s.* épico, epopeia.
**ep.i.dem.ic** *s.* epidemia / *adj.* epidêmico.
**ep.i.lep.sy** *s.* epilepsia.
**ep.i.sode** *s.* episódio.
**e.pis.tle** *s.* epístola, carta, missiva.
**ep.och** *s.* época, era, período.
**eq.ua.ble** *adj.* uniforme, igual.
**e.qual** *s.* semelhante, igual / *adj.* igual, equivalente.

**E**

# equality — 216 — estimate

**e.qual.i.ty** *s.* igualdade.
**e.qual.ize** *v.* igualar.
**eq.ual.ly** *adv.* igualmente.
**e.quate** *v.* equiparar; comparar.
**e.qua.tor** *s.* linha do equador.
**e.qui.lib.ri.um** *s.* equilíbrio.
**e.quip** *v.* equipar, prover,
preparar.
**eq.ui.page** *s.* equipagem.
**e.quip.ment** *s.* equipamento.
**e.quiv.a.lent** *s.* equivalente
/ *adj.* equivalente.
**era** *s.* era, época.
**e.rad.i.cate** *v.* erradicar,
exterminar.
**e.rase** *v.* apagar.
**e.ras.er** *s.* borracha; apagador.
**ere** *conj.* antes de / *prep.* antes.
**e.rect** *adj.* ereto, reto / *v.* levantar,
erguer, erigir.
**e.rec.tion** *s.* ereção.
**e.rode** *v.* causar erosão, corroer,
erodir.
**e.ro.sion** *s.* erosão, desgaste.
**e.rot.ic** *adj.* erótico.
**err** *v.* errar; falhar.
**er.rand** *s.* recado, mensagem;
missão, incumbência.
**er.ror** *s.* erro.
**e.rupt** *v.* entrar em erupção,
estourar.
**e.rup.tion** *s.* erupção, explosão.

**es.ca.late** *v.* intensificar(-se);
aumentar.
**es.ca.la.tor** *s.* escada rolante.
**es.ca.pade** *s.* peripécia, aventura;
fuga, escapadela.
**es.cape** *s.* fuga, evasão
/ *v.* escapar, evadir-se.
**es.chew** *v.* evitar; fugir de.
**es.cort** *s.* escolta; acompanhante
/ *v.* acompanhar, escoltar.
**es.pe.cial.ly** *adv.* sobretudo,
especialmente.
**es.pi.er** *s.* espião.
**es.pi.o.nage** *s.* espionagem.
**es.pla.nade** *s.* esplanada.
**es.pous.al** *s.* casamento, núpcias.
**es.pouse** *v.* casar-se, desposar.
**es.say** *s.* ensaio, redação.
**es.sence** *s.* essência.
**es.sen.tial** *adj.* essencial.
**es.tab.lish** *v.* estabelecer, fundar,
instituir.
**es.tab.lished** *adj.* estabelecido(a),
fundado(a).
**es.tab.lish.ment** *s.*
estabelecimento, instituição,
fundação.
**es.tate** *s.* propriedade; conjunto
de bens, patrimônio.
**es.thet.ic** *adj.* estético.
**es.ti.mate** *s.* estimativa,
avaliação, orçamento / *v.* estimar,
avaliar, orçar.

**es.ti.mation** *s.* cálculo, estimativa; opinião.

**es.tranged** *adj.* separado, alienado, marginalizado.

**etc.** *abrev. de etcetera.*

**etch.ing** *s.* água-forte, gravura ou estampa a água-forte.

**e.ter.nal** *adj.* eterno, perpétuo.

**e.ter.ni.ty** *s.* eternidade, perpetuidade.

**eth.i.cal** *adj.* ético, decente.

**eth.i.cs** *s.* ética.

**E.thi.o.pi.a** *s.* Etiópia.

**eth.nic** *adj.* étnico.

**et.i.quette** *s.* etiqueta.

**eu.lo.gize** *v.* elogiar.

**Eu.rope** *s.* Europa.

**e.vac.u.ate** *v.* evacuar, abandonar.

**e.vade** *v.* sonegar; escapar; evitar.

**e.vader** *s.* fugitivo.

**e.val.u.ate** *v.* avaliar.

**e.val.u.a.tion** *s.* avaliação.

**e.vap.o.rate** *v.* evaporar(-se).

**e.va.sion** *s.* fuga; evasão.

**e.va.sive** *adj.* evasivo(a), ambíguo(a).

**eve** *s.* véspera.

**even** *adj.* plano, liso; par / *adv.* mesmo, até; ainda.

**eve.ning** *s.* noite, anoitecer.

**evening dress** *s.* traje a rigor.

**even.ness** *s.* igualdade; imparcialidade.

**e.vent** *s.* acontecimento, evento, ocorrência.

**e.vent.ful** *adj.* movimentado, cheio de acontecimentos; acidentado.

**e.ven.tu.al** *adj.* final.

**e.ven.tu.al.ly** *adv.* finalmente.

**ev.er** *adv.* sempre; já, alguma vez.

**ev.er.last.ing** *adj.* perpétuo, eterno / *s.* eternidade.

**eve.ry** *adj.* todo(a); cada um(a).

**eve.ry.bod.y** *pron.* todo mundo, todos.

**eve.ry.day** *adj.* diário; todos os dias.

**eve.ry.one** *pron.* todo mundo.

**eve.ry.thing** *pron.* tudo.

**eve.ry.where** *adv.* em todo lugar.

**e.vict** *v.* despejar, desapossar.

**ev.i.dence** *s.* prova, evidência, indício.

**ev.i.dent** *adj.* evidente, óbvio.

**ev.i.dent.ly** *adv.* evidentemente, obviamente.

**e.vil** *s.* maldade, mal / *adj.* mau, má.

**e.vil.do.er** *s.* malfeitor.

**e.vil.ness** *s.* maldade.

**ev.i.ta.ble** *adj.* evitável.

**e.voke** *v.* evocar.

**ev.o.lu.tion** *s.* evolução.

**e.volve** *v.* desenvolver.

**ewe** *s.* ovelha.

**ex.a.cer.bate** *v.* agravar; exacerbar.

**ex.act** *adj.* exato(a), preciso(a).

**ex.act.ing** *adj.* exigente; minucioso.

**ex.act.ly** *adv.* exatamente.

**ex.ag.ger.ate** *v.* exagerar.

**ex.ag.ger.a.tion** *s.* exagero.

**ex.am** *s.* exame.

**ex.am.i.na.tion** *s.* exame; investigação.

**ex.am.ine** *v.* examinar, investigar.

**ex.am.ple** *s.* exemplo.

**ex.as.per.ate** *v.* exasperar, irritar-se.

**ex.as.pe.ra.ting** *adj.* irritante.

**ex.ca.vate** *v.* escavar, cavar.

**ex.ceed** *v.* exceder, ultrapassar.

**ex.ceed.ing.ly** *adv.* extremamente.

**ex.cel** *v.* sobressair; distinguir-se.

**ex.cel.lent** *adj.* excelente, ótimo.

**ex.cept** *prep.* exceto / *v.* excluir.

**ex.cep.tion** *s.* exceção, exclusão.

**ex.cerpt** *s.* trecho, passagem.

**ex.cess** *s.* excesso, demasia.

**ex.ces.sive** *adj.* excessivo.

**ex.change** *s.* troca; intercâmbio / *v.* trocar, cambiar.

**ex.cite** *v.* excitar; agitar.

**ex.cite.ment** *s.* excitação; agitação.

**ex.cit.ing** *adj.* emocionante, excitante.

**ex.claim** *v.* exclamar.

**ex.cla.ma.tion** *s.* exclamação.

**ex.cla.ma.tion mark** *s.* ponto de exclamação.

**ex.clude** *v.* excluir; eliminar.

**ex.clu.sive** *adj.* exclusivo, único.

**ex.cur.sion** *s.* excursão.

**ex.cuse** *s.* desculpa / *v.* desculpar.

**ex.e.cute** *v.* executar.

**ex.e.cu.tion** *s.* execução, realização.

**ex.ec.u.tive** *s.* executivo(a) / *adj.* executivo(a).

**ex.ec.u.tor** *s.* testamenteiro(a).

**ex.emp.tion** *s.* dispensa, isenção.

**ex.er.cise** *s.* exercício / *v.* exercer; fazer exercício.

**ex.ert** *v.* exercer; mostrar.

**ex.hib.it** *s.* obra exposta, exibição, exposição / *v.* exibir, expor.

**ex.hi.bi.tion** *s.* exposição, mostra.

**ex.ile** *s.* exílio / *v.* exilar.

**ex.ist** *v.* existir; viver.

**ex.ist.ence** *s.* existência.

**ex.it** *s.* saída / *v.* sair.

**ex.o.dus** *s.* êxodo.

**ex.on.e.rate** *v.* isentar; exonerar.

**ex.ot.ic** *adj.* exótico.

**ex.pand** *v.* expandir, dilatar; desenvolver.

**ex.panse** *s.* extensão.

**ex.pan.sion** *s.* expansão, dilatação.

**ex.pect** *v.* esperar, aguardar, contar com; supor (coloquial).

**ex.pec.ta.tion** *s.* expectativa.

**ex.pe.di.ence** *s.* conveniência, utilidade.

**ex.pe.di.ent** *adj.* conveniente, útil / *s.* expediente, meio.

**ex.pe.di.tion** *s.* expedição.

**ex.pel** *v.* expelir, expulsar.

**ex.pend** *v.* gastar; despender.

**ex.pen.da.ble** *adj.* prescindível; descartável; dispensável.

**ex.pen.di.ture** *s.* gasto(s).

**ex.pense** *s.* despesa, gasto(s), custo.

**ex.pen.sive** *adj.* caro(a), dispendioso(a), custoso(a).

**ex.pe.ri.ence** *s.* experiência, prática / *v.* experimntar.

**ex.pe.ri.enced** *adj.* experiente.

**ex.per.i.ment** *s.* experimento, tentativa / *v.* fazer experiências, tentar.

**ex.pert** *adj.* perito / *s.* especialista, perito, experto.

**ex.per.tise** *s.* perícia.

**ex.pi.ra.tion** *s.* expiração; vencimento.

**ex.pire** *v.* expirar, vencer, caducar.

**ex.plain** *v.* explicar, elucidar.

**ex.pla.na.tion** *s.* explicação, esclarecimento.

**ex.pli.cit** *adj.* explícito.

**ex.plode** *v.* explodir, estourar.

**ex.ploit** *v.* explorar recursos / *s.* façanha, proeza.

**ex.plore** *v.* explorar um lugar, investigar, examinar.

**ex.plor.er** *s.* explorador(a).

**ex.plo.sion** *s.* explosão, estouro.

**ex.plo.sive** *adj.* explosivo(a) / *s.* explosivo(a).

**ex.port** *s.* exportação / *v.* exportar.

**ex.port.er** *s.* exportador(a).

**ex.pose** *v.* expor, exibir.

**ex.posed** *adj.* exposto(a); desprotegido(a).

**ex.poser** *s.* expositor.

**ex.po.sure** *s.* exposição, exibição.

**ex.pound** *v.* expor, esclarecer.

**ex.press** *adj.* expresso; urgente; rápido / *v.* expressar.

**ex.pres.sion** *s.* expressão, manifestação; fórmula algébrica.

**ex.pres.sive** *adj.* expressivo, significativo.

**ex.press.ly** *adv.* expressamente.

**ex.press.way** *s.* rodovia.

**ex.pul.sion** *s.* expulsão, exclusão.

**ex.pur.gate** *v.* expurgar, limpar, purificar.

**ex.tant** *adj.* existente; sobrevivente.

**ex.tend** *v.* estender, prolongar; prorrogar.

**ex.ten.sion** *s.* extensão; ampliação.

**ex.ten.sive** *adj.* extenso(a), extensivo(a).

**ex.ten.sive.ly** *adv.* extensivamente.

**ex.tent** *s.* alcance, grau.

**ex.te.ri.or** *adj.* externo / *s.* exterior; aspecto.

**ex.ter.nal** *adj.* externo(a), exterior.

**ex.tinct** *adj.* extinto(a).

**ex.tin.guish** *v.* extinguir, apagar.

**ex.tin.guish.er** *s.* extintor.

**ex.tir.pa.tor** *s.* extirpador.

**ex.tort** *v.* extorquir.

**ex.tra** *s.* extraordinário; aumento / *adj.* adicional / *adv.* extra, super.

**ex.tract** *v.* extrair; deduzir / *s.* extrato, resumo, passagem.

**ex.tra.dite** *v.* extraditar.

**ex.traor.di.nar.y** *adj.* extraordinário, notável.

**ex.trav.a.gance** *s.* extravagância.

**ex.trav.a.gant** *adj.* extravagante.

**ex.treme** *adj.* extremo / *s.* extremo.

**ex.treme.ly** *adv.* extremamente.

**ex.tri.cate** *v.* livrar, soltar.

**ex.tro.vert** *s.* extrovertido(a).

**ex.ude** *v.* aparecer.

**eye** *s.* olho / *v.* olhar.

**eye.ball** *s.* globo ocular.

**eye.brow** *s.* sobrancelha.

**eye.lash** *s.* cílio, pestana.

**eye.less** *adj.* sem vista; cego(a).

**eye.lid** *s.* pálpebra.

**eye.shadow** *s.* sombra para os olhos.

**eye.sight** *s.* visão, vista.

**eye.sore** *s.* terçol.

**eye.wit.ness** *s.* testemunha ocular.

# Ff

**F, f** *s.* sexta letra do alfabeto inglês; fá (nota musical).

**fa.ble** *s.* fábula.

**fab.ric** *s.* tecido, pano; fabricação; estrutura; trama; construção.

**fab.ri.cate** *v.* fabricar; confeccionar.

**fab.ri.ca.tion** *s.* fabricação, construção.

**fa.cade** *s.* fachada.

**face** *s.* cara, rosto / *v.* encarar.

**face.less** *adj.* descarado; anônimo; sem rosto.

**fa.ce.tious** *adj.* jocoso, brincalhão.

**face value** *s.* valor nominal.

**fac.ile** *adj.* fácil; simples.

**fa.cil.i.ties** *s. pl.* facilidades; instalações; recursos.

**fac.ing** *s.* material de revestimento; cobertura.

**fac.sim.i.le** *s.* fac-símile, reprodução.

**fact** *s.* fato, acontecimento.

**fac.tor** *s.* fator.

**fac.to.ry** *s.* fábrica.

**fac.tu.al** *adj.* real, efetivo, fatual.

**fac.ul.ty** *s.* faculdade; capacidade; habilidade.

**fad** *s.* mania; moda passageira.

**fade** *v.* desbotar; murchar; enfraquecer.

**fag** *s.* trabalho enfandonho; homossexual (coloquial).

**fail** *v.* reprovar; falhar, fracassar / *s.* reprovação.

**fail.ing** *s.* defeito, falha.

# F

**fail.ure** *s.* falha, deficiência; fracasso; reprovação.

**faint** *s.* desmaio / *v.* desmaiar / *adj.* fraco, leve.

**faint.ness** *s.* fraqueza, debilidade; tontura.

**fair** *s.* feira / *adj.* satisfatório; formoso; louro; justo, imparcial.

**fair-con.di.tioned** *adj.* de boa índole, benigno.

**fair.ly** *adv.* com justiça, honestamente.

**fair.ness** *s.* justiça, integridade, imparcialidade; formosura.

**fair play** *s.* jogo limpo, retidão.

**fair.y** *s.* fada.

**fair.y tale** *s.* conto de fadas.

**faith** *s.* fé, crença.

**faith.ful** *adj.* fiel, leal.

**faith.ful.ly** *adv.* fielmente, lealmente.

**fake** *s.* falsificação; fraude; falso / *v.* fingir; falsificar; imitar.

**fal.con** *s.* falcão.

**fall** *v.* cair / *s.* queda; outono.

**fall.en** *v. pp.* do *v. to fall* / *adj.* caído(a), triste.

**falling star** *s.* estrela cadente.

**fall.out** *s.* partículas radioativas.

**false** *adj.* falso(a).

**false.ness** *s.* falsidade.

**false teeth** *s.* dentadura.

**fal.ter** *s.* vacilação / *v.* vacilar.

**fame** *s.* fama, reputação.

**fa.mil.i.ar** *adj.* familiar; íntimo; conhecido.

**fa.mil.i.ar.ize** *v.* familiarizar-se, habituar-se.

**fam.i.ly** *s.* família; linhagem.

**fam.il.y name** *s.* sobrenome.

**fa.mous** *adj.* famoso, afamado, ilustre.

**fa.mous.ly** *adv.* famosamente.

**fan** *s.* leque, ventilador / *v.* abanar.

**fa.nat.ic** *s.* fanático(a).

**fan.ci.ful** *adj.* extravagante, fantástico(a); fantasioso(a).

**fan.cy** *s.* capricho; fantasia / *adj.* luxuoso(a) / *v.* imaginar, querer (coloquial).

**fan.cy ball** *s.* baile à fantasia.

**fan.cy dress** *s.* fantasia (roupa).

**fang** *s.* dente canino; raiz do dente.

**fan.tas.tic** *adj.* fantástico(a).

**fan.ta.sy** *s.* imaginação, fantasia.

**far** *adj.* distante, remoto(a) / *adv.* muito longe.

**far.a.way** *adj.* remoto(a), longíquo(a); distraído(a), pensativo(a).

**farce** *s.* farsa; pantomima.

**far.ci.cal** *adj.* ridículo(a).

**fare** *s.* tarifa, preço de passagem.

**fare.well** *s.* despedida, adeus / *adj.* de despedida.

**farm** *s.* fazenda / *v.* cultivar.
**farm.er** *s.* fazendeiro(a).
**farm hand** *s.* lavrador(a), trabalhador(a) agrícola.
**farm.house** *s.* casa de fazenda.
**farm.ing** *s.* agricultura, lavoura, cultivo.
**farm.land** *s.* terra de cultivo.
**farm.yard** *s.* pátio de fazenda.
**far-reach.ing** *adj.* de longo alcance.
**fart** *v.* peidar (coloquial). / *s.* peido (coloquial).
**far.ther** *adj.* mais distante, mais afastado / *adv.* mais longe.
**fas.ci.nate** *v.* fascinar, cativar.
**fas.ci.na.tion** *s.* fascinação, encanto.
**fas.cis.m** *s.* fascismo.
**fash.ion** *s.* moda, uso, costume / *v.* modelar, amoldar.
**fash.ion.a.ble** *adj.* da moda, elegante.
**fash.ion show** *s.* desfile de modas.
**fast** *adv.* rapidamente / *adj.* rápido(a) / *s.* jejum / *v.* jejuar.
**fas.ten** *v.* fixar; prender; apertar.
**fas.ten.er** *s.* presilha; prendedor.
**fas.ten.ing** *s.* fecho, gancho, ferrolho.
**fast food** *s.* comida pronta servida rapidamente.

**fas.tid.i.ous** *adj.* fastidioso(a); difícil de contentar; enfadonho.
**fat** *adj.* gordo(a) / *s.* gordura.
**fa.tal** *adj.* fatal.
**fa.tal.i.ty** *s.* fatalidade.
**fa.tal.ly** *adv.* fatalmente.
**fate** *s.* destino; sorte.
**fate.ful** *adj.* fatídico, decisivo.
**fa.ther** *s.* pai, genitor; padre.
**fa.ther.hood** *s.* paternidade.
**fa.ther-in-law** *s.* sogro.
**fa.ther.ly** *adj.* paternal / *adv.* paternalmente.
**fa.tigue** *s.* fadiga, cansaço / *v.* fatigar, cansar.
**fat.ness** *s.* gordura.
**fat.ten** *v.* engordar.
**fat.ty** *s.* gorducho(a) / *adj.* gorduroso, oleoso.
**fau.cet** *s.* torneira.
**fault** *s.* culpa; falta, defeito / *v.* criticar.
**fault.less** *adj.* perfeito, sem falha.
**fault.y** *adj.* defeituoso(a), imperfeito(a).
**fau.na** *s.* fauna.
**faux pas** *s.* gafe, mancada.
**fa.vor** *s.* favor / *v.* favorecer.
**fa.vor.a.ble** *adj.* favorável.
**fa.vor.ite** *adj.* predileto, preferido / *s.* favorito(a).
**fawn** *s.* cervo / *adj.* bege.

**F**

**fax** *s.* fax / *v.* enviar via fax (coloquial).

**FBI** *abrev.* de *Federal Bureau of Investigation* (Agência do Departamento de Justiça Americano).

**fear** *s.* medo, temor / *v.* temer, recear.

**fear.ful** *adj.* terrível, horrendo; medroso, receoso.

**fear.less** *adj.* destemido(a), audaz.

**fea.si.ble** *adj.* viável, factível, exequível.

**feast** *s.* banquete, festa, / *v.* festejar, banquetear.

**feat** *s.* façanha, proeza.

**feath.er** *s.* pena, pluma / *v.* empenar, emplumar-se.

**feath.er.ing** *s.* plumagem.

**fea.ture** *s.* feição, traço, aspecto fisionômico / *v.* apresentar, caracterizar.

**Feb.ru.a.ry** *s.* fevereiro.

**fed** *v. pret.* e *pp.* do *v. to feed.*

**fed.er.al** *adj.* federal.

**fed up** *adj.* de saco cheio, farto (coloquial).

**fee** *s.* taxa; honorários.

**fee.ble** *adj.* ineficaz; fraco, débil.

**fee.ble-mind.ed** *adj.* fraco de espírito.

**feed** *v.* alimentar / *s.* ração, comida.

**feed.back** *s.* retorno; resposta.

**feed.ing bot.tle** *s.* mamadeira.

**feel** *s.* tato; sensação / *v.* sentir; perceber.

**feel.er** *s.* antena de inseto; tentáculo.

**feel.ing** *s.* sentimento.

**fell** *v.* lançar por terra, cortar; *pret.* do *v. to fall* / *s.* derrubada.

**fel.low** *s.* camarada, companheiro.

**fel.low-man** *s.* semelhante, membro da raça humana.

**fel.low.ship** *s.* amizade; comunidade; corporação.

**fel.o.ny** *s.* crime, delito grave.

**felt** *s.* feltro / *v. pret.* e *pp.* do *v. to feel.*

**fe.male** *s.* fêmea / *adj.* do sexo feminino, fêmea.

**fem.i.nine** *adj.* feminino(a) / *s.* feminino(a).

**fem.i.nist** *s.* feminista.

**fence** *s.* cerca, grade, muro / *v.* cercar; esgrimir.

**fenc.ing** *s.* esgrima; cercas.

**fend** *v.* defender-se; desviar.

**fend.er** *s.* paralama; limpa trilhos; guarda, proteção.

**fer.ment** *v.* fermentar / *s.* fermento, levedura.

**fern** *s.* samambaia.

**fer.ret** *s.* furão (animal); cadarço, fita; ferrão.

**ferry** 225 **fighter**

**fer.ry** *s.* balsa / *v.* transportar em balsa.

**fer.ry.boat** *s.* barco de passagem, balsa.

**fer.tile** *adj.* fértil, fecundo.

**fer.ti.lize** *v.* fertilizar, adubar.

**fer.ti.liz.er** *s.* fertilizante, adubo.

**fer.vent** *adj.* ardente; abrasador; intenso.

**fes.ter** *v.* inflamar-se, supurar / *s.* chaga, pústula.

**fes.ti.val** *s.* festival, grande festa.

**fes.tive** *adj.* festivo, alegre.

**fes.tiv.i.ty** *s.* festividade, solenidade.

**fetch** *s.* estratagema; busca / *v.* ir buscar.

**fetch.ing** *adj.* atraente, encantador.

**fet.ish** *s.* fetiche.

**fet.ter** *s.* grilhão; cadeias, algemas (geralmente no plural *felters*).

**feud** *s.* disputa; rixa / *v.* brigar, degladiar-se.

**fe.ver** *s.* febre.

**fe.ver.ish** *adj.* febril.

**fe.ver.ish.ness** *s.* indisposição febril.

**few** *pron.* poucos(as) / *adj.* poucos(as).

**few.er** *adj. (comp. de few)*, menos.

**few.est** *adj. (superl. de few)*, o menor.

**fi.an.cé** *s.* noivo.

**fi.an.cée** *s.* noiva.

**fib** *s.* lorota / *v.* contar lorotas.

**fi.ber.glass** *s.* fibra de vidro.

**fic.tion** *s.* ficção.

**fic.tion.al** *adj.* de ficção, imaginário.

**fic.ti.tious** *adj.* fictício, falso, artificial.

**fid.dle** *s.* violino / *v.* tocar violino.

**fi.del.i.ty** *s.* fidelidade, lealdade, exatidão.

**field** *s.* campo.

**field-glass** *s.* binóculo.

**field.work** *s.* trabalho científico de campo.

**fiend** *s.* demônio; espírito maligno.

**fiend.ish** *adj.* diabólico, cruel (coloquial).

**fierce** *adj.* feroz, selvagem; ardente, fogoso.

**fierce.ness** *s.* ferocidade, fúria.

**fier.y** *adj.* fogoso; furioso.

**fif.teen** *num.* quinze.

**fif.th** *num.* quinto.

**fif.ty** *num.* cinquenta.

**fig** *s.* figo.

**fight** *s.* briga, luta / *v.* lutar, brigar.

**fight.er** *s.* combatente, lutador; avião de caça.

**fight.ing** *s.* batalha, luta / *adj.* combatente, lutador.

**fig.ment** *s.* imaginário, imaginação; ficção.

**fig.u.ra.tive** *adj.* figurado, figurativo, representativo.

**fig.ure** *s.* figura; cifra, número / *v.* figurar; fazer sentido.

**figure out** *v.* compreender; calcular, imaginar.

**filch** *v.* afanar, furtar.

**file** *s.* pasta; arquivo; fio, arame; lima (ferramenta) / *v.* arquivar; limar, lixar.

**fil.ing-cab.i.net** *s.* fichário, arquivo.

**fill** *v.* preencher algo, encher, ocupar; obturar.

**fil.let** *s.* filé (lombo de vitela ou boi); filete, friso; faixa.

**fill.ing** *s.* recheio; obturação.

**filling sta.tion** *s.* posto de gasolina.

**fil.ly** *s.* potranca; garota namoradeira; folgazona (coloquial).

**film** *s.* filme, película / *v.* filmar.

**fil.ter** *s.* filtro / *v.* filtrar.

**fil.ter-tipped** *adj.* filtrado.

**filth.y** *adj.* indecente; corrupto; imundo.

**fin** *s.* barbatana, nadadeira.

**fi.nal** *adj.* final, último, decisivo.

**fi.na.le** *s.* final (música: parte final de uma sinfonia, ópera, peça).

**fi.nal.ize** *v.* concluir, finalizar.

**fi.nal.ly** *adv.* finalmente.

**fi.nance** *s.* finanças / *v.* financiar, custear.

**fi.nan.cial** *adj.* financeiro.

**fi.nan.cier** *s.* financiador(a); financista.

**find** *v.* achar, encontrar; buscar.

**find.ing** *s.* veredicto, decisão; achado, descoberta.

**find out** *v.* descobrir.

**fine** *adj.* fino(a), excelente, refinado(a) / *interj.* ótimo! excelente! / *s.* multa / *v.* multar.

**fine arts** *s.* belas-artes.

**fi.ne.ry** *s.* enfeites, ornatos.

**fi.nesse** *s.* sutileza, finura.

**fin.ger** *s.* dedo.

**fin.ger.print** *s.* impressão digital.

**fin.ger.tip** *s.* ponta do dedo.

**fin.i.cky** *adj.* enjoado(a); fresco(a) (comida) (coloquial).

**fin.ish** *s.* fim; chegada; acabamento / *v.* terminar; concluir.

**Fin.land** *s.* Finlândia.

**Finn** *s.* finlandês.

**Fin.nish** *s.* finlandês(esa) / *adj.* filandês(esa).

**fire** *s.* fogo; incêndio / *v.* atirar, disparar; demitir.

**fire.arm** *s.* arma de fogo.

**fire es.cape** *s.* escada de incêndio.

**fire.fly** *s.* pirilampo, vaga-lume.

**fire.man** *s.* bombeiro.

**fire.place** *s.* lareira.

**fire.proof** *adj.* à prova de fogo.

**fire.side** *s.* lareira.

**fire.wood** *s.* lenha.

**fire.works** *s.* fogos de artifício.

**firing squad** *s.* pelotão de fuzilamento.

**firm** *s.* firma / *adj.* firme / *v.* fixar, firmar.

**firm.ly** *adv.* firmemente.

**first** *adj.* primeiro(a) / *s.* primeiro(a) / *adv.* antes de tudo.

**first aid** *s.* primeiros socorros.

**first-class** *adj.* de primeira classe.

**first-hand** *adj.* de primeira mão.

**first lady** *s.* primeira dama.

**first.ly** *adv.* em primeiro lugar, primeiramente.

**first name** *s.* primeiro nome, prenome.

**fish** *s.* peixe / *v.* pescar.

**fish.er.man** *s.* pescador.

**fish.ing** *s.* pesca, pescaria.

**fish.mon.ger** *s.* peixeiro.

**fist** *s.* punho; mão fechada.

**fit** *adj.* em boa forma, em condições, apto(a), adequado(a) / *v.* caber, servir.

**fit.ness** *s.* aptidão; conveniência.

**fit.ting** *adj.* apropriado, ajustado, adequado / *s.* assentamento, ajuste, encaixe.

**fit.tings** *s.* móveis; utensílios; acessórios.

**fit.ting room** *s.* provador.

**five** *num.* cinco.

**fix** *v.* fixar; consertar / *s.* dificuldade (coloquial).

**fix.a.tion** *s.* fixação, estabilidade.

**fixed** *adj.* fixo, estável.

**fix.ture** *s.* fixação; acessório fixo de uma casa.

**flab.by** *adj.* flácido, balofo (coloquial).

**flag** *s.* bandeira; emblema / *v.* fraquejar, decair, esmorecer.

**flag.pole** *s.* mastro.

**flair** *s.* olfato, faro, instinto.

**flak** *s.* críticas; artilharia antiaérea (militar).

**flake** *s.* floco; lasca / *v.* lascar; esamar; cobrir de flocos.

**flam.boy.ant** *adj.* espalhafatoso(a), extravagante.

**flame** *s.* chama, lume.

**flam.ma.ble** *adj.* inflamável.

**flan** *s.* torta doce.

**flank** *s.* flanco, ala / *v.* ladear, flanquear.

**flan.nel** *s.* flanela.

**flap** *s.* borda, aba, ponta / *v.* ondular, bater, agitar.

**flash** *s.* clarão, lampejo / *v.* brilhar, lampejar.

**flash.back** *s.* lembrança repentina um fato.

**flash bulb** *s.* clarão de lâmpada; *flash* (câmera).

**flash.light** *s.* lanterna, lanterna de bolso; cintilação; clarão de luz; origem de luz artificial.

**flash.y** *adj.* flamejante, cintilante.

**flask** *s.* frasco; cantil; garrafa térmica.

**flat** *s.* apartamento; a parte plana de algo / *adj.* plano, liso, sem relevo.

**flat.food** *s.* pé chato.

**flat.ly** *adv.* terminantemente; de modo chato ou plano.

**flat.ten** *v.* desanimar; achatar, nivelar, alisar.

**flat.ter** *v.* lisonjear; bajular.

**flat.ter.er** *s.* lisonjeador; adulador.

**flat.ter.ing** *adj.* lisonjeiro.

**flat.ter.y** *s.* bajulação; lisonja.

**flaunt** *s.* ostentação, pompa / *v.* ostentar, alardear.

**fla.vor** *s.* sabor, gosto / *v.* aromatizar; temperar, condimentar.

**fla.vor.ing** *s.* aromatizante, condimento, tempero.

**fla.vor.less** *adj.* sem gosto, sem sabor, insípido.

**fla.vor.ous** *adj.* saboroso.

**flaw** *s.* defeito, falha, fenda; furacão, tufão, ventania / *adj.* defeituoso.

**flax** *s.* linho (botânica).

**flax.en** *adj.* de linho, linhoso.

**flea** *s.* pulga.

**fleck** *s.* mancha na pele, pinta.

**flee** *v.* fugir, escapar.

**fleece** *s.* lã / *v.* tosquiar.

**fleet** *s.* frota / *adj.* rápido(a), veloz / *v.* mover-se rapidamente.

**fleet.ing** *adj.* passageiro; fugaz.

**Flem.ish** *adj.* flamengo, habitante da região de Flandres / *s.* flamengo, língua falada na Bélgica.

**flesh** *s.* carne (do homem e dos animais).

**flew** *v. pret.* do *v. to fly.*

**flex.i.ble** *adj.* flexível, adaptável.

**flick** *s.* peteleco / *v.* dar um peteleco.

**flick.er** *v.* tremular / *s.* vislumbre.

**fli.er** *s.* aviador, voador.

**flight** *s.* voo; fuga; lance (de escadas).

**flim.sy** *s.* papel fino, papel de cópia / *adj.* delgado(a), frágil.

**flinch** *v.* vacilar; retroceder-se; esquivar-se / *s.* recuo, desistência, hesitação.

**fling** *s.* arremesso; farra amorosa / *v.* lançar, precipitar-se.

**flip** *s.* sacudidela; gemada / *v.* atirar para o ar; sacudir.

**flip.pant** *adj.* petulante, impertinente.

**flip.per** *s.* nadadeira; barbatana.

**flirt** *v.* flertar, namorar / *s.* paquerador(a), namorador(a).

**flit** *s.* movimento leve / *v.* esvoaçar.

**float** *s.* boia; flutuação / *v.* flutuar.

**float.ing** *adj.* flutuante.

**flock** *s.* rebanho, manada, revoada; floco de lã / *v.* andar em bandos, reunir-se.

**flood** *s.* inundação, enchente / *v.* inundar, transbordar.

**flood.gate** *s.* comporta.

**flood.ing** *s.* inundação.

**flood.light** *s.* holofote.

**floor** *s.* chão, solo, piso; andar / *v.* assoalhar.

**floor.ing** *s.* pavimento, soalho.

**floor lamp** *s.* abajur de pé.

**flop** *v.* fracassar / *s.* fracasso, malogro.

**flop.py** *adj.* frouxo(a), mole, bambo(a) (coloquial).

**flo.ra** *s.* flora.

**flor.id** *adj.* florido(a).

**flo.rist** *s.* florista, floricultor(a).

**flo.rist's** *s.* floricultura.

**flounce** *s.* babado; gesto de impaciência.

**floun.der** *s.* linguado (peixe) / *v.* atrapalhar-se; debater-se.

**flour** *s.* farinha.

**flour.ish** *s.* floreio / *v.* florescer, prosperar.

**flour.ish.ing** *adj.* próspero; notável.

**flout** *v.* desrespeitar, insultar / *s.* escárnio, insulto.

**flow** *s.* fluxo; fluência / *v.* fluir; escorrer.

**flow chart** *s.* fluxograma.

**flow.er** *s.* flor / *v.* florir, desabrochar.

**flow.er bed** *s.* canteiro de flores.

**flo.wer.pot** *s.* vaso de plantas.

**flow.er.y** *adj.* floreado(a), florido(a).

**flow.ing** *adj.* corrente, fluente.

**flown** *v. pp.* do *v. to fly.*

**flu** *s.* gripe, influenza.

**fluc.tu.ate** *v.* flutuar, oscilar.

**flue** *s.* cano de chaminé, fumeiro; penugem; rede / *v.* afunilar.

**flu.ent** *adj.* fluente.

**fluff** *s.* penugem / *v.* afofar.

# fluffy 230 food processor

**fluff.y** *adj.* macio(a); de pelúcia; fofo(a).

**fluid** *s.* fluido, líquido.

**fluke** *s.* sorte, acaso.

**flung** *v. pret.* do *v. to fling.*

**flunk** *s.* fracasso, reprovação / *v.* fracassar, reprovar.

**fluor.ide** *s.* fluoreto.

**flush** *s.* rubor / *v.* corar; dar a descarga.

**flushed** *adj.* corado(a); excitado(a); ansioso(a).

**flus.ter.ed** *adj.* atrapalhado(a); agitado(a), excitado(a).

**flute** *s.* flauta.

**flut.ter** *s.* agitação; palpitação / *v.* palpitar.

**fly** *s.* mosca / *v.* voar.

**fly.ing** *s.* aviação / *adj.* voador; flutuante.

**fly.ing sal.cer** *s.* disco voador.

**foam** *s.* espuma / *v.* espumar.

**fob** *v.* despachar alguém, livrar-se de; enganar.

**fo.cal.ize** *v.* focar, focalizar.

**fo.cal point** *s.* foco, centro.

**fo.cus** *s.* foco / *v.* enfocar, focar.

**fod.der** *s.* forragem / *v.* alimentar (o gado).

**foe** *s.* inimigo, adversário.

**fog** *s.* nevoeiro, ncblina.

**fog light** *s.* farol de neblina.

**foil** *s.* rastro de caça; folha metálica; lâmina delgada / *v.* frustrar.

**fold** *s.* dobra; vinco / *v.* dobrar-se; entrelaçar os dedos.

**fold.er** *s.* pasta de papéis, envoltório.

**fold.ing** *s.* dobragem / *adj.* dobrável.

**fold.ing chair** *s.* cadeira dobradiça.

**fo.li.age** *s.* folhagem, ramagem.

**folk** *s.* povo; gente; nação. / *adj.* folclórico, popular, comum.

**folk dance** *s.* dança folclórica.

**folk.lore** *s.* folclore.

**folk song** *s.* canção popular.

**fol.low** *v.* seguir, suceder.

**fol.low.er** *s.* seguidor(a).

**fol.low.ing** *s.* cortejo, séquito / *adj.* seguinte, próximo.

**fol.ly** *s.* loucura, doidice.

**fond** *adj.* carinhoso, afetuoso; afeiçoado.

**fon.dle** *v.* acariciar, afagar.

**font** *s.* fonte (informática); pia de água benta.

**food** *s.* comida, alimento.

**food poi.son.ing** *s.* intoxicação alimentar.

**food proc.ess.or** *s.* multiprocessador de alimentos.

**food.stuff** *s.* gêneros alimentícios.

**fool** *s.* bobo(a), tolo(a) / *v.* enganar.

**fool.ish** *adj.* tolo, insensato.

**fool.ish.ness** *s.* loucura, insensatez.

**fool.proof** *adj.* infalível, perfeitamente seguro (coloquial).

**foot** *s. (pl. feet)* pé.

**foot.ball** *s.* futebol americano; bola de futebol americano.

**foot.ball match** *s.* partida de futebol.

**foot.bridge** *s.* passarela, ponte para pedestres.

**foot.loose** *adj.* livre, desembaraçado(a).

**foot.note** *s.* nota de rodapé.

**foot.path** *s.* atalho; vereda.

**foot.print** *s.* pegada.

**foot.wear** *s.* calçados.

**for** *prep.* para; por.

**for.age** *s.* forragem.

**for.bad** *v. pret.* do *v. to forbid.*

**for.bear** *v.* conter, reprimir.

**for.bear.ing** *adj.* paciente, indulgente.

**for.bid** *v.* proibir.

**for.bid.den** *v. pp.* do *v. to forbid.*

**for.bid.ding** *adj.* severo; proibitivo(a).

**force** *s.* força / *v.* forçar.

**force.ful** *adj.* vigoroso, forte.

**for.ceps** *s.* fórceps.

**for.ci.bly** *adv.* à força, forçosamente.

**ford** *s.* parte rasa do rio.

**fore** *s.* parte dianteira, frente; proa / *adj.* dianteiro, anterior.

**fore.arm** *s.* antebraço.

**fore.bode** *v.* agourar.

**fore.bod.ing** *s.* agouro, presságio.

**fore.cast** *s.* previsão / *v.* prever, predizer.

**fore.fa.ther** *s.* antepassado.

**fore.fin.ger** *s.* dedo indicador.

**fore.foot** *s.* pata dianteira.

**fore.front** *s.* em primeiro plano, vanguarda; testa.

**fore.go** *v.* anteceder.

**fore.go.ing** *adj.* precedente.

**fore.gone** *adj.* passado, anterior / *v. pp.* do *v. to forego.*

**fore.ground** *s.* primeiro plano.

**fore.head** *s.* testa; fronte.

**for.eign** *adj.* estrangeiro(a).

**for.eign.er** *s.* estrangeiro(a).

**fore.know** *v.* prever.

**fore.leg** *s.* perna dianteira.

**fore.man** *s.* capataz.

**fore.most** *adj.* principal; dianteiro / *adv.* em primeiro lugar.

**fore.name** *s.* prenome.
**fore.run.ner** *s.* precursor(a).
**fore.see** *v.* prever, antever.
**fore.sight** *s.* previdência, prevenção; previsão.
**fore.skin** *s.* prepúcio.
**for.est** *s.* floresta, selva.
**fore.stall** *v.* prevenir, evitar.
**for.est.er** *s.* guarda-florestal.
**for.est.ry** *s.* silvicultura.
**fore.tell** *v.* profetizar, predizer.
**for.ev.er** *adv.* para sempre, eternamente / *s.* eternidade.
**fore.warn** *v.* prevenir, precaver.
**fore.went** *v. pret.* do *v. to forego.*
**fore.word** *s.* prefácio, introdução.
**for.feit** *v.* perder direito / *s.* prevaricação; penalidade, pena.
**for.gave** *v. pret.* do *v. to forgive.*
**forge** *s.* fornalha / *v.* forjar; falsificar.
**forg.er** *s.* falsificador(a), falsário(a); forjador, ferreiro.
**for.ger.y** *s.* falsificação.
**for.get** *v.* esquecer.
**for.get.ful** *adj.* esquecido(a).
**for.get.ful.ness** *s.* esquecimento.
**for.give** *v.* perdoar, desculpar.
**for.give.ness** *s.* perdão.
**for.got** *v. pret.* do *v. to forget.*
**for.got.ten** *v. pp.* do *v. to forget.*

**fork** *s.* garfo; bifurcação / *v.* bifurcar.
**forked** *adj.* bifurcado(a).
**for.lorn** *adj.* desolado(a); abandonado(a).
**form** *s.* formulário, forma, formato / *v.* formar, moldar.
**for.mal** *adj.* formal. cerimônia.
**for.mal.i.ty** *s.* formalidade.
**for.mal.ly** *adv.* formalmente, cerimoniosamente.
**for.mat** *s.* formato; formatar (informática).
**form.er** *adj.* anterior.
**for.mer.ly** *adv.* anteriormente, antigamente, outrora.
**for.mi.da.ble** *adj.* formidável, tremendo.
**for.mu.la** *s.* fórmula.
**for.sake** *v.* abandonar, renunciar a.
**fort** *s.* forte, fortificação, castelo.
**forth** *adv.* adiante; para frente.
**for.ti.fy** *v.* fortalecer, fortificar.
**for.ti.tude** *s.* fortaleza, coragem, resistência.
**fort.night** *s.* quinzena.
**for.tress** *s.* fortaleza, castelo forte.
**for.tu.nate** *adj.* felizardo(a), afortunado(a), venturoso(a).

**for.tu.nate.ly** *adv.* felizmente, afortunadamente.

**for.tune** *s.* fortuna; sina, sorte.

**for.tune.tell.er** *s.* adivinho(a), cartomante.

**for.ty** *num.* quarenta.

**for.ward** *adj.* para frente, dianteiro; avançado / *v.* enviar; avançar.

**fos.sil** *s.* fóssil.

**fought** *v. pret.* do *v. to fight.*

**foul** *s.* infração, falta / *adj.* desonesto(a), ilícito(a).

**found** *v.* fundar; *v. pret.* do *v. to find.*

**foun.da.tion** *s.* fundação; fundamento, alicerce.

**found.er** *s.* fundador(a).

**found.ing** *s.* exposto(a); enjeitado(a).

**foun.dry** *s.* fundição.

**foun.tain** *s.* chafariz, fonte, bebedouro.

**foun.tain-pen** *s.* caneta-tinteiro.

**four** *num.* quatro.

**four.teen** *num.* catorze.

**four.th** *num.* quarto(a).

**fox** *s.* raposa.

**frac.tion** *s.* fração.

**frac.ture** *s.* fratura / *v.* fraturar.

**frag.ile** *adj.* frágil, quebradiço, delicado.

**frag.ment** *s.* fragmento / *v.* fragmentar.

**fra.grant** *adj.* perfumado(a), fragrante.

**frame** *s.* estrutura; moldura; armação / *v.* emoldurar.

**frame of mind** *s.* estado de espírito, disposição.

**frame.work** *s.* armação; treliça.

**France** *s.* França.

**fran.chise** *s.* concessão, franquia.

**frank** *adj.* franco, honesto / *v.* franquear.

**frank.ly** *adv.* francamente.

**frank.ness** *s.* franqueza, sinceridade.

**fran.tic** *adj.* frenético; furioso; desesperado.

**fra.ter.ni.ty** *s.* fraternidade.

**fraud** *s.* fraude, embuste; impostor(a), embusteiro.

**fray** *s.* rixa, briga / *v.* esfiapar, desfiar.

**freak** *s.* anormal, excentricidade, aberração / *adj.* esquisito(a), grotesco(a).

**freck.le** *s.* sarda (na pele).

**freck.led** *adj.* sardento(a).

**free** *adj.* livre; grátis / *v.* livrar; libertar.

**free.dom** *s.* liberdade.

**free gift** *s.* brinde.

**free.hand** *s.* carta branca, plenos poderes / *adj.* a mão livre.

**free.lance** *s.* colaborador, trabalhador independente.

**free.ly** *adv.* livremente.

**Free.ma.son** *s.* maçom, membro da maçonaria.

**free.ma.son.ry** *s.* maçonaria.

**free.post** *s.* porte pago.

**free trade** *s.* comércio livre.

**free.way** *s.* autoestrada, rodovia.

**free-will** *s.* livre arbítrio.

**freeze** *s.* congelamento / *v.* congelar.

**freez.er** *s.* congelador.

**freez.ing** *s.* congelação / *adj.* glacial, frio.

**freight** *s.* frete, carga.

**French** *s.* francês (esa) / *adj.* francês (esa).

**French fries** *s.* batatas fritas.

**fren.zy** *s.* frenesi, furor.

**fre.quent** *adj.* frequente / *v.* frequentar.

**fre.quent.ly** *adv.* frequentemente.

**fresh** *adj.* fresco.

**fresh.en up** *v.* refrescar-se.

**fresh.ly** *adv.* com aspecto sadio, juvenil; recentemente.

**fresh.man** *s.* calouro; estudante novato.

**fresh.ness** *s.* frescor, frescura.

**fresh water** *adj.* de água doce.

**fret** *s.* lamúria, choradeira, aborrecimento / *v.* amofinar-se, irritar-se.

**fri.ar** *s.* frade, monge.

**fric.tion** *s.* fricção, atrito.

**Fri.day** *s.* sexta-feira.

**fridge** *s.* geladeira.

**fried** *adj.* frito / *v. pret.* e *pp.* do *v. to fry.*

**friend** *s.* amigo(a).

**friend.ly** *adj.* amigável / *adv.* amigavelmente.

**friend.ship** *s.* amizade; afeição.

**fright.en** *v.* assustar, amedrontar.

**fright.ened** *adj.* com medo, aterrorizado(a).

**fright.en.ing** *adj.* assustador(a).

**fright.ful** *adj.* assustador(a), espantoso(a).

**frill** *s.* franja de tecido; franja de cabelo; enfeite.

**fringe** *s.* franja.

**frisk** *s.* pulo, cambalhota / *v.* saltar, pular.

**frisk.y** *adj.* animado(a), brincalhão(ona), travesso(a).

**frizz.y** *adj.* crespo(a), encrespado(a).

**frog** *s.* rã.

**frol.ic** *s.* brincadeira, travessura / *v.* brincar, traquinar.

**from** *prep.* de; proveniente de.

**front** *s.* frente; dianteira.

**front.age** *s.* fachada.

**fron.tier** *s.* fronteira.

**frost** *s.* geada / *v.* gear.

**frost.ed** *adj.* fosco; coberto de geada.

**frost.ing** *s.* glacê para cobertura de bolos.

**frost.y** *adj.* coberto de geada; gelado(a).

**froth** *s.* espuma / *v.* espumar.

**froze** *v. pret.* do *v. to freeze.*

**fro.zen** *v. pp.* do *v. to freeze* / *adj.* congelado(a).

**fruit** *s.* fruto, fruta, produto.

**fruit.er.er** *s.* fruteiro, vendedor de frutas.

**fruit.ful** *adj.* proveitoso(a); frutífero(a); fecundo(a).

**frus.tate** *v.* frustrar; malograr.

**fry** *s.* fritada / *v.* fritar.

**fry.ing pan** *s.* frigideira.

**fud.dy-dud.dy** *s.* careta.

**fuel** *s.* combustível / *v.* abastercer com combustível.

**fu.gi.tive** *s.* fugitivo(a), foragido(a) / *adj.* fugitivo(a), fugaz.

**ful.fil** *v.* cumprir a palavra, satisfazer um desejo.

**ful.fill.ment** *s.* satisfação; cumprimento; realização.

**full** *adj.* cheio(a), lotado(a).

**full age** *s.* maioridade.

**full grown** *adj.* maduro(a); adulto(a).

**full moon** *s.* lua cheia.

**full.name** *s.* nome completo.

**full.ness** *s.* plenitude, abundância.

**full-time** *adj.* por tempo integral / *adv.* por tempo integral.

**ful.ly** *adv.* completamente, inteiramente.

**ful.some** *adj.* enjoativo(a), grosseiro(a), repugnante.

**fume** *s.* fumo / *v.* fumegar.

**fumes** *s.* gases.

**fun** *s.* diversão, brincadeira / *adj.* engraçado.

**func.tion** *s.* função / *v.* funcionar.

**func.tion.al** *adj.* prático(a), funcional.

**fund** *s.* fundo, capital, valor disponível.

**fun.da.men.tal** *adj.* fundamental.

**fun.da.men.tal.ist** *s.* fundamentalista.

**fu.ner.al** *s.* funeral, enterro.

**fun.fair** *s.* parque de diversões.

**fun.gus** *s.* fungo; cogumelo.

**funk** *s.* medo, pavor / *v.* atemorizar, intimidar.

**fun.nel** *s.* funil.

**fun.ny** *adj.* divertido(a), engraçado(a); esquisito(a), estranho(a).

**fur** *s.* pelo de animal; pele, peliça.

**fur-coat** *s.* casaco de peles.

**fu.ri.ous** *adj.* furioso(a), irado(a).

**fur.lough** *s.* licença / *v.* licenciar, conceder licença a.

**fur.nace** *s.* forno, fornalha.

**fur.nish** *v.* mobiliar, suprir.

**fur.nish.ings** *s. pl.* mobília; guarnições.

**fur.ni.ture** *s.* móveis, mobília.

**fur.row** *s.* sulco; ranhura / *v.* sulcar, entalhar.

**fur.ry** *adj.* peludo(a).

**fur.ther** *adj.* adicional, outro / *adv.* além disso, demais / *v.* promover.

**fur.ther.more** *adv.* além disso, outrossim, demais.

**fu.ry** *s.* fúria.

**fuse** *s.* fusível / *v.* fundir.

**fuse-box** *s.* caixa de fusíveis.

**fu.se.lage** *s.* fuselagem.

**fuss** *s.* escândalo, espalhafato, alvoroço; preocupação exagerada.

**fuss.y** *adj.* espalhafatoso(a); exigente; meticuloso(a).

**fu.ture** *adj.* futuro(a) / *s.* futuro.

**fuzz** *s.* flocos, penugem, felpa.

**fuzzy** *adj.* flocoso(a), felpudo(a).

# Gg

**G, g** *s.* sétima letra do alfabeto inglês; sol (nota musical); *abrev.* de *gram*.

**gab.ble** *v.* tagarelar / *s.* conversa, tagarelice.

**gab.by** *adj.* conversador, falador.

**gadg.et** *s.* invenção, coisa engenhosa.

**gag** *s.* mordaça / *v.* amordaçar.

**gai.ly** *adv.* alegremente, felizmente.

**gain** *s.* ganho, lucro / *v.* ganhar, obter.

**gain.ful** *adj.* vantajoso, lucrativo.

**gait** *s.* modo de andar, andadura.

**ga.la** *s.* gala, pompa / *adj.* de gala, de festa.

**Ga.lap.a.gos** *s.* Galápagos.

**gal.ax.y** *s.* galáxia.

**gale** *s.* ventania, vento forte.

**gall** *s.* assadura; bílis.

**gal.lant** *adj.* galante, garboso.

**gall blad.der** *s.* vesícula biliar.

**gal.ler.y** *s.* galeria.

**gal.ley** *s.* galera; baleeira; barco grande.

**gal.lon** *s.* galão.

**gal.lop** *s.* galope / *v.* galopar.

**gal.lows** *s.* forca.

**gall.stone** *s.* cálculo biliar.

**ga.lore** *adv.* em abundância / *s.* abundância.

**gal.va.nize** *v.* galvanizar.

**gam.bit** *s.* gambito (no jogo de xadrez).

**gam.ble** *s.* risco / *v.* apostar em jogos de azar.

**gam.bling** s. jogo / adj. referente ao jogo.

**gam.bol** s. cambalhota / v. pular, dar saltos.

**game** s. jogo, partida.

**game.keep.er** s. guarda-caça.

**gan.der** s. ganso macho.

**gang** s. bando, gangue.

**gang.ster** s. gângster, facínora, bandido.

**gang.way** s. corredor, passagem.

**gaol** v. prender / s. cadeia.

**gap** s. brecha, abertura, lacuna.

**gape** s. bocejo / v. ficar boquiaberto.

**gap.ing** adj. muito aberto, escancarado.

**ga.rage** s. garagem.

**garb** s. traje, roupa, veste / v. vestir.

**gar.bage** s. lixo.

**gar.ble** v. deturpar, falsificar, adulterar.

**gar.den** s. jardim, quintal; horta / v. cuidar de jardim.

**gar.den.er** s. jardineiro.

**gar.den.ing** s. jardinagem; horticultura.

**gar.gle** v. gargarejar / s. gargarejo.

**gar.ish** adj. berrante; extravagante.

**gar.land** s. guirlanda, grinalda.

**gar.lic** s. alho.

**gar.ment** s. peça de roupa, vestuário.

**gar.net** s. granada; vermelho--escuro.

**gar.nish** v. enfeitar / s. guarnição, enfeite.

**gar.ri.son** s. guarnição (tropas).

**gas** s. gás; gasolina (coloquial).

**gas cook.er** s. fogão a gás.

**gas cyl.in.der** s. botijão de gás.

**gash** s. talho, corte, ferida profunda / v. talhar.

**gas.ket** s. junta, vedação.

**gas mask** s. máscara contra gases.

**gas-me.ter** s. medidor de gás.

**gas.o.line** s. gasolina.

**gas sta.tion** s. posto de gasolina.

**gas.works** s. fábrica de gás.

**gas.sy** adj. gasoso.

**gate** s. portão, porta, cancela.

**gate.way** s. porta, entrada ou saída; passagem.

**gath.er** s. prega, dobra / v. reunir, juntar.

**gath.er.ing** s. reunião, encontro; ato de reunir.

**gauche** adj. desajeitado.

**gaud.y** adj. afetado, exagerado; ostentoso.

**gaunt** adj. magro, descarnado, esquelético.

gauze     **239**     get in

**gauze** *s.* gaze.

**gave** *v. pret.* do *v. give.*

**gay** *adj.* homossexual; alegre / *s.* homossexual.

**gaze** *s.* olhar fixo / *v.* olhar fixamente, fitar.

**gaz.et.teer** *s.* dicionário geográfico.

**gear** *s.* engrenagem; equipamento / *v.* engrenar.

**gear.box** *s.* caixa de câmbio.

**gear-wheel** *s.* roda dentada.

**gel** *s.* gel.

**geld** *v.* castrar.

**geld.ing** *s.* castração.

**gem** *s.* joia, gema, pedra preciosa.

**Gem.i.ni** *s.* Gêmeos (astrologia).

**gen.der** *s.* gênero.

**gen.er.al** *s.* general / *adj.* geral.

**gen.er.al.ly** *adv.* geralmente.

**gen.er.ate** *v.* gerar, causar.

**gen.er.a.tor** *s.* gerador.

**gen.er.ous** *adj.* generoso.

**ge.ne.tic en.gin.eer.ing** *s.* engenharia genética.

**Ge.ne.va** *s.* Genebra.

**ge.ni.al** *adj.* cordial, amável.

**gen.i.tals** *s.* órgãos genitais.

**ge.ni.us** *s.* gênio, capacidade.

**gen.teel** *adj.* distinto, cavalheiresco.

**gen.tle** *adj.* suave, brando.

**gen.tle.man** *s.* cavalheiro.

**gen.tle.ness** *s.* meiguice; doçura.

**gen.tly** *adv.* gentilmente, suavemente.

**gen.try** *s.* pequena nobreza.

**gents** *s.* banheiro masculino.

**gen.u.ine** *adj.* autêntico.

**ge.og.ra.phy** *s.* geografia.

**ge.ol.o.gy** *s.* geologia.

**ge.om.e.try** *s.* geometria.

**ge.ra.ni.um** *s.* gerânio.

**ger.i.at.ric** *adj.* geriátrico / *s.* geriátrico.

**germ** *s.* micróbio, germe.

**Ger.man** *adj.* alemão (ã) / *s.* alemão (ã).

**Ger.man.y** *s.* Alemanha.

**get** *v.* tornar, receber, obter, ganhar.

**get a.bout** *v.* espalhar-se; circular; viajar muito.

**get a.long** *v.* entender-se com, lidar com; progredir.

**get a.round** *v.* rodear, viajar de lugar em lugar.

**get at** *v.* alcançar, certificar-se.

**get a.way** *v.* partir, ir embora, escapar / *s.* fuga.

**get back** *v.* voltar, receber de volta, regressar.

**get by** *v.* passar despercebido.

**get down** *v.* abaixar, descer.

**get in** *v.* entrar.

**get off** *v.* sair, decolar / *s.* decolagem.

**get on** *v.* subir.

**get out** *v.* sair.

**get-to.geth.er** *v.* reunir-se / *s.* reunião informal.

**get up** *v.* levantar da cama.

**get-up** *s.* enfeite, arranjo.

**ghast.ly** *adj.* horrível, medonho.

**ghost** *s.* fantasma, alma.

**gi.ant** *s.* gigante / *adj.* gigantesco.

**gid.dy** *adj.* com tontura, zonzo.

**gift** *s.* presente; dom, dádiva / *v.* presentear.

**gift.ed** *adj.* dotado, talentoso.

**gilt** *s.* dourado / *adj.* dourado.

**gim.mick** *s.* macete, truque.

**gin** *s.* gim.

**gin.ger** *s.* gengibre; pessoa ruiva.

**gin.ger.ly** *adv.* cuidadosamente, cautelosamente.

**gip.sy** *s.* cigano(a).

**gi.raffe** *s.* girafa.

**gir.der** *s.* viga mestra, suporte principal.

**girl** *s.* menina, garota.

**girl.friend** *s.* namorada; amiga.

**gist** *s.* essência, ponto principal.

**give** *v.* dar.

**give back** *v.* devolver.

**give in** *v.* ceder.

**give up** *v.* desistir; renunciar.

**giz.zard** *s.* moela.

**gla.ci.er** *s.* geleira.

**glad** *adj.* contente, alegre.

**glade** *s.* clareira.

**glad.ly** *adv.* com muito prazer.

**glam.our** *s.* encanto, deslumbramento.

**glam.or.ous** *adj.* glamoroso, deslumbrante.

**glance** *s.* relance, olhadela / *v.* dar uma olhada rápida, lançar os olhos.

**glanc.ing** *adj.* oblíquo.

**gland** *s.* glândula.

**glare** *s.* luminosidade, clarão; olhar penetrante / *v.* olhar com raiva.

**glass** *s.* vidro; copo.

**glass-house** *s.* estufa; fábrica de vidros.

**glass-ware** *s.* objetos de vidro.

**glaze** *s.* verniz; esmalte / *v.* envidraçar, vitrificar.

**glazed** *adj.* vitrificado.

**gla.zi.er** *s.* vidraceiro.

**gleam** *v.* brilhar, reluzir / *s.* lampejo, vislumbre.

**glean** *v.* colher aos poucos, obter.

**glee** *s.* regozijo, alegria.

**glen** *s.* vale estreito e profundo.

**glib** *adj.* lisonjeiro, volúvel.

# glide / godsend

**glide** *s.* deslizamento / *v.* planar, deslizar.

**glid.er** *s.* planador (piloto ou avião).

**glid.ing** *s.* voo sem motor.

**glim.mer** *s.* lampejo, luz trêmula / *v.* vislumbrar.

**glint** *s.* raio de luz, lampejos / *v.* cintilar; reluzir.

**glis.ten** *v.* brilhar / *s.* brilho, resplendor.

**glit.ter** *s.* brilho / *v.* reluzir.

**glob.al** *adj.* mundial; total, integral.

**globe** *s.* globo, esfera.

**gloom** *s.* escuridão; tristeza / *v.* escurecer, estar triste.

**gloom.y** *adj.* escuro; sombrio, triste.

**glo.ri.fy** *v.* glorificar, honrar.

**glo.ri.ous** *adj.* glorioso, ilustre.

**glo.ry** *s.* glória; beleza.

**gloss** *s.* brilho, lustro; brilho para os lábios (cosmético) / *v.* polir, lustrar.

**glos.sa.ry** *s.* glossário.

**gloss.y** *adj.* lustroso, reluzente.

**glove** *s.* luva.

**glove com.part.ment** *s.* porta--luvas.

**glow-worm** *s.* pirilampo, vaga--lume.

**glu.cose** *s.* glicose.

**glue** *s.* cola / *v.* colar.

**glum** *adj.* carrancudo, de mau humor.

**glut** *s.* fartura, abundância / *v.* fartar, saturar.

**glut.ton** *s.* glutão(ona), comilão(ona).

**glut.ton.y** *s.* gula, glutonaria.

**gnarled** *adj.* retorcido; áspero.

**gnat** *s.* mosquito.

**gnaw** *v.* roer algo; atormentar alguém.

**go ahead** *v.* ir em frente, avançar.

**go away** *v.* ir embora.

**go back** *v.* voltar.

**go on** *v.* continuar.

**goal** *s.* meta, objetivo; gol.

**goal.keep.er** *s.* goleiro(a).

**goal.post** *s.* trave de gol.

**goat** *s.* cabra, bode; Capricórnio (astrologia).

**gob.ble down** *v.* devorar.

**go-be.tween** *s.* intermediário(a).

**gob.let** *s.* cálice, taça.

**god** *s.* deus, ídolo.

**God** *s.* Deus.

**god.child** *s.* afilhado(a).

**god.daughter** *s.* afilhada.

**god.dess** *s.* deusa.

**god.fa.ther** *s.* padrinho.

**god.like** *adj.* divino.

**god.moth.er** *s.* madrinha.

**god.send** *s.* dádiva do céu.

**god.son** *s.* afilhado.

**go.ing** *s.* andamento; curso da vida / *adj.* andante, em movimento.

**gold** *s.* ouro.

**gold.en** *adj.* dourado, de ouro.

**gold.fish** *s.* peixe-dourado.

**gold mine** *s.* mina de ouro.

**gold.smith** *s.* ourives.

**golf** *s.* golfe.

**golf.er** *s.* jogador de golfe.

**gone** *v. pp.* do *v. to go*.

**gong** *s.* gongo.

**good** *adj.* bom, boa.

**good-bye** *interj.* até logo! adeus!

**Good Fri.day** *s.* Sexta-feira Santa.

**good-for-noth.ing** *s.* pessoa inútil.

**good-hu.moured** *adj.* bem--humorado.

**good-look.ing** *adj.* bonito.

**good-na.tured** *adj.* de boa índole.

**good.ness** *s.* bondade / *interj.* céus!

**goods** *s. pl.* mercadorias; bens, posses.

**good.will** *s.* boa vontade, benevolência.

**good.y** *s.* velhinha; beata; gulodice.

**goof** *s.* bobo, pateta (coloquial).

**goon** *s.* pessoa estúpida (coloquial).

**goose** *s. (pl. geese)* ganso.

**goose.ber.ry** *s.* groselha espinhosa.

**gorge** *s.* garganta, goela (anatomia); desfiladeiro, garganta (geografia).

**gor.geous** *adj.* magnífico, deslumbrante.

**go.ril.la** *s.* gorila.

**gorse** *s.* tojo.

**go.ry** *adj.* sangrento, ensanguentado.

**gosh** *interj.* Deus!; caramba!

**go-slow** *s.* operação tartaruga; greve branca.

**gos.pel** *s.* evangelho / *adj.* evangélico.

**gos.sip** *s.* fofoca, fofoqueiro(a) / *v.* fofocar.

**got** *v. pret.* do *v. to get*.

**got.ten** *v. pp.* do *v. to get*.

**gout** *s.* gota (doença).

**gov.ern** *v.* governar, administrar.

**gov.er.ness** *s.* governanta.

**gov.ern.ment** *s.* governo, administração.

**gov.er.nor** *s.* governador(a).

**gown** *s.* vestido longo; beca, toga.

**grab** *v.* agarrar.

**grace** *s.* graça, elegância / *v.* adornar.

**grace.ful** *adj.* gracioso, elegante.

**gra.cious** *adj.* afável; elegante, luxuoso.

# grade / gravel

**grade** *s.* classe; grau
/ *v.* classificar.

**grade cross.ing** *s.* passagem de nível.

**grade school** *s.* escola primária.

**gra.di.ent** *s.* declive, inclinação.

**grad.u.al** *adj.* gradual.

**grad.u.al.ly** *adv.* gradualmente, paulatinamente.

**grad.u.ate** *s.* graduado, diplomado / *v.* formar-se, graduar-se.

**grad.u.a.tion** *s.* formatura, graduação, colação de grau.

**graf.fi.ti** *s.* pichação, grafite.

**graft** *s.* enxerto / *v.* enxertar.

**grain** *s.* grão.

**grained** *adj.* granulado.

**gram** *s.* grama (unidade de massa).

**gram.mar** *s.* gramática.

**gram.mat.i.cal** *adj.* gramatical.

**grand** *adj.* esplêndido, formidável.

**grand.child** *s.* neto(a).

**grand.daugh.ter** *s.* neta.

**gran.deur** *s.* grandeza.

**grand.fa.ther** *s.* avô.

**gran.di.o.se** *adj.* grandioso, imponente.

**grand.ness** *s.* grandeza.

**grand.moth.er** *s.* avó.

**grand.par.ents** *s.* avós.

**grand pi.a.no** *s.* piano de cauda.

**grand.son** *s.* neto.

**gran.ger** *s.* granjeiro.

**gran.ite** *s.* granito.

**gran.ny** *s.* vovó, vó.

**grant** *v.* conceder / *s.* subsídio, subvenção.

**gran.u.lat.ed** *adj.* granulado.

**grape** *s.* uva; videira.

**grape.fruit** *s.* toranja.

**graph** *s.* gráfico.

**graph.ic** *adj.* gráfico.

**graph.ic arts** *s.* artes gráficas.

**grap.ple** *s.* agarramento, luta
/ *v.* atracar-se com.

**grasp** *v.* agarrar, pegar.

**grasp.ing** *adj.* avaro; ganancioso.

**grass** *s.* grama, gramado.

**grass.hop.per** *s.* gafanhoto.

**grass roots** *s.* povo comum, zonas rurais.

**grate** *v.* ralar; ranger.

**grate.ful** *adj.* agradecido, grato.

**grat.er** *s.* ralador.

**grat.ing** *adj.* rangedor, rilhador
/ *s.* grade, barras de ferro.

**grat.i.tude** *s.* gratidão.

**gra.tu.i.ty** *s.* gratificação, gorjeta.

**grave** *s.* cova, sepultura
/ *adj.* sério, grave / *v.* gravar, esculpir.

**grav.el** *s.* cascalho, pedregulho.

G

gravestone     **244**     groggy

**grave.stone** *s.* lápide, túmulo.

**grave.yard** *s.* cemitério.

**grav.i.ty** *s.* gravidade (física), seriedade ( formal).

**gra.vy** *s.* molho ou caldo de carne.

**gray, grey** *adj.* cinzento, cinza / *s.* cinza.

**grease** *s.* gordura, banha; graxa / *v.* engraxar; lubrificar.

**greas.y** *adj.* gorduroso, oleoso.

**great** *adj.* genial; grande, vasto; formidável.

**great grand.daught.er** *s.* bisneta.

**great grand.father** *s.* bisavô.

**great grand.mother** *s.* bisavó.

**great grand.son** *s.* bisneto.

**great.ly** *adv.* imensamente, muito.

**great.ness** *s.* grandeza.

**Greece** *s.* Grécia.

**greed** *s.* ganância; gula.

**Greek** *s.* grego / *adj.* grego.

**green** *adj.* verde; imaturo, inexperiente / *s.* verde.

**green card** *s.* autorização de residência nos EUA.

**green.gro.cer** *s.* verdureiro, quitandeiro.

**green.ery** *s.* verdura, hortaliças.

**green.house** *s.* estufa.

**green.ish** *adj.* esverdeado.

**Green.land** *s.* Groenlândia.

**greens** *s. pl.* verduras.

**greet** *v.* acolher; saudar, cumprimentar.

**greet.ing** *s.* saudação, cumprimento.

**greet.ing(s) card** *s.* cartão comemorativo; saudação.

**gre.nade** *s.* granada.

**grew** *v. pret.* do *v.* to grow.

**grey** *adj.* cinzento, cinza / *s.* cinza.

**grey-haired** *adj.* grisalho.

**grid** *s.* grade; grelha; linhas (de coordenadas).

**grid.dle** *s.* forma redonda para bolo.

**grief** *s.* pesar, aflição.

**griev.ance** *s.* queixa, mágoa.

**grieve** *v.* afligir; chorar a perda de alguém.

**grill** *s.* grelha / *v.* grelhar.

**grille** *s.* grade (de proteção).

**grim** *adj.* desagradável, carrancudo, severo.

**grim.y** *adj.* encardido.

**grind** *v.* moer, triturar.

**grip** *s.* aderência, cabo, alça / *v.* agarrar.

**gripe** *s.* aperto, agarramento.

**gripp.ing** *adj.* fascinante.

**gris.ly** *adj.* medonho, terrível.

**gris.tle** *s.* nervo; cartilagem.

**griz.zly bear** *s.* urso-pardo (EUA).

**groan** *s.* gemido / *v.* gemer.

**gro.cer** *s.* dono de mercearia.

**gro.cer.ies** *s.* mantimentos.

**gro.cer.y** *s.* mercearia.

**grog.gy** *adj.* grogue, embriagado; tonto, zonzo.

groin *s.* virilha.

groom *s.* noivo.

groove *s.* ranhura, entalhe, sulco / *v.* entalhar, sulcar.

gross *s.* grosa (doze dúzias) / *adj.* inteiro, total, bruto / *v.* totalizar.

gross.ly *adv.* inteiramente, extremamente; grosseiramente.

gro.tesque *adj.* grotesco.

grot.to *s.* gruta, caverna.

grot.ty *adj.* repugnante.

ground *s.* terreno, terra, chão, solo; fundamento / *v.* fundamentar, basear.

ground-floor *s.* andar térreo.

ground.ing *s.* base, fundamentos; primeira demão (pintura).

ground.work *s.* preparação; base, princípio fundamental.

grouse *s.* galo silvestre / *v.* resmungar.

grout *s.* reboco / *v.* rebocar.

grove *s.* arvoredo, bosque.

grov.el *v.* abaixar-se, humilhar-se, rastejar.

grow *v.* crescer; cultivar; aumentar.

grow up *v.* tornar-se adulto, desenvolver-se.

grow.ing *adj.* crescente / *s.* crescimento.

growl *v.* rosnar, rugir / *s.* rosnado, rugido.

grown *v. pp.* do *v. to grow* / *adj.* crescido, adulto.

growth *s.* crescimento, aumento

grub *s.* larva, lagarta; boia (comida) (coloquial).

grub.by *adj.* sujo, imundo.

grudge *v.* ter rancor; invejar alguém / *s.* rancor, ressentimento.

gru.el.ing *adj.* árduo, cansativo, penoso.

grue.some *adj.* horrível, medonho.

gruff *adj.* rude, brusco; áspero.

grum.ble *v.* resmungar / *s.* queixa.

grump.y *adj.* rabugento, resmungão.

grunt *s.* grunhido / *v.* grunhir, resmungar.

guar.an.tee *s.* garantia / *v.* garantir.

guard *s.* guarda, vigia / *v.* vigiar, proteger.

guard.ed *adj.* cauteloso, precavido.

guard.i.an *s.* tutor(a), guardião(o).

guard.i.an.ship *s.* tutela.

guard-rail *s.* trilho ou grade de segurança.

**Gua.te.ma.la** *s.* Guatemala.

**gua.va** *s.* goiaba.

**guer.ril.la** *s.* guerrilheiro(a).

**guess** *v.* adivinhar, imaginar / *s.* suposição.

**guest** *s.* convidado(a); hóspede.

**guest.room** *s.* quarto de hóspedes.

**guf.faw** *v.* gargalhar / *s.* gargalhada.

**guid.ance** *s.* orientação; supervisão.

**guide** *s.* guia (pessoa ou livro) / *v.* guiar, orientar.

**guide-book** *s.* guia (livro).

**guider** *s.* guia, condutor.

**guide.line** *s.* orientação, diretriz.

**guile** *s.* astúcia, malícia, fraude.

**guile.less** *adj.* sincero, sem malícia, ingênuo.

**guilt** *s.* culpa.

**guilt.less** *adj.* inocente.

**guilt.y** *adj.* culpado (a).

**guinea pig** *s.* porquinho-da-índia.

**gui.tar** *s.* violão, guitarra.

**gulf** *s.* golfo.

**gull** *s.* gaivota / *v.* enganar.

**gul.let** *s.* esôfago, garganta, goela.

**gul.ly** *s.* rego, bueiro.

**gulp** *v.* engolir, tragar / *s.* trago, gole.

**gum** *s.* goma, chiclete; gengiva (geralmente no plural *gums*).

**gum.boots** *s.* galochas.

**gump.tion** *s.* juízo; bom senso.

**gun** *s.* arma, pistola, espingarda / *v.* atirar.

**gun.fire** *s.* tiroteio.

**gun.man** *s.* pistoleiro.

**gun.point** *s.* ponta ou mira de arma.

**gun.pow.der** *s.* pólvora.

**gurk** *s.* arroto / *v.* arrotar.

**gu.ru** *s.* guru.

**gust** *s.* rajada de vento; gosto, gozo, deleite.

**gus.to** *s.* garra, entusiasmo (coloquial).

**gut** *s.* intestino, tripa ♦ ~*s* coragem (coloquial).

**gut.ter** *s.* calha; sarjeta; rego.

**guy** *s.* cara, sujeito, rapaz (coloquial).

**Guy.an.a** *s.* Guiana.

**guz.zle** *s.* bebedeira / *v.* empaturrar-se, encher a cara de.

**gym** *s. abrev.* de *gymnasium*

**gym.na.sium** *s.* ginástica; ginásio de esporte.

**gym.nast** *s.* ginasta.

**gym.nas.tics** *s.* ginástica.

**gy.ne.col.ogist** *s.* ginecologista.

**gyp** *s.* trapaceiro (coloquial) / *v.* lograr, enganar.

**gyve** *s.* algema (geralmente no plural *gyves*) / algemar.

# Hh

**H, h** s. oitava letra do alfabeto inglês.

**ha** v. zumbir / *interj.* ai!, ah!

**hab.er.dash.er.y** s. loja de armarinho; loja de roupas masculinas.

**hab.it** s. hábito, costume.

**ha.bit.u.al** *adj.* habitual.

**hack** s. corte / v. cortar; invadir algo ilegalmente (coloquial).

**hack.er** s. pirata de computador (coloquial).

**hack.neyed** *adj.* corriqueiro; vulgar.

**had** v. *pret.* e *pp.* do v. *to have.*

**had.dock** s. hadoque.

**hadn't** contração de *had not.*

**hail** s. granizo; saudação / v. chover granizo; saudar.

**hail.stone** s. pedra de granizo.

**hair** s. cabelo; pelo.

**hair.brush** s. escova de cabelo.

**hair.cut** s. corte de cabelo.

**hair.do** s. penteado de mulher (coloquial).

**hair.dress.er** s. cabeleireiro(a).

**hair.pin** s. grampo de cabelo.

**hair-rais.ing** *adj.* horripilante, de arrepiar os cabelos.

**hair spray** s. laquê.

**hair.y** *adj.* peludo; cabeludo.

**hale** *adj.* vigoroso, são / v. puxar, levantar.

**half** s. (pl. *halves*) metade, meio / *adj.* meio, metade de / *adv.* pela metade.

**half-baked** *adj.* meio assado (pão); inexperiente.

# half-bred — hangman

**248**

**half-bred** *adj.* raça mista, bastardo.

**half.caste** *s.* mestiço(a).

**half-mast** *s.* meio-mastro; pôr a bandeira a meio-mastro.

**half.moon** *s.* meia-lua.

**hall** *s.* saguão; entrada.

**hall.mark** *s.* marca de qualidade (de metais preciosos).

**hal.lowed** *adj.* sagrado.

**Hal.low.een** *s.* dia das bruxas.

**hall.way** *s.* corredor, entrada.

**halt** *s.* parada, interrupção; descanso / *v.* deter-se, parar.

**hal.ter** *s.* cabresto / *v.* amarrar com corda.

**halve** *v.* dividir ao meio.

**ham** *s.* presunto.

**ham.burg.er** *s.* hambúrguer; almôndega.

**ham.let** *s.* lugarejo; vilarejo.

**ham.mer** *s.* martelo / *v.* martelar.

**ham.mock** *s.* rede (de dormir).

**ham.per** *s.* cesto grande; empecilho, estorvo / *v.* impedir, tolher.

**ham.ster** *s.* hamster.

**hand** *s.* mão / *v.* dar, entregar.

**hand.bag** *s.* bolsa (de mulher); maleta.

**hand.bill** *s.* folheto.

**hand.book** *s.* manual.

**hand.brake** *s.* freio de mão.

**hand.cuff** *s.* algema / *v.* algemar.

**hand.ful** *s.* punhado.

**hand.i.cap** *s.* incapacidade, deficiência / *v.* prejudicar.

**hand.i.craft** *s.* artesanato; habilidade manual.

**hand.i.work** *s.* obra, trabalho manual.

**hand.ker.chief** *s.* lenço de bolso.

**han.dle** *s.* maçaneta, asa, alça, cabo da xícara / *v.* manusear, lidar com.

**han.dle bars** *s.* guidão de bicicleta.

**hand.made** *adj.* feito à mão.

**hand.out** *s.* doação, donativo; folheto.

**hand.rail** *s.* corrimão.

**hand.shake** *s.* aperto de mão.

**hand.some** *adj.* atraente, bonito; generoso.

**hand.writ.ing** *s.* caligrafia.

**hand.y** *adj.* habilidoso, prático; à mão.

**hand.y.man** *s.* biscateiro.

**hang** *v.* pendurar; enforcar.

**hang on** *v.* esperar, aguardar.

**han.gar** *s.* hangar, galpão.

**hang.er** *s.* cabide.

**hang.ing** *s.* enforcamento.

**hang.man** *s.* carrasco.

**hang.o.ver** *s.* ressaca.

**hang-up** *s.* problema, grilo (coloquial).

**hap.haz.ard** *adj.* por acaso / *adv.* casualmente.

**hap.pen** *v.* acontecer, ocorrer.

**hap.pen.ing** *s.* acontecimento, ocorrência.

**hap.pi.ly** *adv.* felizmente, alegremente.

**hap.pi.ness** *s.* felicidade, alegria.

**hap.py** *adj.* feliz, alegre.

**ha.rass** *v.* importunar, molestar, incomodar.

**har.ass.ment** *s.* perseguição, assédio, tormento.

**har.bor** *s.* porto; abrigo, refúgio / *v.* abrigar, proteger.

**hard** *adj.* duro; difícil.

**hard disk** *s.* disco rígido (informática).

**hard.en** *v.* endurecer.

**hard.ly** *adv.* dificilmente.

**hard.ness** *s.* dureza.

**hard.ship** *s.* privação, dificuldade.

**hard up** *adj.* sem dinheiro; em apuros.

**hard.ware** *s.* ferragens; *hardware* (informática).

**hard-wear.ing** *adj.* resistente, durável.

**hard-working** *adj.* trabalhador(a), aplicado.

**hard.y** *adj.* resistente, robusto.

**hare** *s.* lebre.

**hare-brained** *adj.* maluco.

**har.lot** *s.* prostituta.

**harm** *s.* dano / *v.* prejudicar.

**harm.ful** *adj.* prejudicial.

**harm.less** *adj.* inofensivo.

**har.mon.i.ca** *s.* gaita; harmônio.

**har.mo.ni.ous** *adj.* harmonioso.

**har.mo.ny** *s.* harmonia.

**har.ness** *s.* correia, arreios / *v.* arrear (cavalo).

**harp** *s.* harpa / *v.* tocar harpa.

**har.poon** *s.* arpão.

**har.row** *s.* rastelo, ancinho.

**harsh** *adj.* desarmonioso; áspero; estridente; duro.

**har.vest** *s.* colheita / *v.* colher.

**has** *v. 3ª pess. sing. pres.* do *v. to have*.

**hash** *s.* picadinho, guisado.

**hash.ish** *s.* haxixe.

**hasn't** contração de *has not*.

**has.sle** *s.* complicação, trabalhão (coloquial).

**haste** *s.* pressa / *v.* apressar.

**has.ten** *v.* acelerar, apressar-se.

**hast.ily** *adv.* depressa, apressadamente.

**hast.y** *adj.* ligeiro, rápido, apressado; precipitado.

**hat** *s.* chapéu.

**hatch** *s.* ninhada; escotilha; abertura / *v.* sair do ovo; chocar, incubar.

**hatch.et** *s.* machadinha.

**hate** *s.* ódio / *v.* odiar.

**hate.ful** *adj.* odioso, detestável.

**ha.tred** *s.* ódio, aversão.

**haul** *v.* puxar, arrastar.

**haunt** *v.* assombrar / *s.* abrigo, lugar preferido.

**have** *v.* ter, possuir.

**ha.ven** *s.* porto, ancoradouro; refúgio / *v.* abrigar.

**haven't** contração de *have not.*

**hav.er.sack** *s.* mochila; farnel.

**hav.oc** *s.* destruição, devastação / *v.* destruir, devastar.

**Ha.wai.i** *s.* Havaí.

**hawk** *s.* falcão, gavião.

**hay** *s.* feno.

**hay-loft** *s.* palheiro.

**haystack** *s.* monte de feno.

**haz.ard** *s.* perigo, risco / *v.* aventurar, arriscar (jogos).

**haz.ard.ous** *adj.* perigoso, arriscado.

**haze** *s.* neblina, cerração / *v.* enevoar, obscurecer; judiar, maltratar.

**ha.zel.nut** *s.* avelã.

**haz.y** *adj.* nebuloso; vago, confuso.

**he** *pron.* ele.

**head** *s.* cabeça / *v.* encabeçar.

**head.ache** *s.* dor de cabeça.

**head.ing** *s.* cabeçalho, título.

**head.light** *s.* farol de automóvel.

**head.line** *s.* título, manchete (de jornal).

**head-on** *adv.* de ponta-cabeça; de frente.

**head.phone** *s.* fone de ouvido.

**head.quarters** *s.* quartel-general; sede.

**head.strong** *adj.* teimoso, obstinado.

**head.y** *adj.* estonteante, inebriante; violento, irrefletido; forte.

**heal** *v.* curar, cicatrizar, sarar.

**health** *s.* saúde.

**health.y** *adj.* saudável, sadio(a).

**heap** *s.* pilha / *v.* empilhar.

**hear** *v.* ouvir, escutar.

**hear.ing** *s.* audição; interrogatório.

**hear.ing aid** *s.* aparelho para surdez.

**hear.say** *s.* boato, rumor.

**hearse** *s.* carro funerário.

**heart** *s.* coração.

**heart.ache** *s.* mágoa.

**heart at.tack** *s.* ataque cardíaco.

**heart.beat** *s.* batida do coração.

**heart.break.ing** *adj.* angustiante, de partir o coração.

**heart.brok.en** *adj.* angustiado, de coração partido.

**heart.burn** *s.* azia; inveja.

**heart.en** *v.* animar.

**heart fail.ure** *s.* parada cardíaca.

**heart.felt** *adj.* sincero, cordial.

**heart.land** *s.* área central.

**heart.less** *adj.* sem coração, insensível.

**heat** *s.* calor / *v.* aquecer.

**heat.ed** *adj.* aquecida.

**heat.er** *s.* aquecedor.

**hea.then** *s.* pagão(ã).

**heat.ing** *s.* aquecimento, calefação.

**heat stroke** *s.* insolação.

**heat wave** *s.* onda de calor.

**heav.en** *s.* paraíso, céu.

**heav.en.ly** *adj.* divino, celestial.

**heav.i.ly** *adj.* muito, em grande quantidade; pesadamente.

**heav.y** *adj.* pesado; cansativo.

**heav.y.weight** *s.* peso-pesado.

**He.brew** *s.* hebreu, hebraico, / *adj.* hebraico.

**hec.tic** *adj.* frenético; febril; corado / *s.* tísica.

**hedge** *s.* cerca viva, cerca, sebe / *v.* cercar, restringir.

**heed** *s.* cuidado, atenção / *v.* prestar atenção.

**heel** *s.* calcanhar; salto de sapato.

**hef.ty** *adj.* robusto, pesado, forte.

**heif.er** *s.* novilha, bezerra.

**height** *s.* altura, altitude.

**height.en** *v.* elevar, intensificar, levantar.

**heir** *s.* herdeiro.

**heir.ess** *s.* herdeira.

**heir.loom** *s.* relíquia de família, peça de herança.

**held** *v. pret. e pp.* do *v. to hold*.

**hel.i.cop.ter** *s.* helicóptero.

**hel.i.port** *s.* heliporto.

**he.li.um** *s.* hélio (química).

**hell** *s.* inferno; droga! (coloquial).

**hell.ish** *adj.* terrível, infernal.

**hel.lo** *interj.* olá! oi! alô!

**helm** *s.* leme, direção, timão (navio).

**hel.met** *s.* capacete.

**help** *s.* ajuda, auxílio, socorro / *v.* ajudar, auxiliar.

**help.er** *s.* ajudante.

**help.ful** *adj.* prestativo, útil.

**help.ing** *s.* porção (de comida); ajuda.

**help.less** *adj.* indefeso; desamparado.

**help.mate** *s.* ajudante.

**hem** *s.* bainha / *v.* fazer a bainha.

**hem.i.sphere** *s.* hemisfério.

**hem.or.rhage** *s.* hemorragia.

**hem.or.rhoids** *s.* hemorroidas.

**hen** *s.* galinha; fêmea de qualquer ave.

**hence** *adv.* portanto, por isso.

**hence.forth** *adv.* de agora em diante.

**hench.man** *s.* capanga.

**hep.a.ti.tis** *s.* hepatite.

**her** *adj. poss.* dela / *pron.* lhe, a ela, sua, seu, a.

**her.ald** *s.* precursor(a); mensageiro / *v.* anunciar, trazer notícias.

**herb** *s.* erva; forragem, capim.

**herd** *s.* rebanho, manada.

**here** *adv.* aqui, cá.

**here.a.bout(s)** *adv.* por aqui.

**here.af.ter** *adv.* daqui por diante, depois / *s.* futuro.

**here.by** *adv.* por este meio, por isto.

**he.red.i.ty** *s.* hereditariedade.

**her.e.sy** *s.* heresia.

**her.e.tic** *s.* herege / *adj.* herege.

**her.i.tage** *s.* patrimônio; herança.

**her.met.ic.ally** *adv.* hermeticamente.

**her.mit** *s.* eremita.

**her.ni.a** *s.* hérnia.

**he.ro** *s.* herói; protagonista.

**her.o.in** *s.* heroína (droga).

**her.o.ine** *s.* heroína (pessoa); protagonista.

**he.ron** *s.* garça.

**her.ring** *s.* arenque (peixe).

**hers** *pron. poss.* dela, seu, sua.

**her.self** *pron.* ela mesma, se, a si mesma.

**hes.i.tant** *adj.* indeciso, hesitante.

**hes.i.tate** *v.* hesitar, vacilar.

**hes.i.ta.tion** *s.* indecisão, hesitação.

**het.e.ro.sex.u.al** *adj.* heterossexual.

**hew** *v.* cortar com machado, derrubar.

**hey.day** *s.* auge, apogeu.

**hi** *interj.* oi!

**hi.ber.nate** *v.* hibernar.

**hic.cough, hic.cup** *v.* soluçar / *s.* soluço.

**hick** *s.* caipira (coloquial).

**hid** *v. pret.* do *v. to hide*.

**hide** *v.* esconder, ocultar.

**hide-and-seek** *s.* esconde-esconde.

**hide.a.way** *s.* esconderijo, refúgio.

**hi.er.ar.chy** *s.* hierarquia.

**hi-fi** *adj.* alta-fidelidade / *s.* aparelho (de alta-fidelidade) (coloquial).

**high** *adj.* alto, elevado, superior.

**high.born** *adj.* de alta linhagem; de nascimento ilustre.

**high.brow** *s.* intelectual, erudito.

| | |
|---|---|
| **high chair** *s.* cadeira alta, cadeira de bebê. | **hind.er** *v.* retardar, atrapalhar. |
| **higher ed.u.ca.tion** *s.* ensino superior. | **hin.drance** *s.* estorvo, obstáculo, impedimento. |
| **high-hat** *adj.* grã-fino, arrogante. | **hind.sight** *s.* retrospecto; compreensão tardia. |
| **high-heeled** *adj.* de salto alto | **Hin.du** *adj.* hindu / *s.* hindu. |

**high chair** *s.* cadeira alta, cadeira de bebê.

**higher ed.u.ca.tion** *s.* ensino superior.

**high-hat** *adj.* grã-fino, arrogante.

**high-heeled** *adj.* de salto alto

**high.light** *v.* realçar, ressaltar; iluminar / *s.* ponto alto, melhor momento.

**high.ly** *adv.* altamente, muito, extremamente.

**High.ness** *s.* alteza.

**high school** *s.* escola secundária.

**high seas.on** *s.* alta temporada.

**high.way** *s.* estrada, rodovia.

**hi.jack** *v.* sequestrar (avião).

**hi.jack.er** *s.* sequestrador (de avião).

**hike** *s.* caminhada / *v.* caminhar.

**hik.er** *s.* andarilho(a), aquele(a) que caminha bastante.

**hi.lar.i.ous** *adj.* hilário, hilariante, divertido.

**hill** *s.* colina, ladeira, morro.

**hill.side** *s.* encosta.

**hill.y** *adj.* montanhoso.

**hilt** *s.* cabo, punho (de faca ou de espada).

**him.self** *pron.* ele mesmo, se, a si mesmo.

**hind** *s.* corça (fêmea do veado) / *adj.* traseiro posterior.

**hind.er** *v.* retardar, atrapalhar.

**hin.drance** *s.* estorvo, obstáculo, impedimento.

**hind.sight** *s.* retrospecto; compreensão tardia.

**Hin.du** *adj.* hindu / *s.* hindu.

**hinge** *s.* dobradiça / *v.* colocar em dobradiças.

**hip** *s.* quadril; anca.

**hip.po.pot.a.mus** *s.* hipopótamo.

**hire** *s.* aluguel, arrendamento / *v.* alugar, arrendar, contratar.

**his** *adj. poss.* dele / *pron.* dele, seu(s), sua(s).

**hiss** *s.* assobio, silvo / *v.* assobiar, sibilar.

**his.to.ri.an** *s.* historiador(a).

**his.tor.ic(al)** *adj.* histórico(a).

**his.to.ry** *s.* história, narração.

**hit** *v.* bater, acertar, atingir / *s.* golpe, pancada.

**hitch.hike** *v.* pedir carona.

**hi-tech** *s.* alta tecnologia.

**hive** *s.* colmeia.

**hoar.frost** *s.* geada.

**hoarse** *adj.* rouco.

**hob** *s.* placa de aquecimento (de fogão).

**hob.ble** *v.* mancar; impedir.

**hob.by** *s.* passatempo preferido.

**hock.ey** *s.* hóquei.

**hoe** *s.* enxada.

**hog** *s.* porco capado.

**hoist** *v.* içar, levantar.

**hold** *v.* segurar, pegar.

**hold.er** *s.* recipiente, vasilhame; portador(a); titular, proprietário.

**hold.ing** *s.* participação ♦ ~ *company* sociedade teto.

**hold on** *v.* esperar; firmar, segurar.

**hold up** *s.* assalto à mão armada; atraso; engarrafamento.

**hole** *s.* buraco, orifício, toca / *v.* esburacar, furar.

**hol.i.day** *s.* folga, feriado, dia santo; férias.

**ho.li.ness** *s.* santidade.

**Hol.land** *s.* Holanda.

**hol.low** *adj.* oco, vazio / *s.* cavidade, buraco.

**hol.ly** *s.* azevinho (botânica).

**hol.o.caust** *s.* holocausto, destruição.

**ho.ly** *adj.* sagrado, santo.

**hom.age** *s.* homenagem.

**home** *s.* casa, lar / *adv.* para casa.

**home ad.dress** *s.* endereço residencial.

**home com.put.er** *s.* computador doméstico.

**home.less** *adj.* desabrigado, sem lar / *s.* mendigo.

**home.made** *adj.* caseiro, feito em casa.

**home.town** *s.* cidade natal.

**home.work** *s.* lição de casa.

**ho.mo.ge.ne.ous** *adj.* homogêneo.

**ho.mo.sex.u.al** *adj.* homossexual / *s.* homossexual.

**Hon.du.ras** *s.* Honduras.

**hon.est** *adj.* honesto, franco, sincero.

**hon.est.ly** *adv.* honestamente, francamente.

**hon.es.ty** *s.* honestidade, honradez, franqueza.

**hon.ey** *s.* mel; doçura, querido(a) (coloquial).

**hon.ey.comb** *s.* favo de mel.

**hon.ey.moon** *s.* lua de mel.

**honk** *v.* buzinar.

**ho.nor** *v.* honrar / *s.* honra, dignidade.

**hon.or.a.ble** *adj.* honrado, honesto, ilustre, decente.

**hon.or.ar.y** *adj.* honorário.

**hood** *s.* capuz; capô.

**hood.wink** *v.* tapear, enganar, lograr; vendar os olhos.

**hoof** *s.* casco, pata.

**hook** *s.* gancho; anzol (pesca); / *v.* prender, fisgar.

**hoo.li.gan** *s.* desordeiro(a), vândalo.

**hoop** *s.* arco (de barril), aro, argola.

**hoot** *s.* vaia; pio (coruja); barulho (de buzina) / *v.* piar; buzinar; vaiar.

**hoot.er** *s.* buzina, sirene.

**hoo.ver** *s.* aspirador de pó / *v.* aspirar (com o aspirador).

**hop** *s.* pulo / *v.* pular em um pé só.

**hope** *v.* esperar, ter esperança / *s.* esperança.

**hope.ful** *adj.* esperançoso, otimista.

**hope.ful.ly** *adv.* esperançosamente, com otimismo.

**hope.less** *adj.* desesperado; inútil; impossível.

**horde** *s.* multidão, horda.

**ho.ri.zon** *s.* horizonte ♦ ~s perspectiva.

**hor.i.zon.tal** *adj.* horizontal.

**hor.mone** *s.* hormônio.

**horn** *s.* chifre, corno; buzina (carro); trompa, corneta (música).

**hor.net** *s.* vespão.

**horn.y** *adj.* córneo, caloso; excitado sexualmente (coloquial).

**hor.o.scope** *s.* horóscopo.

**hor.ri.ble** *adj.* horrível.

**hor.rid** *adj.* terrível, antipático.

**hor.ri.fy** *v.* horrorizar.

**hor.ror** *s.* horror, pavor.

**horse** *s.* cavalo.

**horse.back** *s.* garupa de cavalo / *adv.* a cavalo.

**horse.fly** *s.* mutuca.

**horse.hair** *s.* crina de cavalo.

**horse.shoe** *s.* ferradura.

**hor.ti.cul.ture** *s.* horticultura.

**hose** *s.* mangueira.

**hos.pice** *s.* asilo; hospício.

**hos.pi.ta.ble** *adj.* hospitaleiro.

**hos.pi.tal** *s.* hospital.

**hos.pi.tal.i.ty** *s.* hospitalidade.

**host** *s.* anfitrião; apresentador; hóstia (religião) / *v.* hospedar, receber.

**hos.tage** *s.* refém.

**hos.tel** *s.* albergue, hospedaria.

**host.ess** *s.* anfitriã; recepcionista.

**hos.tile** *adj.* hostil, inimigo.

**hos.til.i.ty** *s.* hostilidade.

**hot** *adj.* quente; ardente, picante.

**hot-blood.ed** *adj.* de sangue quente, fogoso.

**hot dog** *s.* cachorro-quente.

**ho.tel** *s.* hotel.

**ho.tel.i.er** *s.* hoteleiro(a).

**hot.house** *s.* estufa de plantas.

**hot line** *s.* linha direta.

**hot.ly** *adv.* ardentemente, calorosamente.

**hot.plate** *s.* chapa elétrica.

**hound** *s.* cão de caça / *v.* caçar, perseguir.

**hour** *s.* hora.

**hour.ly** *adj.* de hora em hora / *adv.* de hora em hora.

**house** *s.* casa, residência / *v.* alojar, acomodar.

**house ar.rest** *s.* prisão domiciliar.

**house.break.ing** *s.* arrombamento, furto.

**house.keep.er** *s.* governanta.

**house.maid** *s.* doméstica, arrumadeira.

**house.warm.ing** *s.* festa de inauguração de uma casa nova.

**housewife** (*pl. housewives*) *s.* dona de casa.

**house.work** *s.* trabalhos domésticos.

**hous.ing** *s.* alojamento, moradia.

**hov.el** *s.* cabana, choupana.

**how** *adv.* como, de qual maneira.

**how.ev.er** *adv.* de qualquer modo / *conj.* contudo, porém, todavia.

**howl** *s.* uivo, urro, grito / *v.* uivar, berrar.

**hub** *s.* cubo (da roda); centro.

**hub.bub** *s.* algazarra, tumulto.

**hub.cap** *s.* calota.

**huff** *s.* raiva; mau humor / *v.* gritar, xingar.

**hug** *s.* abraço / *v.* abraçar; acariciar.

**huge** *adj.* enorme, imenso.

**huge.ness** *s.* vastidão, imensidão.

**hull** *s.* casco (de navio); casca (de ervilha, vagem) / *v.* descascar.

**hu.man** *s.* humano / *adj.* humano.

**hu.man be.ing** *s.* ser humano.

**hu.man.i.tar.i.an** *adj.* humanitário.

**hu.man.i.ty** *s.* humanidade.

**hum.ble** *v.* humilhar / *adj.* humilde, modesto; submisso.

**hum.ble.ness** *s.* humildade, modéstia.

**hu.mid** *adj.* úmido.

**hu.mid.i.ty** *s.* umidade.

**hu.mil.i.ate** *v.* humilhar.

**hu.mil.i.ty** *s.* humildade.

**hum.ming.bird** *s.* beija-flor.

**hu.mor** *s.* humor, graça.

**hump** *s.* corcunda, corcova, giba / *v.* corcovar, curvar.

**hunch** *s.* pressentimento, palpite; corcova, corcunda / *v.* corcovar.

**hunch.back** *s.* corcunda.

**hun.dred** *num.* cem, cento

**hung** *v. pret.* e *pp.* do *v. to hang*.

**Hun.ga.ri.an** *s. adj.* húngaro.

**hun.ger** *s.* fome.

**hun.ger strike** *s.* greve de fome.

**hun.gry** *adj.* faminto, com fome.

**hunt** *s.* caça, caçada / *v.* caçar, perseguir.

**hunt.er** *s.* caçador(a).

**hunt.ing** *s.* caça.

**hur.dle** *s.* barreira (no esporte); obstáculo.

**hur.ri.cane** *s.* furacão, tufão.

**hur.ried** *adj.* apressado.

**hur.ry** *s.* pressa / *v.* apressar.

**hurt** *s.* ferida, dor / *v.* ferir, machucar, ofender.

**hurt.ful** *adj.* ofensivo.

**hus.band** *s.* marido.

**hush** *s.* silêncio / *v.* silenciar / *interj.* quieto! silêncio!

**husk** *s.* casca; exterior.

**husk.y** *adj.* rouco; forte, robusto / *s.* cão esquimó; idioma dos esquimós.

**hut** *s.* cabana; barraca.

**hy.brid** *s.* híbrido.

**hy.drant** *s.* hidrante.

**hy.draul.ic** *adj.* hidráulico.

**hy.dro.e.lec.tric** *adj.* hidroelétrico.

**hy.dro.gen** *s.* hidrogênio.

**hy.e.na** *s.* hiena.

**hy.giene** *s.* higiene.

**hymn** *s.* hino, cântico.

**hype** *s.* exageração (coloquial).

**hy.per.mar.ket** *s.* hipermercado.

**hyp.no.sis** *s.* hipnose.

**hyp.no.tist** *s.* hipnotizador(a).

**hyp.no.tize** *v.* hipnotizar.

**hyp.o.crite** *s.* hipócrita.

**hy.po.ther.mi.a** *s.* hipotermia.

**hy.poth.e.sis** *s.* hipótese.

**hys.ter.i.cal** *adj.* histérico.

**hys.ter.ics** *s.* histeria.

# Ii

**I, i** *s.* nona letra do alfabeto inglês; representa o número um em algarismos romanos.

**I** *pron.* eu.

**ice** *s.* gelo / *v.* gelar.

**ice.berg** *s. iceberg.*

**ice.box** *s.* geladeira.

**ice cream** *s.* sorvete.

**ice cube** *s.* cubo de gelo.

**iced** *adj.* gelado.

**Ice.land** *s.* Islândia.

**ice lol.ly** *s.* picolé.

**ice rink** *s.* rinque de patinação, pista de gelo.

**ice-skate** *v.* patinar no gelo.

**ic.ing** *s.* glacê.

**ic.y** *adj.* gelado.

**I'd** contração de *I should, I had, I would.*

**i.de.a** *s.* ideia, plano.

**i.de.al** *s.* ideal / *adj.* ideal.

**i.deal.ize** *v.* idealizar.

**i.den.ti.cal** *adj.* idêntico.

**i.den.ti.fi.ca.tion** *s.* identificação.

**i.den.ti.fy** *v.* identificar.

**i.den.ti.ty** *s.* identidade.

**id.i.om** *s.* idioma; expressão idiomática.

**id.i.ot** *s.* idiota.

**id.i.ot.ic** *adj.* idiota.

**i.dle** *adj.* ocioso; fútil; desempregado; à toa.

**i.dol** *s.* ídolo.

**i.dyl** *s.* idílio; amor poético.

**if** *conj.* se.

**if so** *loc.* neste caso, se assim for.

**ig.nite** *v.* acender, incendiar.

**ig.ni.tion** *s.* ignição; combustão.

**ig.ni.tion key** *s.* chave de ignição.

**ig.no.rance** *s.* ignorância.

**ig.no.rant** *adj.* ignorante.

**ig.nore** *v.* ignorar.

**I'll** contração de *I will, I shall.*

**ill** *adj.* doente, indisposto / *s.* mal, desgosto.

**ill-ad.vised** *adj.* imprudente, mal-aconselhado.

**ill-affected** *adj.* mal-intencionado.

**ill bred** *adj.* malcriado, mal--educado.

**il.le.gal** *adj.* ilegal, ilegítimo.

**il.leg.i.ble** *adj.* ilegível.

**il.le.git.i.mate** *adj.* ilegítimo, bastardo.

**ill feeling** *s.* má vontade; rancor.

**il.lit.er.ate** *adj.* analfabeto, iletrado, ignorante.

**ill-luck** *s.* desgraça, infortúnio.

**ill-man.nered** *adj.* mal-educado, rude, grosseiro.

**ill.ness** *s.* doença.

**il.lo.gi.cal** *adj.* ilógico, incoerente.

**ill-tem.pered** *s.* mal-humorado, resmungão.

**ill-treat.ment** *s.* maus tratos.

**il.lu.mi.nate** *v.* iluminar / *adj.* iluminado, culto.

**il.lu.mi.na.tion** *s.* iluminação.

**il.lu.sion** *s.* ilusão.

**il.lu.so.ry** *adj.* ilusório, enganador.

**il.lus.tra.te** *v.* ilustrar, esclarecer / *adj.* renomado, ilustre.

**il.lus.tra.tion** *s.* ilustração; esclarecimento.

**I'm** contração de *I am.*

**im.age** *s.* imagem.

**i.ma.gine** *v.* imaginar, supor.

**im.bal.ance** *s.* desequilíbrio.

**im.bibe** *v.* absorver, embeber.

**im.bue** *v.* embeber.

**im.i.tate** *v.* imitar, copiar.

**im.i.ta.tion** *s.* imitação, cópia.

**im.mac.u.late** *adj.* impecável, imaculado.

**im.ma.te.ri.al** *adj.* irrelevante.

**im.ma.ture** *adj.* imaturo.

**im.me.di.ate** *adj.* imediato, urgente.

**im.me.di.ate.ly** *adv.* imediatamente; diretamente.

**im.mense** *adj.* imenso, enorme.

**im.merse** *v.* submergir.

**im.mer.sion** *s.* imersão.

**im.mi.grant** *s.* imigrante / *adj.* imigrante.

**im.mi.gra.tion** *s.* imigração.

**im.mi.nent** *adj.* iminente.

**im.mo.bile** *adj.* imóvel.

**im.mo.bi.lize** *v.* imobilizar.

**im.mor.al** *adj.* imoral.

**im.mor.tal** *adj.* imortal.

**im.mune** *adj.* imune.
**im.mu.ni.ty** *s.* imunidade.
**im.mu.nize** *v.* imunizar.
**imp** *s.* criança levada.
**im.pact** *s.* impacto, colisão, choque.
**im.pair** *v.* prejudicar, deteriorar.
**im.part** *v.* dar, conceder.
**im.par.tial** *adj.* imparcial, neutro.
**im.pass.a.ble** *adj.* impraticável.
**im.pas.sive** *adj.* impassível.
**im.pa.tience** *s.* impaciência.
**im.pay.a.ble** *adj.* impagável.
**im.peach** *v.* acusar, contestar; impedir.
**im.peach.ment** *s.* impedimento legal de exercer mandato; contestação.
**im.pen.e.tra.ble** *adj.* impenetrável.
**im.per.a.tive** *s.* imperativo / *adj.* premente.
**im.per.fect** *adj.* imperfeito, defeituoso / *s.* imperfeito.
**im.per.me.a.ble** *adj.* impermeável.
**im.pe.ri.al** *adj.* imperial.
**im.per.son.al** *adj.* impessoal.
**im.per.son.ate** *v.* personificar, representar.
**im.per.ti.nent** *adj.* impertinente.
**im.pet.u.ous** *adj.* impetuoso.
**im.pi.e.ty** *s.* impiedade.

**im.plac.a.ble** *adj.* implacável.
**im.ple.ment** *v.* executar, implementar / *s.* instrumento.
**im.pli.cate** *s.* implicante / *v.* implicar, envolver.
**im.pli.ca.tion** *s.* implicação, envolvimento.
**im.plore** *v.* implorar, suplicar.
**im.ply** *v.* inferir, deduzir.
**im.po.lite** *adj.* indelicado, grosseiro.
**im.port** *v.* importar / *s.* importação.
**im.por.tance** *s.* importância.
**im.por.tant** *adj.* importante.
**im.por.ter** *s.* importador(a).
**im.por.tune** *v.* importunar.
**im.pose** *v.* impor.
**im.pos.ing** *adj.* imponente, grandioso.
**im.po.si.tion** *s.* imposição.
**im.pos.si.ble** *adj.* impossível.
**im.pos.si.bil.ity** *s.* impossibilidade.
**im.po.tent** *adj.* impotente, incapaz.
**im.pound** *v.* confiscar; encerar.
**im.pov.er.ished** *adj.* empobrecido.
**im.prac.ti.ca.ble** *adj.* impraticável.
**im.prac.ti.cal** *adj.* pouco prático.
**im.pre.cise** *adj.* impreciso.
**im.preg.nate** *v.* impregnar; emprenhar / *adj.* impregnado; prenhe.

**im.press** *v.* impressionar; imprimir; incutir.

**im.pres.sion** *s.* impressão.

**im.pres.sion.ist** *s.* impressionista.

**im.press.ive** *adj.* impressionante.

**im.print** *s.* impressão; marca; carimbo / *v.* imprimir, carimbar.

**im.pris.on** *v.* encarcerar, prender.

**im.prop.er** *adj.* impróprio, inconveniente.

**im.prove** *v.* melhorar, progredir, aperfeiçoar.

**im.prove.ment** *s.* melhora, melhoria; progresso.

**im.pro.vise** *v.* improvisar.

**im.pru.dent** *adj.* imprudente.

**im.pulse** *s.* impulso.

**im.pu.ni.ty** *s.* impunidade.

**im.pure** *adj.* impuro.

**in** *prep* em, dentro de / *abrev.* de *inch*.

**in.a.bil.i.ty** *s.* incapacidade.

**in.ac.ces.si.ble** *adj.* inacessível.

**in.ac.cu.rate** *adj.* impreciso, inexato.

**in.ad.e.quate** *adj.* inadequado, insuficiente.

**in.an.i.mate** *adj.* inanimado.

**in.ap.pro.pri.ate** *adj.* inadequado, impróprio.

**in.apt** *adj.* inapto, incapaz.

**in.ar.tic.u.late** *adj.* inarticulado.

**in.as.much as** *adv.* na medida em que, visto que.

**in.at.ten.tive** *adj.* desatento.

**in.au.gu.ra.tion** *s.* inauguração.

**in-be.tween** *adj.* intermediário.

**in.born** *adj.* inato, inerente.

**in.bred** *adj.* congênito.

**in.cal.cu.la.ble** *adj.* incalculável.

**in.can.ta.tion** *s.* encantamento, feitiçaria.

**in.ca.pa.ble** *adj.* incapaz; incapacitado.

**in.ca.pa.ci.tate** *v.* incapacitar, desqualificar.

**in.cense** *s.* incenso / *v.* enraivecer; perfumar.

**in.cen.tive** *s.* incentivo, estímulo.

**in.ces.sant** *adj.* incessante.

**in.ces.sant.ly** *adv.* incessantemente, sem parar.

**inch** *s.* polegada (equivalente a 2,54 cm).

**in.ci.dence** *s.* incidência.

**in.ci.dent** *s.* incidente, acontecimento.

**in.ci.den.tal.ly** *adv.* a propósito; incidentalmente.

**in.cite** *v.* provocar, incitar.

**in.cli.na.tion** *s.* tendência, inclinação.

**in.cline** *s.* inclinação, declive / *v.* inclinar.

# include · 262 · indicator

**in.clude** *v.* incluir.
**in.clud.ing** *adj.* inclusivo.
**in.clu.sive** *adj.* incluído.
**in.co.her.ent** *adj.* incoerente.
**in.come** *s.* renda, rendimento, salário.
**income tax** *s.* imposto de renda.
**in.com.ing** *adj.* de chegada; de entrada, entrante.
**in.com.pa.ra.ble** *adj.* incomparável.
**in.com.pe.tent** *adj.* incompetente.
**in.com.plete** *adj.* incompleto.
**in.con.sid.er.ate** *adj.* sem consideração.
**in.con.sis.tent** *adj.* inconsistente.
**in.con.ve.ni.ence** *s.* inconveniência / *v.* incomodar.
**in.con.ve.ni.ent** *adj.* inconveniente, inoportuno.
**in.cor.po.rate** *v.* incorporar, unir / *adj.* incorporado, unido.
**in.cor.po.rat.ed com.pa.ny** *s.* sociedade anônima.
**in.cor.rect** *adj.* incorreto, errado.
**in.crease** *s.* aumento / *v.* aumentar.
**in.creas.ing** *adj.* crescente.
**in.creas.ing.ly** *adv.* progressivamente, de modo crescente.
**in.cred.i.ble** *adj.* incrível, inacreditável.
**in.cred.u.lous** *adj.* incrédulo.

**in.cre.ment** *s.* aumento, incremento.
**in.crim.i.nate** *v.* incriminar.
**in.cu.ba.tor** *s.* incubadora, chocadeira (elétrica).
**in.cum.bent** *s.* titular; beneficiado.
**in.cur** *v.* incorrer; atrair sobre si.
**in.da.gate** *v.* indagar.
**in.debt.ed** *adj.* em dívida com alguém, endividado.
**in.de.ci.sive** *adj.* indeciso, hesitante.
**in.deed** *adv.* certamente, de fato, realmente.
**in.def.i.nite** *adj.* indefinido, vago.
**in.def.i.nite.ly** *adv.* indefinidamente.
**in.de.pen.dence** *s.* independência.
**in.de.pen.dent** *adj.* independente.
**in.de.scrib.a.ble** *adj.* indescritível.
**in.de.struc.ti.ble** *adj.* indestrutível.
**in.dex** *s.* *(pl. indexes)* índice / *v.* indexar.
**In.di.a** *s.* Índia.
**In.di.an O.cean, the** *s.* Oceano Índico.
**in.di.cate** *v.* indicar, sinalizar.
**in.di.ca.tion** *s.* indício, indicação.
**in.dic.a.tive** *s.* indicativo.
**in.di.ca.tor** *s.* indicador, pisca--pisca.

**indict** *v.* acusar, culpar.
**in.dict.ment** *s.* acusação, incriminação.
**in.dif.fer.ence** *s.* indiferença.
**in.dif.fer.ent** *adj.* indiferente.
**in.di.ges.tion** *s.* indigestão.
**in.dig.nant** *adj.* indignado.
**in.dig.na.tion** *s.* indignação.
**in.dig.ni.ty** *s.* indignidade, humilhação.
**in.di.go** *s.* anil; índigo / *adj.* azul-escuro.
**in.di.rect** *adj.* indireto.
**in.dis.creet** *adj.* indiscreto.
**in.dis.crim.i.nate** *adj.* indiscriminado.
**in.dis.pu.ta.ble** *adj.* incontestável, indisputável.
**in.dis.tinct** *adj.* indistinto, confuso.
**in.di.vid.u.al** *s.* indivíduo / *adj.* individual.
**in.di.vid.u.al.ly** *adv.* individualmente.
**in.di.vid.u.al.ize** *v.* individualizar.
**in.di.vis.i.ble** *adj.* indivisível.
**in.doc.tri.nate** *v.* doutrinar.
**in.do.lent** *adj.* preguiçoso, indolente.
**In.do.ne.si.a** *s.* Indonésia.
**in.doors** *adv.* no interior, dentro de casa, em lugar fechado.

**in.duce** *v.* induzir, persuadir.
**in.duce.ment** *s.* incentivo, persuasão.
**in.duct** *v.* introduzir; iniciar.
**in.dus.tri.al** *adj.* industrial / *s.* industrial.
**in.dus.tri.ous** *adj.* trabalhador(a), diligente.
**in.dus.try** *s.* indústria.
**in.ef.fec.tive** *adj.* ineficaz, ineficiente.
**in.ef.fi.ciency** *s.* ineficiência.
**in.ef.fi.cient** *adj.* ineficiente.
**in.ept** *adj.* inepto.
**in.e.qual.i.ty** *s.* desigualdade.
**in.ert** *adj.* inerte.
**in.ev.i.ta.ble** *adj.* inevitável.
**in.ev.i.ta.bly** *adv.* inevitavelmente.
**in.ex.cus.a.ble** *adj.* imperdoável, indesculpável.
**in.ex.pen.sive** *adj.* barato, econômico.
**in.fal.li.ble** *adj.* infalível.
**in.fa.mous** *adj.* infame.
**in.fan.cy** *s.* infância.
**in.fant** *s.* criança pequena.
**in.fan.tile** *adj.* infantil.
**in.fan.try** *s.* infantaria.
**in.fant school** *s.* pré-escola.
**in.fect** *v.* contagiar, infectar.
**in.fec.tion** *s.* infecção.

**in.fec.tious** *adj.* contagioso, infeccioso.

**in.fer** *v.* deduzir, inferir.

**in.fer.ence** *s.* dedução, conclusão, inferência.

**in.fe.ri.or** *adj.* inferior / *s.* subalterno(a).

**in.fe.ri.or.i.ty** *s.* inferioridade.

**in.fe.ri.or.i.ty com.plex** *s.* complexo de inferioridade.

**in.fight.ing** *s.* conflitos internos.

**in.fil.trate** *v.* infiltrar, penetrar.

**in.fi.nite** *adj.* infinito.

**in.fin.i.tive** *s.* infinitivo.

**in.fin.i.ty** *s.* infinito, infinidade.

**in.firm** *adj.* enfermo, débil.

**in.fir.ma.ry** *s.* enfermaria.

**in.fir.mi.ty** *s.* fraqueza, enfermidade.

**in.flamed** *adj.* inflamado.

**in.flam.ma.ble** *adj.* inflamável.

**in.flam.ma.tion** *s.* inflamação.

**in.flat.a.ble** *adj.* inflável.

**in.flate** *v.* inflar, encher de ar.

**in.fla.tion** *s.* inflação.

**in.flex.i.ble** *adj.* inflexível.

**in.flu.ence** *s.* influência / *v.* influenciar.

**in.flu.en.tial** *adj.* influente.

**in.flu.en.za** *s.* gripe, influenza.

**in.flux** *s.* afluxo; influxo.

**in.form** *v.* informar.

**in.for.mal** *adj.* informal.

**in.for.mal.i.ty** *s.* informalidade.

**in.form.ant** *s.* informante.

**in.for.ma.tion** *s.* informação, conhecimento.

**in.for.ma.tive** *adj.* informativo.

**in.form.er** *s.* informante, delator(a).

**in.fringe.ment** *s.* violação, infração.

**in.fu.ri.at.ing** *adj.* enfurecedor.

**in.ge.ni.ous** *adj.* engenhoso.

**in.ge.nu.i.ty** *s.* engenho, talento, habilidade.

**in.gen.u.ous** *adj.* ingênuo, simples.

**in.gest** *v.* ingerir.

**in.gre.di.ent** *s.* ingrediente.

**in.gress** *s.* ingresso, entrada.

**in.grown** *adj.* encravado.

**in.hab.it** *v.* habitar.

**in.hab.i.tant** *s.* habitante.

**in.hale** *v.* inalar, tragar.

**in.her.ent** *adj.* inerente, inato.

**in.her.it** *v.* herdar.

**in.her.i.table** *adj.* hereditário.

**in.her.i.tance** *s.* herança.

**in.hu.man** *adj.* desumano, cruel.

**in.iq.ui.ty** *s.* injustiça, maldade.

**i.ni.tial** *adj.* inicial / *s.* inicial.

**i.ni.tial.ly** *adv.* inicialmente.

**in.i.ti.ate** *v.* iniciar.

**initiation**     **265**     **insistent**

**in.i.ti.ation** *s.* iniciação, começo.

**in.i.tia.tive** *s.* iniciativa.

**in.ject** *v.* injetar.

**in.jec.tion** *s.* injeção.

**in.junc.tion** *s.* injunção, determinação.

**in.jure** *v.* ferir, machucar.

**in.jured** *s.* ferido, machucado.

**in.ju.ry** *s.* ferimento, lesão.

**in.jus.tice** *s.* injustiça.

**ink** *s.* tinta de escrever.

**ink.pot** *s.* tinteiro.

**in-laws** *s.* parentes por afinidade.

**in.let** *s.* enseada, baía.

**in.most** *adj.* íntimo, interno.

**inn** *s.* hospedaria, estalagem.

**in.nate** *adj.* inato.

**in.ner** *adj.* íntimo, interior.

**in.ner ci.ty** *s.* metrópole.

**in.ner tube** *s.* câmara de ar.

**in.nings** *s.* turno, a vez de jogar.

**in.no.cence** *s.* inocência.

**in.no.cent** *adj.* inocente.

**in.no.va.tion** *s.* inovação, novidade.

**i.noc.u.lation** *s.* inoculação, vacinação.

**in-pa.tient** *s.* paciente interno.

**in.put** *s.* entrada; contribuição, produção.

**in.quest** *s.* inquérito, sindicância.

**in.quire** *v.* perguntar, investigar.

**in.quir.y** *s.* inquérito, investigação, inquirição.

**in.sane** *adj.* insano, demente.

**in.san.i.ty** *s.* insanidade, loucura.

**in.scrip.tion** *s.* inscrição; dedicatória.

**in.scru.ta.ble** *adj.* impenetrável, inescrutável.

**in.sect** *s.* inseto.

**in.sec.ti.cide** *s.* inseticida.

**in.se.cure** *adj.* inseguro.

**in.se.cu.ri.ty** *s.* insegurança.

**in.sem.i.na.tion** *s.* inseminação.

**in.sen.si.ble** *adj.* inconsciente.

**in.sen.si.tive** *adj.* insensitivo, insensível.

**in.sert** *v.* inserir, introduzir.

**in.ser.tion** *s.* inserção, anúncio.

**in-ser.vice** *adj.* contínuo; relativo a cursos de treinamento na empresa.

**in.side** *s.* interior / *adj.* interior / *adv.* dentro.

**in.sight** *s.* discernimento; perspicácia, argúcia; percepção.

**in.sig.ni.a** *s.* insígnias, emblemas.

**in.sig.nif.i.cant** *adj.* insignificante.

**in.sin.cere** *adj.* falso.

**in.sin.u.ate** *v.* insinuar.

**in.sip.id** *adj.* insípido, sem graça.

**in.sist** *v.* insistir, persistir.

**in.sis.tent** *adj.* insistente.

I

insole        266        intelligent

**in.sole** *s.* palmilha.

**in.so.lent** *adj.* insolente.

**in.som.ni.a** *s.* insônia.

**in.spect** *v.* inspecionar.

**in.spec.tion** *s.* inspeção, fiscalização.

**in.spec.tor** *s.* inspetor(a), fiscal.

**in.spi.ra.tion** *s.* inspiração.

**in.spire** *v.* inspirar.

**in.stall** *v.* instalar, empossar.

**in.stal.la.tion** *s.* instalação, emposse.

**in.stall.ment** *s.* prestação, parte; fascículo, capítulo.

**in.stance** *s.* exemplo, caso.

**in.stant** *s.* instante, momento / *adj.* imediato, instantâneo.

**in.stant.ly** *adv.* instantaneamente, imediatamente.

**in.stead** *adv.* em vez, em lugar (de).

**in.step** *s.* dorso do pé.

**in.sti.gate** *v.* instigar.

**in.stinct** *s.* instinto.

**in.sti.tute** *s.* instituto, associação / *v.* instituir, iniciar.

**in.sti.tu.tion** *s.* instituição, instituto; costume.

**in.struct** *v.* instruir, ensinar.

**in.struc.tion** *s.* instrução, instruções (para fazer algo); ensino.

**in.struc.tive** *adj.* instrutivo.

**in.struc.tor** *s.* instrutor.

**in.stru.ment** *s.* instrumento.

**in.stru.men.tal** *adj.* instrumental.

**in.suf.fe.ra.ble** *adj.* insuportável.

**in.suf.fi.cient** *adj.* insuficiente.

**in.suf.flate** *v.* insuflar, encher de ar.

**in.su.lar** *adj.* estreito, bitolado.

**in.su.late** *v.* isolar; separar.

**in.su.la.tion** *s.* isolamento.

**in.su.lin** *s.* insulina.

**in.sult** *s.* ofensa, insulto / *v.* insultar.

**in.sult.ing** *adj.* ofensivo, insultante.

**in.su.pe.ra.ble** *adj.* insuperável.

**in.sur.ance** *s.* seguro.

**in.sur.ance pol.i.cy** *s.* apólice de seguro.

**in.sure** *v.* segurar; assegurar.

**in.tact** *adj.* intato, ileso.

**in.take** *s.* quantidade que entra, consumo.

**in.te.gral** *adj.* integral, integrante, essencial / *s.* integral, total.

**in.te.grate** *v.* integrar, incorporar.

**in.teg.ri.ty** *s.* integridade, honestidade, totalidade.

**in.tel.lect** *s.* intelecto, inteligência.

**in.tel.lec.tu.al** *adj.* intelectual, inteligente / *s.* intelectual.

**in.tel.li.gence** *s.* inteligência.

**in.tel.li.gent** *adj.* inteligente.

**in.tel.li.gi.ble** *adj.* inteligível, compreensível.

**in.tend** *v.* pretender, planejar, ter a intenção de.

**in.tend.ed** *adj.* pretendido / *s.* futuro marido, futura esposa, pretendente.

**in.tense** *adj.* intenso.

**in.tense.ly** *adv.* extremamente, intensamente.

**in.ten.si.fy** *v.* intensificar.

**in.ten.sive** *adj.* intensivo.

**in.tent** *s.* intenção, intento / *adj.* intencionado, atento.

**in.ten.tion** *s.* intenção.

**in.ten.tion.al** *adj.* intencional.

**in.ten.tion.al.ly** *adv.* de propósito, intencionalmente.

**in.tent.ly** *adv.* atentamente.

**in.ter** *v.* enterrar, sepultar; entre.

**in.ter.act** *v.* interagir.

**in.ter.ac.tion** *s.* interação, relacionamento.

**in.ter.ac.tive** *adj.* interativo.

**in.ter.cept** *v.* interceptar.

**in.ter.change** *s.* intercâmbio, troca / *v.* intercambiar.

**in.ter.change.a.ble** *adj.* permutável, intercambiável.

**in.ter.com** *s.* interfone (coloquial).

**in.ter.course** *s.* relações sexuais.

**in.terest** *s.* interesse; vantagem; juros / *v.* interessar-se.

**in.terest.ing** *adj.* interessante.

**in.ter.face** *s.* interface.

**in.ter.fere** *v.* interferir, intervir.

**in.ter.fer.ence** *s.* intromissão, interferência.

**in.ter.im** *adj.* interino, provisório / *s.* ínterim.

**in.te.ri.or** *s.* interior / *adj.* interno, interior.

**in.ter.jec.tion** *s.* interjeição.

**in.ter.lace** *v.* entrelaçar-se.

**in.ter.lock** *v.* engrenar.

**in.ter.lop.er** *s.* intruso(a).

**in.ter.lude** *s.* interlúdio (música), intervalo.

**in.ter.me.di.ate** *adj.* intermediário / *v.* intermediar.

**in.ter.mi.na.ble** *adj.* interminável.

**in.ter.mis.sion** *s.* intervalo, intermissão.

**in.ter.mit.tent** *adj.* intermitente.

**in.ter.mix** *v.* misturar.

**in.tern** *v.* internar / *s.* médico interno.

**in.ter.nal** *adj.* interno.

**in.ter.na.tion.al** *adj.* internacional.

**in.tern.ment** *s.* internação, internamento.

**in.ter.play** *s.* interação.

**in.ter.pose** *v.* interpor.

**in.ter.pret** *v.* interpretar, traduzir.

**in.ter.pret.er** *s.* intérprete, tradutor.

**in.ter.re.lated** *adj*. inter-relacionado, ligado.
**in.ter.ro.gate** *v*. interrogar.
**in.ter.ro.ga.tion** *s*. interrogatório.
**in.ter.rog.a.tive** *adj*. interrogativo.
**in.ter.rupt** *v*. interromper.
**in.ter.rup.tion** *s*. interrupção.
**in.ter.sect** *v*. cruzar, dividir.
**in.ter.sec.tion** *s*. cruzamento, intersecção.
**in.ter.twine** *v*. entrelaçar.
**in.ter.val** *s*. intervalo.
**in.ter.vene** *v*. intervir, interpor.
**in.ter.ven.tion** *s*. intervenção.
**in.ter.view** *s*. entrevista / *v*. entrevistar.
**in.ter.view.er** *s*. entrevistador(a).
**in.tes.tine** *s*. intestino.
**in.ti.ma.cy** *s*. intimidade.
**in.ti.mate** *v*. insinuar, sugerir; intimar, notificar / *adj*. íntimo, familiar.
**in.tim.i.date** *v*. intimidar.
**in.to** *prep*. em; dentro; para dentro.
**in.tol.er.a.ble** *adj*. intolerável.
**in.tol.er.ant** *adj*. intolerante / *s*. intolerante.
**in.to.na.tion** *s*. entonação.
**in.tox.i.cat.ed** *adj*. embriagado.
**in.tox.i.cation** *s*. intoxicação, embriaguez.
**in.trac.ta.ble** *adj*. intratável.

**in.tran.si.tive** *adj*. intransitivo.
**in.tra.ven.ous** *adj*. intravenoso.
**in.tri.cate** *adj*. complicado, complexo.
**in.trigue** *s*. intriga / *v*. intrigar.
**in.tro.duce** *v*. introduzir; apresentar alguém.
**in.tro.duc.tion** *s*. introdução, apresentação.
**in.tro.duc.to.ry** *adj*. introdutório.
**in.tro.vert** *s*. introvertido(a) / *v*. introverter / *adj*. introvertido.
**in.trud.er** *s*. intruso.
**in.tu.i.tion** *s*. intuição, percepção.
**in.un.date** *v*. inundar.
**in.vade** *v*. invadir.
**in.vader** *s*. invasor.
**in.va.lid** *s*. inválido(a) / *adj*. nulo.
**in.val.ua.ble** *adj*. inestimável.
**in.var.i.a.bly** *adv*. invariavelmente.
**in.va.sion** *s*. invasão.
**in.veigh** *v*. injuriar, censurar.
**in.vent** *v*. inventar.
**in.ven.tion** *s*. invenção, invento.
**in.ven.tor** *s*. inventor(a).
**in.ven.tory** *s*. inventário; estoque.
**in.vert** *v*. inverter.
**in.vert.ed com.ma** *s*. aspas.
**in.vest** *v*. investor.
**in.ves.ti.gate** *v*. investigar.
**in.ves.ti.ga.tion** *s*. investigação.
**in.vest.ment** *s*. investimento.
**in.ves.tor** *s*. investidor(a).

**invidious**     **269**     **isle**

**in.vid.i.ous** *adj.* invejoso; hostil; odioso.

**in.vi.gi.la.tor** *s.* fiscal (de exame), vigilante.

**in.vig.or.at.ing** *adj.* revigorante.

**in.vin.ci.ble** *adj.* invencível.

**in.vis.i.ble** *adj.* invisível.

**in.vi.ta.tion** *s.* convite.

**in.vite** *v.* convidar.

**in.vit.ing** *adj.* convidativo, tentador.

**in.voice** *s.* fatura / *v.* faturar.

**in.voke** *v.* invocar, chamar.

**in.vol.un.ta.ry** *adj.* involuntário.

**in.volve** *v.* envolver, incluir, implicar, comprometer.

**in.volved** *adj.* complexo, complicado; envolvido, incluído.

**in.volve.ment** *s.* envolvimento, comprometimento.

**in.ward** *adj.* íntimo, interior.

**i.o.dine** *s.* iodo.

**I.ran** *s.* Irã.

**I.raq** *s.* Iraque.

**i.rate** *adj.* irado, colérico.

**ire** *s.* ira, raiva.

**Ire.land** *s.* Irlanda.

**i.ris** *s.* íris.

**I.rish** *adj.* irlandês(esa) / *s.* irlandês(esa).

**i.ron** *s.* ferro / *v.* passar roupa / *adj.* de ferro.

**i.ron.ic(al)** *adj.* irônico, sarcástico.

**i.ron.ing** *s.* roupa passada / *v.* passar (a ferro).

**i.ron.ing board** *s.* tábua de passar roupa.

**iron.mon.ger** *s.* ferreiro, ferrageiro.

**iron.ware** *s.* ferragens.

**i.ron.y** *s.* ironia, sarcasmo.

**ir.ra.tion.al** *adj.* irracional.

**ir.rec.on.cil.a.ble** *adj.* irreconciliável.

**ir.reg.u.lar** *adj.* irregular.

**ir.rel.e.vant** *adj.* irrelevante.

**ir.re.place.a.ble** *adj.* insubstituível.

**ir.re.pres.si.ble** *adj.* irrefreável, irreprimível.

**ir.re.sis.ti.ble** *adj.* irresistível.

**ir.re.spon.si.ble** *adj.* irresponsável.

**ir.rev.e.rent** *adj.* irreverente.

**ir.ri.gate** *v.* irrigar.

**ir.ri.gation** *s.* irrigação.

**ir.ri.ta.ble** *adj.* irritável.

**ir.ri.tate** *v.* irritar, provocar.

**ir.ri.tat.ing** *adj.* irritante.

**ir.ri.ta.tion** *s.* irritação.

**is** *v.* 3ª *pess. sing. pres. indic.* do *v. to be.*

**Is.lam** *s.* islã, islamismo.

**is.land** *s.* ilha.

**isle** *s.* ilhota, ilha.

**isn't** contração de *is not.*
**i.so.lat.ed** *adj.* isolado.
**i.so.la.tion** *s.* isolamento.
**Is.rael** *s.* Israel.
**Is.rae.li** *s.* israelense / *adj.* israelense.
**is.sue** *s.* questão; edição; tema, assunto / *v.* distribuir; emitir.
**it** *pron.* o, a, lhe, ele, ela (substitui um animal ou um objeto).
**I.tal.ian** *s.* italiano / *adj.* italiano.
**i.tal.ics** *s.* itálico (tipografia).
**It.a.ly** *s.* Itália.
**itch** *s.* comichão, coceira / *v.* coçar, desejar.

**itch.y** *adj.* que coça.
**i.tem** *s.* item; assunto.
**i.tem.ize** *v.* especificar, relacionar.
**i.tin.e.rant** *adj.* itinerante.
**i.tin.e.ra.ry** *s.* itinerário.
**it'll** contração de *it will.*
**its** *adj. poss.* dele(s), dela(s) / *pron.* dele(a).
**it's** contração de *it is.*
**it.self** *pron.* ele(a) mesmo(a), a si mesmo(a).
**I've** contração de *I have.*
**i.vo.ry** *s.* marfim / *adj.* de marfim.
**i.vy** *s.* hera (botânica).

**J. j** s. décima letra do alfabeto inglês.
**jab** s. golpe, estocada, espetada / v. cutucar, espetar, ferir com a ponta de algo.
**jack** s. macaco (mecânica); valete (baralho).
**jack.al** s. chacal.
**jack.ass** s. asno, burro.
**jack.et** s. jaqueta, casaco curto.
**jack-in-the-box** s. caixa de surpresa.
**jack.pot** s. bolada, sorte grande.
**jack-straw** s. boneco de palha, espantalho.
**jail** s. cadeia, prisão / v. encarcerar.
**jam** s. geleia; congestionamento, engarrafamento / v. amontoar, apinhar-se.
**Ja.mai.ca** s. Jamaica.
**jamb** s. ombreira, jamba, batente.
**jan.i.tor** s. zelador.
**Jan.u.a.ry** s. janeiro.
**Ja.pan** s. Japão.
**Jap.a.nese** s. japonês(esa) / adj. japonês(esa).
**jar** s. jarro, pote, frasco / v. destoar; irritar.
**jar.gon** s. jargão / v. tagarelar.
**jas.min(e)** s. jasmim.
**jaunt** s. excursão, caminhada / v. perambular, vaguear.
**jaun.ty** adj. animado, vivo.
**jave.lin** s. dardo de arremesso, lança.
**jaw** s. maxilar, mandíbula.
**jay.walk.er** s. pedestre imprudente.

**jazz** *s. jazz.*
**jazz up** *v.* animar.
**jeal.ous** *adj.* ciumento(a).
**jeal.ous.y** *s.* ciúme.
**jean** *s.* fustão de algodão.
**jeans** *s. pl.* calças de brim.
**jeep** *s.* jipe.
**jeer** *s.* zombaria, vaia / *v.* zombar, vaiar.
**jel.ly** *s.* gelatina, geleia.
**jel.ly.fish** *s.* água-viva.
**jerk** *s.* empurrão; sacudida; idiota (coloquial) / *v.* sacudir.
**jer.kin** *s.* jaqueta.
**jerk.y** *adj.* aos trancos; idiota (coloquial).
**jer.sey** *s.* suéter de lã; jérsei (tecido).
**jest** *s.* gracejo / *v.* gracejar.
**Je.sus** *s.* Jesus.
**jet** *s.* jato, jorro, esguicho.
**jet.ty** *s.* molhe, quebra-mar.
**Jew** *s.* judeu / *adj.* judaico.
**jew.el** *s.* joia, pedra preciosa, gema.
**jew.el.er** *s.* joalheiro.
**jew.el.er's** *s.* joalheria.
**jew.el.ry** *s.* joias, joalheria.
**Jew.ess** *s.* judia / *adj.* judia.
**Jew.ish** *adj.* judaico, hebreu.
**jif.fy** *s.* instante, momento (coloquial).
**jig.saw** *s.* quebra-cabeça.

**jilt** *v.* namorar, flertar.
**jim.my** *s.* pé de cabra, alavanca.
**jin.gle** *s.* música de propaganda / *v.* tilintar, soar.
**job** *s.* emprego; tarefa.
**job.ber.y** *s.* agiotagem, especulação.
**job.cen.ter** *s.* agência de emprego.
**job.less** *adj.* desempregado.
**jock.ey** *s.* jóquei; impostor.
**joc.und** *adj.* alegre, divertido.
**jog** *s.* sacudida / *v.* cutucar, empurrar; correr.
**jog.ging** *s.* corrida.
**join** *s.* ligação; junção / *v.* juntar, ligar.
**join.er** *s.* marceneiro.
**joint** *s.* junta, articulação, união / *adj.* articulado; conjunto.
**joint ac.count** *s.* conta conjunta.
**joke** *s.* piada, gracejo, brincadeira / *v.* brincar.
**jok.er** *s.* curinga (cartas); brincalhão.
**jol.ly** *adj.* alegre, divertido / *adv.* muito, bastante (coloquial).
**Jor.dan** *s.* Jordânia.
**jos.tle** *s.* colisão, choque / *v.* acotovelar, empurrar.
**jour.nal** *s.* jornal especializado, revista, diário.
**jour.nal.is.m** *s.* jornalismo.

**jour.nal.ist** *s.* jornalista.

**jour.ney** *s.* viagem, jornada.

**jowl** *s.* mandíbula.

**joy** *s.* alegria, felicidade.

**joy.ful** *adj.* alegre, jovial.

**joy-ride** *s.* passeio temerário (de automóvel).

**joy.stick** *s.* alavanca de controle.

**ju.bi.lee** *s.* jubileu.

**judge** *s.* juiz, árbitro / *v.* julgar, avaliar, criticar.

**judge.ment** *s.* julgamento, crítica.

**ju.di.cial** *adj.* judicial, forense.

**ju.di.ci.ar.y** *s.* poder judiciário; comarca; jurisdição.

**ju.do** *s.* judô.

**jug** *s.* jarro, jarra; moringa; canto do rouxinol.

**jug.gler** *s.* malabarista.

**juice** *s.* suco, sumo.

**juic.y** *adj.* suculento; picante; interessante.

**juke.box** *s.* máquina que toca música quando põe-se dinheiro nela.

**Ju.ly** *s.* julho.

**jum.ble** *s.* desordem, confusão / *v.* remexer, confundir.

**jum.ble sale** *s.* bazar, venda de artigos em saldos.

**jum.bo** *s.* colosso (coloquial) / *adj.* colossal, gigantesco.

**jump** *s.* salto, pulo / *v.* saltar, pular.

**jump.er** *s.* saltador; avental; suéter.

**jump.ing-board** *s.* trampolim.

**jump-leads** *s.* cabo para bateria.

**junc.tion** *s.* cruzamento, entroncamento.

**junc.ture** *s.* conjuntura, momento.

**June** *s.* junho.

**jun.gle** *s.* selva; bagunça.

**ju.ni.or** *s.* jovem / *adj.* mais novo; subalterno.

**ju.ni.or school** *s.* escola primária.

**junk** *s.* sucata, refugo.

**junk food** *s.* comida sem valor nutritivo.

**junk.ie** *adj.* drogado(a), viciado(a).

**Ju.pi.ter** *s.* Júpiter.

**ju.ror** *s.* jurado.

**ju.ry** *s.* júri.

**just** *adj.* justo, correto / *adv.* justamente, exatamente, quase, apenas.

**just right** *adj.* perfeito.

**jus.tice** *s.* justiça.

**jus.ti.fi.ca.tion** *s.* justificativa, causa.

**jus.ti.fy** *v.* justificar.

**jut** *v.* sobressair.

**jute** *s.* juta.

**ju.ve.nile** *s.* jovem, menor / *adj.* juvenil, imaturo.

# K k

**K, k** *s.* décima primeira letra do alfabeto inglês.

**Kam.pu.che.a** *s.* Camboja.

**kan.ga.roo** *s.* canguru (zoologia).

**ka.ra.te** *s.* caratê.

**ke.bab** *s.* espetinho, churrasquinho.

**keek** *s.* olhadela / *v.* olhar, mirar.

**keen** *adj.* entusiasmado, muito interessado; penetrante; intenso.

**keep** *v.* guardar; manter, conservar; ficar, permanecer.

**keep.er** *s.* guardião(ã), zelador(a).

**keep.ing** *s.* cuidado, custódia; manutenção, sustento.

**keep.sake** *s.* lembrança, dádiva, presente.

**ken.nel** *s.* canil; casinha de cachorro.

**Ken.ya** *s.* Quênia.

**kept** *v. pret.* e *pp.* do *v. to keep*.

**kerb** *s.* meio-fio.

**ker.nel** *s.* amêndoa (o miolo comestível de uma semente); parte central.

**ketch.up** *s.* molho picante de tomate.

**ket.tle** *s.* chaleira; caldeira.

**key** *s.* chave; tecla / *adj.* essencial, fundamental.

**key.board** *s.* teclado.

**key.hole** *s.* buraco da fechadura.

**key.ring** *s.* chaveiro (porta-chaves).

**kha.ki** *adj.* cáqui (cor) / *s.* caqui.

**kick** *v.* chutar, dar pontapé, espernear / *s.* pontapé, chute.

**kick.off** *s.* chute inicial (futebol).

**kid** *s.* criança; cabrito / *v.* brincar.

**kid.dy** *s.* criança pequena.

kidnap     275     knighthood

**kid.nap** *v.* sequestrar, raptar.

**kid.nap.per** *s.* sequestrador(a).

**kid.nap.ping** *s.* sequestro, rapto.

**kid.ney** *s.* rim.

**kill** *v.* matar, abater.

**kill.er** *s.* assassino(a).

**kill.ing** *s.* assassinato; matança.

**kil.o.gram** *s.* quilograma.

**kil.o.me.ter** *s.* quilômetro.

**kil.o.watt** *s.* quilowatt.

**kilt** *s.* saiote escocês.

**kin** *s.* parente.

**kind** *adj.* generoso, amável / *s.* espécie, classe, tipo.

**kin.der.gar.ten** *s.* jardim de infância.

**kind-heart.ed** *adj.* bom coração, bondoso.

**kin.dle** *v.* acender, iluminar; dar cria (ninhada).

**kind.ly** *adv.* amavelmente, gentilmente.

**kind.ness** *s.* bondade, gentileza.

**kin.dred** *s.* família, parentes / *adj.* aparentado, afim.

**king** *s.* rei.

**king.dom** *s.* reino, monarquia; domínio.

**king.ly** *adj.* real, majestoso / *adv.* majestosamente, regiamente.

**king-size** *adj.* tamanho grande, maior do que o tipo comum.

**kin.less** *adj.* sem parentes.

**kin.ship** *s.* parentesco, afinidade.

**ki.osk** *s.* quiosque.

**kip.per** *s.* arenque defumado.

**kir.mess** *s.* quermesse.

**kiss** *s.* beijo / *v.* beijar.

**kit** *s.* estojo; equipamento (de soldado ou de viagem).

**kitch.en** *s.* cozinha.

**kitch.en sink** *s.* pia de cozinha.

**kitch.en.ware** *s.* utensílios de cozinha.

**kite** *s.* papagaio de papel, pipa.

**kit.ten** *s.* gatinho.

**kit.ty** *s.* gatinho; montante em dinheiro arrecadado para um fim (vaquinha).

**km** *abrev.* de *kilometer*.

**knee** *s.* joelho.

**knee.cap** *s.* rótula (anatomia).

**kneel** *v.* ajoelhar-se.

**knelt** *v. pret.* e *pp.* do *v.* to kneel.

**knew** *v. pret.* do *v.* to know.

**knick.ers** *s.* calcinha.

**knick-knack** *s.* bagatela; bugiganga.

**knife** *s. (pl. knives)* faca / *v.* esfaquear.

**knife-grinder** *s.* amolador de faca.

**knight** *s.* cavaleiro; cavalo do xadrez.

**knight.hood** *s.* fidalguia, nobreza.

K

**knit** *v.* tricotar; entrelaçar.
**knit.ting** *s.* tricô.
**knit.ting ma.chine** *s.* máquina de tricotar.
**knit.ting nee.dle** *s.* agulha de tricô.
**knit.wear** *s.* roupa de malha.
**knob** *s.* maçaneta, puxador.
**knock** *s.* pancada, batida / *v.* bater.
**knock.out** *s.* nocaute / *v.* nocautear.
**knock over** *v.* atropelar.
**knot** *s.* nó, laço; grupo de pessoas / *v.* atar, amarrar.
**knot.ty** *adj.* cheio de nós, nodoso.

**know** *v.* saber, conhecer, entender.
**know-all** *s.* sabichão(ona).
**know-how** *s.* experiência, prática, conhecimento.
**knowl.edge** *s.* conhecimento, instrução.
**knowl.edge.a.ble** *adj.* versado, instruído.
**known** *v. pp.* do *v. to know*.
**knuck.le** *s.* nó dos dedos, junta, articulação.
**Ko.ran** *s.* Alcorão.
**Ko.re.a** *s.* Coreia.

# Ll

**L, l** *s.* décima segunda letra do alfabeto inglês; *abrev.* de *liter*; representa o número 50 em algarismos romanos.

**lab** *abrev.* de *laboratory*.

**la.bel** *s.* etiqueta, rótulo / *v.* rotular, etiquetar.

**la.bor** *s.* trabalho / *v.* trabalhar.

**la.bor.a.tory** *s.* laboratório.

**la.bored** *adj.* forçado; elaborado.

**la.bor.er** *s.* operário, trabalhador.

**lace** *s.* renda; cadarço / *v.* amarrar (sapatos).

**lack** *s.* falta, carência / *v.* faltar.

**lack.a.dai.si.cal** *adj.* apático; lânguido.

**lacquer** *s.* fixador; verniz.

**lad** *s.* rapaz, moço.

**lad.der** *s.* escada de mão.

**lad.die** *s.* rapazinho.

**lad.en** *adj.* carregado, onerado / *v. pp.* do *v.* to *lade*.

**lad.ing** *s.* carregamento.

**ladle** *s.* concha de sopa.

**la.dy** *s. (pl. ladies)* senhora; dama.

**la.dy.bird, la.dy.bug** *s.* joaninha.

**la.dy.like** *adj.* refinado, elegante.

**la.dy.love** *s.* amada.

**la.dy.ship** *s.* senhoria.

**lag** *s.* atraso, demora / *v.* ficar para trás, retardar-se, demorar-se.

**lag.gard** *s.* retardatário / *adj.* vagaroso.

**la.goon** *s.* lagoa, laguna.

**laid-back** *adj.* descontraído.

**lain** *v. pp.* do *v.* to *lie*.

**lair** *s.* covil, toca.

**lake** *s.* lago.

**lamb** *s.* cordeiro.

**lame** *adj.* manco, coxo / *v.* mancar.

**la.ment** *s.* lamento, queixa / *v.* lamentar-se.

**lam.i.nate** *s.* laminado / *v.* laminar / *adj.* laminado.

**lamp** *s.* lâmpada, lanterna.

**lamp.post** *s.* poste de iluminação.

**lamp.shade** *s.* abajur.

**lance** *s.* lança / *v.* lançar.

**land** *s.* terra; região; terras, solo / *v.* pousar, desembarcar.

**land-holder** *s.* proprietário (de terras).

**land.ing** *s.* aterrissagem; desembarque.

**land.la.dy** *s.* proprietária (de estalagem), senhoria.

**land.lord** *s.* proprietário (de estalagem), senhorio.

**land.mark** *s.* lugar conhecido, marco, baliza.

**land.own.er** *s.* latifundiário(a).

**land.scape** *s.* paisagem, cenário.

**land.slide** *s.* desmoronamento, deslizamento de terra.

**lane** *s.* caminho, raia, pista.

**lan.guage** *s.* língua, linguagem, idioma.

**lan.guid** *adj.* lânguido.

**lan.guish** *v.* debilitar, adoecer, definhar.

**lank** *adj.* liso; magro, delgado / *v.* decair.

**lank.y** *adj.* magro, esbelto.

**lan.tern** *s.* lanterna.

**lap** *s.* volta; colo; regaço; lambida / *v.* marulhar; beber algo às lambidas.

**la.pel** *s.* lapela.

**Lap.land** *s.* Lapônia.

**lapse** *s.* lapso de tempo; erro, deslize / *v.* escoar, decorrer.

**lap.top** *s.* computador portátil.

**lar.ce.ny** *s.* apropriação indébita.

**lard** *s.* banha de porco.

**lar.der** *s.* despensa.

**large** *adj.* grande, abundante, amplo.

**large.ly** *adv.* em grande parte, amplamente.

**large-scale** *adj.* em grande escala.

**lar.gess** *s.* presente, dádiva.

**lark** *s.* brincadeira, travessura; cotovia.

**lar.yn.gi.tis** *s.* laringite.

**lar.ynx** *s.* laringe.

**la.ser** *s.* raio *laser*.

**la.ser print.er** *s.* impressora a *laser*.

**lash** *s.* chicotada / *v.* chicotear.

**lass** *s.* moça.

**last** *adj.* último / *adv.* em último lugar / *v.* durar.

**last.ing** *adj.* duradouro, durável.

**last.ly** *adv.* finalmente, por último.

**last min.ute** *s.* última hora / *adj.* última hora.

**latch** *s.* trinco / *v.* trancar.

**late** *adj.* atrasado / *adv.* tarde, tardio.

**late.com.er** *s.* retardatário(a).

**late.ly** *adv.* ultimamente, recentemente.

**lat.er** *adj.* posterior / *adv.* mais tarde.

**la.test** *adj.* último.

**lathe** *s.* torno mecânico.

**lath.er** *s.* espuma (de sabão) / *v.* ensaboar.

**Lat.in** *s.* latim / *adj.* latino.

**Lat.in A.mer.i.ca** *s.* América Latina.

**Lat.in A.mer.i.can** *adj.* latino-americano.

**lat.i.tude** *s.* latitude; largura.

**lat.tice** *s.* treliça.

**laud** *s.* louvor, elogio / *v.* louvar, elogiar.

**lau.da.ble** *adj.* louvável.

**laugh** *s.* riso, risada / *v.* rir, gargalhar.

**laugh.a.ble** *adj.* ridículo, risível.

**laugh.ing** *s.* riso, risada / *adj.* risonho.

**laugh.ing.stock** *s.* alvo de riso.

**laugh.ter** *s.* risada, riso.

**launch** *s.* lancha; lançamento, inauguração / *v.* lançar.

**laun.der** *v.* lavar e passar (roupa).

**laun.dress** *s.* lavadeira.

**laun.dry** *s.* lavanderia, roupa para lavar.

**lav.a.to.ry** *s.* lavatório, banheiro, vaso sanitário.

**lav.en.der** *s.* lavanda.

**lav.ish** *adj.* generoso, abundante.

**law** *s.* lei, direito, regra.

**law court** *s.* tribunal de justiça.

**law.ful** *adj.* lícito, legal.

**law.less** *adj.* ilegal; sem lei.

**lawn** *s.* gramado, relvado.

**lawn mow.er** *s.* cortador de grama.

**law school** *s.* faculdade de direito.

**law.suit** *s.* ação judicial, processo.

**law.yer** *s.* advogado(a).

**lax** *s.* diarreia / *adj.* relaxado, frouxo.

**lax.a.tive** *s.* laxante / *adj.* laxativo.

**lay** *adj.* leigo / *v.* colocar, pôr, derrubar.

**lay.a.bout** *s.* vadio(a).

**lay-by** *s.* acostamento.

**lay.er** *s.* camada; estrato (geologia).

**lay.ette** *s.* enxoval de bebê.

**layman**     280     **leeway**

**lay.man** *s.* leigo.
**lay.out** *s.* desenho, plano, esquema.
**laze** *v.* vadiar / *s.* ócio.
**la.zy** *adj.* preguiçoso.
**lb.** *abrev.* de *pound*.
**lead** *s.* chumbo; dianteira; conduta / *v.* liderar; conduzir.
**lead.en** *adj.* cinzento; feito de chumbo.
**lead.er** *s.* líder; guia.
**lead.er.ship** *s.* liderança, comando.
**lead-free** *adj.* sem chumbo.
**lead.ing** *adj.* principal.
**lead.ing light** *s.* destaque.
**lead singer** *s.* vocalista.
**leaf** *s.* *(pl. leaves)* folha (de planta, livro).
**leaf through** *v.* folhear rapidamente.
**leaf.less** *adj.* desfolhado.
**leaf.let** *s.* folheto.
**leaf.y** *adj.* frondoso.
**league** *s.* liga, aliança; légua.
**leak** *s.* vazamento, goteira, escape / *v.* vazar, gotejar, escapar.
**lean** *adj.* magro, delgado (animal, pessoa) / *s.* inclinação / *v.* inclinar.
**lean.ing** *s.* inclinação, propensão.
**leap** *s.* salto / *v.* pular.

**leap.frog** *s.* jogo de pular sela.
**leap year** *s.* ano bissexto.
**learn** *v.* aprender.
**learn.ed** *adj.* instruído / *v. pret.* e *pp.* do *v. to learn*.
**learn.er** *s.* principiante, discípulo, aprendiz.
**learn.ing** *s.* saber, erudição; aprendizagem.
**lease** *s.* arrendamento / *v.* arrendar.
**leash** *s.* correia, trela.
**least** *adj.* menor, mínimo / *adv.* pelo menos, menos / *s.* menor, mínimo.
**leath.er** *s.* couro.
**leave** *v.* deixar, partir, abandonar / *s.* licença, permissão.
**leave be.hind** *v.* deixar para trás.
**leav.en** *s.* levedura, fermento.
**leave out** *v.* omitir.
**Leb.a.non** *s.* Líbano.
**lech.er.ous** *adj.* lascivo, luxurioso.
**lec.ture** *s.* palestra, preleção / *v.* dar uma palestra.
**lec.tur.er** *s.* palestrante, conferencista, professor.
**ledge** *s.* peitoril, saliência, orla.
**led.ger** *s.* lápide.
**leech** *s.* sanguessuga.
**leek** *s.* alho-poró.
**lee.way** *s.* liberdade de ação, deriva.

left *v. pret.* do *v. leave*
/ *s.* esquerda / *adj.* esquerdo
/ *adv.* à esquerda.

**left-hand.ed** *adj.* canhoto.

**left.o.ver** *s.* sobra, resto.

**left-wing** *s.* ala esquerdista
/ *adj.* esquerdista.

**leg** *s.* perna.

**leg.a.cy** *s.* legado, herança.

**le.gal** *adj.* legal, legítimo.

**leg.al.ize** *v.* legalizar.

**leg.al.ly** *adv.* legalmente.

**le.gend** *s.* lenda; legenda.

**le.gen.da.ry** *adj.* legendário.

**le.gis.la.tion** *s.* legislação.

**le.gis.la.ture** *s.* legislatura,
assembleia legislativa.

**le.git.i.mate** *adj.* legítimo,
autêntico / *v.* legitimar, legalizar.

**leg.room** *s.* espaço para as pernas.

**lei.sure** *s.* lazer, prazer.

**lei.sure.ly** *adj.* calmo, vagaroso
/ *adv.* vagarosamente.

**lem.on** *s.* limão.

**lem.on.ade** *s.* limonada.

**lend** *v.* emprestar para.

**length** *s.* comprimento; duração.

**lens** *s.* lente.

**Lent** *s.* quaresma.

**lent** *v. pret.* e *pp.* do *v. to lend.*

**len.til** *s.* lentilha.

**Leo** *s.* Leão (astrologia).

**leop.ard** *s.* leopardo.

**lep.er** *s.* leproso, hanseniano.

**lep.ro.sy** *s.* lepra, mal de Hansen.

**les.bi.an** *s.* lésbica / *adj.* lésbico.

**less** *s.* inferior, menor, menos
/ *adj.* inferior, menor, menos
/ *adv.* menos / *prep.* sem, menos.

**less.en** *v.* diminuir, reduzir.

**less.er** *adj.* menor, inferior
/ *adv.* menos.

**les.son** *s.* aula, lição.

**let** *v.* deixar, permitir; alugar.

**let down** *v.* baixar, humilhar.

**let.down** *s.* desapontamento,
humilhação.

**le.thal** *adj.* letal, mortal.

**let's go** contração de *let us go*
(vamos).

**let.ter** *s.* letra; carta.

**let.ter bomb** *s.* carta bomba.

**let.ter.box** *s.* caixa de correio.

**let.ter.head** *s.* cabeçalho.

**let.ter.ing** *s.* letras; inscrição.

**let.tuce** *s.* alface.

**let-up** *s.* diminuição, pausa,
intervalo.

**leu.ke.mia** *s.* leucemia.

**lev.el** *s.* nível; superfície plana
/ *adj.* plano, nivelado / *v.* nivelar.

**lev.er** *s.* alavanca.

**lev.i.ty** *s.* leviandade, inconstância.

**lev.y** *s.* coleta, taxação.

**liability**     282     **likelihood**

**li.a.bil.i.ty** *s.* responsabilidade; obrigação.

**li.a.ble** *adj.* responsável.

**li.aise** *v.* estabelecer contato, ligação.

**li.ar** *s.* mentiroso(a).

**li.bel** *s.* difamação, calúnia / *v.* difamar.

**lib.e.ral** *s.* liberal / *adj.* liberal.

**lib.e.rate** *v.* libertar, liberar.

**lib.e.ration** *s.* liberação, libertação.

**lib.er.ty** *s.* liberdade.

**Li.bra** *s.* Libra (astrologia).

**li.brar.i.an** *s.* bibliotecário(a).

**li.brar.y** *s.* biblioteca.

**Lib.y.a** *s.* Líbia.

**li.cense** *s.* licença, autorização.

**li.censed** *adj.* licenciado, autorizado.

**li.cense plate** *s.* placa (de carro).

**lick** *s.* lambida / *v.* lamber.

**lid** *s.* tampa.

**lie** *s.* mentira / *v.* jazer, deitar-se; mentir.

**lieu.ten.ant** *s.* tenente.

**life** *s.* (*pl. lives*) vida.

**life.belt** *s.* cinto de segurança.

**life.boat** *s.* barco salva-vidas.

**life.guard** *s.* salva-vidas.

**life in.sur.ance** *s.* seguro de vida.

**life.jacket** *s.* colete salva-vidas.

**life.less** *adj.* sem vida, morto.

**life.like** *adj.* natural; tal como a vida.

**life.long** *adj.* que dura a vida toda, vitalício.

**life sen.tence** *s.* pena de prisão perpétua.

**life.span** *s.* duração de vida.

**life.style** *s.* estilo de vida.

**life.time** *s.* tempo de vida, existência.

**lift** *v.* levantar, suspender / *s.* elevador; carona.

**light** *s.* luz / *v.* acender, iluminar / *adj.* claro, leve, delicado.

**lights** *s.* semáforo.

**light.en** *v.* iluminar, acender; tornar mais leve; relampejar.

**light.er** *s.* isqueiro; barcaça, chata.

**light.ing** *s.* iluminação, ignição.

**light.ly** *adv.* ligeiramente, levemente.

**light.ness** *s.* leveza, claridade.

**light.ning** *s.* relâmpago; raio.

**light.ning bug** *s.* vaga-lume.

**light.ning rod** *s.* para-raios.

**light-year** *s.* ano-luz.

**like** *v.* gostar / *prep.* como / *adj.* parecido, semelhante / *s.* igual, semelhante.

**like.a.ble** *adj.* simpático(a), agradável, amável.

**like.li.hood** *s.* probabilidade; semelhança.

**like.ly** *adj.* provável, plausível.
**like mad** *adj.* como louco.
**like.ness** *s.* semelhança, aparência.
**like.wise** *adv.* igualmente, do mesmo modo, também, outrossim.
**lik.ing** *s.* simpatia; preferência.
**li.lac** *s.* lilás / *adj.* lilás.
**lil.y** *s.* lírio; flor-de-lis.
**limb** *s.* membro.
**lim.ber up** *v.* fazer aquecimento.
**lime** *s.* limeira, limão, lima; cal.
**lime.light** *s.* centro das atenções; publicidade.
**lime.stone** *s.* pedra calcária.
**lim.it** *s.* limite / *v.* limitar.
**lim.it.ed** *s.* trem ou ônibus expresso / *adj.* limitado.
**lim.it.ed com.pa.ny** *s.* sociedade anônima.
**limp** *v.* mancar / *adj.* frouxo; flexível; manco.
**line** *s.* linha, corda; fila, reta; linho / *v.* enfileirar-se; riscar.
**lin.e.age** *s.* linhagem, estirpe.
**lined** *adj.* pautado; enrugado.
**lin.en** *s.* linho; roupa (branca) de cama.
**lin.er** *s.* navio ou avião de linha regular.
**lines.man** *s.* juiz de linha, bandeirinha.

**line up** *v.* enfileirar / *s.* alinhamento.
**lin.ger** *v.* demorar, perdurar(-se); persistir.
**lin.ge.rie** *s.* *lingerie*, roupa íntima feminina.
**lin.guis.tics** *s.* linguística.
**link** *s.* elo, conexão, ligação / *v.* unir, conectar, ligar.
**link.up** *s.* conexão, acoplamento; fusão.
**li.on** *s.* leão.
**li.on.ess** *s.* leoa.
**lip** *s.* lábio, beiço.
**lip.stick** *s.* batom.
**liq.ue.fier** *s.* liquidificador.
**li.queur** *s.* licor.
**liq.uid** *s.* líquido, fluido / *adj.* líquido, fluido.
**liq.ui.date** *v.* liquidar, saldar.
**liq.uor** *s.* licor, bebida alcoólica.
**liquor store** *s.* loja de bebidas.
**Lis.bon** *s.* Lisboa.
**lisp** *s.* falar com a língua presa.
**list** *v.* listar / *s.* lista; inclinação (de um navio).
**list.ed** *adj.* tombado; registrado.
**lis.ten** *v.* escutar.
**lis.ten.er** *s.* ouvinte.
**list.less** *adj.* indiferente, desatento.
**lit** *v. pret.* e *pp.* do *v. light.*

**li.ter, li.tre** *s.* litro.

**lit.e.ra.cy** *s.* alfabetização.

**lit.e.ral** *adj.* literal.

**lit.e.ra.ry** *adj.* literário.

**lit.e.rate** *adj.* alfabetizado.

**lit.e.ra.ture** *s.* literatura; folhetos (coloquial).

**lit.ter** *s.* lixo; ninhada; palha ou feno espalhado para cama dos animais ou como cobertura para plantas.

**lit.ter.bin** *s.* lata de lixo.

**lit.tle** *adj.* pequeno, pouco; novo (de idade) / *adv.* pouco, escassamente.

**lit.tle fin.ger** *s.* dedo mindinho.

**live** *v.* viver, morar / *adj.* vivo; ao vivo.

**live.li.hood** *s.* meio de vida, sustento.

**live.long** *adj.* durável.

**live.ly** *adj.* vivo, vigoroso, animado.

**li.ven up** *v.* animar.

**liv.er** *s.* fígado; vivente.

**live.stock** *s.* gado.

**liv.ing** *adj.* vivo / *s.* sustento, modo de vida.

**liv.ing con.di.tions** *s.* condições de vida.

**liv.ing-room** *s.* sala de estar.

**liv.ing stan.dard** *s.* padrão de vida.

**living wage** *s.* salário mínimo.

**liz.ard** *s.* lagarto.

**load** *s.* peso, carga / *v.* carregar.

**load.ed** *adj.* carregado.

**loaf** *s.* filão de pão, pão (de forma, redondo); vadiagem, ociosidade / *v.* vadiar.

**loaf.er** *s.* vadio.

**loan** *s.* empréstimo / *v.* emprestar.

**loan shark** *s.* agiota.

**lob.by** *s.* saguão, vestíbulo; pressão / *v.* pressionar.

**lob.ster** *s.* lagosta.

**lo.cal** *adj.* local.

**lo.cal.i.ty** *s.* localidade.

**lo.cal.ly** *adv.* nos arredores, localmente.

**lo.cate** *v.* localizar, situar; fixar residência.

**lo.ca.tion** *s.* local, localização, posição, locação.

**loch** *s.* lago.

**lock** *s.* fechadura, cadeado / *v.* trancar.

**lock.er** *s.* compartimento com chave.

**lock.et** *s.* medalhão.

**lock.smith** *s.* serralheiro.

**lock.up** *s.* local que serve como prisão / *v.* trancafiar.

**lo.co.mo.tive** *s.* locomotiva / *adj.* locomotivo.

**lo.cust** *s.* gafanhoto.

**lodge** *s.* guarita; residência temporária; alojamento / *v.* alojar.

**loft** *s.* sótão; apartamento pequeno e de luxo.

**log** *s.* tora, lenha; diário de bordo ou de voo / *v.* registrar.

**log-book** *v.* registrar / *s.* livro de registro, diário.

**loge** *s.* camarote de teatro.

**lo.gic** *s.* lógica.

**lo.gic.al** *adj.* lógico.

**lo.go** *s.* logotipo.

**loin** *s.* lombo.

**loi.ter** *v.* perder tempo, tardar.

**loll** *v.* refestelar-se; pôr a língua para fora.

**lol.li.pop** *s.* pirulito.

**Lon.don** *s.* Londres.

**Lon.don.er** *s.* londrino(a).

**lone** *adj.* solitário.

**lone.li.ness** *s.* solidão, isolamento.

**lone.ly** *adj.* só, solitário.

**long** *adj.* longo, comprido / *adv.* muito tempo / *v.* ansiar por algo, desejar.

**long-distance** *adj.* longa distância / *adv.* de longa distância.

**long-haired** *adj.* peludo, cabeludo.

**long.hand** *s.* escrita manual.

**long.ish** *adj.* um tanto longo.

**long-life** *adj.* longa vida.

**long-range** *adj.* de longo alcance.

**long-term** *adj.* a longo prazo.

**loo** *s.* banheiro.

**look** *v.* olhar; parecer / *s.* olhar; aparência.

**look for** *v.* procurar.

**look out** *v.* tomar cuidado.

**look over** *v.* examinar.

**loom** *s.* tear / *v.* assomar, surgir.

**loon.y** *s.* débil mental / *adj.* maluco (coloquial).

**loop** *s.* laço, laçada / *v.* enlaçar.

**loose** *s.* liberdade / *adj.* solto, folgado, vago / *v.* soltar, desamarrar.

**loose.ly** *adv.* folgadamente, livremente.

**loos.en** *v.* afrouxar, desatar, soltar.

**loot** *v.* saquear, pilhar / *s.* saque, pilhagem.

**lop off** *v.* podar, cortar.

**lop-sid.ed** *adj.* torto, distorcido.

**Lord** *s.* Deus.

**lord** *s.* o senhor, lorde.

**lord.like** *adj.* nobre, senhoril; arrogante.

**lor.ry** *s.* caminhão.

**lose** *v.* perder.

**los.er** *s.* perdedor(a).

**loss** *s.* perda, dano prejuízo.

**lost** *v. pret.* e *pp.* do *v. lose* / *adj.* perdido(a), desorientado(a).

**lot** *s.* porção; lote; destino / *v.* lotear, dividir.

lotion     **286**     lush

**lo.tion** *s.* loção.

**lot.ter.y** *s.* loteria.

**loud** *adj.* alto; barulhento / *adv.* alto, em voz alta.

**loud-hail.er** *s.* megafone.

**loud.ly** *adv.* ruidosamente, em voz alta.

**loud.speak.er** *s.* alto-falante.

**lounge** *s.* saguão; bar social / *v.* espreguiçar-se, vadiar.

**louse** *s.* (*pl. lice*) piolho.

**lous.y** *adj.* piolhento; vil, torpe.

**lov.e.ble** *adj.* adorável, amável.

**love** *s.* amor / *v.* amar.

**love a.ffair** *s.* caso de amor.

**love life** *s.* vida sentimental.

**love.less** *adj.* sem amor.

**love.ly** *adj.* encantador(a), gracioso(a).

**lov.er** *s.* amante.

**lov.ing** *adj.* carinhoso(a).

**low** *adj.* baixo / *adv.* baixo.

**low-cut** *adj.* decotado.

**low.er** *adj.* inferior; mais baixo / *v.* reduzir, baixar.

**low-fat** *adj.* magro, de baixa caloria.

**low.ing** *s.* mugido.

**low.land** *s.* planície.

**low.ly** *adj.* humilde, modesto; vil, inferior.

**low-spir.it.ed** *adj.* deprimido.

**low tide** *s.* maré-baixa.

**loy.al** *adj.* leal, fiel.

**loy.al.ty** *s.* lealdade, fidelidade.

**lu.bri.cate** *v.* lubrificar.

**luck** *s.* sorte; acaso.

**luck.i.ly** *adv.* felizmente, afortunadamente.

**luck.y** *adj.* sortudo(a), afortunado(a).

**lug** *s.* puxão, arranco / *v.* puxar pelas orelhas.

**lug.gage** *s.* bagagem.

**luggage rack** *s.* porta-bagagem.

**lull** *s.* calmaria, bonança / *v.* acalmar, acalentar.

**lul.la.by** *s.* canção de ninar / *v.* ninar.

**lum.ber** *s.* restos de madeira / *v.* mover-se com dificuldade.

**lum.ber.ing** *adj.* pesado.

**lum.ber.jack** *s.* lenhador.

**lu.mi.nous** *adj.* luminoso.

**lump** *s.* torrão; inchação, inchaço.

**lu.na.tic** *s.* louco(a), lunático(a) / *adj.* louco(a), lunático(a).

**lunch** *s.* almoço / *v.* almoçar.

**lunch time** *s.* hora do almoço.

**lung** *s.* pulmão.

**lurch** *s.* desamparo; balanço brusco / *v.* dar uma guinada, cambalear.

**lurk** *v.* espreitar; emboscar.

**lush** *adj.* viçoso, exuberante.

**lust** *s.* luxúria / *v.* cobiçar.
**lus.ter** *s.* lustre, brilho.
**lust.y** *adj.* robusto, vigoroso.
**Lux.em.bourg** *s.* Luxemburgo.
**lux.u.ry** *s.* luxo / *adj.* de luxo.
**ly.ing** *s.* mentira / *adj.* mentiroso(a).

**ly.ing-in** *s.* resguardo, situação de estar deitado.
**lynch** *v.* linchar.
**lyr.i.cal** *adj.* lírico.
**lyr.ics** *s.* letra de música.

**L**

# Mm

**M, m** *s.* décima terceira letra do alfabeto inglês; representa o número 1000 em algarismos romanos.

**ma' am** *abrev.* de *madam*.

**mach.i.nate** *v.* maquinar.

**ma.chine** *s.* máquina.

**ma.chi.ne-gun** *s.* metralhadora.

**ma.chin.e.ry** *s.* maquinaria; maquinismo.

**mack.in.tosh** *s.* capa impermeável, tecido impermeável.

**mad** *adj.* louco, demente, insensato; furioso.

**mad.am** *s.* senhora, madame.

**mad.den** *v.* enlouquecer, enfurecer.

**made** *adj.* feito, fabricado / *v. pret. pp.* do *v. to make*.

**made-to-or.der** *adj.* feito sob medida, sob encomenda.

**mad-up** *adj.* inventado, mentiroso.

**mad.house** *s.* hospício.

**mad.ly** *adv.* loucamente.

**mad.man** *s.* louco, alienado.

**mad.ness** *s.* loucura; raiva.

**mag.a.zine** *s.* revista, periódico.

**ma.gic** *s.* magia / *adj.* mágico.

**mag.is.trate** *s.* magistrado, juiz(íza).

**mag.nate** *s.* magnata.

**mag.net** *s.* ímã, magneto.

**mag.net.ic** *adj.* magnético.

**maid** *s.* criada, empregada; virgem.

**maid.en** *s.* solteirona, donzela.

**maid.en.hood** *s.* virgindade.

**maid.en name** *s.* nome de solteira.

**maid.ser.vant** *s.* criada.

**mail** *s.* correio; correspondência / *v.* mandar, expedir, enviar pelo correio.

**mail.box** *s.* caixa de correio.

**mail.man** *s.* carteiro.

**maim** *s.* lesão, mutilação / *v.* mutilar, desfigurar.

**main** *s.* condutor de gás / *adj.* principal, essencial.

**main.te.nance** *s.* sustento; manutenção.

**maize** *s.* milho.

**ma.jes.tic** *adj.* majestoso, grandioso.

**ma.jor** *s.* major; maior de idade / *adj.* muito importante.

**ma.jor.i.ty** *s.* maioria; maioridade.

**make** *v.* fazer, fabricar, produzir / *s.* marca, fabricação.

**make-up** *s.* maquiagem, composição; constituição.

**mak.ing** *s.* fabricação.

**ma.laise** *s.* mal-estar, indisposição.

**male** *s.* macho, varão / *adj.* masculino, macho.

**mal.ice** *s.* malícia.

**ma.lign** *v.* caluniar, difamar / *adj.* maligno.

**mal.le.a.ble** *adj.* maleável.

**mal.treat** *v.* maltratar.

**mam.mal** *s.* mamífero.

**man** *s.* (*pl. men*) homem.

**man.a.cle** *s.* algema; constrangimento / *v.* algemar; restringir.

**man.age** *v.* administrar, gerenciar, dirigir.

**man.age.a.ble** *adj.* maneável; controlável; dócil.

**man.age.ment** *s.* administração, gerência, direção; gestão, conduta.

**man.ag.er** *s.* gerente, diretor, administrador.

**man.di.ble** *s.* mandíbula, queixada.

**mane** *s.* crina, juba.

**man.go** *s.* manga (fruta).

**man.hood** *s.* humanidade; virilidade.

**man.i.fest** *v.* manifestar / *adj.* manifesto, evidente / *s.* manifesto.

**ma.nip.u.late** *v.* manipular, manejar.

**man.kind** *s.* gênero humano; humanidade.

**man.ly** *adj.* másculo, viril.

**man.ner** *s.* modo, maneira.

**man.ner.less** *adj.* sem modos, indelicado.

**man.pow.er** *s.* potencial humano, mão de obra.

**man.u.al** *adj.* manual, feito com as mãos / *s.* manual.

**man.u.fac.ture** *v.* manufaturar, fabricar / *s.* manufatura, fabricação.

**man.u.fac.tur.er** *s.* fabricante.

**man.y** *pron.* muito(s), muita(s) / *adj.* muito(s), muita(s).

**map** *s.* mapa / *v.* mapear; planejar.

**mar** *v.* frustar, arruinar.

**mar.ble** *s.* mármore ♦ ~s bolinha de gude.

**March** *s.* março.

**march** *s.* marcha / *v.* marchar.

**mare** *s.* égua.

**mar.ga.rine** *s.* margarina.

**mar.gin** *s.* margem (rio, papel).

**mar.i.jua.na** *s.* maconha, haxixe.

**mar.i.ner** *s.* marinheiro.

**marish** *s.* pântano / *adj.* pantanoso.

**mark** *s.* marca, sinal; nota escolar / *v.* marcar, assinalar, corrigir.

**mar.ket** *s.* mercado.

**mar.ket.ing** *s.* ação de comprar e vender, *marketing*.

**mar.quis** *s.* marquês.

**mar.quise** *s.* marquesa.

**mar.riage** *s.* casamento, matrimônio.

**mar.ried** *adj.* casado(a).

**Mars** *s.* Marte.

**marsh** *s.* pântano, brejo.

**mar.shal** *s.* marechal.

**mar.tyr** *s.* mártir.

**mar.vel** *s.* maravilha / *v.* maravilhar-se.

**mar.vel.ous** *adj.* maravilhoso.

**mash** *s.* purê de batatas, mistura, papa (coloquial) / *v.* triturar, espremer.

**mask** *s.* máscara; disfarce / *v.* mascarar.

**masked ball** *s.* baile de máscaras.

**ma.son** *s.* pedreiro; maçom.

**mass** *s.* multidão, massa; missa / *v.* juntar-se, amontoar-se.

**mas.sage** *s.* massagem / *v.* fazer massagem em.

**mass me.di.a** *s.* meios de comunicação de massa.

**mas.ter** *s.* mestre, dono, senhor / *v.* dominar, controlar.

**mas.ter.piece** *s.* obra-prima.

**mat** *s.* esteira, capacho, tapete.

**match** *s.* fósforo; jogo, partida; igual; companheiro / *v.* combinar.

**match.box** *s.* caixa de fósforo.

**mate** *s.* companheiro, colega / *v.* dar xeque-mate no xadrez.

**ma.te.ri.al** *s.* matéria, material, substância; tecido / *adj.* material, essencial.

# matrix — memory

**ma.trix** *s.* matriz.

**ma.tron** *s.* matrona.

**matt** *adj.* fosco, sem brilho.

**mat.ter** *s.* questão, assunto, matéria / *v.* importar, significar.

**mat.tress** *s.* colchão.

**ma.ture** *adj.* maduro / *v.* amadurecer.

**ma.tu.ri.ty** *s.* maturidade.

**mawk.ish** *adj.* enjoativo, repugnante.

**max.im** *s.* máxima.

**May** *s.* maio.

**may** *v. modal* poder, ter permissão.

**may.be** *adv.* talvez, possivelmente.

**mayor** *s.* prefeito.

**maze** *s.* labirinto.

**me** *pron.* me, mim, comigo.

**mead.ow** *s.* prado, campina.

**meal** *s.* refeição.

**mean** *adj.* avarento; médio / *s.* meio, média / *v.* significar, querer dizer.

**mean.ing** *s.* sentido, significado / *adj.* expressivo, significativo.

**mean.ing.less** *adj.* sem sentido.

**mean.time** *adv.* entretanto, enquanto isso.

**mean.while** *adv.* entretanto, enquanto isso.

**mea.sles** *s.* sarampo.

**meas.ly** *adj.* miserável, vil; atacado de sarampo.

**meas.ure** *v.* medir; comparar; tirar as medidas / *s.* medida.

**meat** *s.* carne (alimento).

**me.chan.ic** *s.* mecânico / *adj.* mecânico.

**med.al** *s.* medalha.

**med.dle** *v.* intrometer-se.

**me.di.a** *s.* meios de comunicação, mídia.

**me.dic.a.ment** *s.* medicamento.

**medi.cine** *s.* medicina, remédio.

**me.di.o.cre** *adj.* medíocre.

**me.di.um** *adj.* médio, moderado / *s.* meio.

**med.ley** *s.* mistura, miscelânea, confusão / *v.* misturar / *adj.* misturado.

**meek** *adj.* manso, submisso, meigo.

**meet** *v.* encontrar; reunir-se; conhecer.

**meet.ing** *s.* reunião; encontro.

**meg.a.phone** *s.* megafone.

**mel.o.dy** *s.* melodia.

**mel.on** *s.* melão.

**mem.ber** *s.* membro; sócio, associado.

**mem.o** *s.* memorando, circular.

**mem.o.ra.ble** *adj.* memorável, notável.

**mem.o.rize** *v.* memorizar, decorar.

**mem.o.ry** *s.* memória, lembrança, recordação.

menace 292 military

**men.ace** *s.* ameaça / *v.* ameaçar.
**mend** *v.* remendar, consertar, reparar / *s.* remendo, conserto, reparo.
**men.tal** *adj.* mental.
**men.u** *s.* cardápio, *menu*.
**mer.ce.nar.y** *adj.* mercenário; interesseiro.
**mer.chan.dise** *s.* mercadoria(s).
**mer.ci.ful** *adj.* misericordioso, piedoso, clemente.
**mer.ci.less** *adj.* impiedoso.
**Mercury** *s.* Mercúrio (planeta); Mercúrio (deus dos romanos).
**mer.cu.ry** *s.* mercúrio.
**mer.cy** *s.* piedade, misericórdia.
**mere** *s.* lago, lagoa, charco / *adj.* mero, simples.
**me.rid.i.an** *s.* meridiano / *adj.* meridiano.
**mer.it** *s.* mérito / *v.* merecer.
**mer.maid** *s.* sereia.
**mer.ry** *adj.* alegre.
**merry-go-round** *s.* carrossel.
**mess** *s.* confusão, desordem, bagunça / *v.* bagunçar, sujar, desarrumar (coloquial).
**mes.sage** *s.* mensagem, recado.
**mes.sen.ger** *s.* mensageiro(a).
**mess.y** *adj.* sujo, desarrumado, bagunçado.
**met.al.lur.gy** *s.* metarlugia.

**me.ter** *s.* metro, medidor / *v.* medir.
**meth.od** *s.* método.
**me.trop.o.lis** *s.* metrópole.
**met.tle** *s.* ânimo, vigor.
**mew** *s.* gaivota; miado / *v.* miar.
**Mex.i.can** *s.* mexicano. / *adj.* mexicano.
**mi.crobe** *s.* micróbio.
**mid** *adj.* meio, meados; semi.
**mid.day** *s.* meio-dia.
**mid.dle** *s.* meio, centro, metade / *adj.* médio, central.
**mid.dle age** *s.* meia-idade / *adj.* de meia-idade.
**midge** *s.* mosquito.
**midg.et** *s.* anão(ã); pigmeu.
**mid.night** *s.* meia-noite.
**mid.wife** *s.* parteira.
**might** *s.* força, poder / *v. pret.* de *may*.
**might.y** *adj.* poderoso, potente.
**mi.graine** *s.* enxaqueca.
**mi.grate** *v.* migrar, emigrar.
**mild** *adj.* brando, meigo; ameno, suave.
**mil.den** *v.* abrandar, suavizar.
**mild.ness** *s.* suavidade, brandura.
**mile** *s.* milha.
**mil.i.tant** *adj.* militante, combativo / *s.* militante.
**mil.i.ta.ry** *adj.* militar.

milk *s.* leite / *v.* ordenhar.

**milk.y** *adj.* leitoso, com bastante leite.

**Milky Way** *s.* Via Láctea.

**mill** *s.* moinho, engenho, fábrica / *v.* moer, triturar.

**mil.len.ni.um** *s.* milênio.

**mill.ing** *s.* moagem, moedura.

**mil.lion** *s.* milhão / *adj.* milhão.

**mill.stone** *s.* mó, pedra de moinho; carga pesada.

**mime** *s.* mímica / *v.* imitar, fazer mímicas.

**mim.ic** *s.* mímico, imitador / *adj.* mímico, imitativo / *v.* imitar.

**mince** *s.* picadinho de carne / *v.* moer, picar.

**mind** *s.* mente, intelecto / *v.* concentrar-se, dedicar-se.

**mine** *s.* mina / *pron. poss.* meu(s), minha(s) / *v.* minerar, extrair.

**min.er** *s.* mineiro.

**min.ia.ture** *s.* miniatura / *adj.* miniatura.

**min.im** *s.* mínima.

**min.is.ter** *s.* ministro; sacerdote, pastor.

**min.is.try** *s.* ministério; clero.

**mi.nor** *adj.* menor, secundário, de pouca importância / *s.* menor (de idade).

**mint** *s.* hortelã, menta; casa da moeda.

**mi.nus** *s.* sinal de menos (-) / *adj.* menos, negativo.

**min.ute** *s.* minuto.

**minx** *s.* rapariga, mulher à toa.

**mir.a.cle** *s.* milagre.

**mi.rage** *s.* miragem.

**mire** *s.* lodo, lama / *v.* atolar; envolver-se em dificuldades.

**mir.ror** *s.* espelho / *v.* espelhar, refletir.

**mis.ad.ven.ture** *s.* desgraça, infelicidade, infortúnio.

**mis.ap.ply** *v.* empregar mal, desviar.

**mis.cel.la.ne.ous** *adj.* variado, misto.

**mi.ser** *s.* avarento, sovina / *adj.* avarento, sovina.

**mis.e.ra.ble** *adj.* triste, infeliz, desgraçado, miserável.

**mis.e.ry** *s.* miséria, penúria; tristeza, aflição.

**mis.fit** *s.* traje que não veste bem / *v.* assentar mal.

**mis.for.tune** *s.* infortúnio, desgraça, infelicidade.

**mis.giv.ing** *s.* apreensão; pressentimento.

**mis.guide** *v.* desencaminhar.

**mis.han.dle** *v.* maltratar, manejar mal.

**Miss** *s.* senhorita, moça.
**miss** *s.* falha, erro / *v.* perder (não acertar, não compreender); sentir falta.
**mis.sile** *s.* míssil, projétil.
**miss.ing** *adj.* ausente, extraviado, que falta, desaparecido.
**mis.sion** *s.* missão.
**mis.sive** *s.* missiva, carta.
**mis.take** *s.* erro / *v.* errar.
**Mis.ter** *s.* senhor.
**mis.treat** *v.* maltratar.
**Mis.tress** *s.* senhora, título dado à mulher casada.
**mis.tress** *s.* ama, dona de casa; amante, concubina.
**mis.trust** *s.* desconfiança / *v.* desconfiar.
**mist.y** *adj.* nebuloso.
**mis.un.der.stand** *v.* entender mal, interpretar mal.
**mis.un.der.stand.ing** *s.* equívoco, mal-entendido, desavença.
**mix** *v.* misturar, mesclar / *s.* mistura, mescla.
**mixed-up** *s.* confusão / *adj.* confuso.
**mix.er** *s.* batedeira, misturador.
**mo.bile** *adj.* móvel.
**mo.bil.i.ty** *s.* mobilidade.
**mode** *s.* modo, maneira, meio.

**mod.el** *s.* modelo, maquete / *v.* modelar, moldar.
**mod.e.rate** *adj.* moderado, módico / *v.* moderar.
**mod.ern** *adj.* moderno.
**mod.est** *adj.* modesto.
**moist** *s.* umidade.
**moist.en** *v.* umedecer.
**mole** *s.* verruga, pinta; porto, dique; toupeira / *v.* cavar, escavar.
**mol.e.cule** *s.* molécula.
**mo.lest** *v.* molestar, importunar; agredir.
**mol.ten** *adj.* fundido.
**mo.ment** *s.* momento, instante.
**mon.arch** *s.* monarca.
**Mon.day** *s.* segunda-feira.
**mon.e.ta.ry** *adj.* monetário.
**mon.ey** *s.* dinheiro.
**mon.eyed** *adj.* endinheirado.
**monk** *s.* monge, frade.
**mon.key** *s.* macaco.
**monkey busi.ness** *s.* macaquice; trapaça.
**mon.ster** *s.* monstro.
**mon.tage** *s.* montagem.
**month** *s.* mês.
**mon.u.ment** *s.* monumento.
**mood** *s.* humor, disposição.
**moon** *s.* lua.
**moon.light** *s.* luar / *adj.* iluminado pela lua, enluarado.

**moot** *s.* debate, disputa / *v.* debater.

**mop.pet** *s.* boneca de pano.

**mor.al** *s.* moral.

**mo.ral.i.ty** *s.* moralidade.

**mor.al.ize** *v.* moralizar.

**mor.bid** *adj.* doentio, mórbido.

**more** *adj.* mais / *adv.* além do mais; ainda.

**more.o.ver** *adv.* além disso, além do mais.

**morgue** *s.* necrotério.

**morn.ing** *s.* manhã / *adj.* matinal, da manhã.

**mor.tar** *s.* argamassa; morteiro (militar); pilão.

**mort.gage** *s.* hipoteca / *v.* hipotecar.

**mo.sa.ic** *s.* mosaico.

**moss** *s.* musgo.

**most** *s.* maior parte de, maioria de / *adv.* o(a) mais, muito / *adj.* mais.

**mote** *s.* partícula (de pó), molécula.

**moth** *s.* traça; mariposa.

**moth.er** *s.* mãe; madre, freira.

**moth.er.hood** *s.* maternidade.

**moth.er-in-law** *s.* sogra.

**moth.er.land** *s.* pátria.

**mo.tive** *s.* motivo, razão.

**mot.ley** *adj.* variado, multicolor / *s.* roupa colorida usada pelos bufões.

**mo.tor** *s.* motor.

**mould** *s.* mofo, bolor, fungo; molde, modelo, forma / *v.* mofar; moldar.

**mould.y** *adj.* mofado, bolorento.

**moun.tain** *s.* montanha.

**moun.tain range** *s.* cordilheira, cadeia de montanhas.

**mouse** *s.* (*pl. mice*) camundongo.

**mouse.trape** *s.* ratoeira.

**mouth** *s.* boca; foz.

**mouth.ful** *s.* bocado.

**move** *s.* movimento / *v.* mover.

**mov.ie** *s.* filme.

**mov.ies** *s.* cinema.

**mov.ing** *adj.* comovente, tocante / *adj.* de mudança.

**mow** *s.* celeiro / *v.* aparar, cortar, ceifar.

**Mr.** *abrev.* de *Mister.*

**Mrs.** *abrev.* de *Mistress.*

**Ms.** *abrev.* de *Miss.*

**much** *adv.* muito / *s.* grande quantidade.

**muck** *s.* sujeira, porcaria; esterco.

**muck.y** *adj.* imundo, sujo; vil.

**muff** *s.* pessoa desajeitada.

**muf.fle** *s.* focinho.

**muf.fler** *s.* luva de boxe; amortecedor.

**mug** *s.* caneca; otário (coloquial).

**mug.gy** *adj.* abafado.
**mul.ber.ry** *s.* amora; amoreira.
**mulct** *v.* multar / *s.* multa, penalidade.
**mule** *s.* mula; chinelo de quarto.
**mul.ti.ple** *s.* múltiplo / *adj.* múltiplo.
**mul.ti.ply** *v.* multiplicar.
**mum.my** *s.* múmia; mamãe (coloquial).
**mumps** *s.* cachumba.
**mur.der** *s.* assassinato, homicídio / *v.* assassinar, matar.
**mus.cle** *s.* músculo.

**mu.se.um** *s.* museu.
**mush.room** *s.* cogumelo.
**mu.sic** *s.* música.
**must** *s.* obrigação, dever, necessidade / *v. aux.* dever, ter que, ser obrigado a.
**must.y** *adj.* mofado, bolorento.
**my** *pron.* meu(s), minha(s).
**my.self** *pron.* me, eu mesmo, mim mesmo, a mim.
**mys.te.ri.ous** *adj.* misterioso.
**mys.tic** *s.* místico / *adj.* místico.
**myth** *s.* mito; fábula.

**M**

# Nn

**N, n** *s.* décima quarta letra do alfabeto inglês.

**nail** *s.* unha; prego / *v.* pregar, cravar.

**na.ked** *adj.* nu(a), exposto, despido.

**na.ked.ness** *s.* nudez.

**name** *s.* nome / *v.* nomear, dar nome a.

**nap** *s.* soneca, sesta; penugem / *v.* cochilar, dormitar.

**nape** *s.* nuca.

**nap.kin** *s.* guardanapo.

**nap.py** *s.* fralda.

**nar.cot.ic** *s.* narcótico / *adj.* narcótico.

**nar.rate** *v.* narrar, contar.

**nar.ra.tor** *s.* narrador.

**nar.row** *adj.* estreito; limitado / *v.* estreitar, apertar; limitar.

**nar.row.ness** *s.* estreiteza.

**nas.ty** *adj.* vil, sórdido, repugnante.

**na.tion** *s.* nação.

**na.tion.al** *adj.* nacional.

**na.tive** *s.* natural, nativo(a) / *adj.* natural, nativo(a).

**nat.u.ral** *adj.* natural; nato, inato.

**na.ture** *s.* natureza, universo; caráter, índole.

**naugh.ty** *adj.* malcriado(a); travesso; malicioso(a).

**na.vy** *s.* marinha; frota / *adj.* marinho.

**near** *adj.* próximo(a); vizinho(a). / *adv.* perto, a pouca distância / *prep.* junto a.

**ne.ces.sa.ry** *adj.* necessário.

**ne.ces.si.ty** *s.* necessidade; pobreza; artigo de primeira necessidade.

**neck** *s.* pescoço.

**neck.lace** *s.* colar.

**need** *s.* necessidade, precisão / *v.* precisar, necessitar.

**need.ful** *adj.* necessário, indispensável.

**nee.dle** *s.* agulha (de costura, de bússola).

**need.less** *adj.* desnecessário.

**neg.a.tive** *s.* negativo / *adj.* negativo.

**ne.glect** *s.* negligência, desleixo / *v.* negligenciar.

**neg.li.gence** *s.* negligência, descuido.

**neigh.bor** *s.* vizinho, próximo / *adj.* vizinho, próximo.

**nei.ther** *pron.* nenhum / *conj.* nem / *adv.* tampouco.

**neph.ew** *s.* sobrinho.

**Nep.tune** *s.* Netuno.

**nerve** *s.* nervo; ousadia.

**ner.vous** *adj.* nervoso.

**nest** *s.* ninho.

**nes.tle** *v.* aninhar-se, acomodar-se.

**net** *s.* rede; armadilha / *adj.* líquido / *v.* obter um lucro líquido de; apanhar.

**Neth.er.lands** *s.* Holanda, Países Baixos.

**net.work** *s.* rede, cadeia.

**neu.tral** *adj.* neutro.

**nev.er** *adv.* nunca, jamais.

**new** *adj.* novo; recente; outro.

**new.born** *s.* recém-nascido.

**news** *s.* notícia(s), novidade(s); informação ♦ *the* ~ o noticiário.

**news.pa.per** *s.* jornal.

**next** *s.* o próximo; o seguinte / *adj.* próximo, ao lado de, a seguir.

**nib.ble** *v.* beliscar, mordiscar.

**nice** *adj.* simpático, agradável, bonito.

**nick** *s.* pequeno corte, entalhe ♦ *the* ~ a prisão / *v.* cortar, entalhar.

**nick.name** *s.* apelido, alcunha / *v.* apelidar.

**niece** *s.* sobrinha.

**night** *s.* noite.

**night.fall** *s.* anoitecer.

**night.mare** *s.* pesadelo.

**night-walker** *s.* sonâmbulo.

**nine** *num.* nove.

**nine.teen** *num.* dezenove.

**nine.ty** *num.* noventa.

**ninth** *num.* nono.

**nip.per** *s.* garra; pinça; alicate; aquele que belisca.

**Nip.pon** *s.* Japão.

**no** *adv.* não, nenhum / *adj.* nenhum / *s.* não, recusa / *pron.* nenhum, nenhuma.

**no.bil.i.ty** *s.* nobreza.
**no.bod.y** *pron.* ninguém.
**no.how** *adv.* de modo algum.
**noise** *s.* ruído, barulho.
**none** *adv.* de modo algum
/ *pron.* ninguém, nenhum, nada
/ *adj.* nenhum.
**non.sense** *s.* absurdo, besteira.
**non-stop** *adj.* contínuo, direto,
sem parada.
**noon** *s.* meio-dia.
**nor** *conj.* nem, também não
/ *adv.* nem, também não.
**north** *s.* norte / *adj.* do norte.
**north.east** *adj.* nordeste
/ *adv.* em direção ao nordeste
/ *s.* nordeste.
**nose** *s.* nariz; focinho; faro.
**nos.tril** *s.* narina.
**not** *adv.* não ♦ ~ *yet* ainda não.
**no.ta.ble** *adj.* notável
/ *s.* celebridade, pessoa notável.
**note** *s.* nota (bilhete, música,
dinheiro); tom / *v.* notar, observar.
**note.book** *s.* caderno; computador
portátil.
**noth.ing** *s.* nada, ninharia,
nulidade / *adv.* de modo algum,
em vão.

**no.tice** *s.* anúncio, notificação,
aviso / *v.* notar, perceber; avisar,
notificar.
**nought** *s.* nada, zero.
**noun** *s.* substantivo.
**No.vem.ber** *s.* novembro.
**now** *adv.* agora, já, presentemente
/ *conj.* assim sendo.
**now.a.days** *adv.* hoje em dia,
atualmente.
**no.way** *adv.* de modo algum.
**nude** *adj.* nu(a) (artístico ou
erótico).
**nud.ist** *s.* nudista / *adj.* nudista.
**num.ber** *s.* número; algarismo
/ *v.* numerar.
**num.er.ous** *adj.* numeroso,
abundante.
**nurse** *s.* enfermeiro(a)
/ *v.* cuidar de.
**nur.se.ry** *s.* berçário, creche,
escola maternal; viveiro de plantas.
**nut** *s.* noz; porca (de parafuso);
maluco(a) (coloquial).
**nut.meg** *s.* noz-moscada.
**nu.tri.ent** *s.* nutriente
/ *adj.* nutritivo, nutriente.
**nymph** *s.* ninfa.

# Oo

**O, o** *s.* décima quinta letra do alfabeto inglês.

**oak** *s.* carvalho.

**oar** *s.* remo / *v.* remar.

**oars.man** *s.* remador.

**oat** *s.* aveia.

**oath** *s.* juramento; praga.

**oat.meal** *s.* farinha ou mingau de aveia.

**o.be.di.ence** *s.* obediência.

**o.be.si.ty** *s.* obesidade.

**o.bey** *v.* obedecer.

**ob.ject** *s.* objeto; propósito / *v.* objetar, ser contra.

**ob.li.ga.tion** *s.* obrigação, compromisso.

**ob.li.ga.to.ry** *adj.* obrigatório.

**ob.scene** *adj.* obsceno.

**ob.scure** *adj.* obscuro / *v.* obscurecer.

**ob.serve** *v.* observar, cumprir; notar, reparar.

**ob.ses.sion** *s.* obsessão.

**ob.sta.cle** *s.* obstáculo, empecilho.

**ob.sti.nate** *adj.* teimoso, obstinado.

**ob.tain** *v.* obter, conseguir, alcançar.

**ob.vi.ous** *adj.* óbvio, evidente.

**oc.cult** *adj.* oculto, secreto / *v.* ocultar, esconder.

**oc.cu.pa.tion** *s.* ocupação, profissão.

**oc.cu.py** *v.* ocupar.

**oc.cur** *v.* ocorrer, acontecer.

**o.cean** *s.* oceano.

**Oc.to.ber** *s.* outubro.

**odd** *adj.* estranho; esquisito; ímpar,

**odd.ness** *s.* extravagância, esquisitice.

**of** *prep.* de, do.

**off** *adj.* desligado, apagado, livre / *adv.* embora / *prep.* fora, fora de / *interj.* saia!

**of.fense** *s.* ofensa, insulto, afronta, delito.

**of.fen.sive** *adj.* ofensivo, agressivo, insultante / *s.* ofensiva, ataque.

**of.fer** *s.* oferta / *v.* ofertar.

**of.fer.ing** *s.* oferecimento, oferenda.

**of.fice** *s.* escritório.

**of.fi.cial** *adj.* autorizado, oficial / *s.* funcionário(a) público(a).

**off.set** *s.* compensação, equivalência / *v.* compensar, equiparar.

**off.side** *s.* impedimento / *adj.* impedido (esporte).

**of.ten** *adv.* frequentemente, muitas vezes.

**oil** *s.* óleo; petróleo / *v.* lubrificar.

**O.K., okay** *adj.* certo, correto / *adj.* bem / *interj.* tudo certo!

**old** *adj.* velho, antigo, idoso.

**old age** *s.* velhice.

**old- fash.ioned** *adj.* antiquado, fora de moda.

**ol.ive** *s.* azeitona; oliveira.

**o.lym.pic** *adj.* olímpico.

**O.lym.pic games** *s.* olimpíadas, jogos olímpicos.

**o.mit** *v.* omitir.

**on** *prep.* sobre, em cima de; no, na, nos, nas / *adv.* sobre, em cima de, a partir de.

**once** *s.* uma vez / *conj.* uma vez que / *adv.* outrora, uma vez.

**once again** *adv.* mais uma vez.

**one** *num.* um, uma.

**on.ly** *adv.* somente, apenas / *adj.* único, só / *conj.* só que, exceto.

**onus** *s.* responsabilidade, carga, peso.

**o.pen** *adj.* aberto; livre, desimpedido / *v.* abrir.

**o.pen.ing** *s.* abertura; início; inauguração.

**op.e.rate** *v.* fazer funcionar, operar.

**op.e.ra.tion** *s.* operação, funcionamento.

**op.e.ra.tor** *s.* operador; telefonista.

**o.pin.ion** *s.* opinião, parecer.

**op.por.tune** *adj.* oportuno, conveniente.

**op.por.tu.ni.ty** *s.* oportunidade.

**op.pose** *v.* opor-se, resistir.

**op.po.site** *adj.* oposto, contrário / *s.* oposto, oponente.

**op.tion** *s.* opção, alternativa.

**op.u.lent** *adj.* opulento, farto.

**or** *conj.* ou, senão.

**or.a.cle** *s.* oráculo.

**or.ange** *s.* laranja / *adj.* alaranjado.

**or.ange.ade** *s.* laranjada.

**or.chard** *s.* pomar.

**or.ches.tra** *s.* orquestra.

**or.chid** *s.* orquídea.

**or.der** *s.* ordem, comando; pedido / *v.* encomendar, pedir, ordenar.

**or.gan.i.za.tion** *s.* organização.

**o.ri.ent** *s.* oriente / *v.* orientar.

**o.rig.i.nal** *adj.* original, primeiro, primitivo / *s.* original.

**os.cil.late** *v.* oscilar; vibrar.

**os.trich** *s.* avestruz.

**oth.er** *pron.* outro(s), outra(s) / *adv.* de outra maneira.

**oth.er.wise** *adv.* de outra maneira, por outro lado / *conj.* senão.

**ot.ter** *s.* lontra.

**ought** *s.* dever, obrigação / *v.* ♦ ~ to dever, convir.

**ounce** *s.* onça (animal); onça (medida de peso equivalente a 28, 35 gramas).

**our(s)** *adj.* nosso(s), nossa(s).

**out** *adv.* fora, para fora / *interj.* fora! saia!

**out.back** *s.* interior, área distante, cafundó.

**out.door** *adj.* ao ar livre.

**out.line** *s.* contorno, esboço / *v.* delinear, esboçar.

**out.side** *s.* exterior / *adj.* externo / *adv.* lá fora, para fora / *prep.* fora de.

**out.size** *adj.* de tamanho extra grande.

**ov.en** *s.* forno.

**o.ver** *prep.* por cima de, sobre / *adj.* excedente, acabado / *adv.* de novo.

**o.ver.all** *adj.* geral, absoluto.

**o.ver.coat** *s.* sobretudo, capote.

**o.ver.do** *v.* execeder, exagerar.

**o.ver.dose** *s.* dose excessiva.

**o.ver.flow** *s.* inundação / *v.* transbordar, inundar.

**o.ver.head** *s.* gastos gerais / *adj.* elevado, suspenso / *adv.* em cima.

**o.ver.lay** *s.* revestimento / *v.* revestir.

**o.ver.night** *adv.* durante a noite / *adj.* noturno.

**o.ver.shad.ow** *v.* eclipsar, ofuscar, ensombrecer, obscurecer.

**owe** *v.* dever, ter dívidas.

**owl** *s.* coruja.

**own** *v.* possuir, ter / *adj.* próprio.

**ox** *s.* (*pl.* oxen) boi.

**ox.y.gen** *s.* oxigênio.

**oy.ster** *s.* ostra.

**o.zone** *s.* ozônio.

# Pp

**P, p** *s.* décima sexta letra do alfabeto inglês; *abrev.* de *penny*.
**pace** *s.* passo; compasso.
**pace up and down** *v.* andar de um lado para o outro.
**pa.cif.ic** *adj.* pacífico, sossegado.
**Pacific Ocean, the** *s.* Oceano Pacífico.
**pac.i.fist** *s.* pacifista / *adj.* pacifista.
**pac.i.fy** *v.* acalmar, pacificar.
**pack** *v.* empacotar / *s.* pacote, embrulho; bando, quadrilha; matilha.
**pack.age** *s.* pacote, embrulho.
**pack.ing case** *s.* caixa de embalagem.
**pact** *s.* pacto, trato.
**pad** *s.* almofada (de carimbo).

**pad.dle** *s.* remo curto / *v.* remar.
**pad.dock** *s.* cercado para cavalos.
**pad.lock** *s.* cadeado.
**pae.di.at.rics** *s.* pediatria.
**pa.gan** *s.* pagão.
**page** *s.* página; mensageiro; pajem.
**pag.eant** *s.* cortejo; desfile alegórico.
**page boy** *s.* mensageiro.
**pa.go.da** *s.* pagode (templo pagão).
**paid** *v. pret., pp.* do *v. pay* / *adj.* pago.
**pail** *s.* balde.
**pain** *s.* dor, sofrimento.
**pain.ful** *adj.* doloroso.
**pain.less** *adj.* sem dor.
**paint** *s.* pintura, tinta / *v.* pintar.

pair *s.* par, dupla / *v.* juntar, unir.
**pair of shoes** *s.* par de sapatos.
**Pa.kis.tan** *s.* Paquistão
/ *adj.* paquistanês.
**pal** *s.* camarada, companheiro.
**pal.ace** *s.* palácio.
**pale** *adj.* pálido / *v.* empalidecer.
**pale.face** *s.* cara pálida.
**Pal.es.tine** *s.* Palestina.
**pal.ette** *s.* palheta.
**pal.ing** *s.* estaca; cerca.
**palm** *s.* palma da mão; palmeira;
palmo (medida).
**pal.sied** *adj.* paralítico, paralisado.
**pam.per** *v.* mimar.
**pan** *s.* panela, caçarola.
**Pan.a.ma** *s.* Panamá.
**pan.cake** *s.* panqueca.
**pan.de.mo.ni.um** *s.* pandemônio,
confusão, caos.
**pan.der** *v.* favorecer.
**pan.ic** *s.* pânico.
**pan.o.ram.a** *s.* panorama.
**pan.ther** *s.* pantera.
**pants** *s. pl.* calças.
**pa.per** *s.* papel; jornal; exame
(escrito).
**pa.per-mill** *s.* fábrica de papel.
**pap.ri.ka** *s.* páprica
(condimento), pimentão.
**par.a.chute** *s.* paraquedas.
**pa.rade** *s.* desfile, parada
/ *v.* desfilar.

**par.a.dise** *s.* paraíso.
**par.a.dox** *s.* paradoxo.
**par.a.graph** *s.* parágrafo.
**par.al.lel** *s.* paralela, linha
paralela; semelhança / *adj.* paralelo.
**par.a.lyse** *v.* paralizar.
**pa.ral.y.sis** *s.* paralisia.
**par.a.mount** *adj.* primordial;
de suma importância.
**par.a.ple.gic** *s.* paraplégico(a).
**par.a.site** *s.* parasita.
**par.a.troop.er** *s.* paraquedista.
**par.cel** *s.* pacote, embrulho
/ *v.* embrulhar.
**parch** *v.* secar, ressecar; tostar.
**par.don** *s.* perdão / *v.* perdoar.
**par.ent** *s.* pai ou mãe ♦ ~s pais.
**pa.ren.the.sis** *s.* parêntese.
**Pa.ris** *s.* Paris.
**par.ish** *s.* paróquia.
**Pa.ris.i.an** *s.* parisiense
/ *adj.* parisiense.
**par.i.ty** *s.* paridade, igualdade.
**park** *s.* parque / *v.* estacionar.
**parking lot** *s.* estacionamento.
**par.lia.ment** *s.* parlamento.
**par.lor, par.lour** *s.* sala de
visitas, salão.
**pa.ro.chi.al** *adj.* paroquial,
paroquiano.
**par.o.dy** *s.* paródia / *v.* parodiar.
**par.rot** *s.* papagaio.

parry | 305 | pay

**par.ry** v. desviar (de golpes), evitar, evadir.

**pars.ley** s. salsa, salsinha.

**par.son** s. pároco, vigário.

**part** s. parte, pedaço / v. partir, repartir; ir-se embora.

**par.tial** adj. parcial.

**par.tic.i.pant** s. participante. / adj. pacifista.

**par.ti.ci.ple** s. particípio.

**par.ti.cle** s. partícula, pequena parte.

**par.tic.u.lar** adj. particular, específico, próprio.

**part.ing** s. divisão, separação / adj. de despedida.

**par.ti.san** adj. partidário, sectário.

**par.ti.tion** s. divisão.

**part.ly** adv. em parte, parcialmente.

**part.ner** s. sócio, parceiro.

**part.ner.ship** s. parceria, associação; sociedade.

**part-time** adv. de meio expediente, de meio período / adj. de meio expediente, de meio período.

**par.ty** s. festa; partido, grupo.

**pas.quin** s. sátira afixada em lugar público, pasquim.

**pass** s. passagem / v. passar, ser aprovado.

**pas.sage** s. passagem, corredor; citação.

**pas.sen.ger** s. passageiro, viajante.

**pass.ing** adj. passageiro, fugaz.

**pas.sive** adj. passivo.

**pass.port** s. passaporte.

**pass.word** s. senha.

**past** adj. passado, antigo / s. passado.

**pas.ta** s. macarrão, massa.

**pas.try** s. pastelaria.

**patch** s. retalho; remendo / v. remendar.

**pa.tent** s. patente; direito, licença / adj. patente; óbvio / v. patentear.

**pa.ter.nal** adj. paternal, paterno.

**path** s. caminho, trajetória, trilha.

**pa.thet.ic** adj. patético.

**pa.thol.o.gist** s. patologista.

**path.way** s. caminho, atalho.

**pa.tience** s. paciência.

**pa.tient** s. paciente / adj. paciente.

**pat.ri.ot** s. patriota / adj. patriota.

**pa.trol** s. patrulha / v. patrulhar.

**pause** s. pausa, intervalo / v. pausar, parar.

**pave.ment** s. pavimento, calçada.

**pa.vil.ion** s. pavilhão.

**paw** s. pata, pé (de animal).

**pay** s. pagamento, salário / v. pagar.

payable 306 perceive

**pay.a.ble** *adj.* pagável, a pagar.
**pay.day** *s.* dia de pagamento.
**PC** *abrev.* de *Personal Computer*.
**pea** *s.* ervilha.
**peace** *s.* paz.
**peach** *s.* pêssego.
**pea.cock** *s.* pavão.
**peak** *s.* pico, cume, auge.
**peaked** *adj.* pontudo, pontiagudo.
**pea.nut** *s.* amendoim.
**pear** *s.* pera.
**pearl** *s.* pérola.
**peas.ant** *s.* camponês, agricultor.
**peck** *v.* bicar / *s.* bicada.
**pe.cu.li.ar** *adj.* peculiar, específico; próprio.
**ped.al** *s.* pedal / *v.* pedalar.
**ped.dler** *s.* mascate, vendendor ambulante.
**ped.es.tal** *s.* pedestal.
**pe.des.tri.an** *s.* pedestre.
**ped.i.gree** *s.* raça (de animal), linhagem.
**peek** *v.* espiar, espreitar.
**peel** *s.* casca (de fruta) / *v.* descascar.
**peel.ing** *s.* casca.
**peev.ed** *adj.* irritado.
**pee.vish** *adj.* rabugento, teimoso.
**peg** *s.* pregador (de roupa).
**pe.jo.ra.tive** *adj.* depreciativo (coloquial).

**pel.i.can** *s.* pelicano.
**pen** *s.* caneta.
**pe.nal** *adj.* penal, punível.
**pen.al.ty** *s.* penalidade (esporte); pênalti (futebol); multa, pena.
**pen.ance** *s.* penitência.
**pen.cil** *s.* lápis.
**pen.du.lum** *s.* pêndulo.
**pen.e.trate** *v.* penetrar, infiltrar.
**pen.guin** *s.* pinguim.
**pen.i.cil.lin** *s.* penicilina.
**pe.nin.su.la** *s.* península.
**pe.nis** *s.* pênis.
**pen.i.tence** *s.* penitência.
**pen.knife** *s.* canivete.
**pen.nant** *s.* flâmula.
**pen.ni.less** *adj.* sem dinheiro.
**pen.ny** (*pl.* pence) *s.* moeda divisionária inglesa (1/100 da libra); centavo (EUA) (coloquial).
**pen.sion** *s.* pensão, aposentadoria.
**pen.sive** *adj.* pensativo.
**pen.ta.gon** *s.* pentágono (geometria).
**pent.house** *s.* cobertura (apartamento).
**pent-up** *adj.* reprimido, contido.
**peo.ple** *s.* povo; gente; multidão.
**pep.per** *s.* pimenta.
**per** *prep.* por (por dia, por cento).
**per.ceive** *v.* perceber, compreender.

**per.cen.tage** *s.* porcentagem.

**per.cep.tion** *s.* percepção, ideia, noção.

**per.cus.sion** *s.* percussão.

**pe.ren.ni.al** *adj.* perene.

**per.fect** *adj.* perfeito / *v.* aperfeiçoar.

**per.form** *v.* realizar, fazer, desempenhar; interpretar.

**per.fume** *s.* perfume.

**per.haps** *adv.* talvez.

**pe.rim.e.ter** *s.* perímetro.

**pe.ri.od** *s.* período, época; menstruação; ponto final.

**pe.riph.e.ral** *adj.* periférico.

**per.i.scope** *s.* periscópio.

**per.ish** *v.* perecer, falecer; estragar.

**per.jure** *v.* prestar falso testemunho, perjurar.

**per.ju.ry** *s.* perjúrio.

**perk** *s.* benefício, adicional.

**per.ma.nent** *adj.* permanente, duradouro.

**per.mis.sion** *s.* permissão, autorização.

**per.mis.sive** *adj.* permissivo.

**per.mu.ta.tion** *s.* permutação, troca.

**per.ni.cious** *adj.* pernicioso, nocivo, maligno.

**per.pen.dic.u.lar** *adj.* perpendicular.

**per.pet.u.al** *adj.* perpétuo, eterno.

**per.plex.i.ty** *s.* perplexidade, atordoamento.

**per.se.cute** *v.* perseguir.

**per.se.vere** *v.* perseverar, persistir.

**Per.sian** *s.* persa, pérsico (natural da Pérsia, atual Irã) / *adj.* persa, pérsico.

**per.sist** *v.* persistir; subsistir.

**per.son** *s.* pessoa, indivíduo.

**per.so.nal com.put.er** *s.* computador pessoal.

**per.spec.tive** *s.* perspectiva.

**per.spi.ra.tion** *s.* transpiração, suor.

**per.suade** *v.* persuadir, convencer.

**pert** *adj.* atrevido(a), ousado(a).

**per.tain.ings** *s. pl.* pertences.

**per.ti.nent** *adj.* pertinente, adequado.

**pert.ness** *s.* atrevimento, ousadia.

**per.turb** *v.* perturbar.

**Pe.ru** *s.* Peru.

**Pe.ru.vi.an** *s.* peruano / *adj.* peruano(a).

**per.verse** *adj.* perverso, maldoso.

**per.vert** *s.* pervertido / *v.* perverter, corromper.

**pes.si.mis.m** *s.* pessimismo.

**pest** *s.* peste, praga.

**pes.ter** *v.* incomodar, importunar / *s.* importuno.

**pes.ti.cide** *s.* pesticida.

**pet** *s.* animal de estimação.

**pet.al** *s.* pétala.

**pe.ti.tion** *s.* petição.

**pet.ri.fied** *adj.* petrificado, paralisado.

**pet.rol** *s.* gasolina.

**pe.tro.le.um** *s.* petróleo.

**pet shop** *s.* loja de venda de animais de estimação.

**phan.tom** *s.* fantasma.

**phar.aoh** *s.* faraó.

**phar.ma.cist** *s.* farmacêutico(a).

**phase** *s.* fase, etapa.

**phe.nom.e.non** *s.* (*pl. phenomena*) fenômeno.

**phi.lan.thro.pist** *s.* filantropo(a).

**phi.lat.e.ly** *s.* filatelia.

**Phil.ip.pine** *s.* filipino / *adj.* filipino.

**phi.los.o.pher** *s.* filósofo.

**pho.bi.a** *s.* fobia.

**phone** *s. abrev.* de *telephone* (coloquial) / *v.* telefonar.

**pho.net.ics** *s.* fonética.

**phos.phate** *s.* fosfato (química).

**pho.to** *s.* foto, fotografia.

**phrase** *s.* frase.

**phys.i.cal** *adj.* físico.

**phys.ics** *s.* física.

**phys.i.ol.o.gy** *s.* fisiologia.

**pi.a.nist** *s.* pianista.

**pi.an.o** *s.* piano.

**pick** *v.* apanhar, pegar.

**pick.er** *s.* colhedor, apanhador.

**pick.et** *s.* piquete, estaca.

**pick.le** *s.* picles.

**pick.up** *s.* caminhonete.

**pic.nic** *s.* piquenique.

**pic.ture** *s.* quadro, pintura, tela; retrato.

**pie** *s.* torta, pastelão, empadão.

**piece** *s.* pedaço, fatia; peça.

**pier** *s.* cais, embarcadouro.

**pierce** *v.* penetrar, furar; romper.

**pierc.ing** *adj.* penetrante; perfurante, cortante.

**pi.e.ty** *s.* piedade; abnegação.

**pig** *s.* porco, leitão.

**pi.geon** *s.* pombo.

**pig.ment** *s.* pigmento.

**pig.sty** *s.* chiqueiro, pocilga.

**pike** *s.* posto de pedágio; pico (de montanha).

**pile** *s.* pilha, montão.

**piles** *s.* hemorroidas (coloquial).

**pil.fer** *v.* furtar; afanar.

**pil.grim** *s.* peregrino, romeiro.

**pill** *s.* pílula.

**pil.lar** *s.* pilar, coluna.

**pil.low** *s.* travesseiro.

**pi.lot** *s.* piloto / *v.* pilotar, conduzir.

**pim.ple** *s.* espinha (na pele).

**pin** *s.* alfinete; broche; pino.

**pin.a.fore** *s.* avental para crianças.

**pin.ball** *s.* fliperama.

**pincers** / **play**

**pin.cers** *s.* pinça; alicate.
**pinch** *s.* beliscão.
**pin.cush.ion** *s.* alfineteira, pregadeira.
**pine** *s.* pinheiro.
**pine.ap.ple** *s.* abacaxi.
**pink** *adj.* cor-de-rosa; rosado / *v.* enrubescer.
**pin.na.cle** *s.* cume, pináculo, auge.
**pi.o.neer** *s.* pioneiro, precursor / *adj.* pioneiro, precursor.
**pip** *s.* caroço, semente.
**pipe** *s.* cano, tubo; encanamento; cachimbo.
**pi.quant** *adj.* picante; pungente.
**pi.rate** *s.* pirata.
**Pis.ces** *s.* Peixes (astrologia).
**pis.tol** *s.* pistola.
**pis.ton** *s.* pistão.
**pit** *s.* cova; fossa; mina de carvão.
**pitch** *s.* arremesso; tom (música).
**pitch.er** *s.* jarro, cântaro; arremessador.
**pit.e.ous** *adj.* lastimável, comovente.
**pit.fall** *s.* perigo; armadilha, cilada.
**pit.i.ful** *adj.* comovente, lamentável; deplorável.
**pit.i.less** *adj.* impiedoso, cruel.
**pit.tance** *s.* ninharia; miséria.
**pit.y** *s.* compaixão, pena, piedade.
**piv.ot** *s.* eixo; pino; pivô.

**pix.ie** *s.* duende, elfo.
**plac.ard** *s.* placar.
**pla.cate** *v.* apaziguar.
**place** *s.* lugar; posto; assento / *v.* pôr, colocar; encomendar.
**plac.id** *adj.* plácido, sereno.
**plague** *s.* praga, peste.
**plain** *s.* planície / *adj.* claro, evidente; simples; liso, plano.
**plait** *s.* dobra; trança / *v.* trançar.
**plan** *s.* plano, projeto, esquema / *v.* planejar, projetar.
**plane** *s.* avião; plano (geometria) / *adj.* plano, raso.
**plan.et** *s.* planeta.
**plan.ner** *s.* projetista, planejador.
**plan.ning** *s.* planejamento.
**plant** *s.* planta; fábrica, usina / *v.* plantar, semear.
**plan.ta.tion** *s.* plantação.
**plas.ma** *s.* plasma.
**plas.tic** *s.* plástico / *adj.* plástico.
**plas.tic sur.ge.ry** *s.* cirurgia plástica.
**plat.i.num** *s.* platina / *adj.* de platina.
**pla.toon** *s.* pelotão.
**plat.ter** *s.* travessa (de louça).
**play** *s.* jogo, partida; peça teatral / *v.* jogar, brincar, divertir-se; representar.

# playboy    310    polygamy

**play.boy** *s.* farrista, boêmio (coloquial).

**plea** *s.* apelo; petição; argumento.

**plead** *v.* defender, advogar; apelar, suplicar.

**pleas.ant** *adj.* agradável.

**please** *adv.* por favor / *v.* agradar, dar prazer a.

**pleas.ing** *adj.* agradável, gentil.

**pleas.ure** *s.* prazer, satisfação.

**plen.ty** *s.* abundância, fartura / *adj.* abundante.

**pli.a.ble** *adj.* flexível, maleável.

**plight** *s.* apuro, situação difícil; compromisso.

**plot** *s.* trama, conspiração; lote; enredo de uma história / *v.* tramar; traçar.

**plug** *s.* pino; tomada.

**plum** *s.* ameixa.

**plum.age** *s.* plumagem.

**plumb.er** *s.* encanador.

**plume** *s.* pluma, pena.

**plump** *adj.* roliço, rechonchudo.

**plunge** *s.* salto; mergulho.

**plu.ral** *s.* plural / *adj.* plural.

**plus** *s.* sinal de adição (+) / *prep.* mais / *adj.* positivo.

**plush** *adj.* de pelúcia.

**p.m.** *abrev.* de *post meridiem*.

**pneu.mat.ic** *adj.* pneumático.

**pneu.mo.ni.a** *s.* pneumonia.

**pock.et** *s.* bolso / *adj.* de bolso / *v.* embolsar.

**pod** *s.* vagem (de feijão); bando, cardume.

**podg.y** *adj.* atarracado.

**po.em** *s.* poema.

**po.et** *s.* poeta.

**po.e.try** *s.* poesia.

**poi.gnant** *adj.* comovente, pungente.

**point** *s.* ponto; objetivo; relevância / *v.* indicar, evidenciar.

**poise** *s.* equilíbrio, estabilidade.

**poi.son** *s.* veneno / *v.* envenenar.

**poi.son.ing** *s.* envenenamento.

**poke** *v.* atiçar; cutucar.

**Po.land** *s.* Polônia.

**po.lar** *adj.* polar.

**po.lar.ize** *v.* polarizar.

**po.lice** *s.* polícia / *v.* policiar.

**po.li.o** *s.* poliomielite, pólio.

**Pol.ish** *s.* polonês / *adj.* polonês.

**po.lite** *adj.* gentil, cortês, educado.

**pol.i.tic** *adj.* político, astuto.

**poll** *s.* votação; pesquisa, sondagem.

**pol.len** *s.* pólen.

**pol.lute** *v.* poluir, contaminar.

**pol.y.es.ter** *s.* poliéster.

**po.lyg.a.my** *s.* poligamia.

**pol.y.tech.nic** *s.* politécnica / *adj.* politécnico.

**pom.e.gran.ate** *s.* romã.

**pomp** *s.* pompa, ostentação.

**pom.pous** *adj.* pomposo, empolado.

**pon.der** *v.* ponderar, refletir, considerar.

**pon.tiff** *s.* pontífice.

**pon.tif.i.cate** *v.* pontificar / *s.* pontificado, papado.

**po.ny** *s.* pônei.

**pool** *s.* poça, charco; tanque, reservatório; piscina.

**poor** *adj.* pobre.

**poor.ness** *s.* pobreza.

**pop** *s.* ruído seco; estouro (som), estalo / *v.* estalar, saltar.

**pop.corn** *s.* pipoca.

**pope** *s.* papa.

**pop.eyed** *adj.* com os olhos arregalados.

**pop.py** *s.* papoula.

**pop.u.lar** *adj.* popular; familiar; na moda.

**pop.u.late** *v.* povoar.

**pop.u.lous** *adj.* populoso.

**porce.lain** *s.* porcelana / *adj.* de porcelana.

**porch** *s.* pórtico; varanda, sacada.

**por.cu.pine** *s.* porco-espinho.

**pork.chop** *s.* costeleta de porco.

**por.nog.ra.phic** *adj.* pornográfico.

**po.rous** *adj.* poroso.

**por.poise** *s.* toninha, boto.

**port** *s.* porto, ancoradouro.

**por.ta.ble** *adj.* portátil.

**por.ter** *s.* porteiro; carregador, bagageiro.

**por.tion** *s.* porção, parcela.

**port.ly** *adj.* corpulento; imponente.

**por.trait** *s.* retrato.

**Por.tu.gal** *s.* Portugal.

**Por.tu.guese** *s.* português(esa) / *adj.* português(esa).

**pose** *s.* postura; pose / *v.* posar; propor; fazer posar.

**posh** *adj.* requintado, de luxo, chique.

**po.si.tion** *s.* posição; situação / *v.* posicionar.

**pos.i.tive** *adj.* positivo; certo; definitivo.

**pos.si.bil.i.ty** *s.* possibilidade.

**post** *v.* pôr no correio, postar / *s.* poste, pilar.

**post.er** *s.* cartaz, pôster.

**pos.ter.i.ty** *s.* posteridade.

**post.grad.u.ate** *s.* pós--graduado(a) / *adj.* pós-graduado.

**post me.rid.i.e.m** *adj. loc.* entre o meio-dia e a meia noite.

**post of.fice** *s.* agência do correio.

**pot** *s.* panela, caçarola, pote.

**po.ta.to** *s.* batata.

**po.tent** *adj.* potente, poderoso, forte.

**po.ten.tial** *s.* potencial / *adj.* potencial.

**po.tion** *s.* poção.

**pound** *s.* libra (0,454 quilograma); libra *(£)* / *v.* golpear, socar.

**pov.er.ty** *s.* pobreza; escassez.

**pow.der** *s.* pó / *v.* polvilhar.

**pow.dered milk** *s.* leite em pó.

**pow.er** *s.* poder; força.

**pow.er.ful** *adj.* poderoso; influente.

**prac.ti.cal** *adj.* prático.

**prag.mat.ic** *adj.* pragmático.

**praise** *s.* louvor, elogio / *v.* elogiar, louvar.

**pram** *s.* carrinho de bebê (coloquial).

**prank** *s.* travessura, brincadeira / *v.* brincar, traquinar.

**pray** *v.* rezar, orar.

**preach** *v.* pregar, fazer sermão.

**pre.car.i.ous** *adj.* precário.

**pre.cau.tion** *s.* precaução, prevenção.

**pre.cious** *adj.* precioso, valioso.

**pre.ci.pice** *s.* precipício.

**pre.cip.i.tate** *adj.* precipitado, apressado / *v.* precipitar; apressar.

**pre.cise** *adj.* exato, preciso.

**pref.ace** *s.* prefácio; introdução / *v.* prefaciar.

**pre.fect** *s.* monitor escolar.

**pre.fer** *v.* preferir.

**pre.fix** *s.* prefixo.

**preg.nan.cy** *s.* gravidez.

**prel.ude** *s.* prelúdio (música); introdução.

**pre.ma.ture** *s.* prematuro.

**prem.i.er** *s.* primeiro-ministro / *adj.* principal.

**prem.ise** *s.* premissa.

**pre.mi.um** *s.* prêmio; recompensa.

**pre.oc.cu.pa.tion** *s.* preocupação.

**prep.a.ra.tion** *s.* preparação.

**pre.par.a.to.ry** *adj.* preparatório.

**pre.pare** *v.* preparar.

**prep.o.si.tion** *s.* preposição.

**pre.rog.a.tive** *s.* prerrogativa; privilégio.

**pre.scribe** *v.* prescrever, receitar.

**pres.ence** *s.* presença, comparecimento.

**pres.ent** *s.* presente, atualidade; presente, oferta / *v.* apresentar; presentear.

**pres.er.va.tion** *s.* preservação, conservação.

**pre.ser.va.tive** *s.* preservativo / *adj.* preservativo, conservante.

**pre.serve** *v.* preservar, proteger, conservar.

| preside | **313** | procure |

**pre.side** *v.* presidir.

**pres.i.den.cy** *s.* presidência.

**press** *s.* imprensa, jornalismo (meio de comunicação) / *v.* apertar, pressionar.

**pres.sure** *s.* pressao.

**pres.tige** *s.* prestígio, influência.

**pre.sume** *v.* presumir, supor; inferir, deduzir.

**pre.sup.pose** *v.* pressupor, conjeturar.

**pre.tend** *v.* fingir, simular.

**pre.tend.er** *s.* pretendente, pretensor; embusteiro, simulador.

**pre.ten.sion** *s.* pretensão; ostentação.

**pre.text** *s.* pretexto.

**pret.ty** *adj.* bonito, atraente / *adv.* bastante.

**pre.vail** *v.* prevalecer, imperar.

**pre.vent** *v.* prevenir, evitar, impedir.

**pre.view** *s.* antecipação, pré--estreia.

**pre.vi.ous** *adj.* prévio, anterior; apressado, prematuro.

**price** *s.* preço / *v.* fixar o preço.

**prick** *s.* picada, ferroada / *v.* picar, furar.

**prick.le** *s.* espinho, ferrão.

**pride** *s.* orgulho, soberba; brio.

**priest** *s.* padre, sacerdote.

**pri.ma.ry** *s.* primário; principal; fundamental / *adj.* primário; principal; fundamental.

**pri.mate** *s.* primaz; primata.

**prim.i.tive** *s.* primitivo, aborígene / *adj.* primitivo, rudimentar.

**prince** *s.* príncipe.

**prin.cess** *s.* princesa.

**prin.ci.pal** *s.* chefe, dirigente; diretor de colégio / *adj.* principal.

**prin.ci.ple** *s.* princípio; caráter.

**print** *s.* impressão; cópia; letra / *v.* imprimir; publicar.

**pri.or.i.ty** *s.* prioridade.

**pris.on** *s.* prisão, cárcere, cadeia.

**priv.a.cy** *s.* privacidade; isolamento, retiro.

**pri.vate** *adj.* particular, privado / *s.* soldado raso.

**priv.i.lege** *s.* privilégio.

**prize** *s.* prêmio, recompensa / *adj.* premiado.

**prob.a.bil.i.ty** *s.* probabilidade.

**prob.lem** *s.* problema.

**pro.ce.dure** *s.* procedimento, método; norma.

**pro.ceed** *v.* proceder; prosseguir, avançar.

**proc.ess** *s.* processo / *v.* tratar, processar.

**pro.cure** *v.* obter, conseguir.

**prod.i.gy** *s.* prodígio.

**prod.uct** *s.* produto.

**pro.file** *s.* perfil; contorno.

**pro.found** *adj.* profundo.

**pro.gram** *s.* programa / *v.* programar.

**pro.gress** *s.* progresso, avanço, desenvolvimento / *v.* progredir, evoluir.

**proj.ect** *s.* projeto, plano / *v.* projetar.

**pro.jec.tor** *s.* projetor.

**pro.long** *v.* prolongar, estender.

**prom.e.nade** *s.* passeio / *v.* passear.

**prom.ise** *s.* promessa / *v.* prometer.

**pro.mote** *v.* promover.

**prompt** *adj.* pronto, rápido, pontual / *v.* induzir, incitar.

**pro.noun** *s.* pronome.

**pro.nounce** *v.* pronunciar, declarar.

**pro.nun.ci.a.tion** *s.* pronúncia.

**proof** *s.* prova; evidência.

**prop.er.ty** *s.* propriedade; posses, bens.

**proph.e.cy** *s.* profecia, predição.

**pro.pose** *v.* propor; pedir em casamento.

**pro.sa.ic** *adj.* prosaico, trivial.

**prose** *s.* prosa.

**pros.per** *v.* prosperar, progredir.

**pros.ti.tute** *s.* prostituta, meretriz.

**pro.tect** *v.* proteger, amparar.

**pro.tein** *s.* proteína.

**pro.test** *s.* protesto / *v.* protestar.

**pro.to.col** *s.* protocolo / *v.* protocolizar.

**proud** *adj.* orgulhoso; imponente; soberbo.

**prove** *v.* testar; provar.

**prov.erb** *s.* provérbio.

**pro.vide** *v.* prover, munir, suprir.

**prov.ince** *s.* província; o interior.

**prov.o.ca.tion** *s.* provocação; estímulo; incitamento.

**pro.voke** *v.* provocar, desafiar, afrontar.

**prow** *s.* proa.

**psy.chi.a.tric** *adj.* psiquiátrico.

**psy.cho.log.i.cal** *adj.* psicológico.

**psy.chol.o.gist** *s.* psicólogo(a).

**pub** *abrev.* de *public house* (bar, botequim).

**pub.lic** *s.* público / *adj.* público, notório.

**pub.li.ca.tion** *s.* publicação.

**pub.lic.i.ty** *s.* publicidade.

**pub.lish** *v.* publicar, divulgar, difundir.

**puff** *s.* sopro; baforada / *v.* soprar, bufar.

**puff.y** *adj.* inchado(a); balofo.

**pull** *v.* puxar / *s.* puxão.

**pull.o.ver** *s.* pulôver.

**pulp** *s.* polpa (de fruta).

**pul.sate** *v.* palpitar, pulsar.

**pul.ver.ize** *v.* pulverizar, vaporizar.

**pum.mel** *v.* esmurrar, socar.

**pump.kin** *s.* abóbora.

**punch** *s.* soco, murro; ponche (bebida alcoólica) / *v.* socar, esmurrar.

**pun.ish** *v.* punir, castigar.

**pu.ny** *adj.* débil, fraco.

**pup.pet** *s.* marionete, fantoche; boneca.

**pup.pet show** *s.* teatro de marionetes.

**pup.py** *s.* filhote de cachorro.

**purchase** *s.* compra, aquisição / *v.* comprar.

**pure** *adj.* puro, imaculado.

**pu.ri.fi.ca.tion** *s.* purificação.

**pur.ist** *s.* purista.

**pu.ri.tan** *s.* puritano(a) / *adj.* puritano.

**pu.ri.ty** *s.* pureza.

**pur.ple** *adj.* roxo, purpúreo / *s.* roxo, púrpura.

**pur.pose** *s.* propósito, finalidade.

**purse** *s.* carteira de mulher; porta-moedas.

**purs.er** *s.* comissário(a) de bordo.

**push** *v.* empurrar / *s.* empurrão.

**pus.sy** *s.* bichano, gatinha.

**put** *v.* pôr, colocar.

**pu.trid** *adj.* podre, putrefato.

**puz.zle** *s.* charada, enigma; quebra-cabeça / *v.* confundir.

**pyr.a.mid** *s.* pirâmide.

**P**

# Qq

**Q, q** *s.* décima sétima letra do alfabeto inglês.

**quaint** *adj.* curioso; esquisito, estranho.

**quake** *v.* tremer, estremecer / *s.* tremor.

**qual.i.fi.ca.tion** *s.* qualificação; habilitação.

**qual.i.fy** *v.* qualificar; capacitar.

**qual.i.ty** *s.* qualidade, propriedade.

**quan.ti.ty** *s.* quantidade, soma.

**quar.rel** *s.* disputa, rixa, briga / *v.* discutir, brigar.

**quar.rel.some** *s.* briguento.

**quar.ter** *s.* quarto, quarta parte, trimestre; quarteirão.

**quartz** *s.* quartzo.

**quash** *v.* anular (sentença).

**queen** *s.* rainha; dama (baralho).

**queer** *adj.* esquisito, estranho; indisposto; homossexual (coloquial).

**quest** *s.* busca, procura.

**ques.tion** *s.* pergunta, dúvida, questão / *v.* indagar, questionar.

**quick** *adj.* rápido, ágil, ligeiro.

**quick.ly** *adv.* rapidamente, depressa.

**quick.ness** *s.* rapidez.

**quid** *s.* libra esterlina (coloquial).
**qui.et** *adj.* calmo, tranquilo / *s.* tranquilidade.
**quilt** *s.* colcha de retalhos / *v.* forrar.
**quit** *v.* renunciar, desistir.

**quite** *adv.* totalmente, completamente; muito, um bocado.
**quiz** *s.* teste, competição (de conhecimento) / *v.* examinar oralmente.

Q

# Rr

**R, r** *s.* décima oitava letra do alfabeto inglês.

**rab.bi** *s.* rabino.

**rab.bit** *s.* coelho.

**race** *s.* corrida; competição; raça humana / *v.* competir.

**ra.cial** *adj.* racial.

**ra.cist** *adj.* racista / *s.* racista.

**rack** *s.* estante; prateleira; suporte.

**rac.y** *adj.* espirituoso(a); vivo(a), esperto(a), animado(a).

**ra.dar** *s.* radar.

**ra.di.ate** *v.* irradiar; emitir / *adj.* radiado.

**ra.di.a.tion** *s.* radiação.

**rad.i.cal** *adj.* radical, extremo.

**ra.di.o** *s.* rádio.

**rad.ish** *s.* rabanete.

**raf.fle** *s.* rifa; sorteio / *v.* rifar, sortear.

**raft** *s.* balsa / *v.* viajar (em balsa ou jangada).

**rag** *s.* trapo, farrapo.

**rage** *s.* raiva, furor, ira / *v.* enfurecer-se.

**rag.ged** *adj.* esfarrapado, maltrapilho.

**raid** *s.* ataque repentino; batida policial.

**rail** *s.* grade; corrimão; trilho.

**rail.road, rail.way** *s.* ferrovia, estrada de ferro.

**rain** *s.* chuva / *v.* chover.

**rain.bow** *s.* arco-íris.

**rain.coat** *s.* capa de chuva.

**rain.drop** *s.* pingo de chuva.

**raise** *s.* elevação, aumento, subida / *v.* surbir, levantar, erguer; criar; educar.

**raisin** — **reader**

**rai.sin** *s.* passa, uva seca.

**ram** *s.* carneiro / *v.* bater, golpear.

**ram.ble** *s.* excursão a pé; caminhada / *v.* vaguear, perambular.

**ramp** *s.* rampa, ladeira.

**ran** *v. pret.* do *v. to run*.

**ranch** *s.* rancho, fazenda.

**ran.dom** *adj.* casual, ao acaso, aleatório / *s.* acaso; impetuosidade.

**rand.y** *adj.* excitado, sensual.

**range** *s.* extensão; alcance; cordilheira / *v.* agrupar, ordenar, estender-se.

**rank** *s.* linha, ordem, grau, fila, fileira / *v.* enfileirar, classificar, ordenar.

**ran.som** *s.* resgate.

**rap** *s.* batida breve e seca; estilo musical.

**rape** *s.* estupro; violação; rapto / *v.* estuprar, violar.

**rap.id** *adj.* rápido, ligeiro / *s.* rápido, correnteza.

**rap.port** *s.* harmonia, conformidade.

**rare** *adj.* raro; mal passado (carne).

**rare.ly** *adv.* raramente.

**rar.i.ty** *s.* raridade.

**rash** *adj.* impetuoso, precipitado / *s.* urticária, irritação na pele.

**rasp.ber.ry** *s.* framboesa.

**rat** *s.* rato / *adj.* pessoa de má índole, vil.

**rate** *s.* preço; taxa; razão, proporção / *v.* avaliar, estimar.

**ra.ther** *adv.* preferivelmente; bastante, muito

**rat.i.fy** *v.* ratificar, endossar.

**ra.tion.al** *adj.* racional / *s.* racional.

**rat trap** *s.* ratoeira; casa velha e descuidada.

**rav.age** *v.* devastar; saquear / *s.* devastação.

**rave** *s.* delírio, desvario; fúria; festa louca e animada / *v.* delirar, enfurecer.

**rav.el** *s.* confusão.

**ra.ven** *s.* corvo.

**rav.e.nous** *adj.* faminto; voraz; ávido.

**rav.ish** *v.* arrebatar, cativar; raptar, violar.

**ray** *s.* raio (de luz, calor).

**raze** *v.* arrasar; aniquilar; demolir; riscar; apagar.

**ra.zor** *s.* navalha usada para remover barba.

**reach** *v.* alcançar, atingir, chegar a / *s.* alcance.

**re.act** *s.* reação / *v.* reagir.

**read** *v.* ler.

**read.er** *s.* leitor(a); livro (de leitura escolar).

R

readily | 320 | reel

**read.i.ly** *adj.* facilmente; prontamente.

**read.ing** *s.* leitura / *adj.* de leitura.

**re.ad.just** *v.* reajustar.

**read.y** *adj.* pronto, preparado, terminado, acabado.

**re.af.firm** *v.* reafirmar, reiterar.

**real** *adj.* real, autêntico, verdadeiro.

**re.al.i.ty** *s.* realidade, verdade.

**rea.li.za.tion** *s.* realização.

**rea.lize** *v.* realizar; dar-se conta de, imaginar, perceber.

**real.ly** *adv.* realmente, de fato; sem dúvida.

**rea.son** *s.* razão, motivo / *v.* raciocinar, pensar.

**rea.so.na.ble** *adj.* razoável, sensato.

**reb.el** *s.* rebelde / *adj.* revoltoso, rebelde / *v.* rebelar-se.

**re.buff** *s.* repulsa, recusa; esnobada / *v.* repelir; esnobar.

**re.call** *v.* recordar; convocar; chamar de volta / *s.* chamada de volta; recolha de produtos com defeitos.

**re.cap** *v.* recapitular / *s.* pneu recauchutado.

**re.cede** *v.* retroceder.

**re.ceive** *v.* receber; acolher.

**rc.cent** *adj.* recente.

**re.cep.tion** *s.* recepção; audiência.

**re.cep.tive** *adj.* receptivo.

**re.ci.pe** *s.* receita.

**re.cip.i.ent** *s.* recipiente, recebedor, destinatário.

**re.cite** *v.* recitar, declamar; relatar, contar.

**reck.less** *adj.* despreocupado, descuidado; imprudente.

**re.cline** *v.* reclinar-se, recostar-se.

**rec.og.nize** *v.* reconhecer; aceitar, admitir.

**re.coil** *v.* retroceder; recuar.

**rec.om.mend** *v.* recomendar.

**rec.om.pense** *s.* recompensa / *v.* recompensar.

**rec.on.cile** *v.* reconciliar.

**re.con.sid.er** *v.* reconsiderar, reavaliar.

**rec.ord** *s.* registro, anotação / *v.* gravar; registrar; gravar em disco.

**re.cre.ate** *v.* recriar.

**re.cre.a.tion** *s.* recreação, passatempo, divertimento.

**red** *adj.* vermelho / *s.* vermelho.

**Re.deem.er** *s.* Redentor.

**red-haired** *adj.* ruivo.

**red pep.per** *s.* malagueta; pimentão.

**re.duce** *v.* reduzir; rebaixar.

**red.wood** *s.* pau-brasil, sequoia.

**reel** *s.* molinete; carretel, bobina / *v.* bobinar, enrolar.

**refer** — 321 — **remove**

**re.fer** *v.* referir-se, reportar; recorrer.

**ref.er.ence** *s.* referência, respeito, menção.

**rc.fill** *s.* carga sobressalente para suprir outra, refil / *v.* reabastecer.

**re.flex** *s.* reflexo; reflexão / *adj.* reflexivo / *v.* recurvar.

**re.form** *s.* reforma, melhoria / *v.* reformar.

**re.fresh** *v.* refrescar, revigorar.

**re.fresh.ment** *s.* refresco; refeição ligeira; descanso, repouso.

**re.fri.ge.ration** *s.* refrigeração.

**re.fri.ge.ra.tor** *s.* geladeira.

**ref.uge** *s.* refúgio, asilo.

**re.fuse** *v.* recusar, rejeitar, negar / *s.* refugo.

**re.fute** *v.* refutar, contradizer.

**re.gard** *s.* consideração, atenção; estima / *v.* considerar, julgar, dizer respeito a.

**re.gard.ing** *prep.* relativo a, a respeito de, com referência a.

**re.gards** *s.* cumprimentos, saudações.

**re.gent** *s.* regente, reinante / *adj.* regente, reinante.

**re.gion** *s.* região, área, território.

**re.gis.ter** *s.* registro, arquivo, lista / *v.* registrar, inscrever.

**re.gret** *s.* arrependimento, remorso / *v.* arrepender, lastimar, lamentar.

**reign** *s.* reinado; domínio / *v.* reinar.

**rein** *s.* rédea.

**rein.deer** *s.* rena.

**re.late** *v.* contar; relacionar.

**re.la.tion** *s.* relação, relacionamento.

**rel.a.tive** *s.* parente / *adj.* relativo.

**re.lax** *v.* relaxar, descontrair, descansar.

**re.lease** *v.* liberar, soltar (nota, publicação) / *s.* soltura, exibição, lançamento.

**re.li.a.ble** *adj.* confiável, de confiança, seguro.

**re.lief** *s.* alívio; relevo, saliência.

**re.li.gion** *s.* religião.

**re.main** *s.* sobra, resto / *v.* permanecer, ficar, restar.

**re.mark** *s.* observação, comentário / *v.* comentar, observar.

**rem.e.dy** *s.* remédio / *v.* remediar.

**re.mem.ber** *v.* lembrar, recordar.

**re.mind.er** *s.* lembrança.

**re.miss** *adj.* remisso, preguiçoso, indolente, lento.

**rem.nant** *s.* resto; retalho.

**re.mote** *adj.* remoto, distante.

**re.move** *v.* tirar; remover.

**re.new** *v.* renovar, refazer, repetir; recomeçar.

**re.new.al** *s.* renovação, recomeço.

**rent** *s.* aluguel / *v.* alugar.

**re.pair** *s.* conserto / *v.* consertar.

**re.peat** *s.* repetição / *v.* repetir.

**re.place** *v.* repor, substituir.

**re.place.ment** *s.* reposição, substituição.

**re.ply** *s.* resposta / *v.* responder, replicar.

**re.port** *s.* relatório; reportagem; boletim de escola / *v.* informar, comunicar.

**re.proach** *s.* repreensão, censura / *v.* repreender.

**re.prove** *v.* reprovar, criticar.

**re.pub.lic** *s.* república.

**re.pulse** *v.* rejeitar, repelir, recusar / *s.* repulsa, recusa, rejeição.

**re.pute** *s.* reputação, fama, renome / *v.* reputar, julgar.

**re.quest** *s.* pedido, requerimento, solicitação / *v.* solicitar, requerer, pedir.

**re.quire** *v.* requerer, exigir, necessitar.

**req.ui.site** *s.* requisito.

**re.sale** *s.* revenda.

**res.cue** *s.* salvamento, resgate / *v.* resgatar, salvar, socorrer.

**re.search** *s.* pesquisa, busca / *v.* pesquisar, examinar, investigar.

**re.sem.ble** *v.* assemelhar-se, parecer-se com.

**re.serve** *s.* reserva, restrição / *v.* reservar, guardar.

**re.side** *v.* residir.

**re.sist** *v.* resistir, opor-se.

**re.solve** *s.* resolução / *v.* resolver, decidir, solucionar.

**re.sort** *s.* local turístico; refúgio.

**re.source** *s.* recurso, meio ♦ ~*s* riquezas.

**re.spect** *s.* respeito, consideração / *v.* respeitar.

**re.spond** *v.* responder, reagir.

**rest** *s.* descanso, repouso; resto, restante, sobra / *v.* descansar; sobrar.

**re.start** *v.* reiniciar, recomeçar / *s.* reinício, recomeço.

**re.stless** *adj.* impaciente.

**re.sult** *s.* resultado, consequência / *v.* resultar.

**re.sume** *v.* reatar, retomar, recuperar.

**re.su.mé** *s.* currículo profissional; resumo, sumário.

**re.tail** *v.* vender a varejo / *s.* varejo.

**re.tain** *v.* reter, manter.

**re.tard** *s.* demora, atraso / *v.* demorar-se, atrasar-se.

**ret.i.cent** *adj.* reticente, reservado.

**re.tire** *v.* aposentar-se, reformar-se.

**re.tort** *s.* réplica / *v.* replicar.

**re.turn** *v.* retornar, regressar, voltar / *s.* retorno, regresso, volta.

**re.venge** *s.* vingança, desforra / *v.* vingar-se.

**re.verse** *s.* contrário, reverso, oposto / *adj.* contrário, reverso, oposto / *v.* revogar, inverter, anular.

**re.view** *v.* rever, revisar, examinar / *s.* revista, revisão, exame, inspeção.

**re.ward** *s.* recompensa, gratificação / *v.* recompensar, retribuir.

**re.write** *v.* reescrever.

**rhi.no.ce.ros** *s.* rinoceronte.

**rhyme, rime** *s.* rima; verso; poesia / *v.* rimar, fazer versos.

**rhyth.m** *s.* ritmo, cadência.

**rib** *s.* costela.

**rib.ald** *adj.* irreverente, devasso, dissoluto.

**rib.bon** *s.* fita, faixa.

**rice** *s.* arroz.

**rich** *adj.* rico.

**rich.es** *pl. s.* riquezas, bens.

**rid** *v.* libertar, livrar-se.

**ride** *s.* passeio / *v.* passear; cavalgar.

**rid.i.cule** *s.* ridículo.

**right** *s.* direito, correto, justo / *adj.* certo, correto, direito; à direita / *adv.* corretamente, justamente.

**ri.gid** *adj.* rígido, firme, duro, inflexível.

**rig.or.ous** *adj.* rigoroso, severo.

**rile** *v.* aborrecer, irritar (coloquial).

**rim** *s.* borda, beira; aro, aba.

**ring** *s.* anel; círculo; toque de campainha ou telefone / *v.* tocar, soar, telefonar.

**rink** *s.* pista de patinação, rinque.

**riot** *s.* desordem, distúrbio / *v.* provocar distúrbios.

**ripe** *adj.* maduro (fruta) / *v.* amadurecer.

**rise** *s.* ação de levantar, ascensão / *v.* ascender, subir, erguer-se.

**rit.u.al** *adj.* ritual, cerimonial.

**riv.er** *s.* rio.

**road** *s.* estrada.

**roar** *v.* rugir, urrar / *s.* rugido, urro.

**roast beef** *s.* rosbife.

**rob** *v.* roubar.

**rob.ber** *s.* ladrão.

**rob.ber.y** *s.* furto, roubo.

**robe** *s.* roupão, robe; manto.

**robot** *s.* robô.

**ro.bust** *adj.* robusto, vigoroso, forte.

**rock** *s.* rocha, pedra; estilo musical / *v.* balançar-se; embalar (criança).

**rock.et** *s.* foguete / *v.* disparar.

**rod** *s.* vara, haste.

**ro.de.o** *s.* rodeio.

**roll.er coast.er** *s.* montanha-russa.

**Roman** *adj.* romano / *s.* romano.

**romance** *s.* romance; caso amoroso; história de amor.

**ro.man.tic** *adj.* romântico.

**roof** *s.* telhado.

**room** *s.* quarto, aposento, sala.

**roost.er** *s.* galo.

**root** *s.* raiz.

**rope** *s.* corda, cabo, cordame.

**rose** *s.* rosa / *v. pret.* do *v. rise*.

**rose.bud** *s.* botão de rosa.

**rose.bush** *s.* roseira.

**rose.ma.ry** *s.* alecrim.

**ro.ta.ry** *adj.* rotativo, giratório.

**rough** *adj.* áspero, tosco; bruto, violento.

**rough.ness** *s.* aspereza, rudeza.

**round** *adj.* redondo / *s.* rodada / *prep.* em volta de, ao redor de / *v.* rodear.

**rou.tine** *s.* rotina, hábito / *adj.* rotineiro, de rotina.

**row** *s.* fileira, fila; briga, motim (coloquial) / *v.* enfileirar; remar; brigar.

**row.er** *s.* remador.

**roy.al** *adj.* real; monárquico.

**rub** *v.* esfregar, friccionar; polir; apagar (com a borracha).

**rub.ber** *s.* borracha; camisinha (coloquial).

**ru.by** *s.* rubi.

**rud.der** *s.* leme.

**rude** *adj.* grosso, grosseiro, rude.

**rum.mage sale** *s.* bazar (de caridade).

**run** *s.* corrida / *v.* correr; administrar, dirigir.

**run.ner** *s.* corredor; aquele que corre.

**runt** *s.* nanico, anão, pigmeu.

**ru.ral** *adj.* rural, campestre.

**rush** *s.* ímpeto, pressa, agitação / *v.* apressar-se, acelerar.

**rush hour** *s.* hora de maior tráfego nas ruas ou estradas.

**Rus.sia** *s.* Rússia.

**rust** *s.* ferrugem / *v.* enferrujar.

**rus.ty** *adj.* enferrujado.

**ruth.less** *adj.* cruel, implacável, desumano.

# S s

**S, s** *s.* a décima nona letra do alfabeto inglês.

**sab.o.tage** *s.* sabotagem / *v.* sabotar.

**sac.ra.ment** *s.* sacramento.

**sac.ri.fice** *s.* sacrifício / *v.* sacrificar.

**sad** *adj.* triste; deplorável.

**sad.ly** *adv.* tristemente; lamentavelmente.

**sad.ness** *s.* tristeza.

**safe** *adj.* seguro / *s.* cofre.

**safe.ty** *s.* segurança.

**safe.ty belt** *s.* cinto de segurança.

**Sag.it.ta.ri.us** *s.* Sagitário (astrologia).

**sail** *s.* vela de navio / *v.* navegar, velejar; deslizar, planar.

**sail.ing** *s.* navegação / *adj.* de vela.

**sai.lor** *s.* marinheiro, marujo.

**saint** *adj.* santo / *s.* santo.

**sal.ad** *s.* salada.

**sal.a.ry** *s.* salário, remuneração.

**sale** *s.* venda, liquidação.

**sa.loon** *s.* bar, botequim, salão (de navio).

**salt** *s.* sal / *v.* salgar.

**salt.ish** *adj.* salgado.

**sal.vage** *s.* salvamento / *v.* salvar.

**same** *adj.* mesmo, igual / *adv.* do mesmo modo / *pron.* o(a) mesmo(a).

**sam.ple** *s.* amostra / *v.* testar, provar.

**sand** *s.* areia.

**san.dal** *s.* sandália.

**sand.wich** *s.* sanduíche.

**sand.y** *adj.* arenoso.

**sane** *adj.* são(ã), sadio(a), sensato(a).

**sarcasm** · 326 · **season**

**sar.cas.m** *s.* sarcasmo, ironia.
**sar.dine** *s.* sardinha.
**sat.ire** *s.* sátira.
**sat.is.fy** *v.* satisfazer; saciar; corresponder.
**Sat.ur.day** *s.* sábado.
**Sat.urn** *s.* Saturno.
**sauce** *s.* molho.
**sau.cer** *s.* pires.
**sauc.y** *adj.* atrevido(a); provocante.
**sau.na** *s.* sauna.
**saus.age** *s.* salsicha; linguiça.
**sav.age** *adj.* cruel; feroz.
**save** *v.* salvar.
**sa.viour** *s.* salvador.
**sax.o.phone** *s.* saxofone.
**saw** *s.* serra, serrote / *v. pret.* do *v. to see.*
**say** *v.* dizer.
**scale** *s.* escala, régua, metro; escama; prato de balança / *v.* escalar; pesar.
**scan.dal** *s.* escândalo.
**scant** *adj.* escasso; insuficiente.
**scar** *s.* cicatriz / *v.* marcar.
**scare** *s.* susto, espanto / *v.* assustar, espantar.
**scarf** *s.* cachecol; lenço de cabeça.
**scar.y** *adj.* assustador.
**scent** *s.* perfume; aroma.
**sched.ule** *s.* horário; lista; programa / *v.* programar.

**schol.ar.ship** *s.* bolsa de estudos.
**school** *s.* escola.
**sci.ence** *s.* ciência.
**scoot.er** *s.* motor pequeno; patinete; lambreta.
**score** *s.* contagem (de pontos) / *v.* marcar (pontos).
**scorn** *s.* desprezo / *v.* desprezar.
**Scor.pi.o** *s.* Escorpião (astrologia).
**Scot** *s.* escocês(esa).
**Scot.land** *s.* Escócia.
**scratch** *s.* arranhão; unhada / *v.* arranhar, coçar.
**scream** *s.* grito / *v.* gritar.
**screen** *s.* tela, tela para cinema.
**screw** *s.* parafuso / *v.* aparafusar.
**script** *s.* escrita; roteiro; manuscrito.
**scrub.ber** *s.* esfregador, esfregão, escovão.
**scuff** *s.* chinelo; ato de arrastar os pés / *v.* esfolar; arrastar os pés.
**sea** *s.* mar.
**seal** *s.* foca; brasão, escudo / *v.* selar, fechar com lacre.
**sea.man** *s.* marinheiro, marujo.
**sea.quake** *s.* maremoto.
**search** *s.* busca, procura; pesquisa, exame / *v.* procurar; investigar.
**sea.son** *s.* época, período, estação do ano / *v.* temperar, condimentar.

**seat** *s.* assento, banco, lugar / *v.* acomodar.

**se.cond** *adj.* segundo(a) / *num.* segundo / *s.* segundo (1/60 de 1 minuto) / *adv.* em segundo lugar.

**sec.re.ta.ry** *s.* secretário(a).

**sec.tion** *s.* seção, parte; artigo.

**sec.u.lar** *adj.* secular.

**se.cure** *adj.* seguro / *v.* prender; assegurar.

**se.cu.ri.ty** *s.* segurança; garantia, fiança.

**se.date** *adj.* sossegado, tranquilo / *v.* sedar.

**sed.i.ment** *s.* sedimento.

**se.duce** *v.* seduzir.

**see** *v.* ver, enxergar, olhar.

**seed** *s.* semente, germe.

**seek** *v.* procurar.

**seep** *v.* penetrar, infiltrar-se.

**see.saw** *s.* gangorra.

**seg.ment** *s.* segmento; gomo (laranja).

**seg.re.gate** *v.* segregar.

**sel.dom** *adv.* raramente.

**se.lect** *adj.* selecionar, escolher.

**self** *s.* eu, ego, a própria pessoa / *pron.* si, mesmo(a).

**sell** *v.* vender.

**se.men** *s.* sêmen, esperma.

**sen.ate** *s.* senado.

**send** *v.* mandar, enviar.

**se.nile** *adj.* senil.

**se.ni.or** *s.* mais velho / *adj.* superior, sênior.

**sen.sa.tion** *s.* sensação.

**sense** *s.* senso, sentido, percepção / *v.* sentir, perceber.

**sen.si.bil.i.ty** *s.* sensibilidade.

**sen.si.ble** *adj.* sensato, sábio, cauteloso.

**sen.si.tive** *adj.* sensível, sensitivo, delicado.

**sen.su.al** *adj.* sensual.

**sen.tence** *s.* sentença, frase, oração.

**sen.try** *s.* sentinela.

**sep.a.rate** *adj.* separado, diferente / *v.* separar.

**Sep.tem.ber** *s.* setembro.

**sep.tic** *adj.* sético, putrefaciente.

**se.quence** *s.* sequência, série.

**ser.e.nade** *s.* serenata.

**ser.geant** *s.* sargento.

**se.ri.al** *s.* seriado, novela / *adj.* serial, em série.

**se.ries** *s.* série; sucessão.

**se.ri.ous** *adj.* sério; grave.

**ser.vice** *s.* serviço; culto.

**ses.sion** *s.* sessão.

**set** *s.* jogo, grupo, conjunto; aparelho / *v.* ajustar; pôr; colocar; estabelecer.

**set.tle** *s.* banco, sofá / *v.* assentar; estabelecer-se, fixar residência; acalmar-se.

**settlement**     **328**     shot

**set.tle.ment** *s.* colonização, assentamento; decisão, acordo.

**set.up** *s.* instalação, configuração, arranjo.

**sev.en** *num.* sete.

**seven.teen** *num.* dezessete.

**sev.enty** *num.* setenta.

**sev.er.al** *adj.* vários, diversos.

**se.vere** *adj.* severo; austero.

**sew** *v.* coser, costurar.

**sew.age** *s.* esgoto.

**sex** *s.* sexo.

**sex.u.al** *adj.* sexual.

**sex.y** *adj.* erótico, excitante.

**shack.le** *s.* algema; obstáculo / *v.* algemar.

**shade** *s.* penumbra, sombra / *v.* escurecer, sombrear.

**shad.ow** *s.* sombra.

**shad.y** *adj.* sombreado.

**shag.gy** *adj.* felpudo; peludo.

**shake** *v.* sacudir, tremer, agitar.

**shal.low** *adj.* raso; superficial.

**shame** *s.* vergonha; uma pena, uma lástima (coloquial). / *v.* envergonhar.

**sham.poo** *s.* xampu / *v.* lavar os cabelos.

**shan.ty.town** *s.* favela.

**shape** *s.* forma, figura, contorno / *v.* formar, dar forma.

**share** *s.* parte, porção; cota, ação / *v.* dividir.

**shark** *s.* tubarão.

**sharp** *adj.* esperto, perspicaz; afiado, pontudo.

**shave** *v.* barbear, fazer a barba.

**she** *pron.* ela.

**shear** *v.* tosquiar.

**sheep** *s.* ovelha.

**sheet** *s.* lençol; folha (de papel); chapa.

**shelf** *s.* estante, prateleira.

**shell** *s.* concha, casca, casco.

**shel.ter** *s.* abrigo, refúgio / *v.* abrigar, proteger.

**sher.iff** *s.* xerife.

**shin** *s.* canela (da perna).

**shin.bone** *s.* tíbia.

**shine** *s.* brilho / *v.* brilhar.

**shin.y** *adj.* brilhante, lustroso.

**ship** *s.* navio, barco / *v.* embarcar, enviar.

**shirk** *s.* vagabundo / *v.* esquivar-se, faltar ao dever.

**shirt** *s.* camisa.

**shock** *s.* choque, impacto / *v.* chocar, colidir; escandalizar.

**shoe** *s.* sapato.

**shoe.mak.er** *s.* sapateiro.

**shop** *s.* loja / *v.* fazer compras.

**shore** *s.* margem, costa.

**short** *adj.* curto; breve; baixo.

**shot** *s.* tiro, disparo; tentativa; injeção (coloquial).

**shoulder** | 329 | **skin**

**shoul.der** *s.* ombro.

**show** *v.* mostrar, exibir / *s.* mostra, exibição.

**shrimp** *s.* camarão.

**shrub** *s.* arbusto.

**shuf.fle** *v.* embaralhar (cartas) / *s.* truque, embuste.

**shun** *v.* afastar-se de, evitar.

**shunt** *v.* manobrar, desviar / *s.* desvio, manobra.

**shut** *v.* fechar, tapar / *adj.* fechado, tapado.

**shy** *adj.* tímido(a), reservado(a), acanhado(a).

**Si.ci.ly** *s.* Sicília.

**sick** *s.* doente; vômito / *adj.* enjoado, farto.

**sick.le** *s.* foice.

**side** *s.* lado; margem.

**side.walk** *s.* calçada.

**sift** *v.* peneirar.

**sight** *s.* vista; visão.

**sign** *s.* indício; sinal; signo (astrologia) / *v.* assinar, inscrever.

**sig.na.ture** *s.* assinatura.

**sig.ni.fy** *v.* significar.

**si.lence** *s.* silêncio / *v.* silenciar.

**si.lent** *adj.* silencioso(a), calado(a).

**silk** *s.* seda / *adj.* de seda.

**sil.ly** *adj.* bobo(a), idiota, ridículo(a).

**sil.ver** *s.* prata / *adj.* de prata, prateado.

**sim.i.lar** *adj.* parecido, semelhante.

**sim.ple** *adj.* simples, fácil.

**sim.u.late** *v.* simular.

**sin** *s.* pecado / *v.* pecar.

**since** *adv.* desde, desde então / *conj.* desde que, visto que / *prep.* desde, desde então.

**sin.cere** *adj.* sincero.

**sing** *v.* cantar.

**sing.er** *s.* cantor(a).

**sin.gle** *adj.* único, só; solteiro.

**sin.is.ter** *adj.* sinistro; ameaçador.

**sink** *s.* pia / *v.* afundar.

**sin.ner** *s.* pecador(a).

**sir** *s.* senhor.

**sis.ter** *s.* irmã.

**sister.in.law** *s.* cunhada.

**sit** *v.* sentar-se, sentar, acomodar.

**site** *s.* local, lugar.

**sit.u.a.tion** *s.* situação.

**six** *num.* seis.

**six.teen** *num.* dezesseis.

**sixty** *num.* sessenta.

**size** *s.* tamanho, área, dimensão.

**skate** *s.* patim / *v.* patinar.

**skel.e.ton** *s.* esqueleto.

**skid** *s.* derrapagem, escorregão / *v.* derrapar, escorregar.

**skil.ful** *adj.* habilidoso.

**skill** *s.* habilidade, destreza.

**skin** *s.* pele.

S

**skit** s. paródia, sátira.

**skull** s. crânio; caveira.

**skunk** s. gambá.

**sky** s. céu.

**slan.der** s. calúnia / v. difamar, caluniar.

**slang** s. gíria; jargão.

**slap** s. palmada, tapa / v. esbofetear, dar tapas.

**slave** s. escravo.

**slea.zy** adj. sórdido.

**sleep** s. sono / v. dormir.

**sleigh** s. trenó.

**slice** s. fatia, pedaço, porção / v. fatiar, cortar em fatias.

**slick** adj. jeitoso, liso.

**slide** s. escorregador / v. deslizar, escorregar.

**slight** adj. fraco, franzino; mínimo, leve.

**slim** adj. magro / v. emagrecer.

**slip** s. tropeção, escorregão, erro, lapso / v. escapar, fugir, escapulir.

**slip.per** s. chinelo.

**slo.gan** s. frase; lema, moto.

**slop** v. transbordar, derramar / s. lavagem (comida que se dá aos porcos).

**slope** s. ladeira, rampa.

**slow** adj. lento, vagaroso / v. reduzir, diminuir.

**slum.ber** s. sono leve, soneca / v. dormir, tirar uma soneca.

**slur** s. calúnia, insulto / v. desprezar, passar por cima.

**sly** adj. astuto, malicioso.

**small** adj. pequeno.

**small.pox** s. varíola.

**smart** adj. inteligente, esperto; elegante.

**smash** s. quebra, choque / v. despedaçar.

**smell** s. cheiro / v. cheirar.

**smile** s. sorriso / v. sorrir.

**smoke** s. fumaça / v. fumar.

**smooth** adj. macio, suave, liso / v. alisar, suavizar.

**smoth.er** v. sufocar, asfixiar, abafar / s. nuvem de fumaça, de poeira.

**smudge** s. mancha / v. manchar, sujar.

**smug** adj. metido(a), convencido(a).

**smut.ty** adj. obsceno, indecente; sujo.

**snack** s. petisco, lanche.

**snag** s. obstáculo, dificuldade.

**snail** s. lesma, caracol.

**snake** s. cobra, serpente.

**snap** s. estalo / v. estalar.

**snare** s. armadilha, cilada / v. apanhar em armadilha, trair, enganar.

**sneeze** s. espirro / v. espirrar.

**sniff** *s.* farejada, fungada
/ *v.* fungar, cheirar, farejar.
**snoo.ker** *s.* sinuca, bilhar.
**snooze** *s.* soneca / *v.* cochilar.
**snore** *s.* ronco / *v.* roncar.
**snow** *s.* neve / *v.* nevar.
**so** *adv.* tão; desse modo, assim;
de maneira que, logo.
**soak** *v.* encharcar, deixar de molho.
**soap** *s.* sabão.
**sob** *s.* soluço / *v.* soluçar.
**so.ber** *adj.* sóbrio(a); sério(a).
**soc.cer** *s.* futebol.
**so.cia.ble** *adj.* sociável.
**so.cial** *adj.* social.
**so.ci.e.ty** *s.* sociedade.
**so.ci.ol.o.gist** *s.* sociólogo(a).
**sock.et** *s.* tomada, soquete.
**so.da** *s.* refrigerante.
**sod.den** *adj.* encharcado.
**sofa** *s.* sofá.
**soft** *adj.* macio, suave.
**so.lar** *adj.* solar.
**sol.dier** *s.* soldado.
**sol.id** *adj.* sólido.
**sol.i.dar.i.ty** *s.* solidariedade.
**sol.i.ta.ry** *adj.* solitário.
**sol.u.ble** *adj.* solúvel.
**so.lu.tion** *s.* solução.
**some** *pron.* alguns, algumas,
uns, umas.
**some.thing** *pron.* algo, alguma
coisa.

**some.time** *adv.* algum dia.
**some.times** *adv.* às vezes, de vez
em quando.
**son** *s.* filho.
**song** *s.* canção.
**son.net** *s.* soneto.
**soon** *adv.* logo, brevemente, cedo.
**so.phis.ti.cat.ed** *adj.* sofisticado.
**sore** *adj.* doloroso, dolorido,
machucado / *s.* machucado, mágoa.
**sor.ry** *adj.* arrependido / *interj.*
perdão! como? sinto muito!
**soup** *s.* sopa.
**sour** *adj.* azedo; ácido.
**south** *s.* sul / *adj.* do sul
/ *adv.* para o sul.
**Southern Cross** *s.* Cruzeiro
do Sul.
**sou.ve.nir** *s.* lembrança,
recordação.
**spa** *s.* fonte de água; estância
hidromineral.
**space** *s.* espaço, lugar; intervalo.
**spa.ghet.ti** *s.* espaguete.
**Spain** *s.* Espanha.
**Span.ish** *adj.* espanhol
/ *s.* espanhol.
**spank** *v.* dar palmadas; bater,
espancar.
**spare** *adj.* desocupado; de sobra,
extra, disponível / *v.* poupar,
economizar.

**spar.row** *s.* pardal.
**sparse** *adj.* escasso, esparso.
**spas.m** *s.* espasmo.
**spawn** *v.* desovar, criar, gerar / *s.* desova (de peixes), cria, prole.
**speak** *v.* falar.
**spe.cial** *adj.* especial.
**spe.cies** *s.* espécie.
**spe.cif.ic** *adj.* específico, preciso.
**speed** *s.* velocidade, rapidez / *v.* acelerar.
**spell** *v.* soletrar, escrever / *s.* feitiço, encanto; período.
**spend** *v.* gastar, consumir.
**sperm** *s.* esperma.
**spew** *v.* vomitar, lançar / *s.* vômito.
**sphere** *s.* esfera.
**spice** *s.* tempero, condimento / *v.* temperar, condimentar.
**spi.der** *s.* aranha.
**spike** *s.* ponta; espiga.
**spill** *v.* derramar, transbordar.
**spin.ach** *s.* espinafre.
**spine** *s.* espinha dorsal; espinho; lombada (de livro).
**spire** *s.* agulha; pináculo.
**spir.it** *s.* espírito, alma; atitude.
**spir.its** *s.* bebida alcoólica; humor.
**spir.i.tu.al** *adj.* espiritual.
**spit** *v.* cuspir / *s.* cuspe, saliva.
**spite** *s.* rancor, ressentimento.

**spit.tle** *s.* saliva, cuspe.
**spleen** *s.* baço.
**split** *s.* fenda; brecha.
**splut.ter** *v.* gaguejar, balbuciar.
**sponge** *s.* parasita; esponja / *v.* esfregar (com esponja); parasitar.
**spon.sor** *s.* patrocinador.
**spon.sor.ship** *s.* patrocínio.
**spon.ta.ne.ous** *adj.* espontâneo.
**spoon** *s.* colher.
**spo.rad.ic** *adj.* esporádico.
**sport** *s.* esporte.
**spot** *s.* lugar, local; pinta, espinha / *v.* localizar, descobrir (coloquial).
**sprain** *s.* distensão, deslocamento, entorse / *v.* torcer, deslocar.
**spray** *s.* *spray*, borrifador, pulverizador / *v.* borrifar, pulverizar.
**spring** *s.* primavera; mola; nascente; salto.
**sprite** *s.* duende.
**spy** *s.* espião(ã) / *v.* espionar.
**squad** *s.* pelotão, esquadra.
**square** *s.* quadrado; praça / *adj.* quadrado.
**squid** *s.* lula.
**stab** *s.* punhalada, facada / *v.* apunhalar, cravar.
**sta.bil.i.ty** *s.* estabilidade.

**stadium** | 333 | **stink**

**sta.di.um** *s.* estádio.

**staff** *s.* pessoal, empregados.

**stag** *s.* veado adulto.

**stag.nant** *adj.* estagnado.

**staid** *adj.* sério(a); sossegado(a); calmo(a).

**stair** *s.* degrau.

**stairs** *s.* escada.

**stake** *s.* estaca; aposta / *v.* apostar; fixar em estaca ou poste.

**stal.wart** *adj.* robusto, forte; fiel, leal.

**stam.i.na** *s.* resistência, força.

**stamp** *s.* selo, carimbo, marca / *v.* bater o pé, carimbar, selar.

**stand** *s.* posição, postura; barraca, estande, banca / *v.* tolerar, aguentar.

**stan.dard** *s.* padrão / *adj.* padrão, modelo.

**stand by** *s.* alerta, reserva, lista de espera.

**sta.ple** *s.* grampo (de papel) / *adj.* principal / *v.* grampear.

**star** *s.* estrela, astro; celebridade / *v.* estrelar.

**star.fish** *s.* estrela-do-mar.

**stark** *adj.* severo, rigoroso, inflexível.

**star.ry** *adj.* estrelado.

**start** *s.* princípio, começo, início / *v.* começar, iniciar, dar partida.

**state** *s.* estado / *v.* declarar, afirmar.

**stat.ic** *adj.* estático, parado, imóvel / *s.* estática, interferência (rádio).

**sta.tion** *s.* estação (de ônibus, trem); radioemissora.

**sta.tis.tic** *s.* estatística.

**stat.ue** *s.* estátua.

**stat.ute** *s.* estatuto; lei.

**stay** *s.* estada, permanência / *v.* ficar, permanecer.

**steak** *s.* filé, bife.

**steam** *s.* vapor; fumaça / *v.* cozinhar a vapor, emitir vapor.

**steel** *s.* aço / *adj.* de aço.

**step** *s.* passo, degrau; medida / *v.* andar, dar um passo, pisar.

**ster.e.o** *s.* estéreo.

**stern** *adj.* severo, austero, duro.

**stick** *s.* galho; vara; bastão; bengala / *v.* perfurar, espetar; colar, grudar.

**still** *adv.* ainda, ainda assim, contudo / *adj.* quieto(a), calmo(a), parado(a).

**stim.u.late** *v.* estimular.

**sting** *s.* picada, ferroada / *v.* picar.

**stink** *s.* catinga, fedor / *v.* feder.

**S**

**stock** *s.* estoque, reserva / *v.* estocar, armazenar.
**stom.ach** *s.* estômago.
**stone** *s.* pedra, rocha; caroço, semente; pedra preciosa, joia, gema.
**stop** *s.* parada / *v.* parar.
**stop.page** *s.* paralisação, parada, interrupção.
**stor.age** *s.* armazenagem.
**store** *s.* loja, depósito, armazém / *v.* armazenar, pôr em estoque.
**storm** *s.* tempestade, temporal.
**sto.ry** *s.* história, conto, narrativa.
**stove** *s.* fogão.
**straight** *adj.* correto; honrado; direto, reto; liso.
**strain** *s.* tensão, esforço; deslocamento / *v.* esforçar-se; deslocar, luxar.
**strait** *s.* estreito / *adj.* estreito.
**strange** *adj.* desconhecido, estranho.
**stran.gle** *v.* estrangular, sufocar.
**stra.te.gic** *adj.* estratégico.
**strat.e.gy** *s.* estratégia.
**straw.ber.ry** *s.* morango.
**streak** *s.* traço, listra, risca / *v.* riscar.
**stream** *s.* riacho; córrego.
**street** *s.* rua.
**strength** *s.* força, resistência.

**stress** *s.* pressão, tensão, cansaço físico ou mental, esforço / *v.* estressar.
**strife** *s.* luta, conflito.
**strike** *v.* bater, atingir, atacar / *s.* greve; ataque; golpe.
**string** *s.* fio, barbante.
**stroke** *s.* pancada, golpe; derrame, apoplexia.
**strong** *adj.* forte, firme.
**struc.tur.al** *adj.* estrutural.
**stu.dent** *s.* estudante.
**stud.y** *s.* estudo; escritório (em uma casa) / *v.* estudar.
**stu.pid** *s.* estúpido, idiota / *adj.* estúpido, idiota.
**sty** *s.* chiqueiro; terçol.
**style** *s.* estilo, maneira.
**sub.ject** *s.* assunto; matéria; sujeito (gramática) / *v.* sujeitar, submeter.
**sub.ma.rine** *s.* submarino / *adj.* submarine.
**sub.mit** *v.* submeter, apresentar.
**sub.scribe** *v.* fazer a assinatura de, assinar; consentir, concordar.
**sub.stance** *s.* substância, essência.
**sub.sti.tute** *s.* substituto, reserva / *adj.* substituto, reserva / *v.* substituir.
**sub.urb** *s.* subúrbio.
**sub.way** *s.* passagem subterrânea; metrô.

**suc.cess** *s.* sucesso, êxito.

**such** *adj.* desta maneira / *adv.* como tal, assim mesmo / *pron.* semelhante, tal, tão, tanto.

**sue** *v.* processar, acionar.

**suede** *s.* camurça / *adj.* de camurça.

**su.et** *s.* sebo.

**suf.fi.cient** *adj.* suficiente.

**sug.ar** *s.* açúcar.

**suit** *s.* terno (roupa); petição / *v.* processar; cair bem, ficar bem (roupas).

**suit.case** *s.* mala.

**sul.len** *adj.* rabugento(a), teimoso(a), carrancudo(a).

**sum.ma.ry** *s.* resumo; sumário.

**sum.mer** *s.* verão.

**sun** *s.* sol.

**Sun.day** *s.* domingo.

**sun.glass.es** *s.* óculos de sol.

**su.per.mar.ket** *s.* supermercado.

**sup.pli.er** *s.* fornecedor(a).

**sup.ply** *v.* fornecer, abastecer / *s.* fornecimento, abastecimento.

**sup.port** *s.* apoio, suporte, sustento / *v.* apoiar, sustentar.

**sup.pose** *v.* supor, presumir, imaginar.

**sure** *adv.* claro, certo, seguro.

**surf** *s.* surfe.

**sur.ge.ry** *s.* cirurgia.

**sur.name** *s.* sobrenome.

**sur.prise** *s.* surpresa / *v.* surpreender.

**sur.vey** *s.* inspeção, vistoria; pesquisa, levantamento / *v.* pesquisar.

**sur.viv.al** *s.* sobrevivência.

**sus.pect** *adj.* suspeito(a) / *s.* suspeito / *v.* suspeitar, desconfiar.

**sus.pense** *s.* suspense, tensão.

**sus.tain** *v.* sustentar, manter.

**swal.low** *s.* andorinha; gole, trago / *v.* engolir.

**swamp** *s.* pântano, brejo.

**swan** *s.* cisne.

**swap** *s.* permuta, troca / *v.* trocar, permutar.

**swarm** *s.* aglomeração, multidão; enxame (abelhas).

**sweat** *s.* suor, transpiração / *v.* suar, transpirar.

**sweat.y** *adj.* suado(a).

**sweet** *s.* doce / *adj.* doce; amável, gentil.

**swell** *v.* inchar, dilatar.

**swim** *v.* nadar.

**swing** *s.* balanço, oscilação / *v.* balançar, oscilar.

**sym.bol** *s.* símbolo.

**sym.pa.thet.ic** *adj.* solidário(a), compreensivo(a).

**sym.pa.thy** *s.* solidariedade, compreensão, empatia.

**sym.pho.ny** *s.* sinfonia.

**syr.up** *s.* xarope.

**sys.tem** *s.* sistema; organização.

# Tt

**T, t** *s.* vigésima letra do alfabeto inglês.

**ta.ble** *s.* mesa; tabela, lista; tabuada.

**tablet** *s.* tablete, comprimido; placa comemorativa.

**tack.y** *adj.* pegajoso(a), grudento(a).

**tac.tic.al** *adj.* tático(a).

**tag** *s.* etiqueta, identificação, rótulo.

**tail** *s.* rabo, cauda.

**tai.lor** *s.* alfaiate.

**take** *v.* tomar; pegar; levar.

**take-off** *v.* decolar / *s.* decolagem, partida.

**tale** *s.* conto, história; fofoca, fuxico.

**talc** *s.* talco.

**tal.ent** *s.* talento.

**talk** *s.* conversa, papo / *v.* conversar, falar, dizer.

**tall** *adj.* alto(a), grande.

**tan** *s.* bronzeado / *v.* bronzear.

**tang** *s.* sabor forte.

**tan.ge.rine** *s.* tangerina, mexerica.

**tank** *s.* depósito, reservatório; tanque.

**tape** *s.* fita (adesiva); fita magnética / *v.* gravar.

**tape re.cord.er** *s.* gravador.

**tar.get** *s.* alvo, objetivo, meta.

**tar.iff** *s.* tarifa; lista de preços; taxa de importação / *v.* taxar, tarifar.

**taste** *s.* sabor, gosto, paladar / *v.* experimentar, provar, saborear.

**tat.too** *s.* tatuagem / *v.* tatuar.

**Tau.rus** *s.* Touro (astrologia).

**tax** *s.* imposto, tributo, encargo / *v.* tributar, cobrar imposto, taxar.

**tea**

**tea** *s.* chá.

**teach** *v.* ensinar; lecionar.

**team** *s.* time, equipe.

**tear** *s.* rasgão; lágrima / *v.* rasgar; chorar.

**tease** *v.* caçoar, provocar.

**tech.ni.cal** *adj.* técnico.

**tech.no.lo.gi.cal** *adj.* tecnológico.

**te.di.ous** *adj.* chato, maçante, tedioso.

**teen.ag.er** *adj.* adolescente.

**tel.e.gram** *s.* telegrama.

**tel.e.phone** *s.* telefone / *v.* telefonar.

**tel.e.scope** *s.* telescópio.

**tell** *v.* dizer; contar.

**te.me.ri.ty** *s.* temeridade.

**tem.per** *s.* temperamento, humor / *v.* moderar.

**tem.pe.ra.ture** *s.* temperatura; febre.

**tem.ple** *s.* templo.

**tem.po.ra.ry** *adj.* temporário.

**ten** *num.* dez.

**ten.a.ble** *adj.* sustentável, defensável.

**tend** *v.* tender, inclinar-se.

**ten.den.cy** *s.* tendência, propensão.

**ten.nis** *s.* tênis.

**ten.or** *s.* tenor.

**ten.sion** *s.* tensão, pressão.

**tent** *s.* tenda, barraca.

**ten.ta.tive** *s.* tentativa; experiência; provisório, experimental.

**ter.mite** *s.* cupim.

**ter.rl.ble** *adj.* terrível, horrível.

**ter.ri.fy** *v.* aterrorizar.

**ter.ri.to.ry** *s.* território.

**ter.ror** *s.* terror.

**test** *s.* prova, ensaio; teste, exame / *v.* testar, examinar.

**tes.ta.ment** *s.* testamento.

**text** *s.* texto.

**tex.ture** *s.* textura.

**than** *conj.* que, do que.

**thank** *s.* agradecimento ♦ ~s muito obrigado! / *v.* agradecer.

**thank.ful** *adj.* agradecido(a), reconhecido(a).

**that** *pron.* (*pl. those*) isso, esse, essa, aquele, aquela; que / *conj.* que, para que, a fim de que.

**the** *art. def.* o, a, os, as.

**thea.tre** *s.* teatro.

**their** *pron.* seu(s), sua(s), dele(s), dela(s).

**them** *prep.* os, as, a eles, a elas, lhes.

**theme** *s.* tema, tópico.

**them.selves** *pron.* eles mesmos, elas mesmas.

**then** *adv.* então, em seguida, logo.

**there** *adv.* aí, ali, lá.

**there to be** *v. aux.* haver, existir *(there is, there are).*

**ther.mom.e.ter** *s.* termômetro.

**the.sau.rus** *s.* enciclopédia, coleção de palavras ou frases.

**they** *pron.* eles, elas.

**thigh** *s.* coxa.

**thin** *adj.* magro / *v.* afinar.

**thing** *s.* coisa.

**think** *v.* pensar, achar; julgar.

**third** *num.* terceiro.

**thirst** *s.* sede, vontade, ânsia.

**thirst.y** *adj.* sedento(a).

**thir.teen** *num.* treze.

**thir.ty** *num.* trinta.

**this** *pron.* (*pl. these*) este, esta.

**thou.sand** *num.* mil.

**threat** *s.* ameaça, perigo.

**threat.en** *v.* ameaçar.

**three** *num.* três.

**throat** *s.* garganta.

**through** *prep.* por, através de, durante.

**throw** *s.* arremesso, lance / *v.* arremessar, lançar.

**thumb** *s.* polegar.

**thump** *s.* murro, pancada / *v.* golpear, bater.

**thun.der** *s.* trovão / *v.* trovejar.

**Thurs.day** *s.* quinta-feira.

**tick.et** *s.* passagem, bilhete; multa.

**tie** *s.* gravata; empate / *v.* amarrar, atar, empatar.

**ti.ger** *s.* tigre.

**tight** *adj.* esticado(a); apertado(a).

**time** *s.* tempo, hora, momento; espaço de tempo, época, ocasião.

**tire** *v.* cansar, esgotar / *s.* pneu.

**ti.tle** *s.* título.

**to** *prep.* a, para, ao / *adv.* em direção a; partícula utilizada antes do verbo para designar o infinitivo.

**to.day** *s.* hoje / *adv.* hoje.

**toe** *s.* dedo do pé.

**to.geth.er** *adv.* juntos.

**toil.et** *s.* banheiro; vaso sanitário, privada.

**tol.e.rance** *s.* tolerância.

**to.ma.to** *s.* tomate.

**tomb** *s.* tumba, túmulo.

**to.mo.rrow** *s.* amanhã / *adv.* amanhã.

**tone** *s.* tom, tonalidade.

**ton.ic** *s.* tônico.

**to.night** *adv.* esta noite, hoje à noite, à noite / *s.* esta noite.

**too** *adv.* também, igualmente; demais; muito.

**tool** *s.* ferramenta, instrumento.

**tooth** *s.* (*pl. teeth*) dente.

**top** *adj.* mais alto, máximo, principal / *s.* cume, pico, ponto mais alto.

**top.ic** *s.* tópico, assunto.

**tor.ment** *s.* tormento / *v.* torturar.

**tor.toise** *s.* tartaruga (da terra).

**tor.ture** *s.* tortura / *v.* torturar, atormentar.

**toss** *v.* atirar, lançar, chacoalhar, agitar / *s.* agitação, arremesso, sacudida.

**to.tal** *adj.* total / *s.* total, soma.

**touch** *s.* toque, tato / *v.* tocar.

**tough** *adj.* duro, forte, valentão.

**tou.pee** *s.* peruca, topete postiço.

**tour** *s.* viagem, excursão / *v.* excursionar.

**tour.ist** *s.* turista.

**tow.el** *s.* toalha.

**tow.er** *s.* torre, fortaleza.

**town** *s.* cidade.

**tox.ic** *adj.* tóxico(a).

**toy** *s.* brinquedo.

**trace** *s.* traço; indício; rastro, pista / *v.* rastrear, descobrir.

**track** *s.* rastro, pista; trilha; faixa de um CD / *v.* rastrear, localizar.

**trac.tor** *s.* trator.

**trade** *s.* comércio; negócio.

**trade.mark** *s.* marca registrada.

**traf.fic** *s.* trânsito, tráfego; tráfico.

**tra.ge.dy** *s.* tragédia.

**tra.gic** *adj.* trágico(a).

**train** *s.* trem.

**trans.fer** *s.* transferência / *v.* transferir.

**trans.form** *v.* transformar.

**trans.late** *v.* traduzir.

**trans.port** *s.* transporte / *v.* transportar.

**trap** *s.* armadilha, cilada / *v.* prender, aprisionar.

**tra.peze** *s.* trapézio.

**trap.pings** *s.* decoração, ornamento.

**trash** *s.* lixo, refugo; besteira (coloquial); ralé.

**trav.el** *s.* viagem / *v.* viajar.

**tray** *s.* bandeja.

**trea.son** *s.* traição.

**trea.ty** *s.* tratado, acordo, pacto.

**tree** *s.* árvore.

**trem.ble** *s.* tremor / *v.* tremer, estremecer.

**tribe** *s.* tribo.

**trick** *s.* truque, ardil / *v.* enganar, pregar uma peça.

**trip** *s.* viagem, passeio; tropeço / *v.* tropeçar.

**tri.pod** *s.* tripé.

**tri.umph** *s.* triunfo / *v.* triunfar.

**troop** *s.* grupo, bando, tropa.

**tro.phy** *s.* troféu.

**trop.ic** *s.* trópico / *adj.* trópico.

**troub.le** *s.* problema, dificuldade, encrenca / *v.* importunar, incomodar.

**troub.le.some** *adj.* importuno, problemático, desagradável.

**trou.sers** *s.* calças compridas.

**trout** *s.* truta.

**truce** *s.* trégua, folga.

**truck** *s.* caminhão.

**true** *adj.* verdadeiro; legítimo; real.

**tru.ly** *adv.* exatamente, verdadeiramente, sinceramente.

**truss** *v.* atar, amarrar, fixar / *s.* armação, suporte, andaime.

**trust** *s.* confiança, responsabilidade, crédito / *v.* confiar.

**truth** *s.* verdade.

**try** *s.* tentativa / *v.* tentar.

**T-shirt** *s.* camiseta.

**Tues.day** *s.* terça-feira.

**tu.mult** *s.* tumulto.

**tu.nic** *s.* túnica.

**tuning** *s.* sintonização, afinação.

**tun.nel** *s.* túnel.

**tun.ny** *s.* atum.

**tur.ban** *s.* turbante.

**tur.bine** *s.* turbina.

**turn** *s.* volta, giro; vez, ocasião / *v.* girar.

**tur.nip** *s.* nabo.

**turn.o.ver** *s.* faturamento; circulação, rotatividade.

**twelve** *num.* doze.

**twenty** *num.* vinte.

**twice** *adv.* duas vezes.

**twist** *s.* torção, giro, guinada / *v.* retorcer, retorcer.

**two** *num.* dois.

**type** *s.* tipo, espécie, classe.

**type.writ.er** *s.* máquina de escrever.

**typ.i.cal** *adj.* típico, característico.

**T**

# Uu

**U, u** *s.* vigésima primeira letra do alfabeto inglês.

**ug.liness** *s.* feiura.

**ug.ly** *adj.* feio(a); perigoso(a).

**ul.cer** *s.* úlcera.

**um.brel.la** *s.* guarda-chuva.

**un.a.ble** *adj.* ser incapaz, impossibilitado.

**un.ac.com.pa.nied** *adj.* desacompanhado(a).

**u.nan.i.mous** *adj.* unânime.

**un.as.sum.ing** *adj.* modesto(a), despretensioso(a).

**un.a.void.a.ble** *adj.* inevitável.

**un.bal.anced** *adj.* desequilibrado(a), desajustado(a).

**un.bear.a.ble** *adj.* insuportável, intolerável.

**un.beat.en** *adj.* invicto(a), insuperado(a).

**un.be.lie.va.ble** *adj.* inacreditável, incrível.

**un.bro.ken** *adj.* inteiro(a), intato(a).

**un.cer.tain** *adj.* incerto(a), indeciso(a), inseguro(a).

**un.cle** *s.* tio.

**un.com.fort.a.ble** *adj.* incômodo; desconfortável.

**un.com.mon** *adj.* raro, incomum.

**un.con.di.tion.al** *adj.* incondicional.

**un.der** *prep.* debaixo de, embaixo, por baixo, sob.

**un.der.stand** *v.* entender, compreender.

**un.der.wa.ter** *adj.* subaquático.

**un.der.wear** *adj.* roupa de baixo.

# unemployed — upstream

**un.em.ployed** *adj.* desempregado(a).

**un.fair** *adj.* injusto(a).

**un.flag.ging** *adj.* incansável, resistente.

**un.for.get.ta.ble** *adj.* inesquecível.

**un.for.tu.nate** *adj.* infeliz.

**un.for.tu.nate.ly** *adv.* infelizmente.

**un.friend.ly** *adj.* hostil, inamistoso(a), antipático(a) / *adv.* hostilmente.

**un.hap.pi.ness** *s.* tristeza, infelicidade, infortúnio.

**u.ni.form** *adj.* uniforme / *s.* uniforme.

**u.ni.fy** *v.* unificar; unir.

**u.ni.lat.e.ral** *adj.* unilateral.

**u.nion** *s.* união; sindicato trabalhista.

**u.nique** *adj.* único, só, ímpar.

**u.ni.son** *s.* acordo, concordância, harmonia / *adj.* uníssono.

**u.ni.ty** *s.* unidade.

**u.ni.ver.sal** *adj.* universal, ilimitado(a).

**u.ni.verse** *s.* universo, cosmo.

**u.ni.ver.si.ty** *s.* universidade, academia.

**un.just** *adj.* injusto(a).

**un.known** *adj.* desconhecido(a), ignorado(a).

**un.less** *conj.* a menos que, a não ser que.

**un.lock** *v.* destrancar, abrir.

**un.mar.ried** *adj.* solteiro(a).

**un.nat.u.ral** *adj.* artificial; afetado; anormal.

**un.ne.ces.sa.ry** *adj.* desnecessário, inútil.

**un.pleas.ant** *adj.* desagradável, antipático.

**un.plug** *v.* desligar.

**un.pop.u.lar** *adj.* impopular.

**un.real** *adj.* irreal, ilusório.

**un.safe** *adj.* perigoso, inseguro.

**un.suit.a.ble** *adj.* inadequado, impróprio.

**un.sure** *adj.* inseguro, incerto.

**un.til** *prep.* até / *conj.* até que.

**un.u.su.al** *adj.* incomum, inusitado.

**un.wrap** *v.* desembrulhar.

**up** *adj.* avançado, adiantado / *adv.* em cima; para cima, acima / *prep.* em cima, para cima, acima.

**up.date** *v.* atualizar.

**up.grade** *v.* elevar o nível, melhorar / *s.* elevação, melhoria, subida.

**up.keep** *s.* manutenção.

**up.stairs** *adv.* cm cima / *s.* andar de cima / *adj.* do andar superior.

**up.stream** *adv.* rio acima.

| up-to-date | 343 | utter |
|---|---|---|

**up-to-date** *adj.* moderno; atualizado, em dia.

**Ura.nus** *s.* Urano.

**ur.ban** *adj.* urbano, da cidade.

**ur.gency** *s.* urgência, premência.

**u.ri.nate** *v.* urinar.

**us** *pron.* nos, nós.

**us.age** *s.* uso, costume.

**use** *s.* uso (utilidade) / *v.* usar.

**use.ful** *adj.* útil, proveitoso, aproveitável.

**u.su.al** *adj.* usual, habitual, normal.

**u.ten.sil** *s.* utensílio.

**u.til.i.ty** *s.* utilidade.

**u.til ize** *v.* utilizar.

**ut.ter** *adj.* completo(a), total, absoluto(a) / *v.* proferir, expressar, dizer.

U

# V v

**V, v** *s.* vigésima segunda letra do alfabeto inglês; representa o número cinco em algarismos romanos.

**va.can.cy** *s.* vaga, vacância.

**va.ca.tion** *s.* férias.

**vac.cine** *s.* vacina.

**vac.u.um** *s.*vácuo / *v.* limpar com aspirador de pó.

**vain** *adj.* vaidoso(a); vão, fútil.

**Valentine's Day** *s.* dia dos namorados, dia de São Valentim.

**val.id** *adj.* válido, vigente.

**val.ley** *s.* vale.

**val.u.a.ble** *adj.* valioso, precioso.

**val.ue** *s.* valor, preço / *v.* avaliar, calcular o preço de.

**vam.pire** *s.* vampiro(a).

**van** *s.* caminhonete, furgão.

**van.dal** *s.* vândalo, bárbaro.

**va.nil.la** *s.* baunilha.

**van.ish** *v.* desaparecer, sumir.

**van.i.ty** *s.* vaidade.

**var.i.a.ble** *adj.* variável / *s.* variável.

**var.i.a.tion** *s.* variação, alteração.

**va.ri.e.ty** *s.* variedade, diversidade.

**var.i.ous** *adj.* vários(as), diversos.

**var.nish** *s.* verniz, esmalte / *v.* envernizar.

**vase** *s.* vaso, jarra.

**vas.e.line** *s.* vaselina.

**vast** *adj.* vasto, enorme, imenso.

**vault** *s.* abóbada, galeria arqueada; salto, pulo / *v.* pular.

**vege.ta.ble** *s.* vegetal, verdura, hortaliça / *adj.* vegetal.

vegetation 345 vulture

**ve.ge.ta.tion** *s.* vegetação.

**vel.vet** *s.* veludo.

**ven.om** *s.* veneno, peçonha; ódio.

**vent** *s.* abertura, orifício, respiradouro.

**ven.ture** *s.* empreendimento, projeto / *v.* aventurar-se, arriscar-se

**Venus** *s.* Vênus.

**verb** *s.* verbo.

**ver.ba.tim** *adj.* literal, textual / *adv.* palavra por palavra, literalmente, textualmente.

**verge** *s.* limite, margem, beira.

**ver.i.fy** *v.* verificar, conferir.

**ver.sa.tile** *adj.* versátil, volúvel.

**verse** *s.* verso; poesia; estrofe.

**ver.sion** *s.* versão.

**ver.ti.cal** *adj.* vertical.

**ve.ry** *adv.* muito.

**vet.e.ran** *s.* veterano / *adj.* veterano.

**vi.a.ble** *adj.* viável.

**vi.brate** *v.* vibrar, oscilar, tremer.

**view** *s.* vista; cenário / *v.* ver, observar, enxergar.

**view.point** *s.* ponto de vista.

**vi.o.late** *v.* violar, profanar.

**vi.o.lence** *s.* violência, força.

**vi.o.let** *s.* violeta (flor); violeta (cor) / *adj.* violeta, roxo.

**vir.gin** *s.* virgem, donzela / *adj.* virgem, donzela.

**Vir.go** *s.* Virgem (astrologia).

**vir.tue** *s.* virtude; mérito.

**vi.sa** *s.* visto.

**vis.i.ble** *adj.* visível, perceptível.

**vi.sion** *s.* vista; visão.

**vis.it** *s.* visita / *v.* visitar.

**vi.tal** *adj.* essencial, indispensável, vital.

**vit.a.min** *s.* vitamina.

**vo.cab.u.la.ry** *s.* vocabulário.

**vo.ca.tion** *s.* vocação; tendência, inclinação.

**vod.ka** *s.* vodca.

**vogue** *s.* voga, moda.

**voice** *s.* voz.

**void** *s.* vazio, lacuna / *adj.* vazio(a), livre, isento(a).

**volt.age** *s.* voltagem.

**vol.un.ta.ry** *adj.* voluntário, espontâneo.

**vote** *s.* voto / *v.* votar.

**vouch** *v.* garantir, atestar, assegurar, afiançar / *s.* garantia, fiança.

**vow.el** *s.* vogal.

**voy.age** *s.* viagem (espacial ou marítima).

**vul.ture** *s.* abutre, urubu.

**V**

# Ww

**W, w** *s.* vigésima terceira letra do alfabeto inglês.

**wa.fer** *s.* bolacha, biscoito.

**waft** *v.* flutuar, soprar (vento) / *s.* rajada, lufada (vento).

**wag** *v.* sacudir, abanar.

**wa.ger** *s.* aposta / *v.* apostar.

**wag.gon** *s.* carroça, vagão.

**wail** *s.* lamento, gemido / *v.* lamentar-se, gemer.

**wait** *s.* espera, demora / *v.* esperar, aguardar.

**wait.er** *s.* garçom.

**waive** *v.* renunciar a, abrir mão, ceder.

**wake up** *v.* acordar, despertar.

**walk** *s.* passeio, caminhada / *v.* andar a pé, passear.

**wall** *s.* parede, muro / *v.* cercar, murar.

**wal.let** *s.* carteira (de dinheiro).

**wal.lop** *v.* surrar, espancar / *s.* pancada.

**wal.lpa.per** *s.* papel de parede / *v.* revestir (parede) com papel.

**want** *v.* querer, desejar; precisar.

**war** *s.* guerra, conflito.

**ward.er** *s.* carcereiro(a), guarda, sentinela.

**war.drobe** *s.* armário, guarda-roupa.

**ware.house** *s.* armazém.

**warm** *adj.* quente, morno(a), aquecido(a); cordial / *v.* aquecer, esquentar.

**warmth** *s.* calor, quentura; amabilidade, cordialidade.

**warn** *v.* prevenir, avisar, advertir.

**warn.ing** *s.* aviso, prevenção, advertência / *adj.* preventivo(a).

**warranty** 347 **while**

**war.ran.ty** *s.* garantia.

**war.ri.or** *s.* guerreiro.

**wart** *s.* verruga.

**wash** *s.* lavagem / *v.* lavar.

**wash.a.ble** *adj.* lavável.

**wasp** *s.* vespa.

**waste** *s.* perda, sobras; desperdício; lixo / *v.* perder, desperdiçar.

**watch** *s.* relógio (de bolso ou de pulso); cuidado / *v.* olhar, observar.

**wa.ter** *s.* água.

**wa.ter.mel.on** *s.* melancia.

**wave** *s.* onda, ondulação; sinal, aceno / *v.* acenar; ondular.

**wa.ver** *v.* vacilar, fraquejar, hesitar / *s.* oscilação, indecisão.

**wav.y** *adj.* ondulado, ondulante, flutuante.

**wax** *s.* cera / *v.* encerar.

**way** *s.* caminho; modo; forma; maneira.

**we** *pron.* nós.

**wealth** *s.* riqueza, fortuna, abundância.

**wear** *v.* usar (roupa, sapatos, etc.); vestir, trajar.

**wear.y** *adj.* cansado(a), fatigado(a).

**weath.er** *s.* tempo (meteorológico).

**web** *s.* teia; rede; trama.

**wed** *v.* casar-se, unir, ligar.

**wed.ding** *s.* casamento.

**wed.lock** *s.* matrimônio, casamento, união.

**Wednes.day** *s.* quarta-feira.

**week** *s.* semana.

**weigh** *v.* pesar.

**weight** *s.* peso, fadiga.

**weir** *s.* represa, açude.

**wel.come** *s.* acolhimento, recepção / *adj.* bem-vindo / *v.* dar boas vindas.

**weld** *s.* solda / *v.* soldar.

**well** *adv.* bem, estar bem / *s.* fonte, poço.

**west** *s.* oeste / *adj.* ocidental / *adv.* para o oeste.

**wet** *adj.* úmido(a), molhado / *v.* molhar, umedecer.

**whale** *s.* baleia.

**what** *adj.* que, o que, qual / *pron.* quê (interrogativo), qual, quais.

**wheat** *s.* trigo.

**when** *adv.* quando / *pron.* quando / *conj.* quando.

**where** *pron.* onde / *adv.* onde, aonde / *conj.* onde.

**which** *pron.* que, qual / *adj.* que, qual.

**while** *conj.* durante, enquanto.

**W**

**whine** *s.* gemido, lamento, choro / *v.* gemer, choramingar.

**white** *s.* branco / *adj.* branco.

**who** *pron.* que, o qual, quem.

**whole** *adj.* todo, inteiro, completo / *s.* todo, conjunto, totalidade.

**whop.per** *s.* lorota, grande mentira.

**why** *adv.* por que, por quê (interrogativo), por que razão / *pron.* por que, pelo qual / *conj.* por que.

**wick.ed** *adj.* malvado(a), perverso(a).

**wide** *adj.* largo, extenso, amplo.

**wid.ow** *s.* viúva / *adj.* viúva.

**wid.ow.er** *s.* viúvo / *adj.* viúvo.

**wife** *s.* esposa.

**wig** *s.* peruca.

**wild** *adj.* selvagem, agreste; violento, louco(a).

**will.ful** *adj.* teimoso(a), obstinado(a).

**will** *s.* vontade, desejo; testamento / (*v. aux.* na formação do futuro simples).

**will.pow.er** *s.* força de vontade.

**wil.y** *adj.* esperto(a), astuto(a).

**win** *v.* ganhar, vencer.

**wind** *s.* vento.

**win.dow** *s.* janela, vitrine.

**wind.y** *adj.* com vento, ventoso.

**wine** *s.* vinho.

**wing** *s.* asa; ala.

**win.ner** *s.* vencedor, vitorioso.

**win.ter** *s.* inverno.

**wire** *s.* arame.

**wire.less** *s.* rádio (uso antiquado) / *adj.* sem fios, por meio do rádio.

**wir.y** *adj.* resistente, rijo, de arame.

**wis.dom** *s.* sabedoria; ciência; bom senso.

**wise** *adj.* sábio(a); sensato(a), prudente.

**wish** *s.* desejo / *v.* desejar.

**wist.ful** *adj.* pensativo(a), saudoso(a), melancólico(a).

**witch** *s.* bruxa, feiticeira.

**with** *prep.* com.

**with.out** *prep.* sem.

**with.stand** *v.* resistir a.

**wit.ness** *s.* testemunha / *v.* testemunhar, presenciar.

**wit.ty** *adj.* espirituoso(a); engenhoso(a).

**wiz.ard** *s.* feiticeiro, mago.

**wolf** *s.* lobo.

**wom.an** *s.* (*pl. women*) mulher.

**won.der.ful** *adj.* maravilhoso, espetacular.

**wood** *s.* madeira, lenha; floresta, bosque.

**word** *s.* palavra.

**work** *s.* trabalho, emprego, profissão / *v.* trabalhar.
**world** *s.* mundo.
**worm** *s.* verme, lombriga.
**wor.ried** *adj.* preocupado; aflito.
**wor.ry** *s.* preocupação / *v.* preocupar, afligir.
**worse** *adv.* (*comp.* de *bad*) pior / *adj.* pior.

**worst** *s.* o pior / *adv.* (*superl.* de *bad*) pior / *adj.* pior.
**wring** *s.* torção; aperto / *v.* torcer, espremer.
**write** *v.* escrever.
**wrong** *s.* injustiça; erro / *adj.* errado, incorreto, falso / *adv.* erradamente, erroneamente.

**W**

# Xx

**X, x** *s.* vigésima quarta letra do alfabeto inglês; representa o número 10 em algarismos romanos.

**Xmas** *abrev.* de *Christmas.*

**X-ray** *s.* radiografia, raio *s.* X / *v.* tirar chapa, radiografar.

# Y y

**Y, y** *s.* vigésima quinta letra do alfabeto inglês.

**yard** *s.* quintal, pátio; jardim frontal; jarda (unidade de medida equivalente a 91,4 cm).

**yawn** *s.* bocejo / *v.* bocejar.

**year** *s.* ano.

**yearn.ing** *s.* anseio, aspiração, desejo / *adj.* ansioso, desejoso.

**yeast** *s.* levedura, levedo; fermento.

**yell** *s.* grito, berro / *v.* gritar, berrar.

**yel.low** *s.* amarelo / *adj.* amarelo / *v.* amarelar.

**yelp** *s.* latido, ganido / *v.* latir, ganir.

**yes** *s.* sim / *adv.* sim, é mesmo.

**yes.ter.day** *s.* ontem / *adv.* ontem.

**yet** *adv.* ainda / *conj.* porém, contudo, no entanto.

**yield** *s.* rendimento, lucro, produto / *v.* render, produzir.

**yo.ga** *s.* ioga.

**yolk** *s.* gema de ovo.

**yon.der** *adv.* além, acolá, mais longe / *adj.* longínquo.

**you** *pron.* você, tu, vós, vocês.

**young** *adj.* jovem, moço.

**your** *adj. poss.* teu(s), tua(s); seu(s), sua(s).

**your.self** *pron.* teu mesmo, a você mesmo(a), próprio(a).

**youth** *s.* juventude, mocidade.

# Z z

**Z, z** *s.* vigésima sexta letra do alfabeto inglês.

**za.ny** *adj.* tolo(a), bobo(a).

**zeal** *s.* zelo, fervor.

**ze.bra** *s.* zebra.

**ze.ro** *num.* zero.

**zest** *s.* vivacidade, entusiasmo; gosto, sabor; prazer.

**zinc** *s.* zinco / *v.* zincar, galvanizar.

**zip code** *s.* código de endereçamento postal (CEP).

**zo.di.ac** *s.* zodíaco.

**zone** *s.* zona, região.

**zoo** *s.* zoológico.

**zo.ol.o.gist** *s.* zoólogo(a).